IF YOU STEAL

IF YOU STEAL

by JASON

FANTAGRAPHICS BOOKS

For Kim

FANTAGRAPHICS BOOKS
7563 Lake City Way NE
Seattle, WA 98115
Fantagraphics.com

Written and drawn by Jason
Editor: Gary Groth
Series Design: Jason and Covey
Cover Design: Keeli McCarthy
Production: Paul Baresh
Coloring: Hubert
Associate Publisher: Eric Reynolds
Publisher: Gary Groth
Editorial Assistance: RJ Casey,
Daniel Germain, Kim Rost Bridges

To receive a free catalog of fine comics and novels, both prose
and graphic, including all of Jason's other graphic novels
and short stories, call 1-800-657-1100 or visit our website at
Fantagraphics.com.

First printing: August 2015

ISBN 978-1-60699-854-0
Library of Congress Control Number: 2015935148

Printed in Singapore

Jason was born in Norway, oh, quite some time ago. When not drawing he's probably watching a movie or something, while fondling his chess pieces (this is not a euphemism). Sometimes he feels like he lives in a painting by Magritte. Other times not.

CHAPTERS

PRESENTING:

IF YOU STEAL

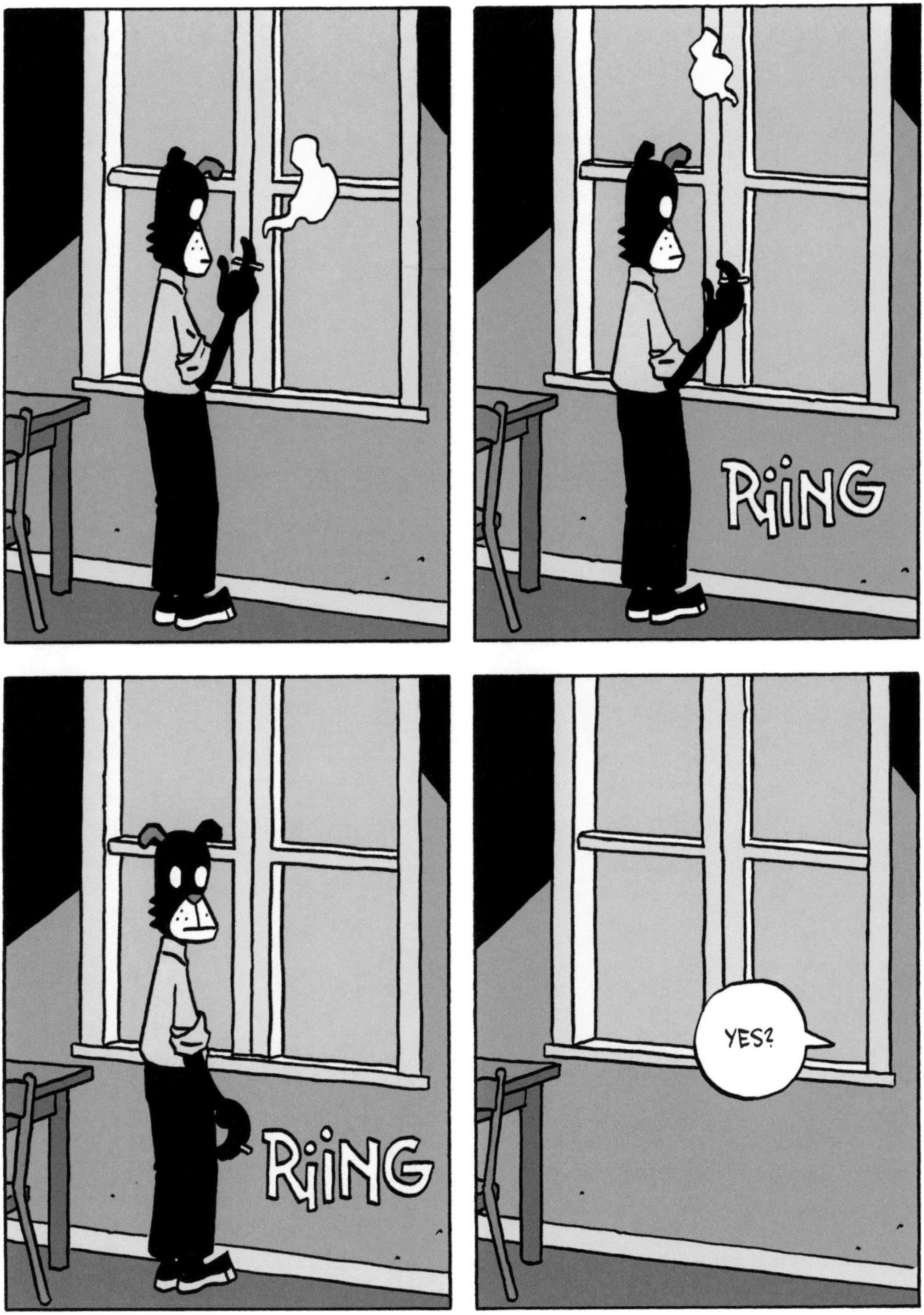
RING
RING
YES?

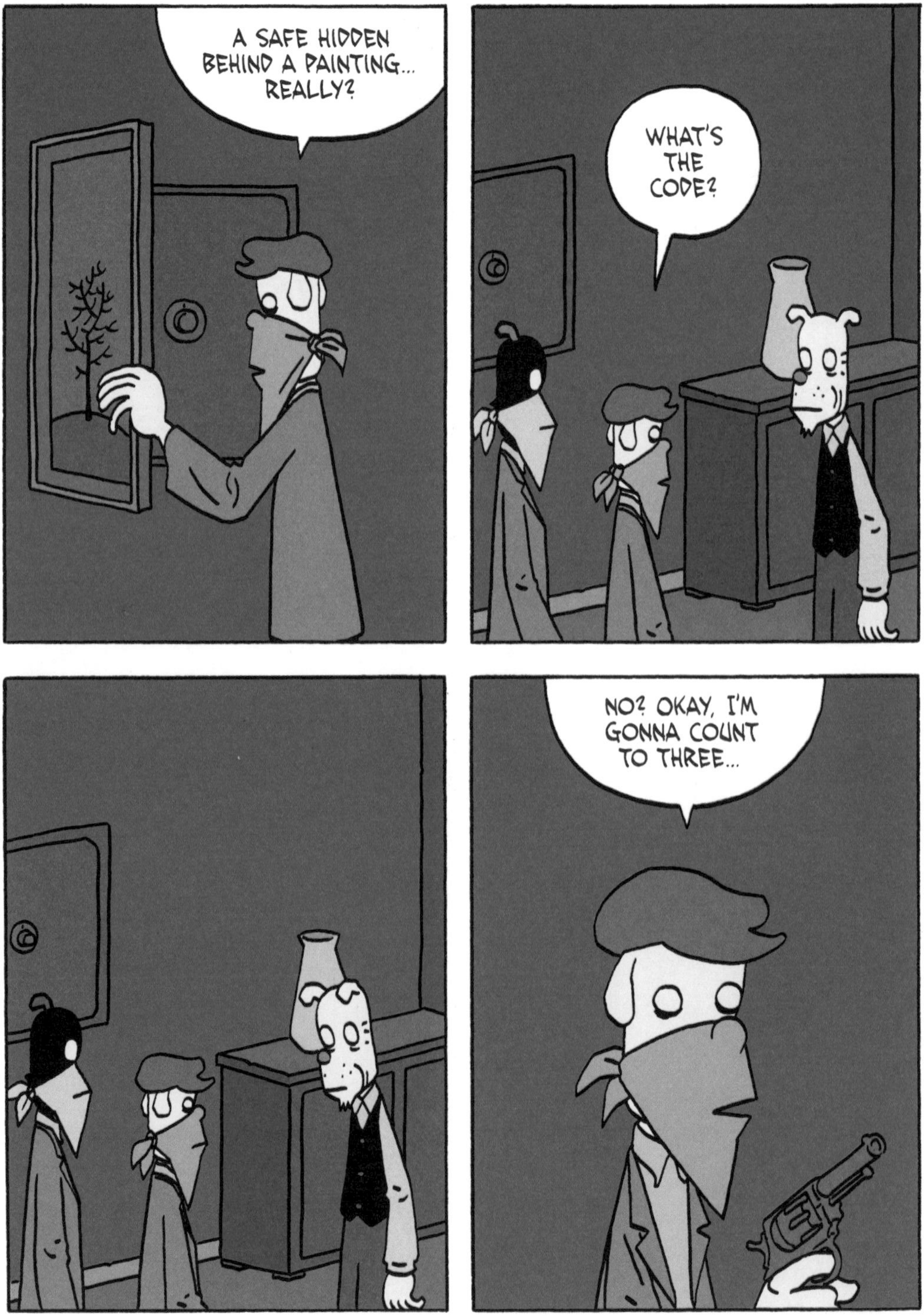
A SAFE HIDDEN BEHIND A PAINTING... REALLY?
WHAT'S THE CODE?
NO? OKAY, I'M GONNA COUNT TO THREE...

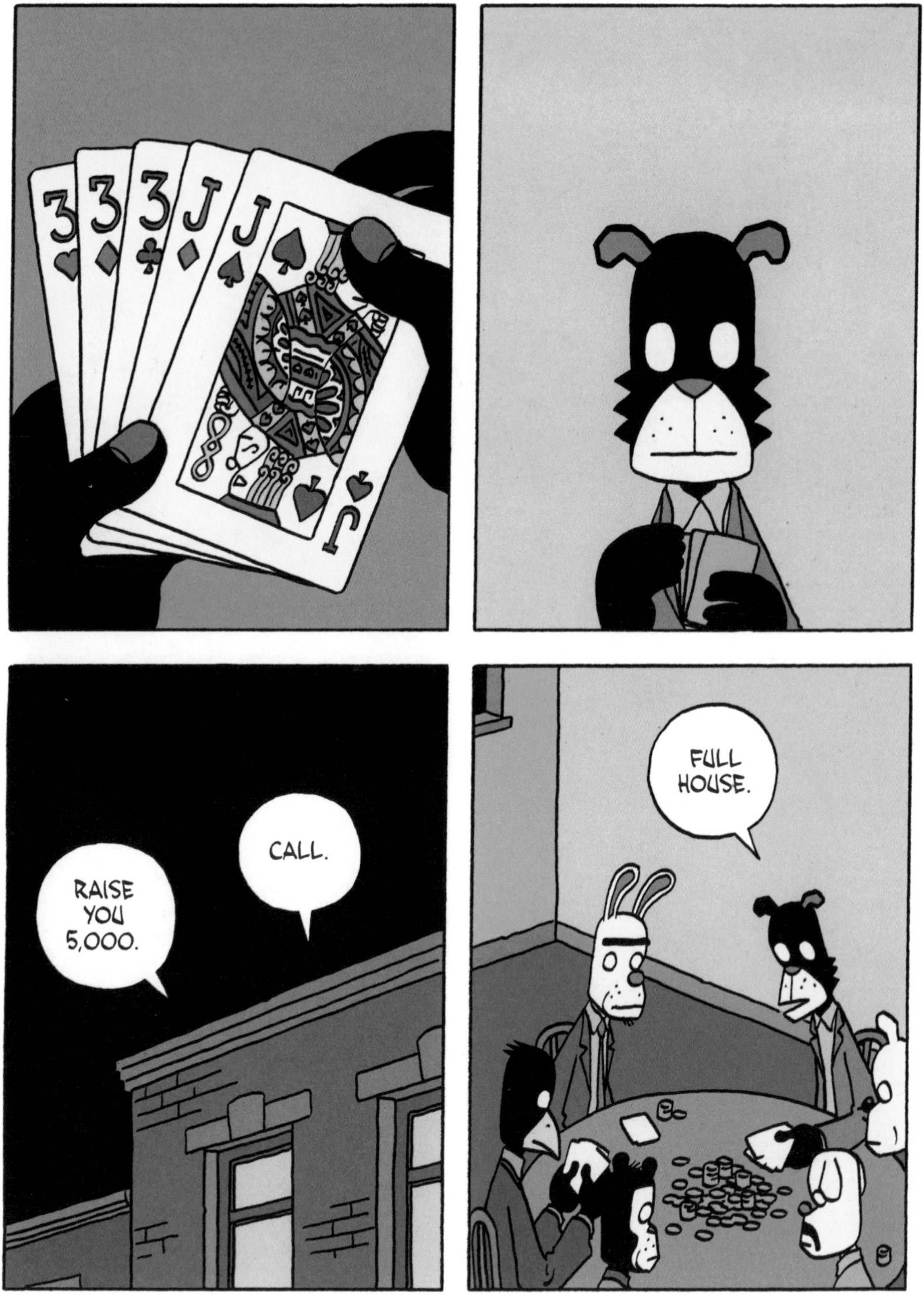
RAISE YOU 5,000.
CALL.
FULL HOUSE.

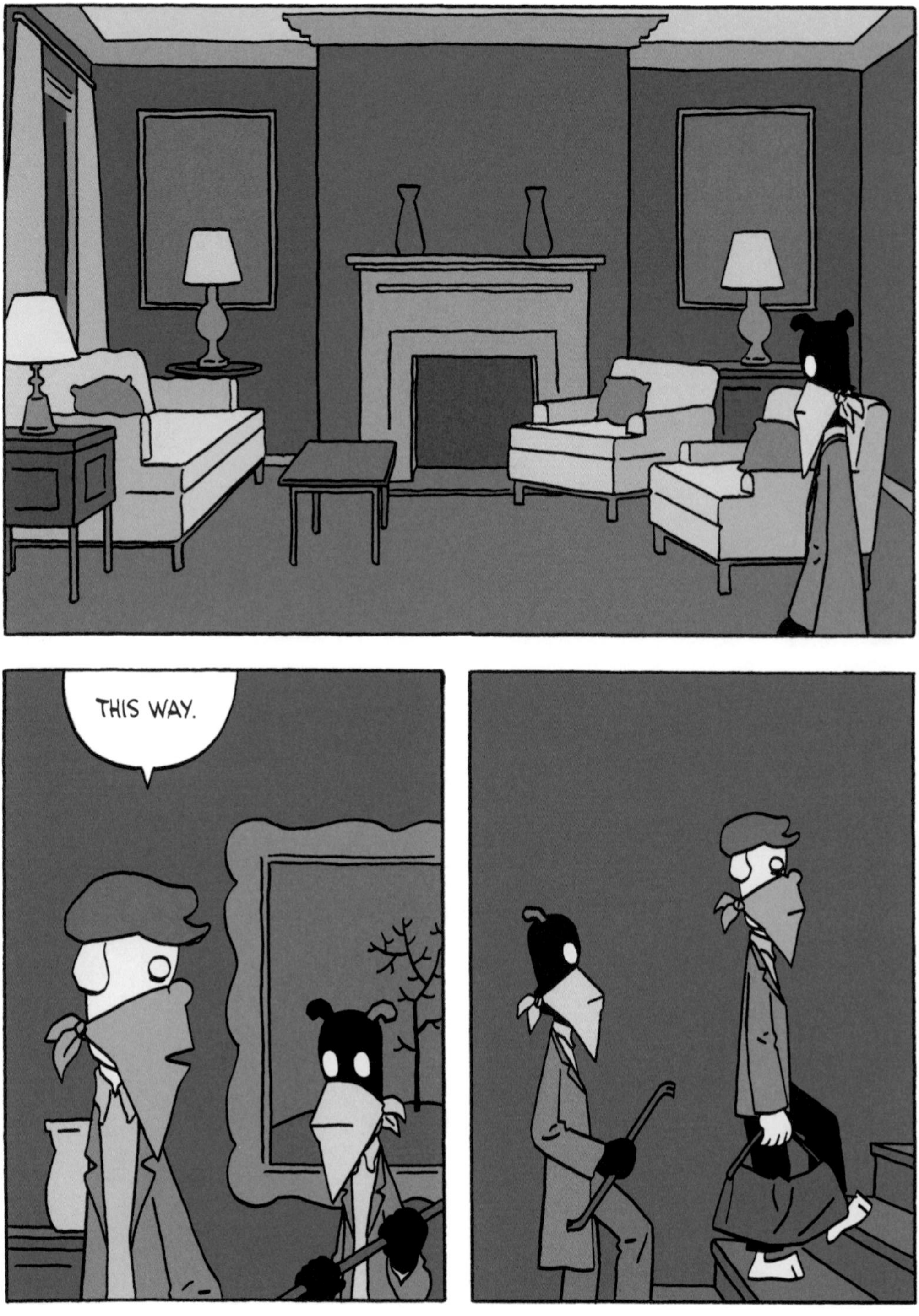
THIS WAY.

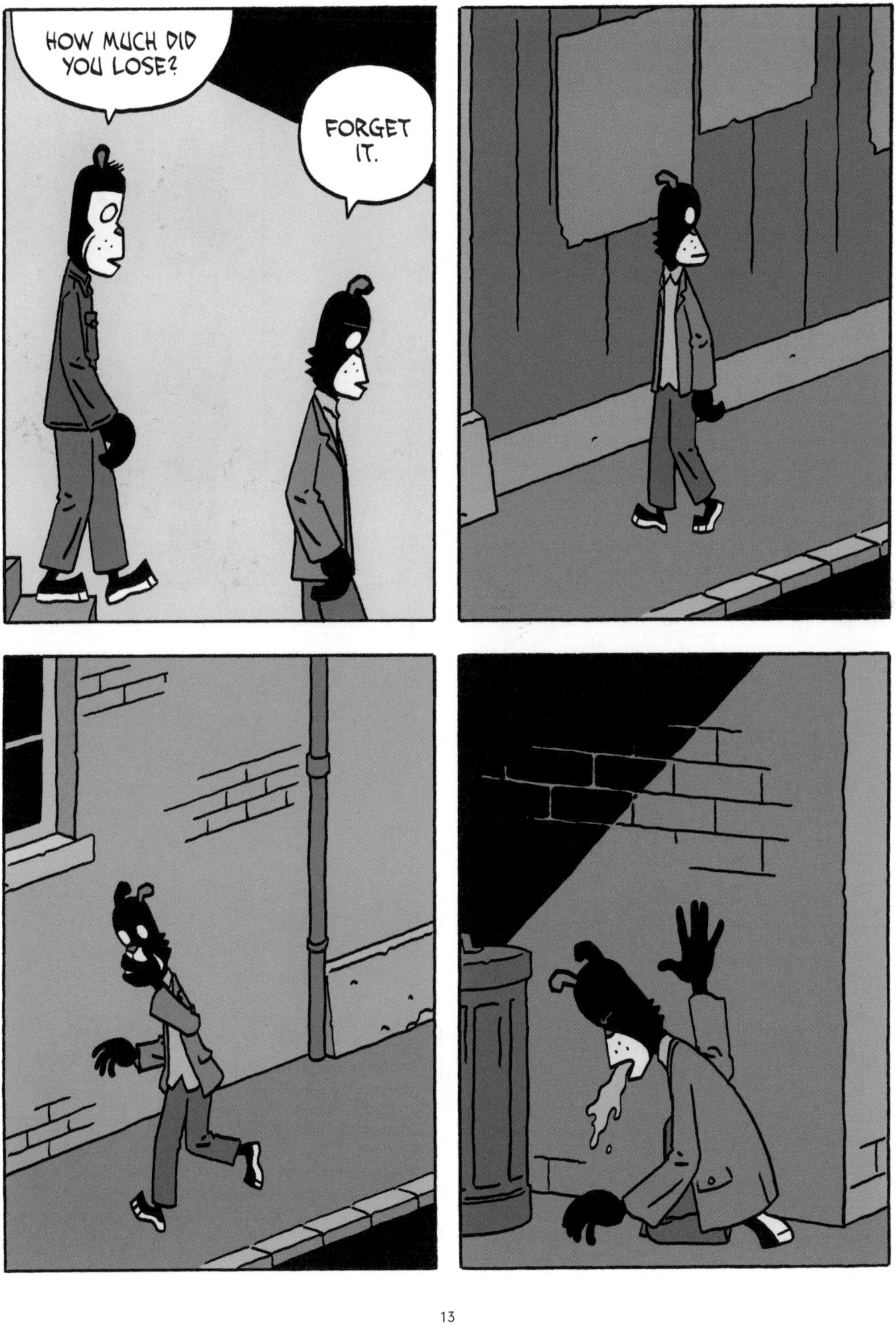
HOW MUCH DID YOU LOSE?
FORGET IT.

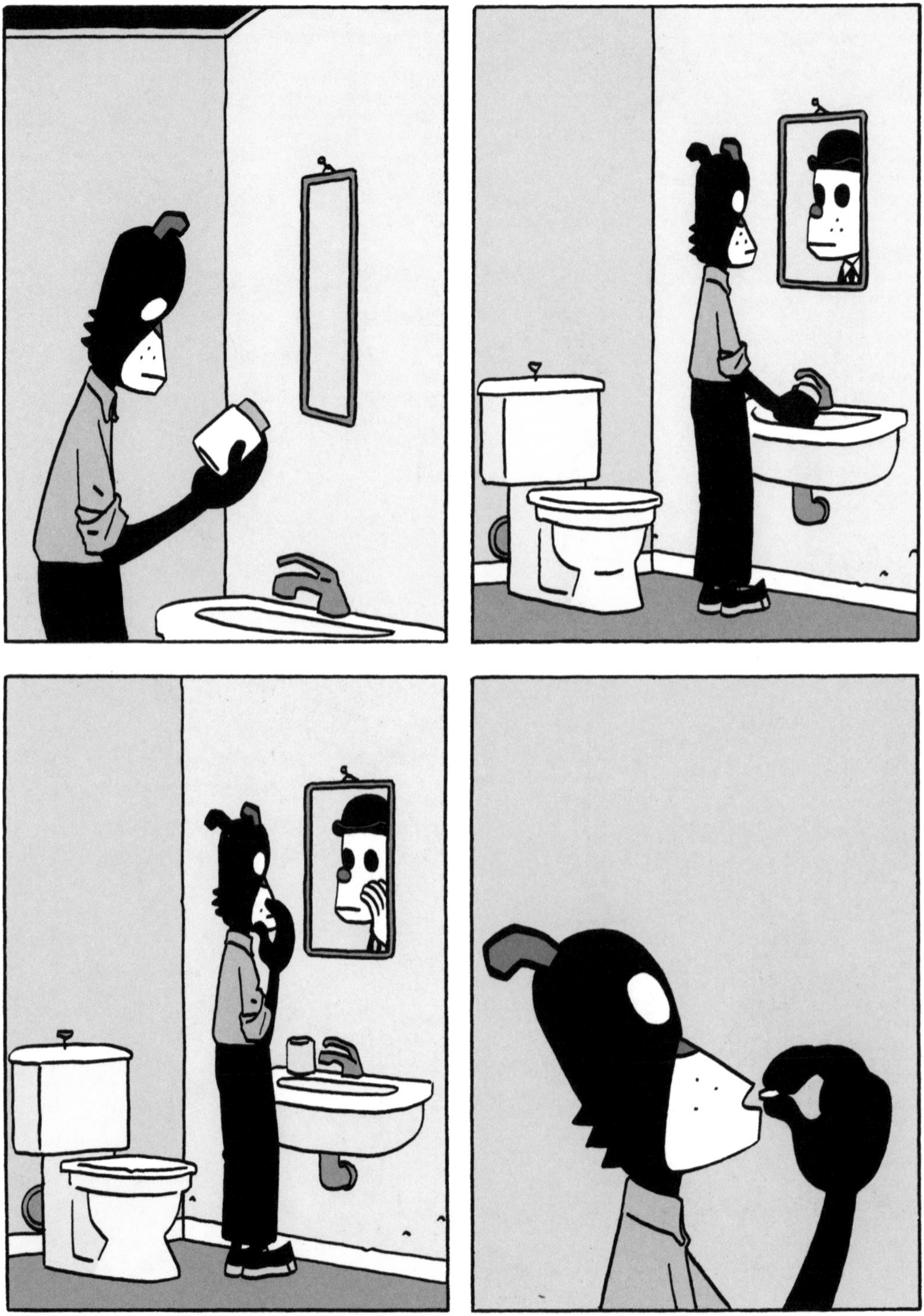

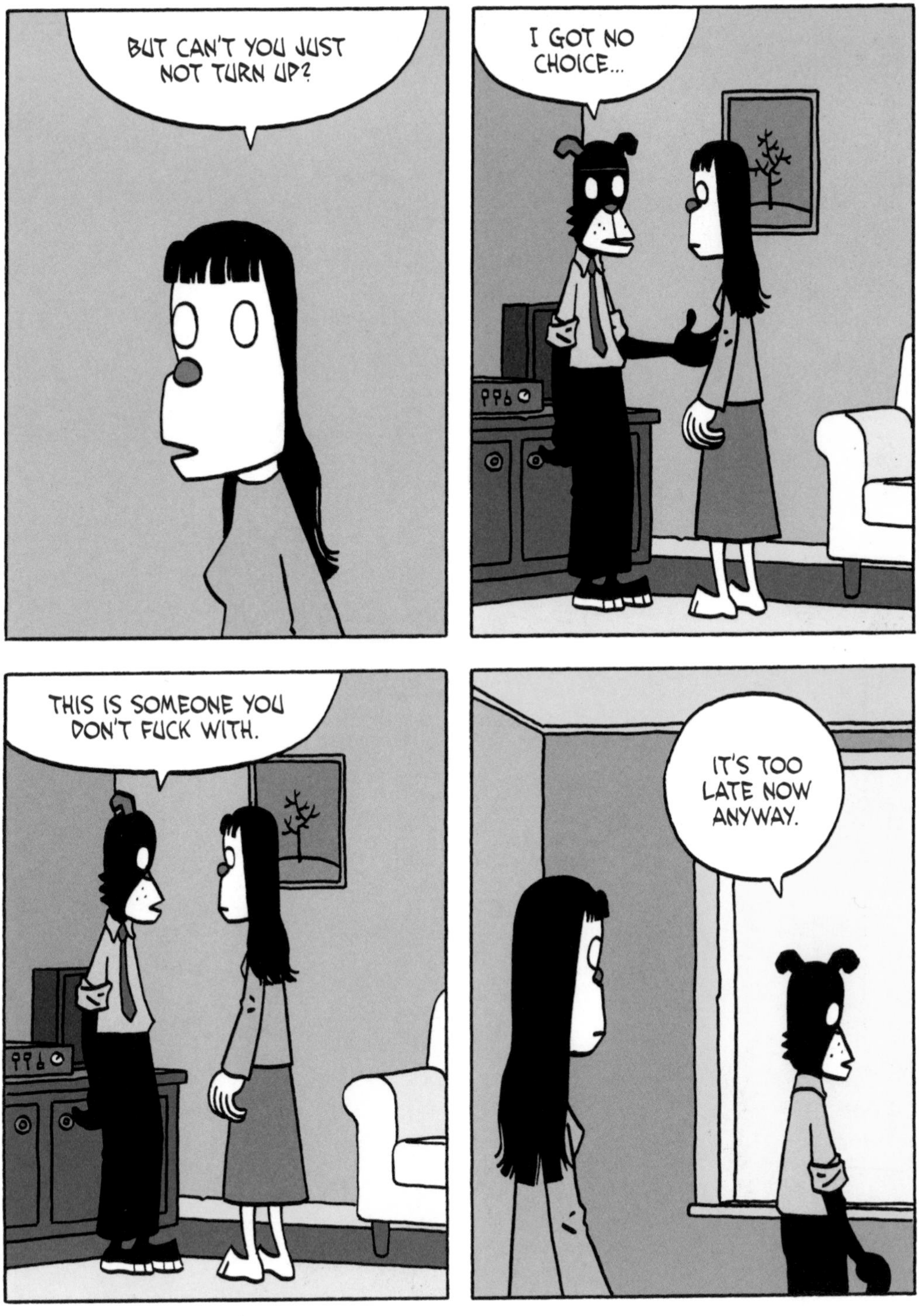
BUT CAN'T YOU JUST NOT TURN UP?
I GOT NO CHOICE...
THIS IS SOMEONE YOU DON'T FUCK WITH.
IT'S TOO LATE NOW ANYWAY.

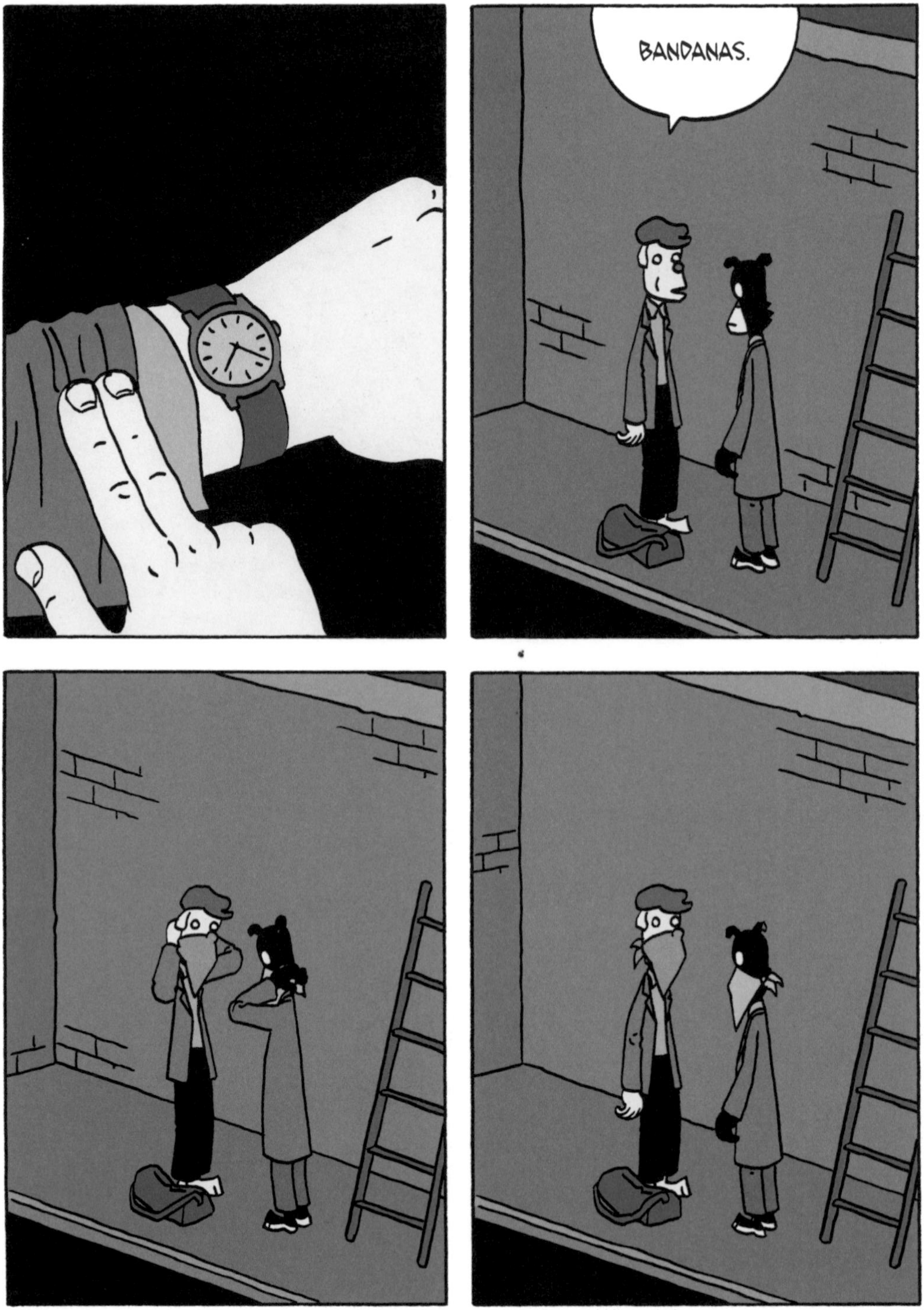
BANDANAS.

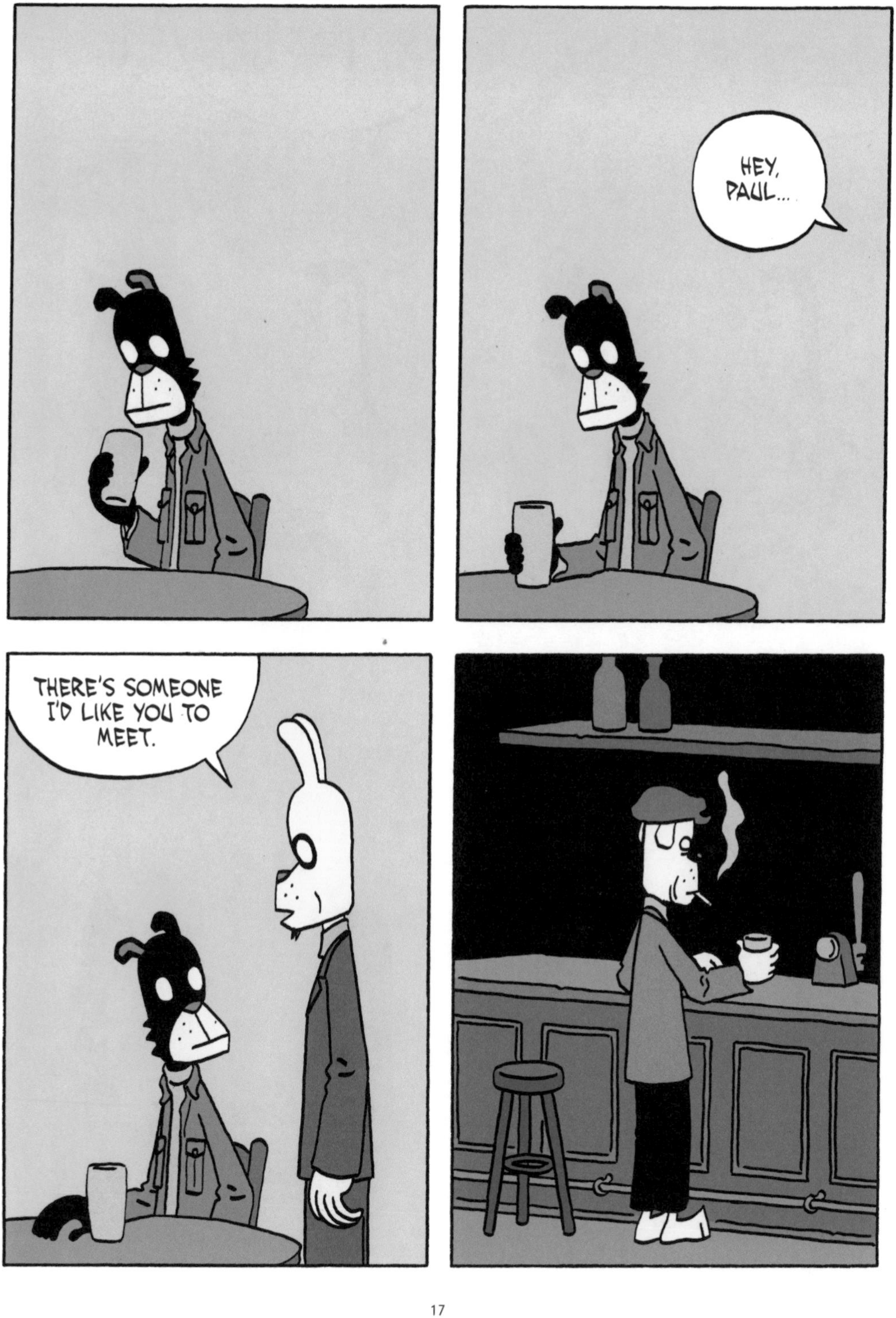
HEY, PAUL...
THERE'S SOMEONE I'D LIKE YOU TO MEET.

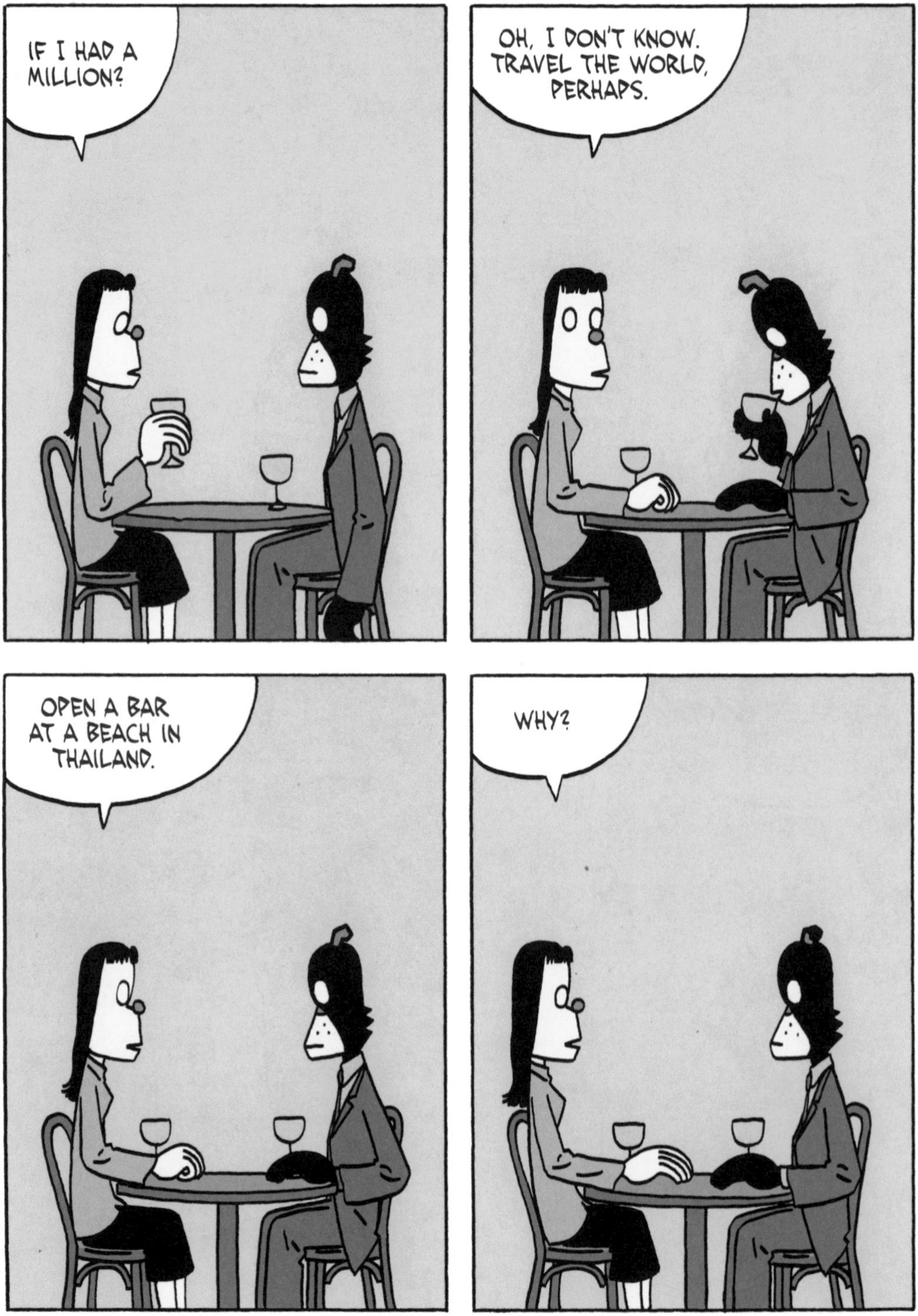
IF I HAD A MILLION?
OH, I DON'T KNOW. TRAVEL THE WORLD, PERHAPS.
OPEN A BAR AT A BEACH IN THAILAND.
WHY?

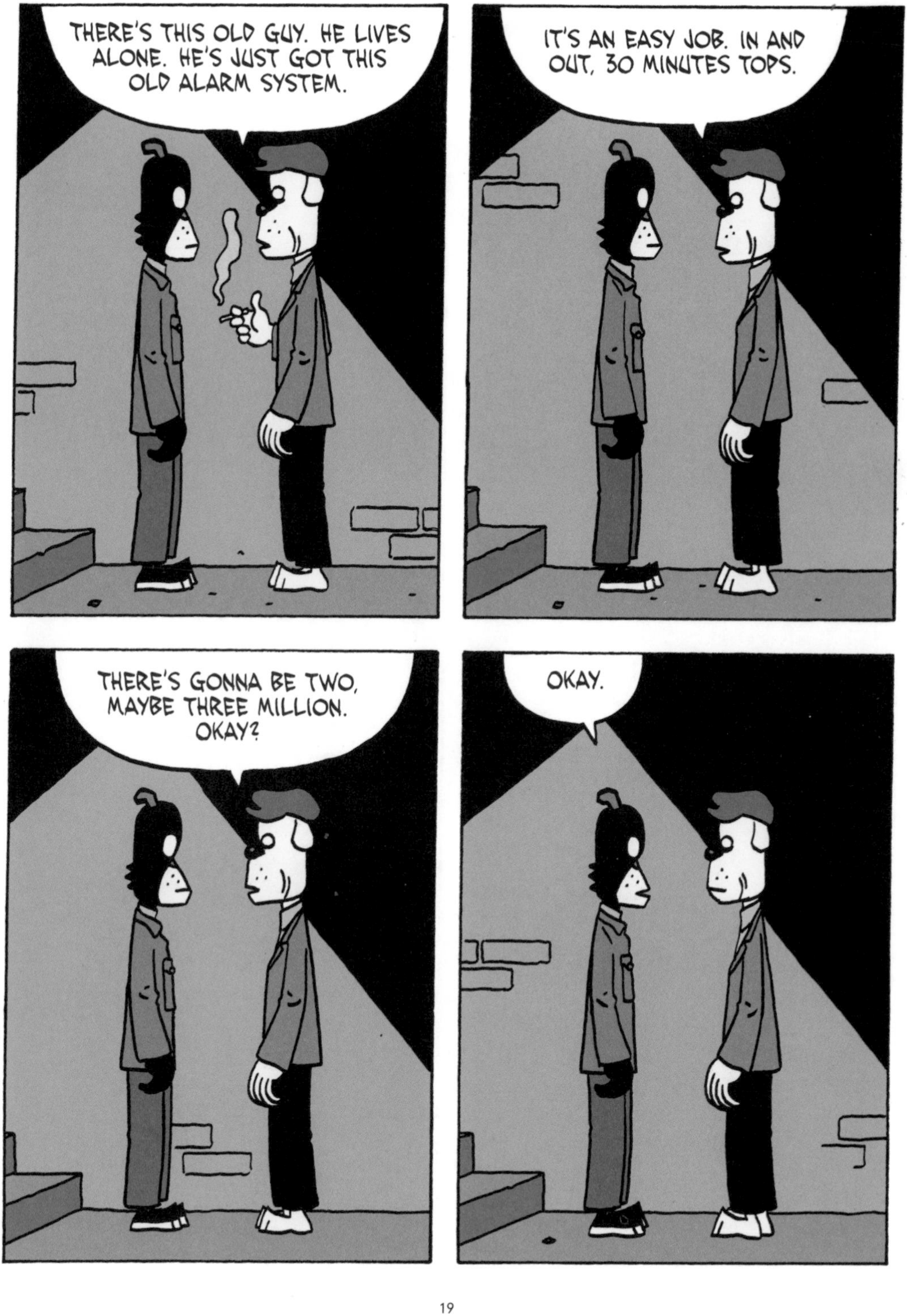
THERE'S THIS OLD GUY. HE LIVES ALONE. HE'S JUST GOT THIS OLD ALARM SYSTEM.
IT'S AN EASY JOB. IN AND OUT, 30 MINUTES TOPS.
THERE'S GONNA BE TWO, MAYBE THREE MILLION. OKAY?
OKAY.

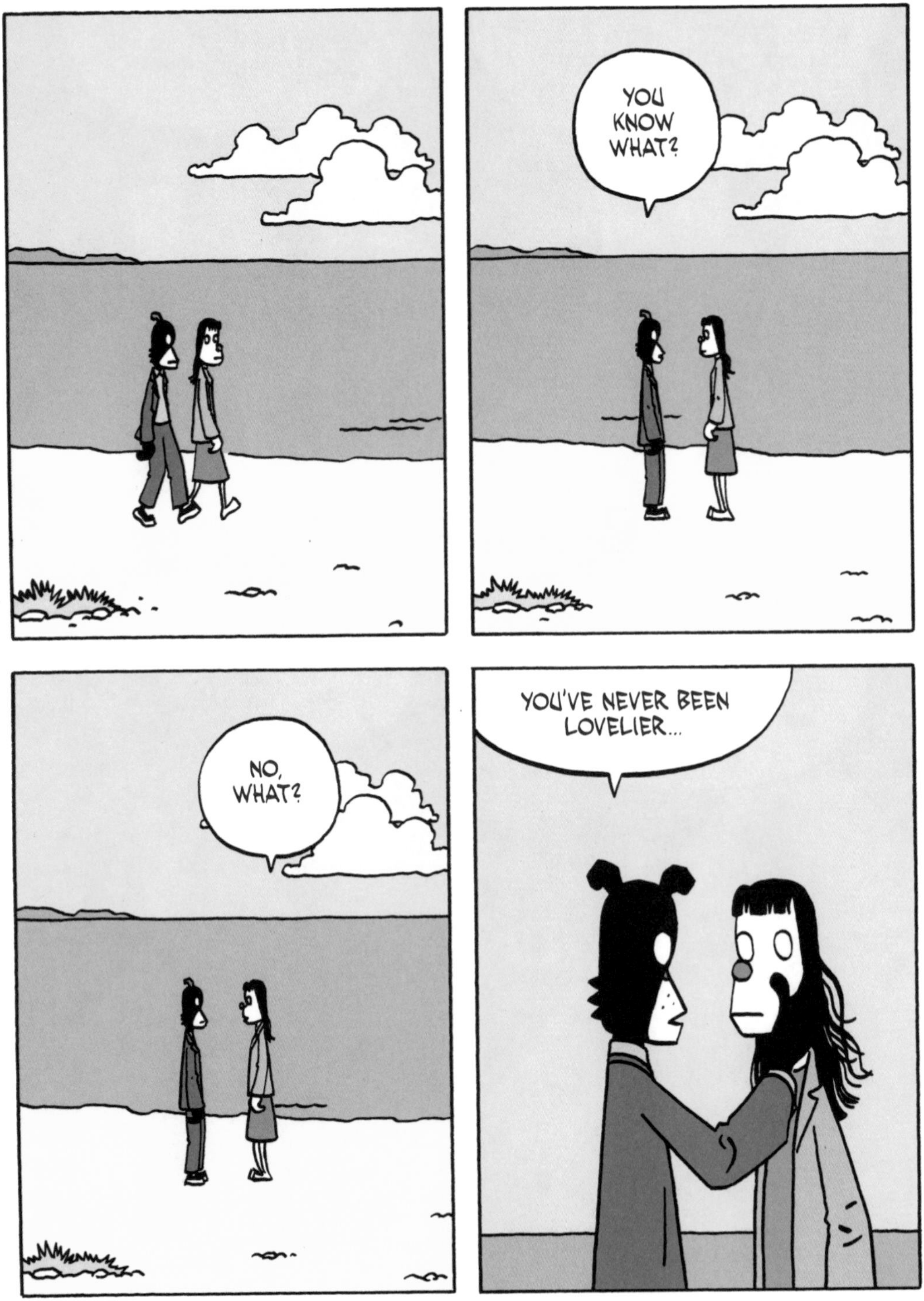
YOU KNOW WHAT?
NO, WHAT?
YOU'VE NEVER BEEN LOVELIER...

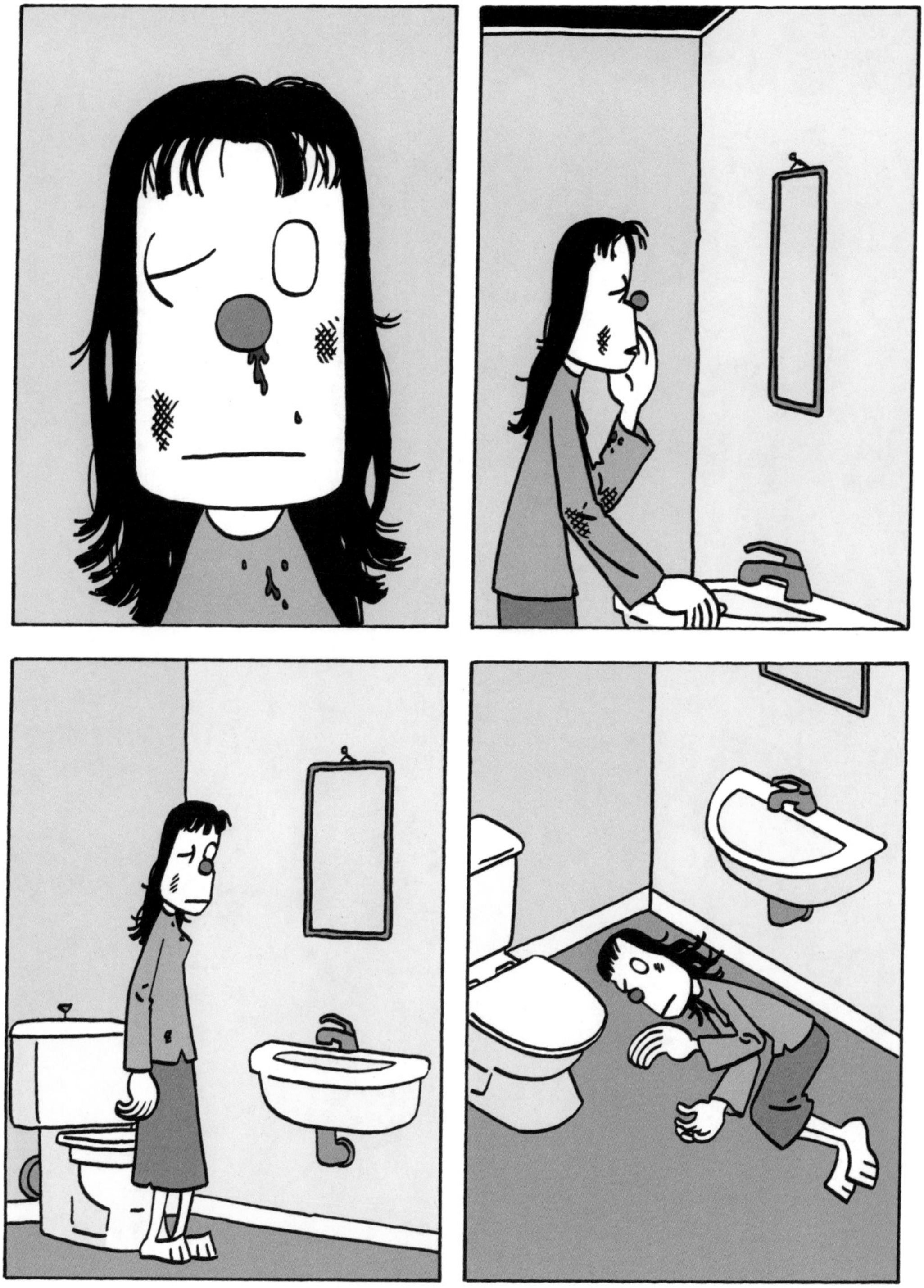

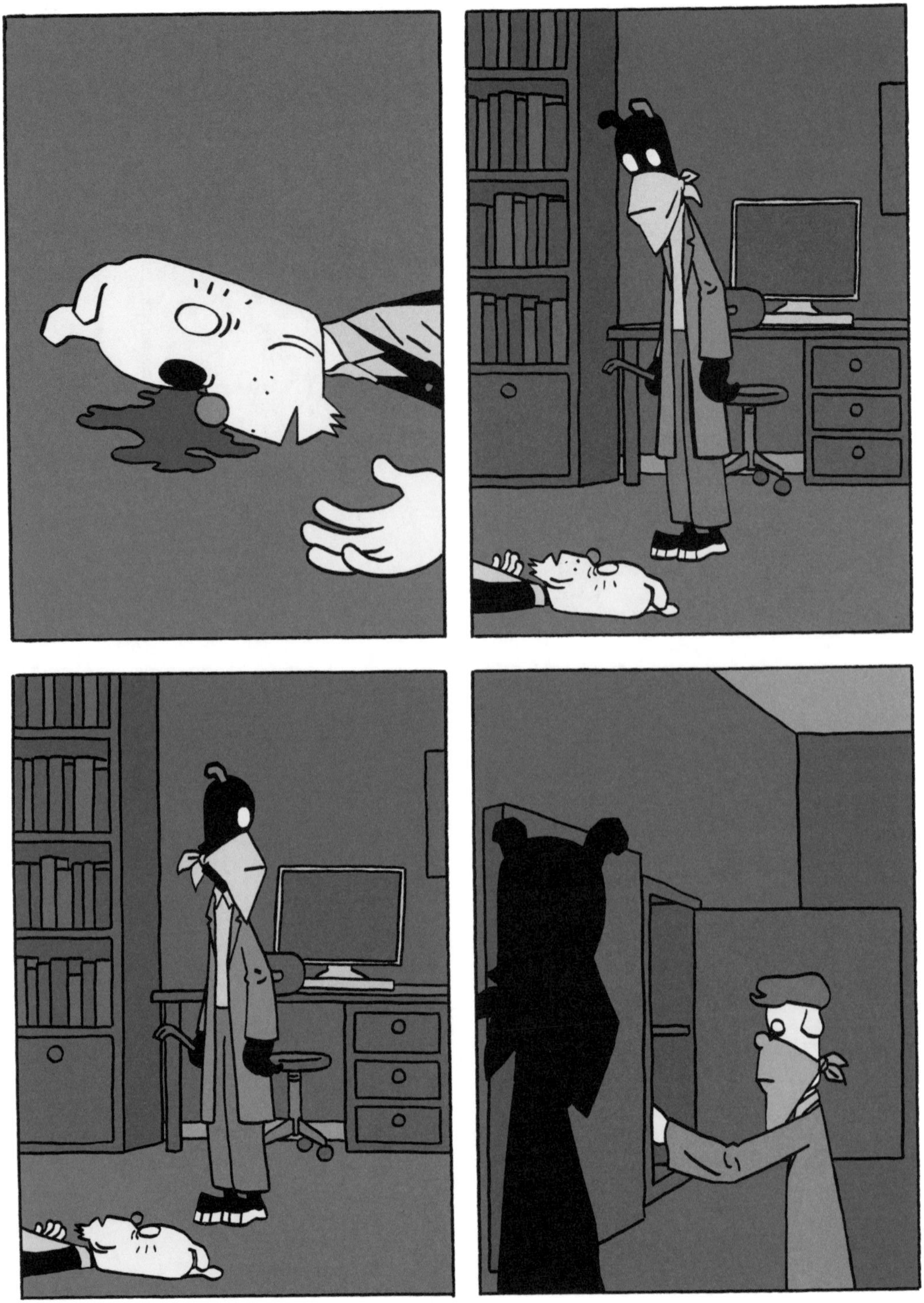

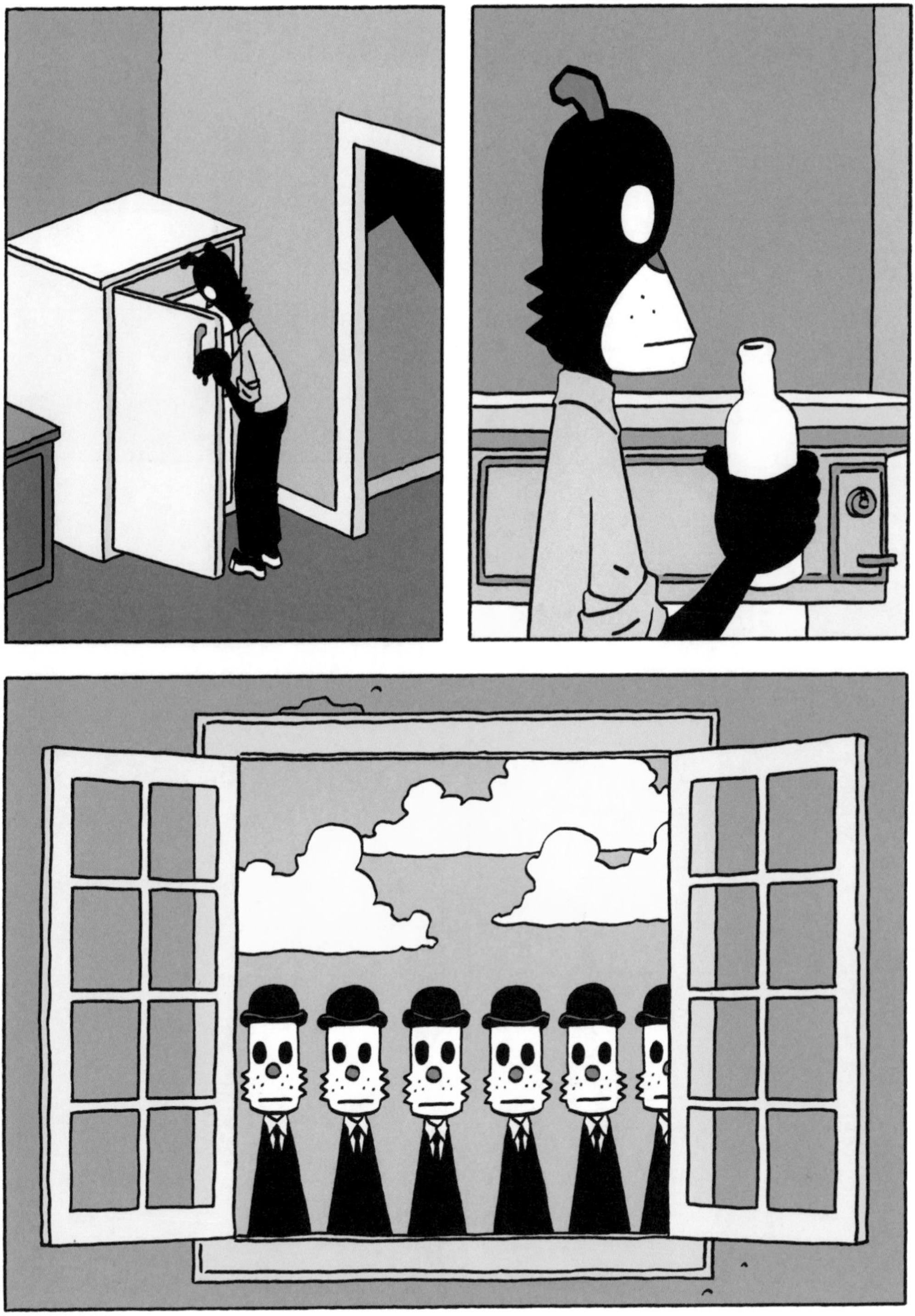

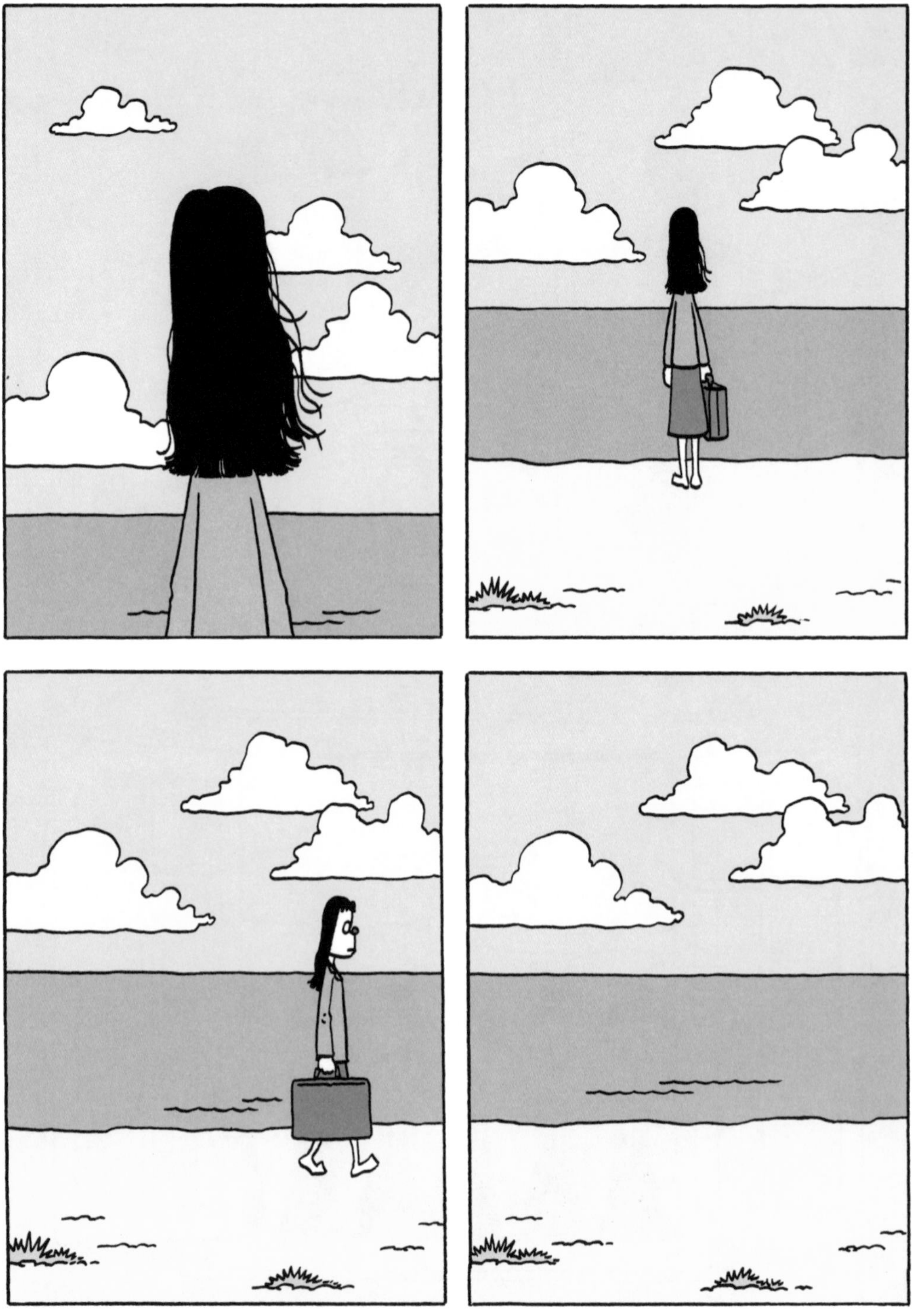

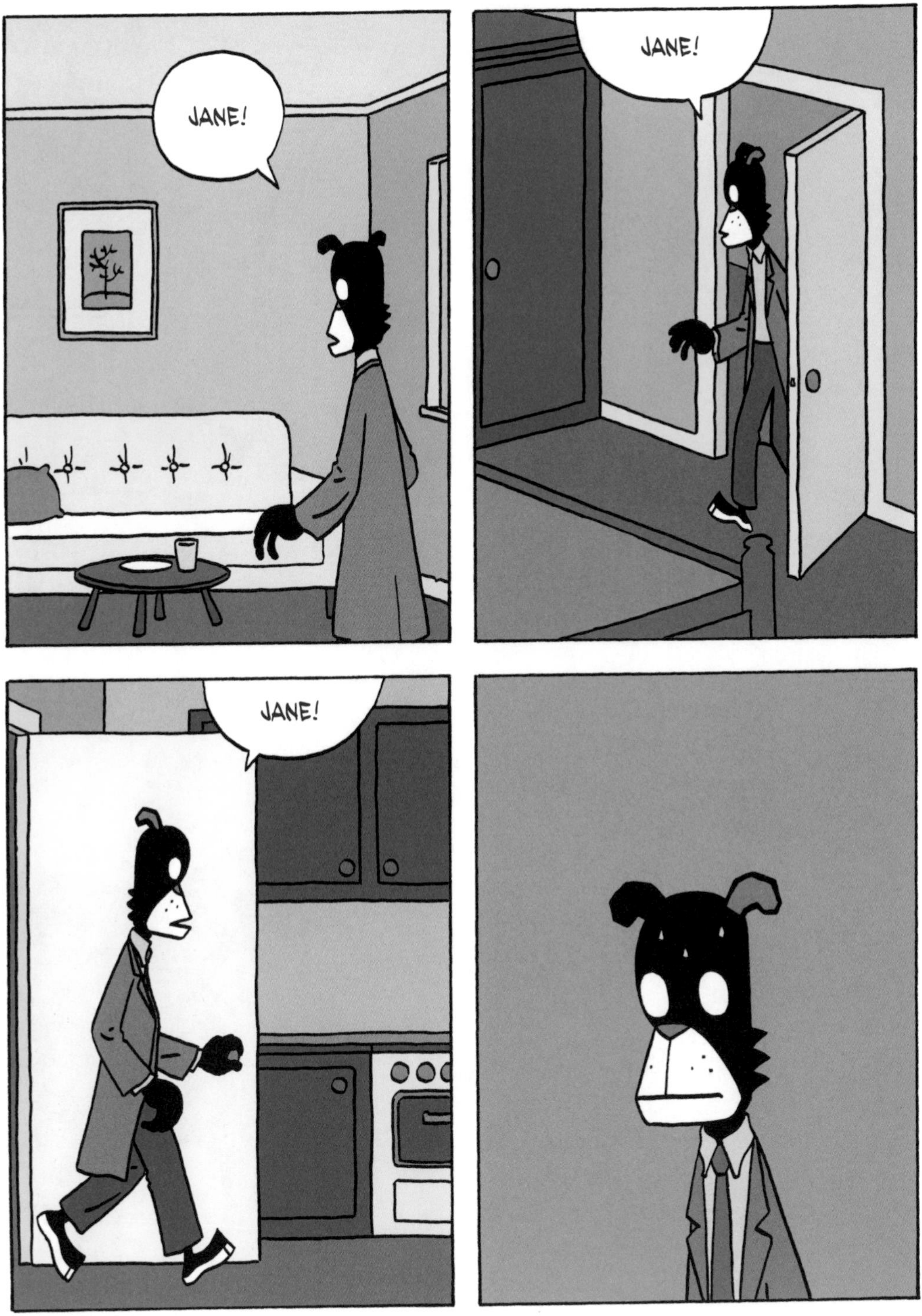
JANE!
JANE!
JANE!

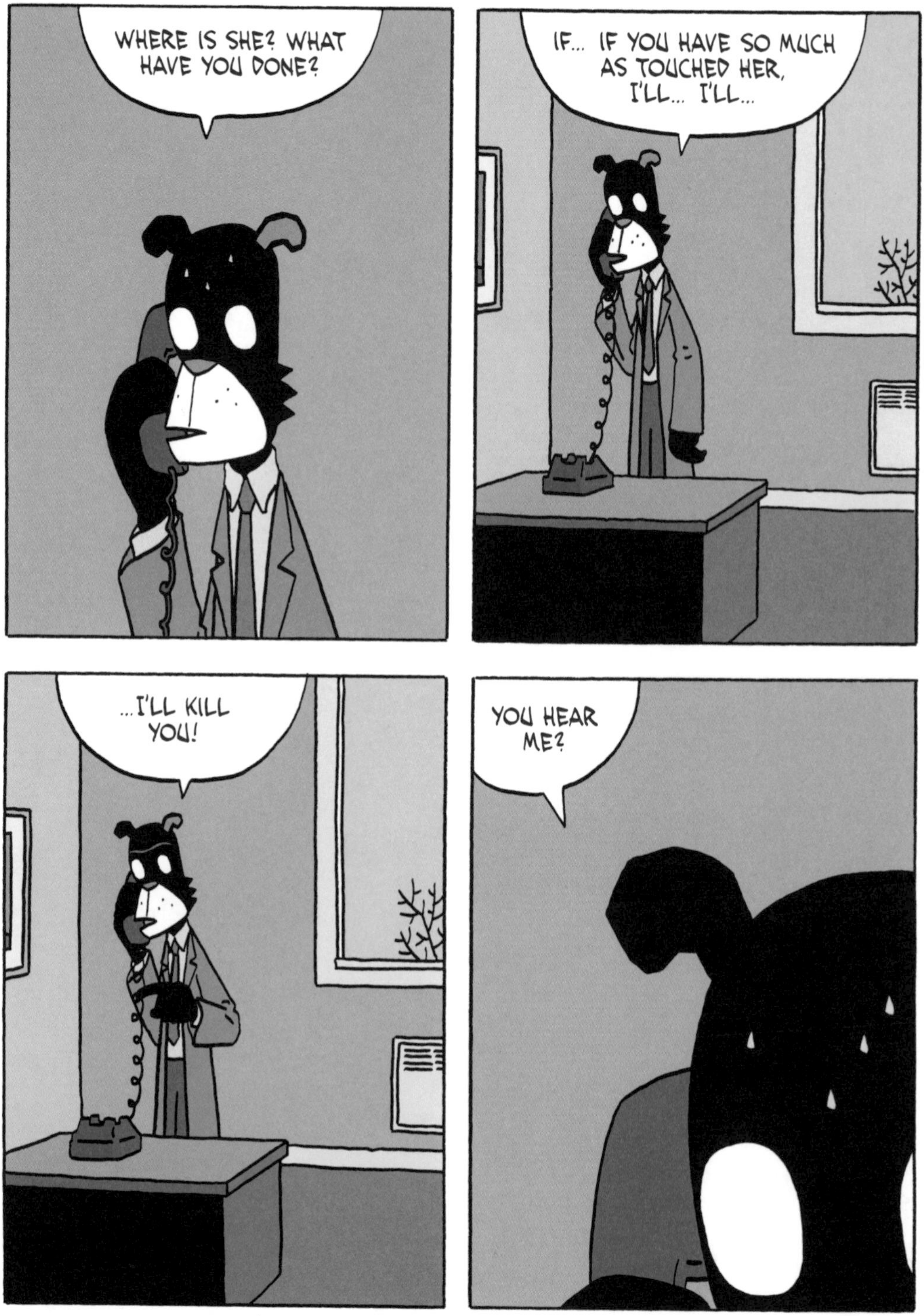
WHERE IS SHE? WHAT HAVE YOU DONE?
IF... IF YOU HAVE SO MUCH AS TOUCHED HER, I'LL... I'LL...
...I'LL KILL YOU!
YOU HEAR ME?

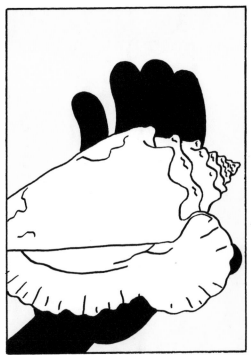

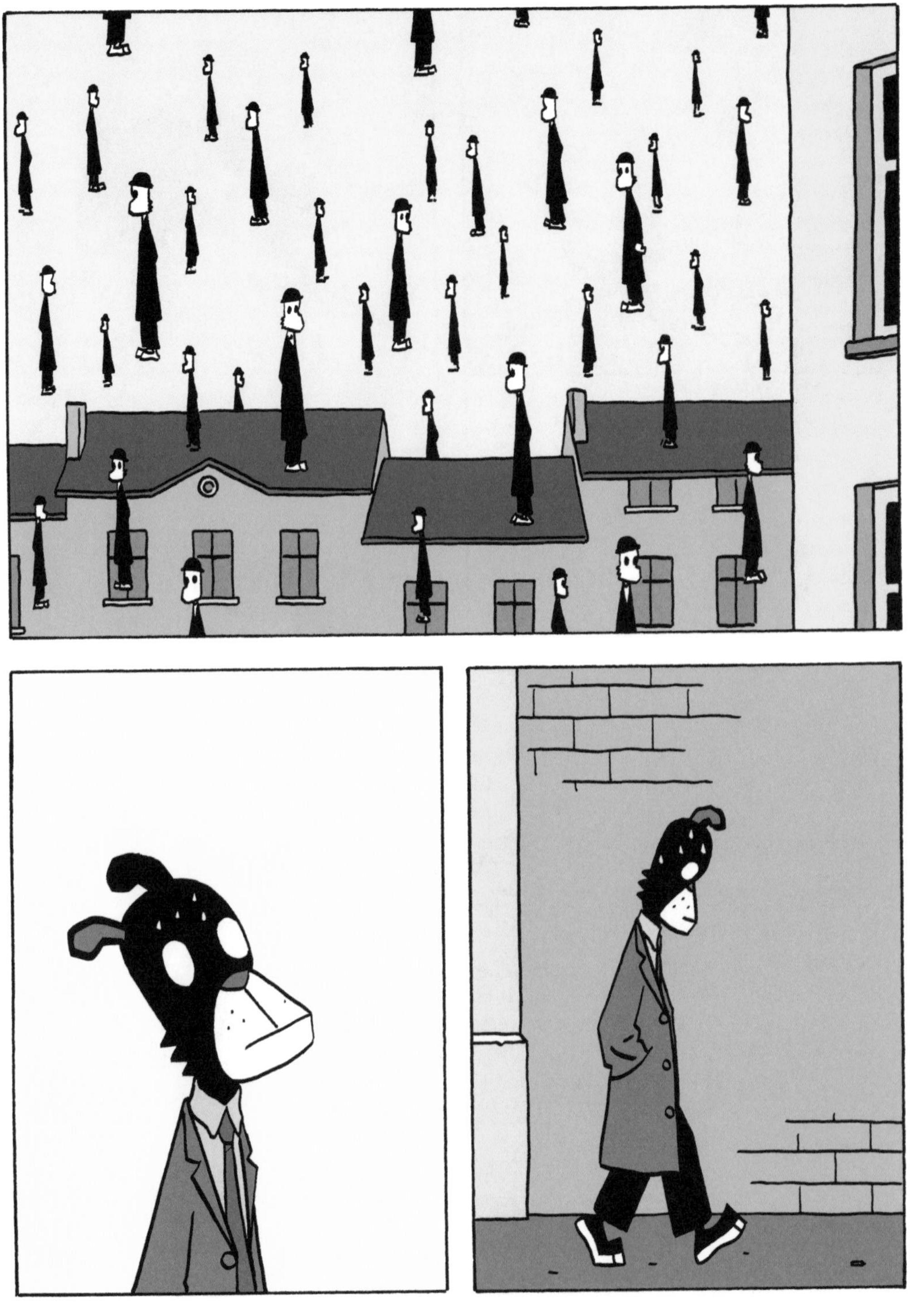

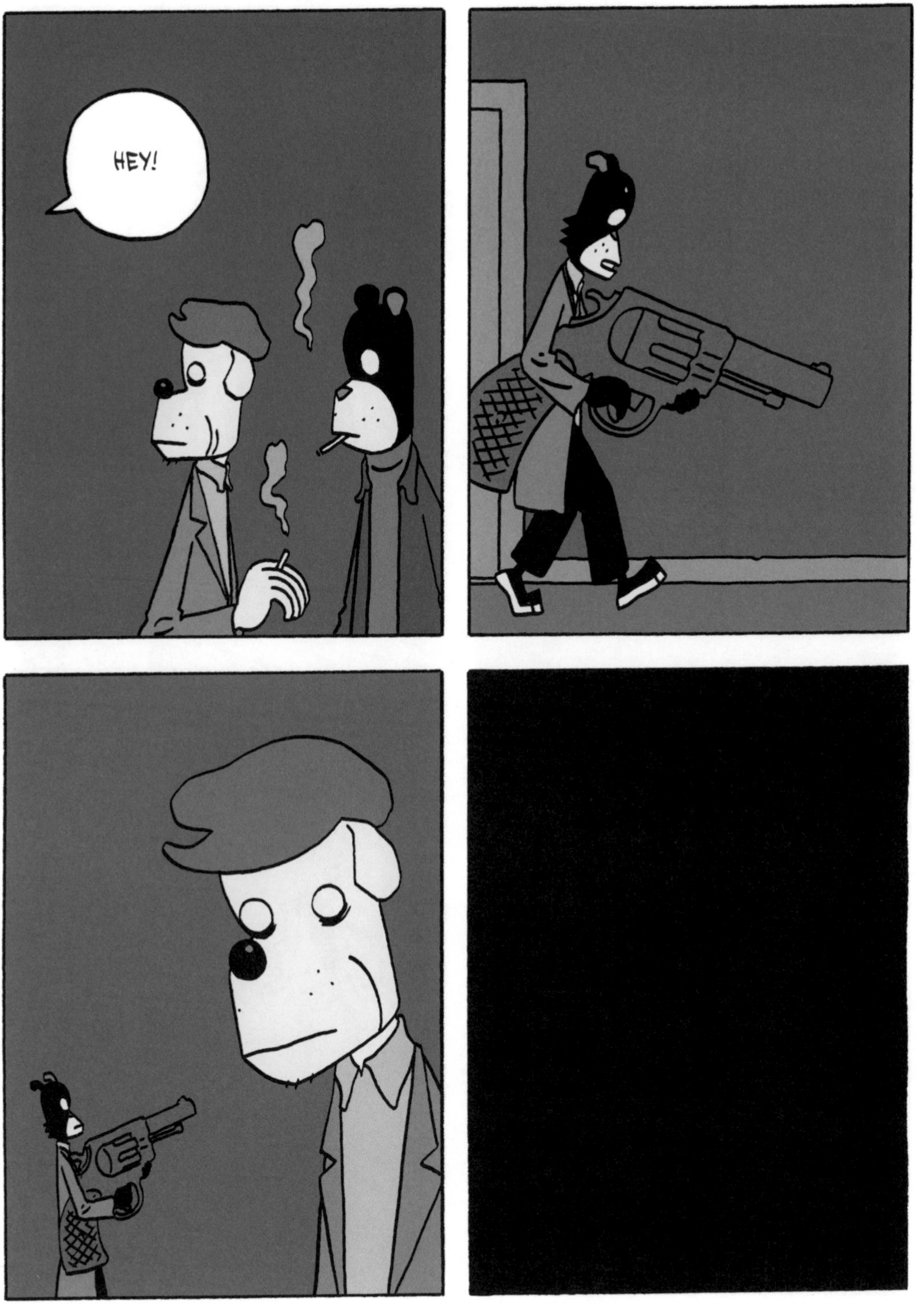
HEY!

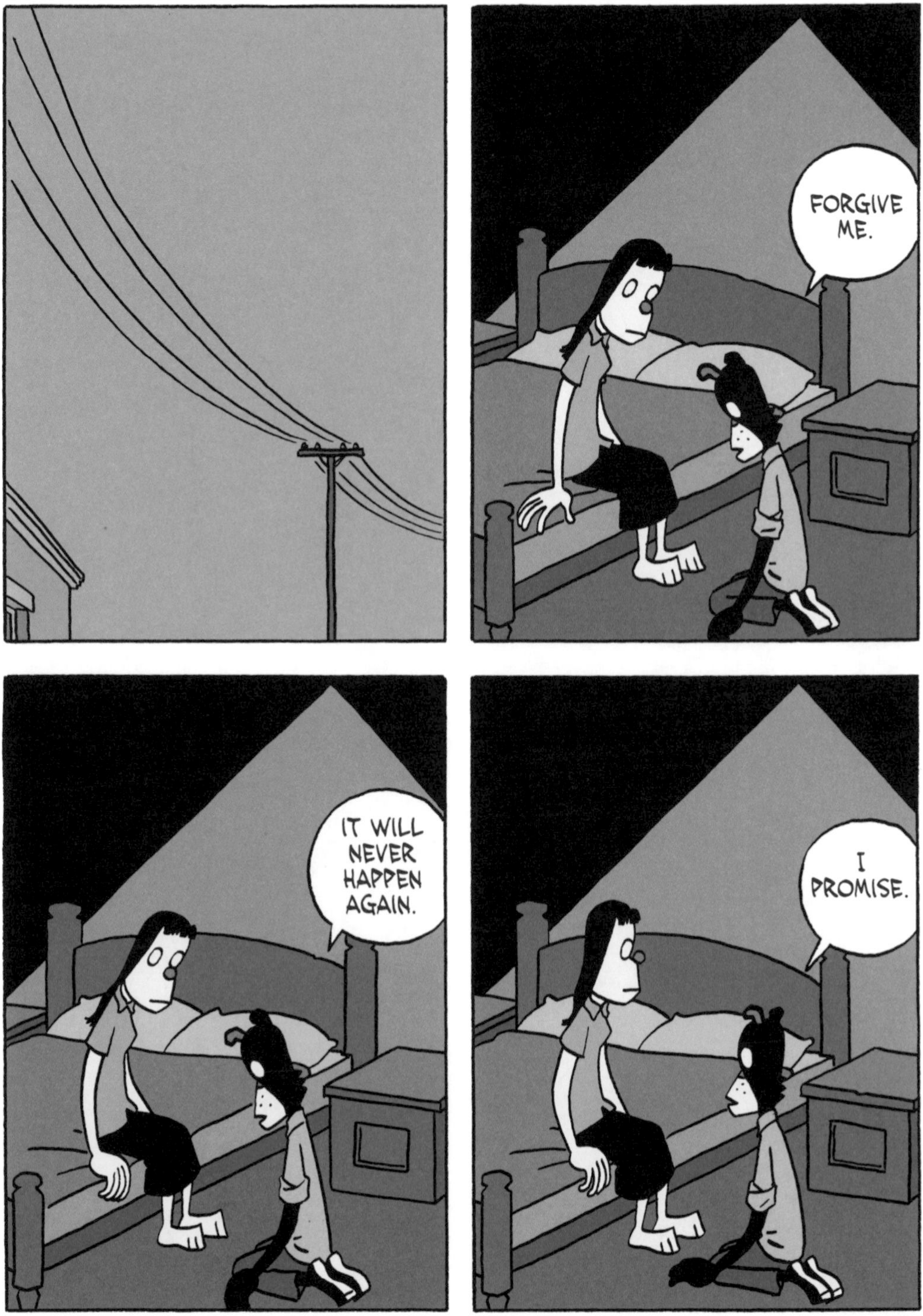
FORGIVE ME.
IT WILL NEVER HAPPEN AGAIN.
I PROMISE.

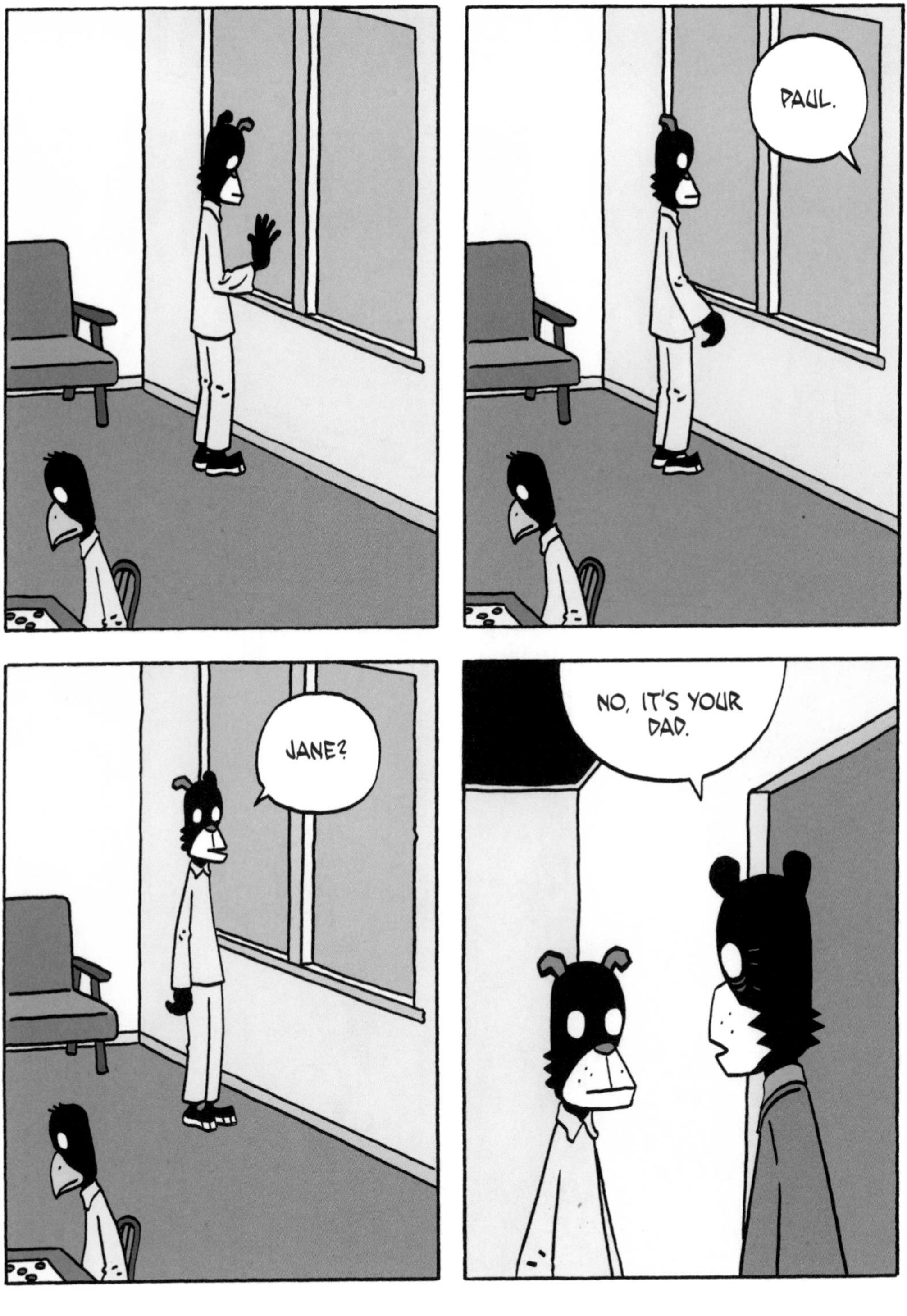
PAUL.
JANE?
NO, IT'S YOUR DAD.

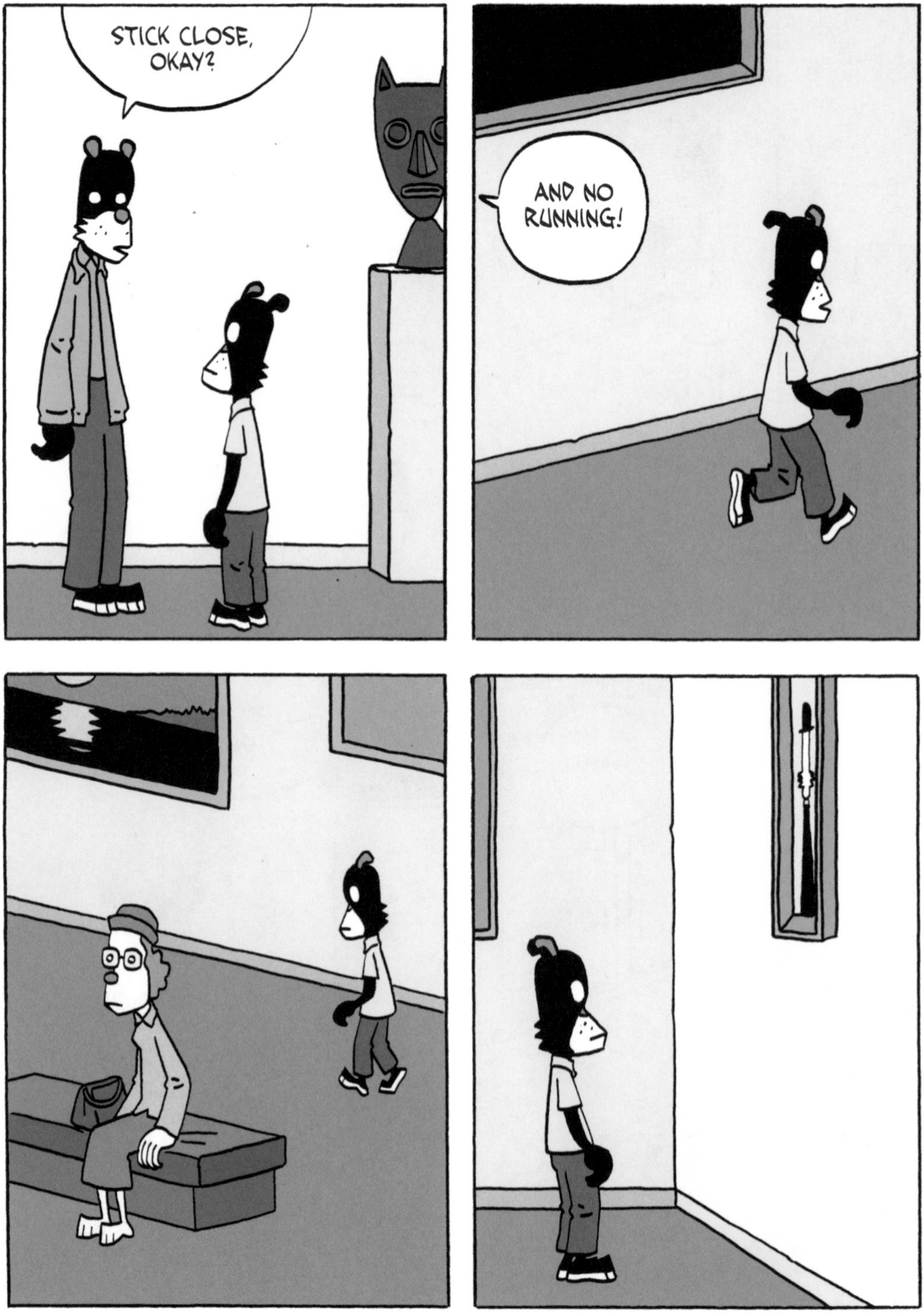
STICK CLOSE, OKAY?
AND NO RUNNING!

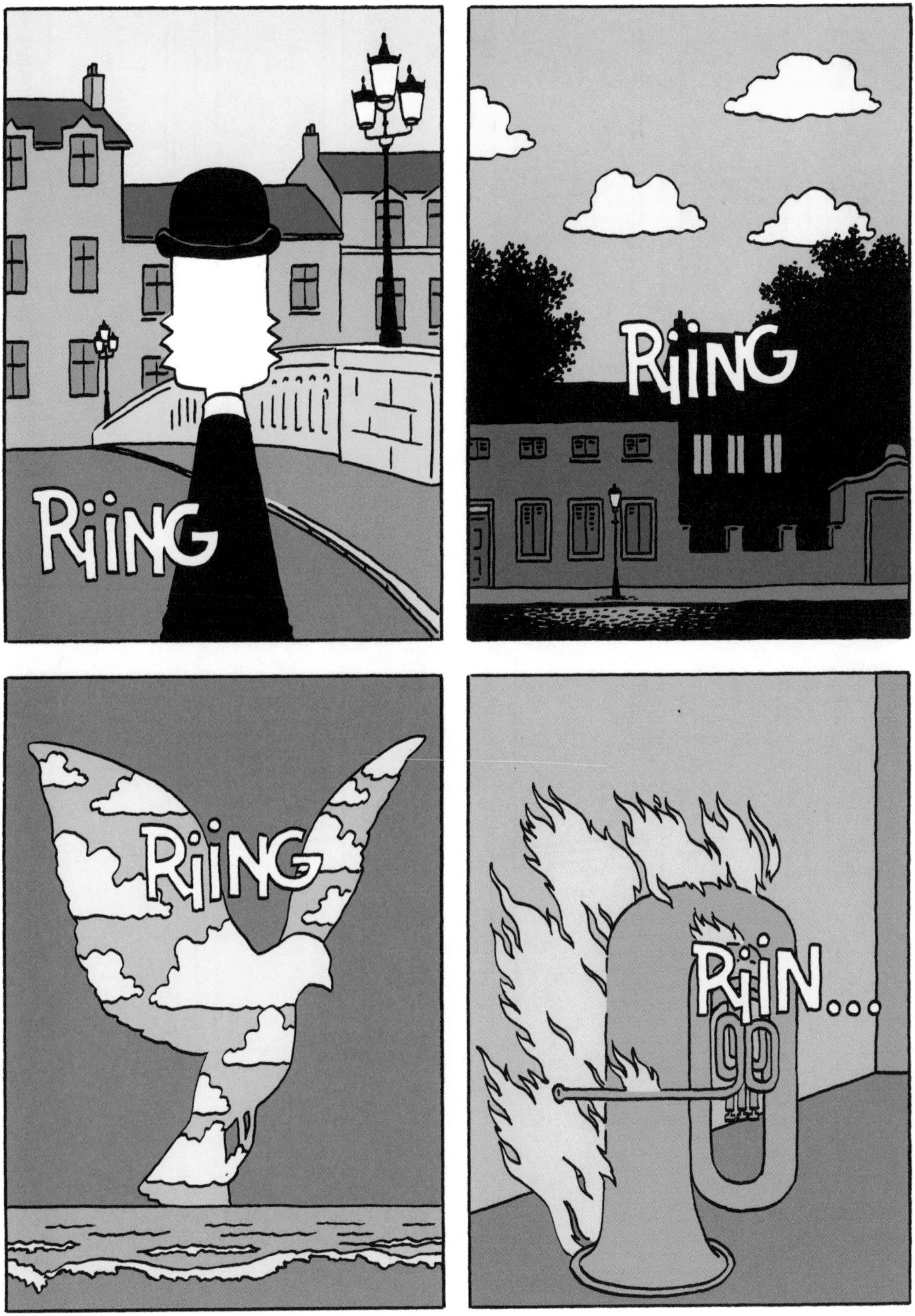
RIING
RIING
RIING
RIIN...

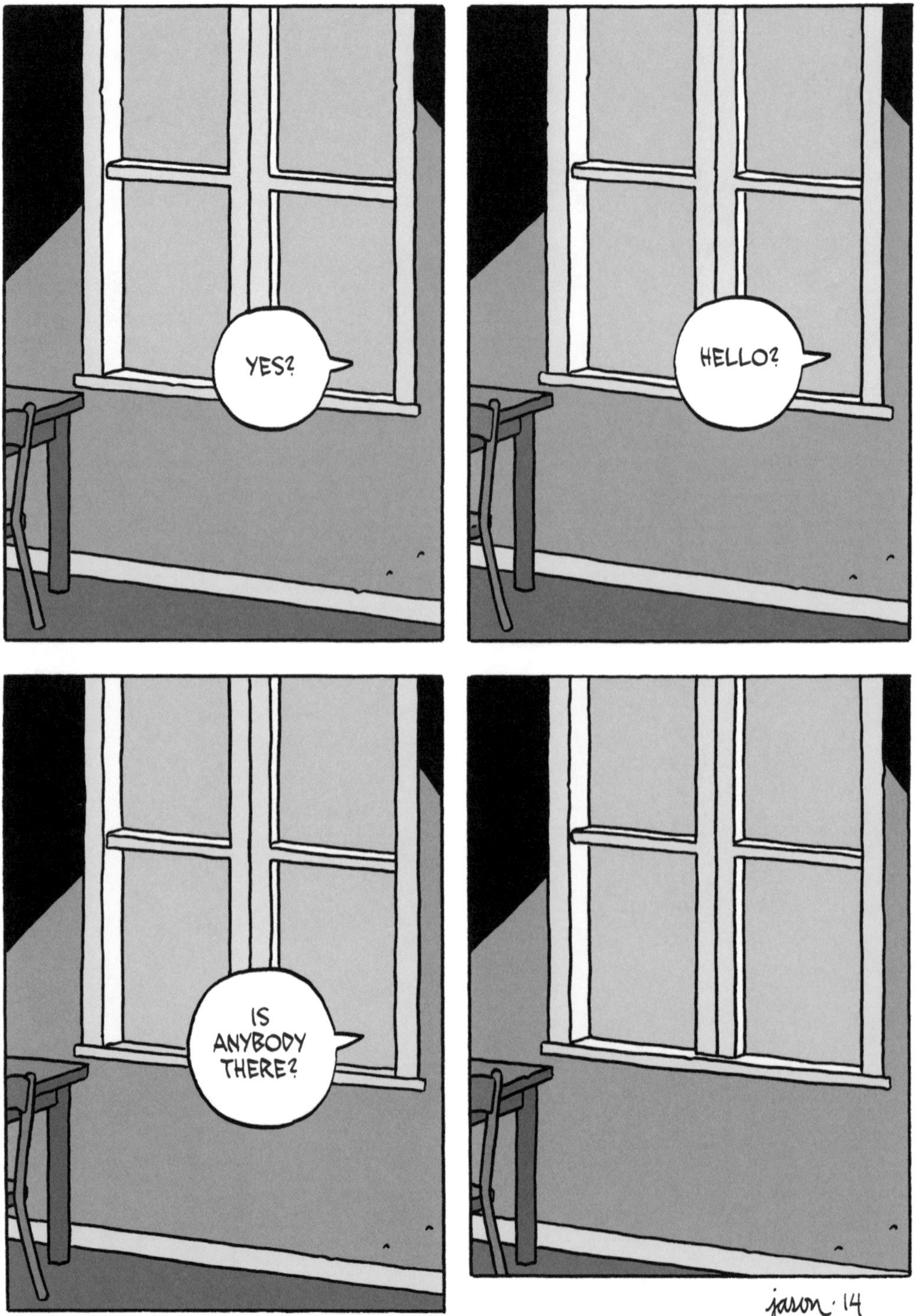
YES?
HELLO?
IS ANYBODY THERE?

jason · 14

PRESENTING:

KARMA CHAMELEON

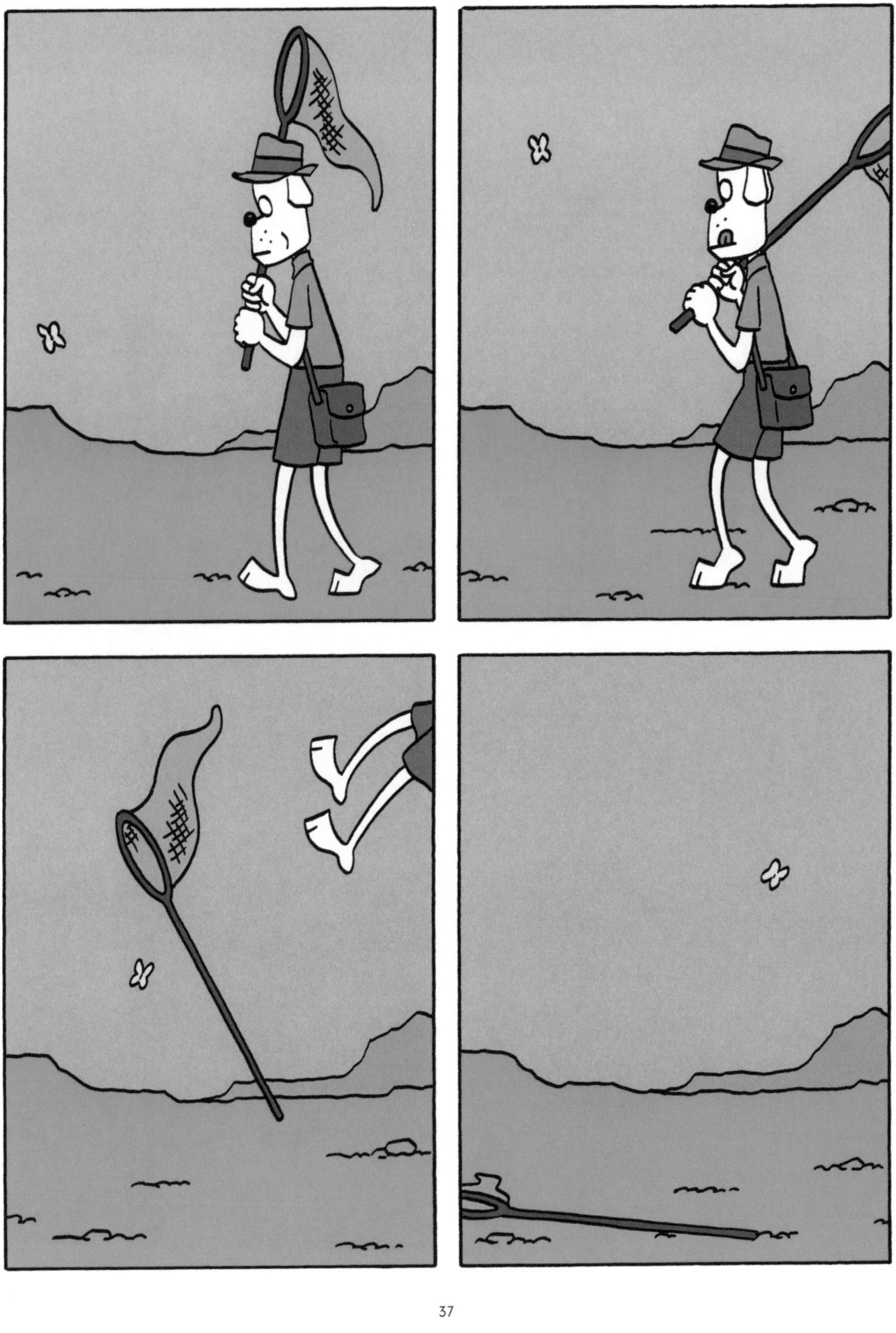

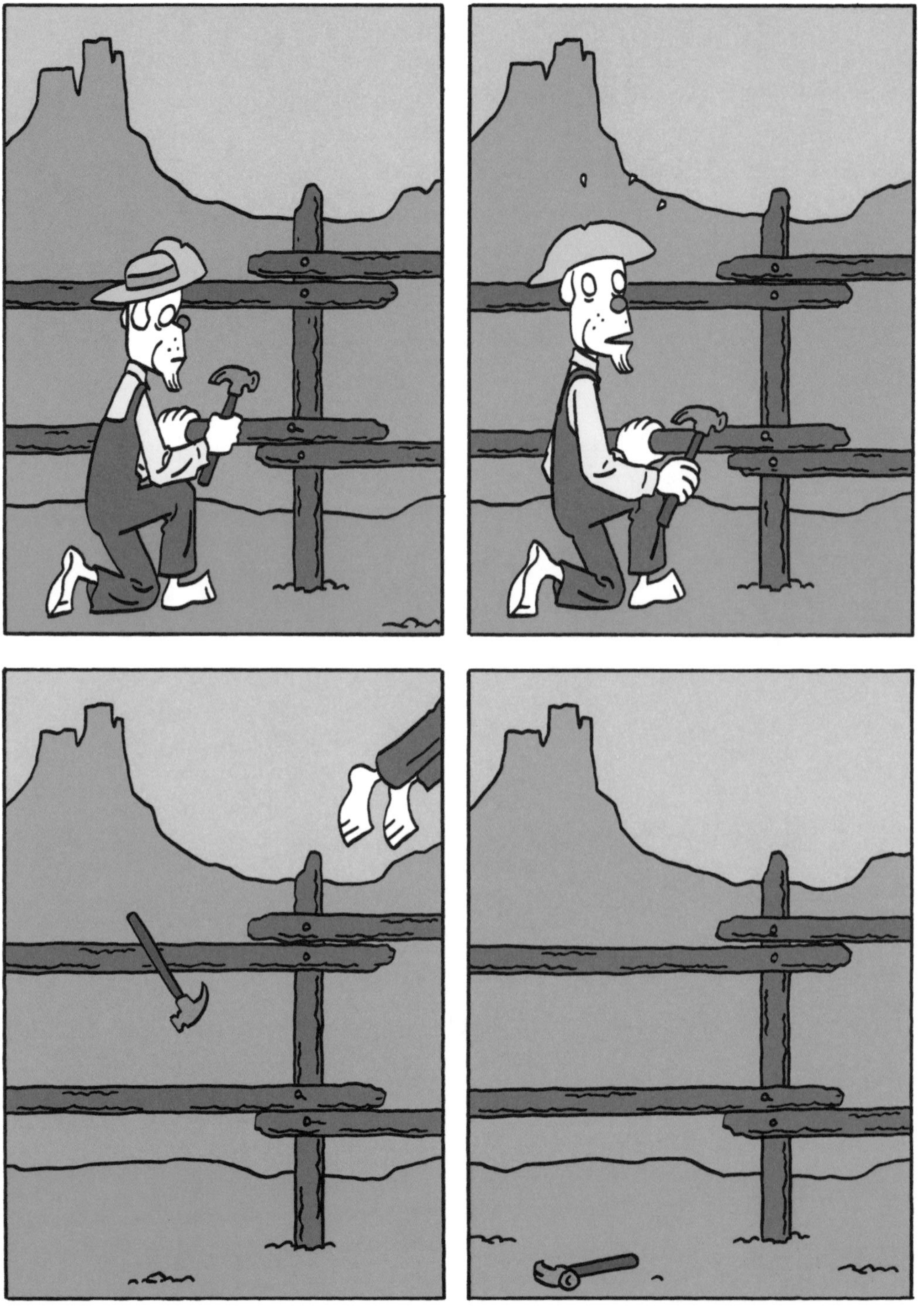

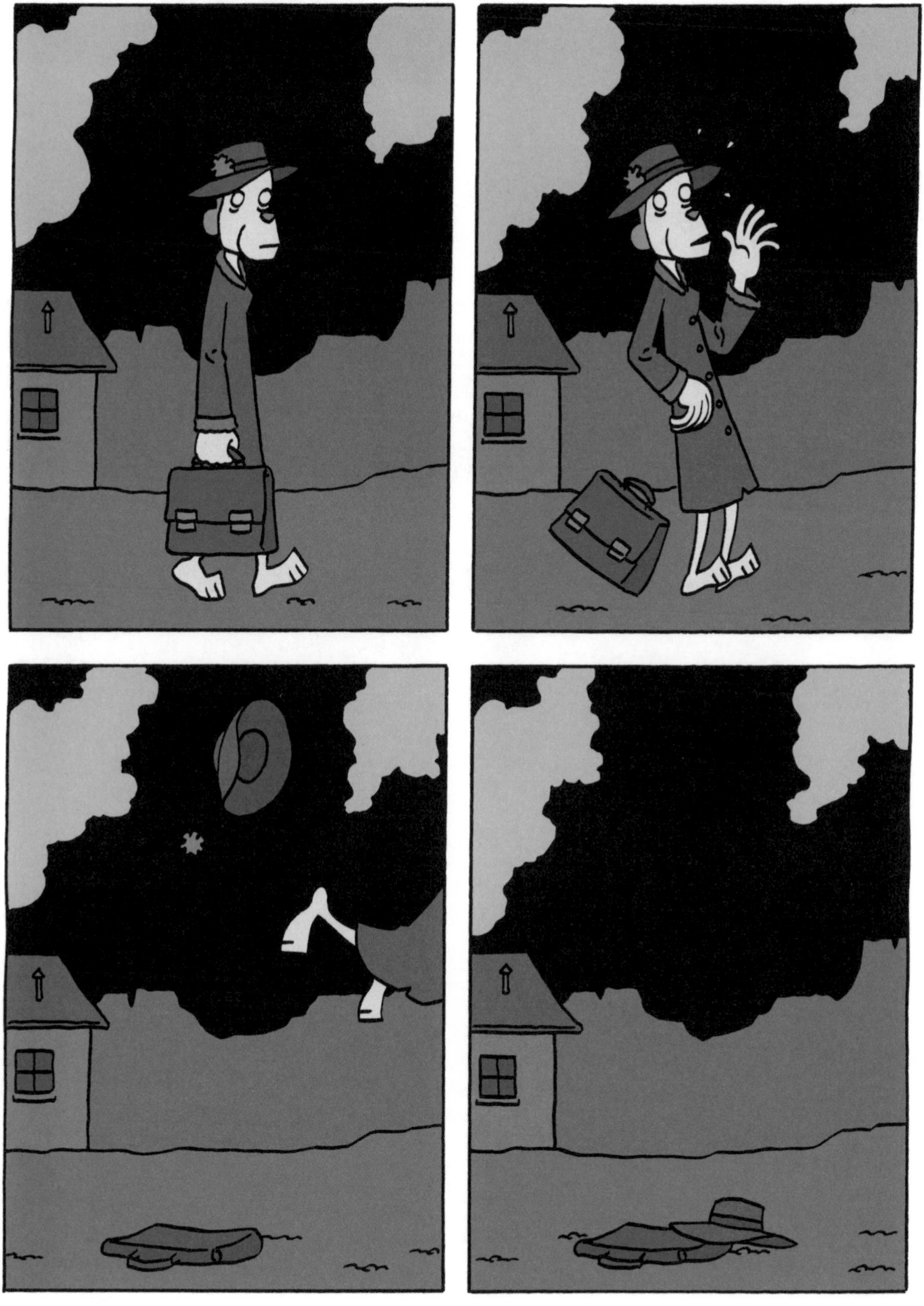

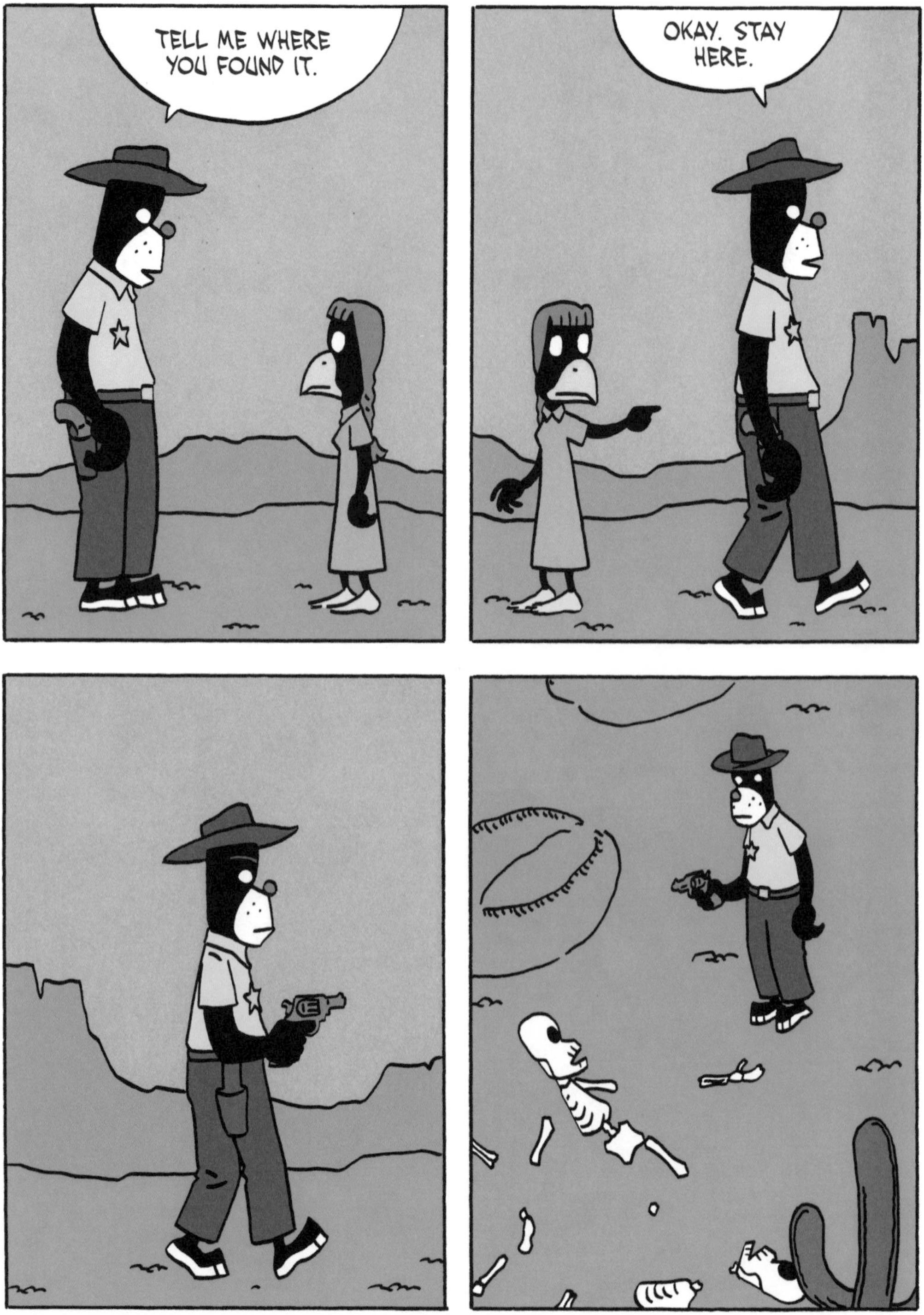
TELL ME WHERE YOU FOUND IT.
OKAY. STAY HERE.

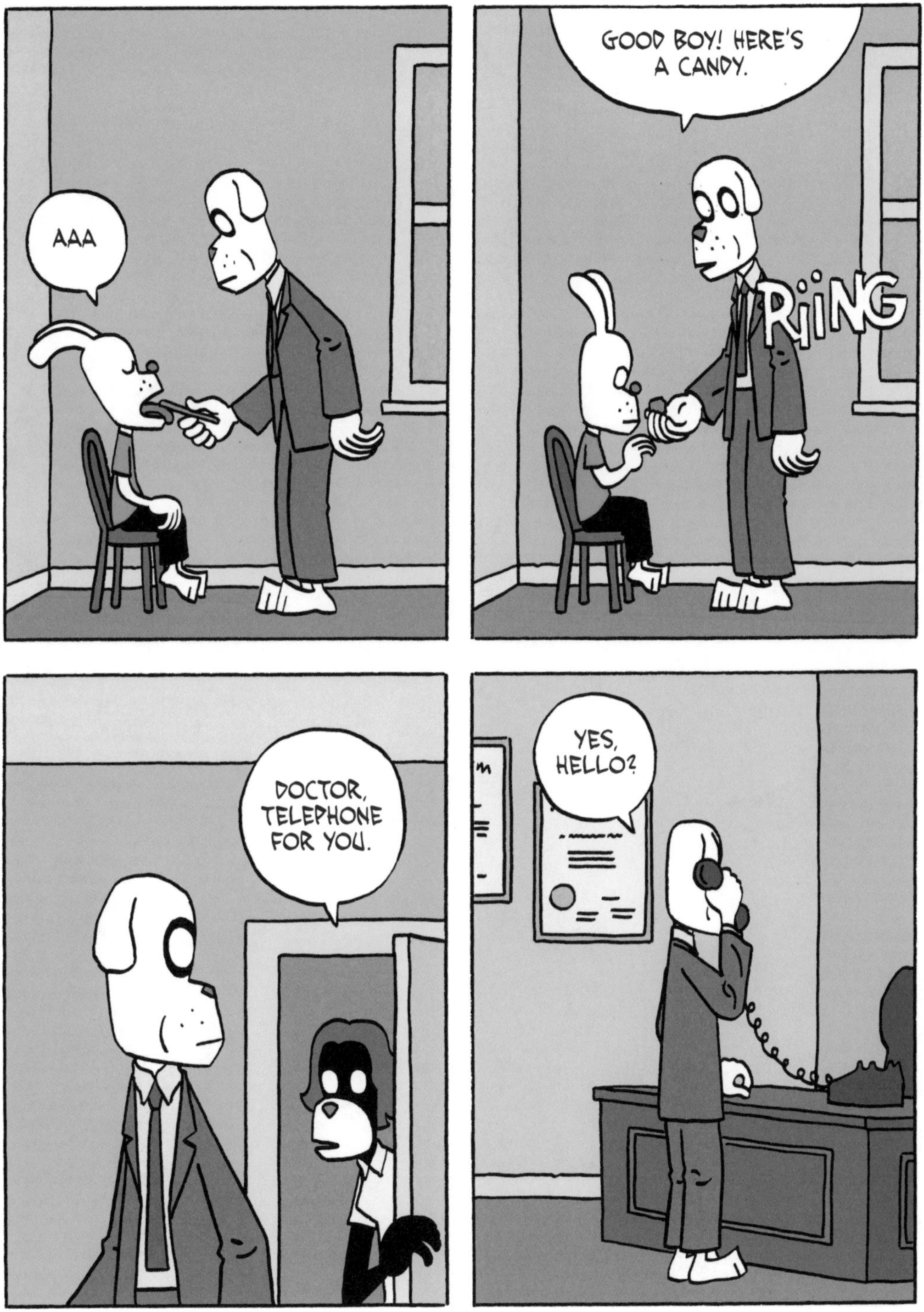
AAA
GOOD BOY! HERE'S A CANDY.
RIING
DOCTOR, TELEPHONE FOR YOU.
YES, HELLO?

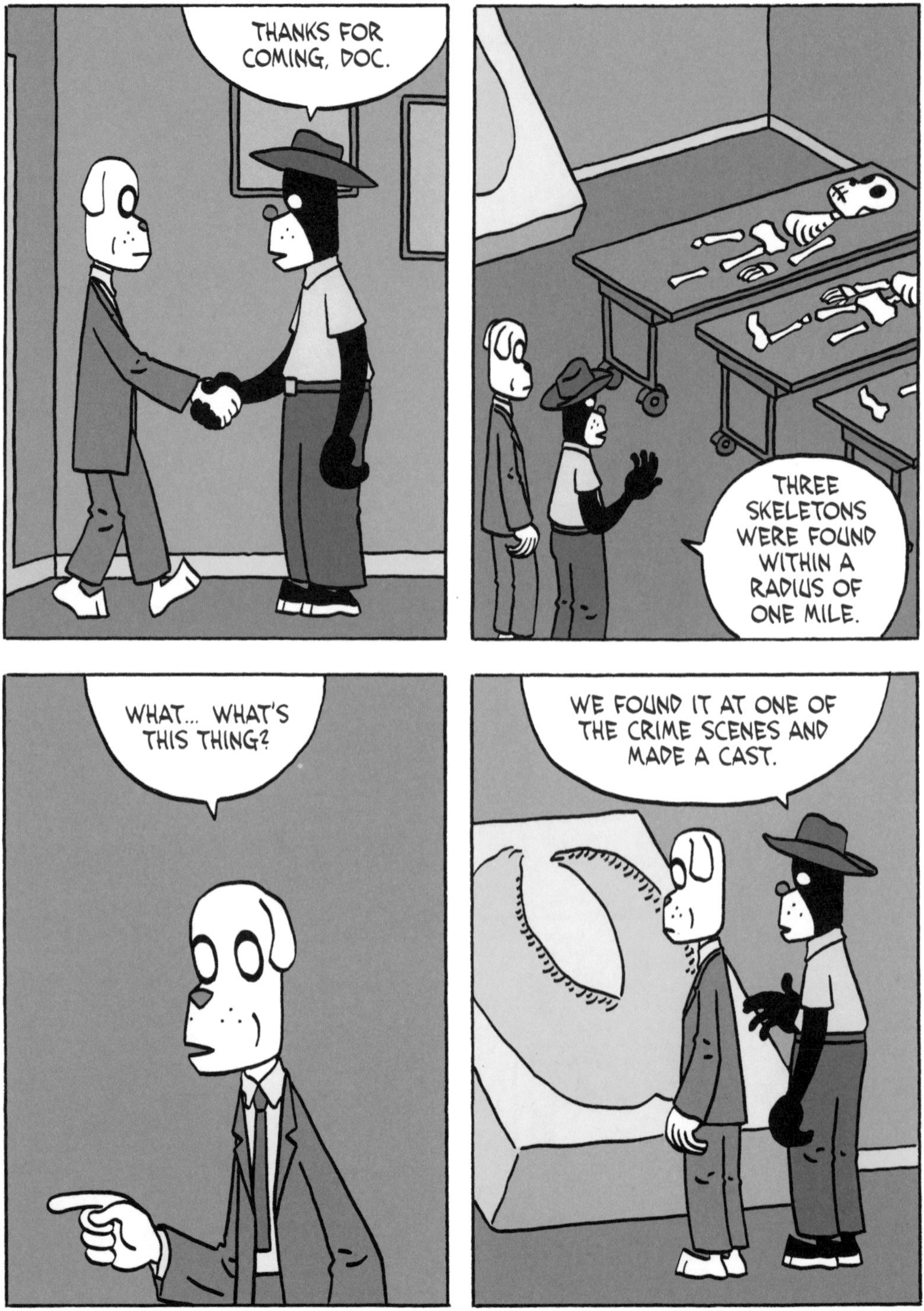
THANKS FOR COMING, DOC.
THREE SKELETONS WERE FOUND WITHIN A RADIUS OF ONE MILE.
WHAT... WHAT'S THIS THING?
WE FOUND IT AT ONE OF THE CRIME SCENES AND MADE A CAST.

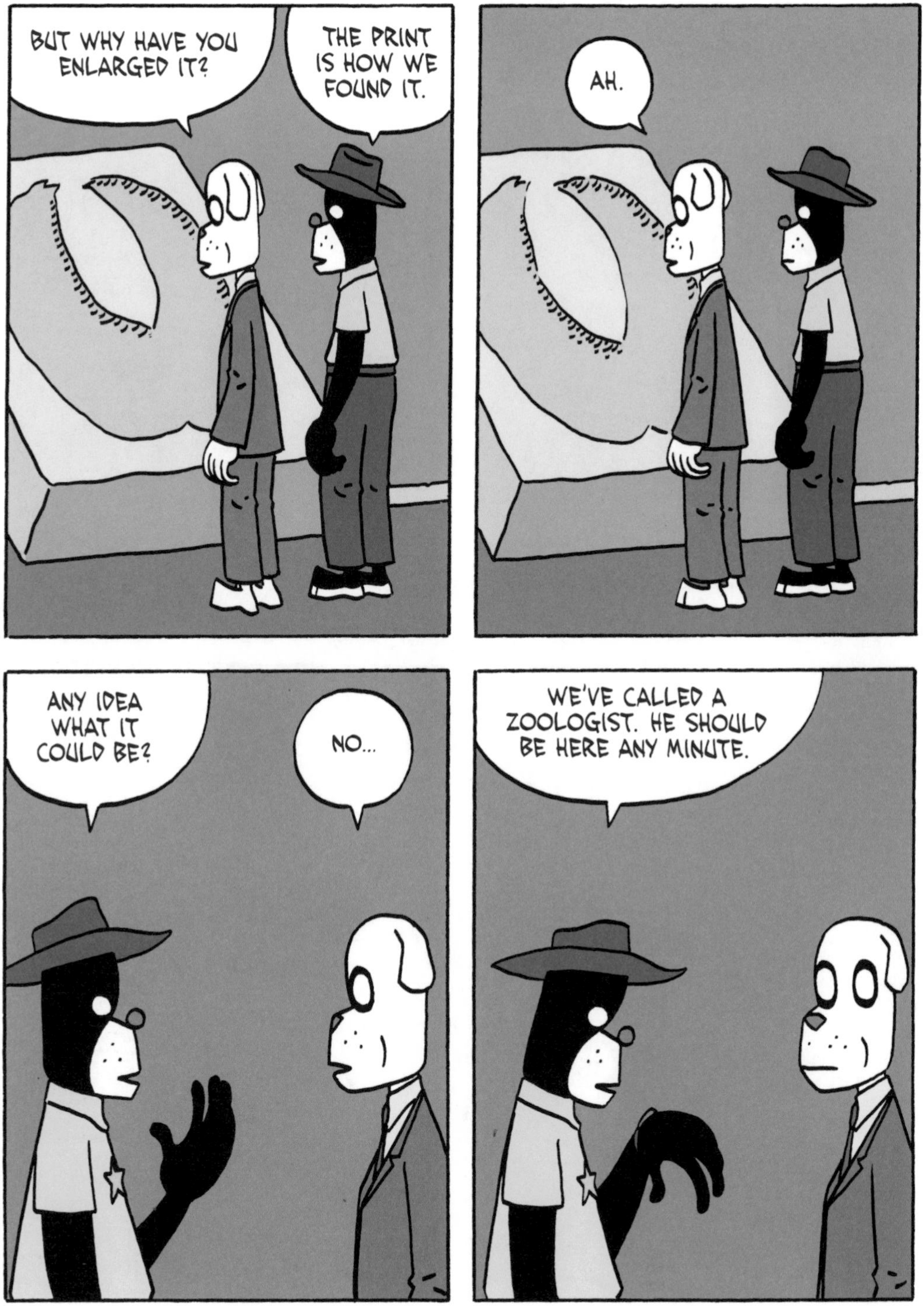
BUT WHY HAVE YOU ENLARGED IT?
THE PRINT IS HOW WE FOUND IT.
AH.
ANY IDEA WHAT IT COULD BE?
NO...
WE'VE CALLED A ZOOLOGIST. HE SHOULD BE HERE ANY MINUTE.

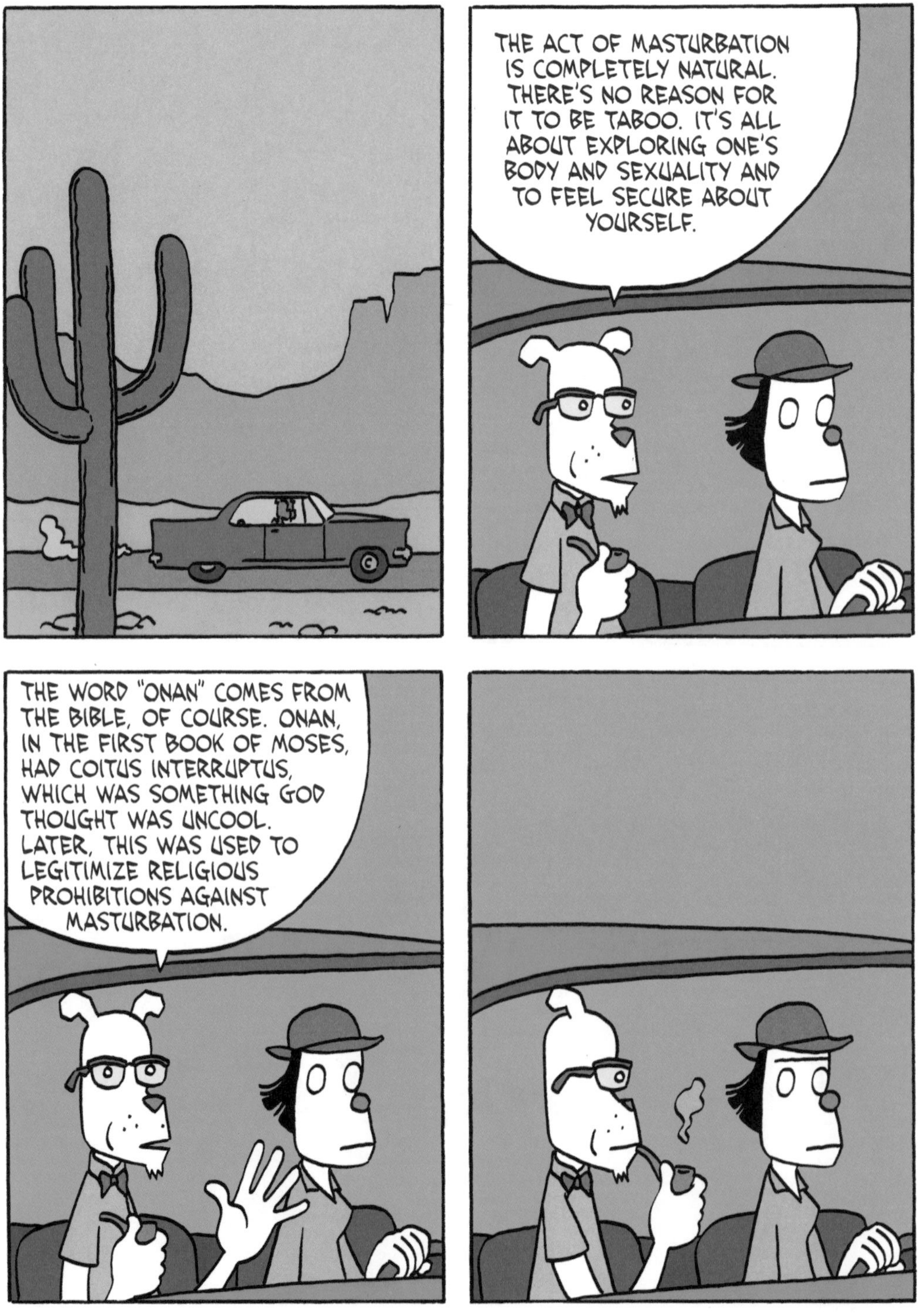
THE ACT OF MASTURBATION IS COMPLETELY NATURAL. THERE'S NO REASON FOR IT TO BE TABOO. IT'S ALL ABOUT EXPLORING ONE'S BODY AND SEXUALITY AND TO FEEL SECURE ABOUT YOURSELF.
THE WORD "ONAN" COMES FROM THE BIBLE, OF COURSE. ONAN, IN THE FIRST BOOK OF MOSES, HAD COITUS INTERRUPTUS, WHICH WAS SOMETHING GOD THOUGHT WAS UNCOOL. LATER, THIS WAS USED TO LEGITIMIZE RELIGIOUS PROHIBITIONS AGAINST MASTURBATION.

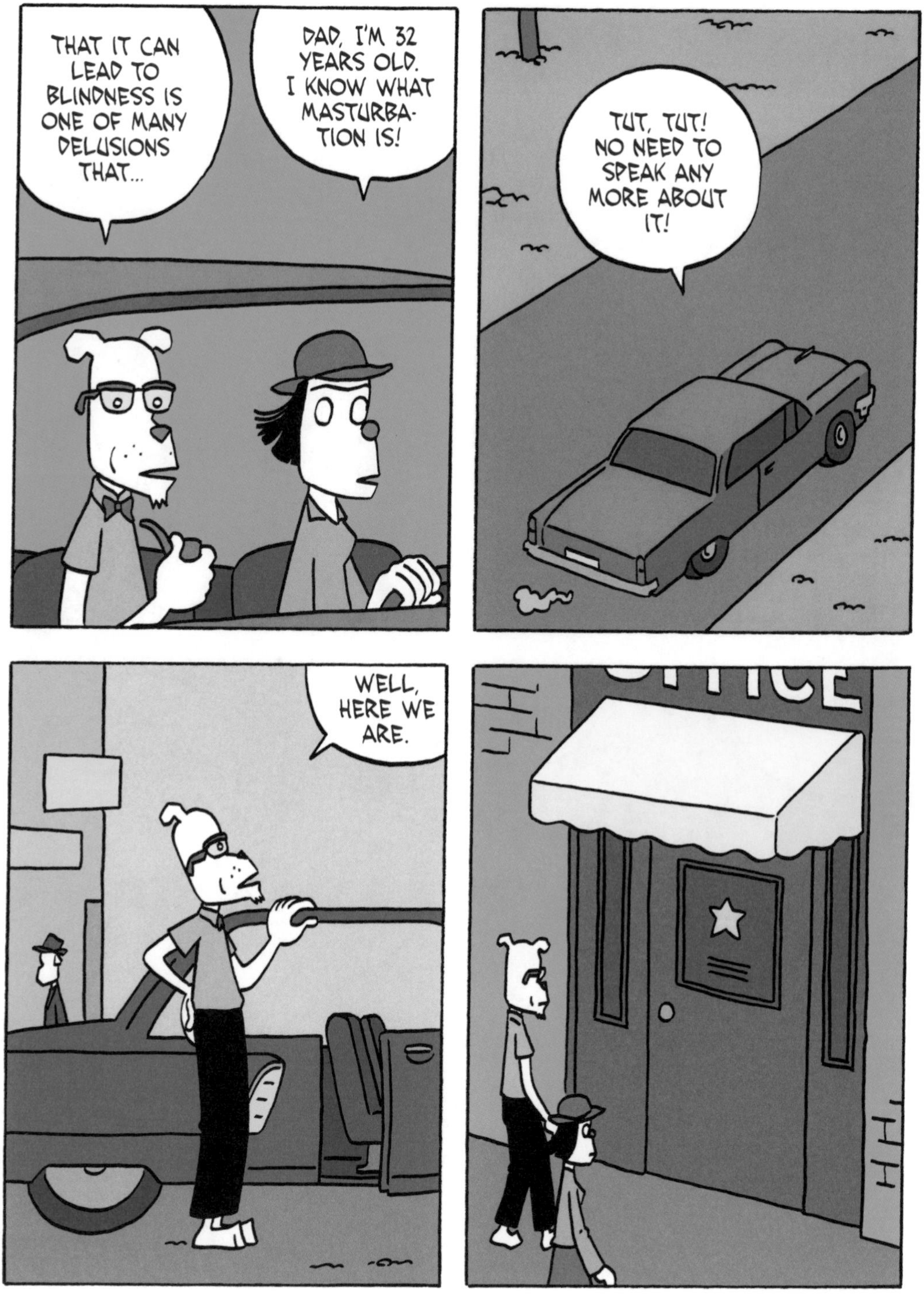
THAT IT CAN LEAD TO BLINDNESS IS ONE OF MANY DELUSIONS THAT...
DAD, I'M 32 YEARS OLD. I KNOW WHAT MASTURBA-TION IS!
TUT, TUT! NO NEED TO SPEAK ANY MORE ABOUT IT!
WELL, HERE WE ARE.
OFFICE

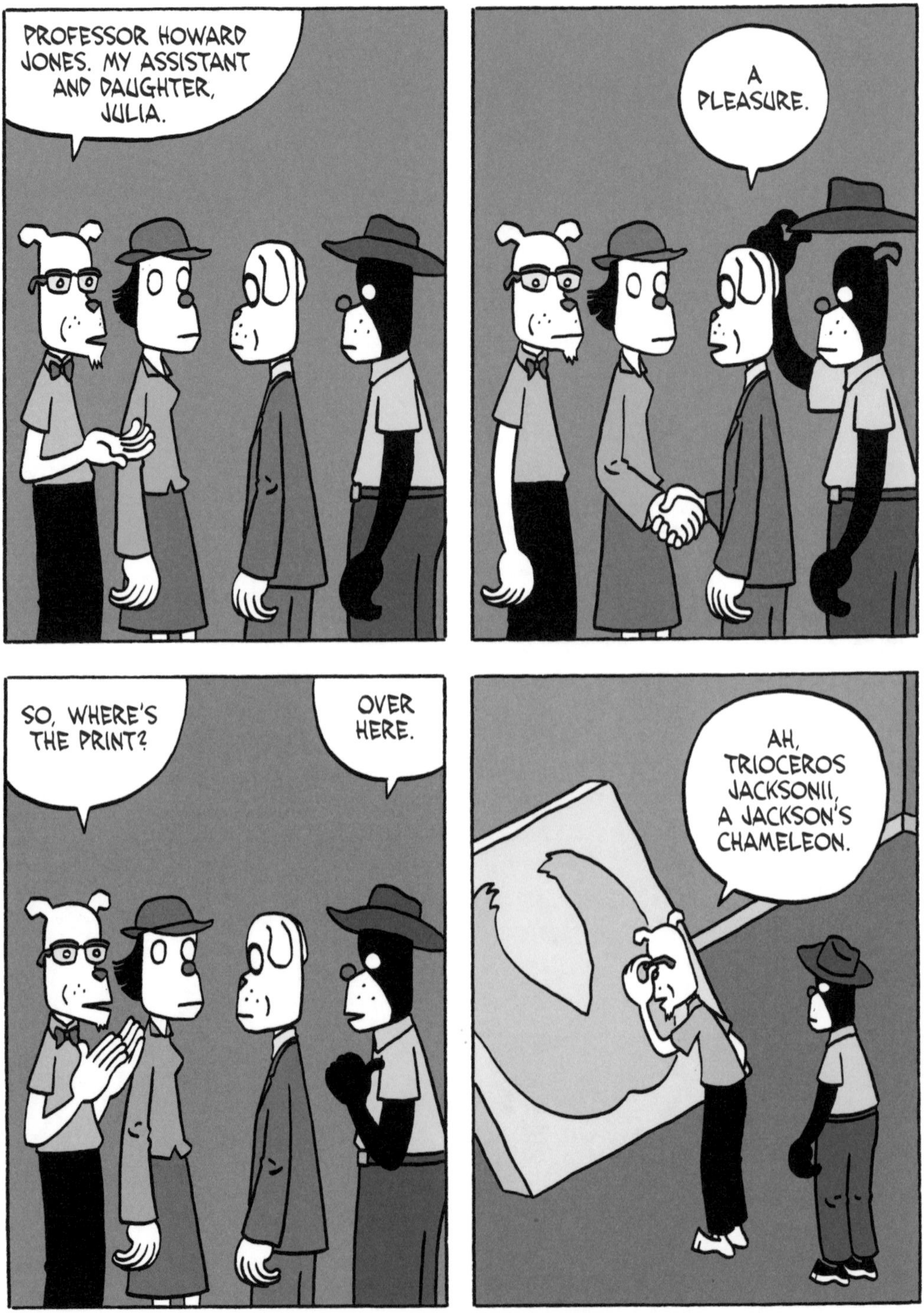
PROFESSOR HOWARD JONES. MY ASSISTANT AND DAUGHTER, JULIA.
A PLEASURE.
SO, WHERE'S THE PRINT?
OVER HERE.
AH, TRIOCEROS JACKSONII, A JACKSON'S CHAMELEON.

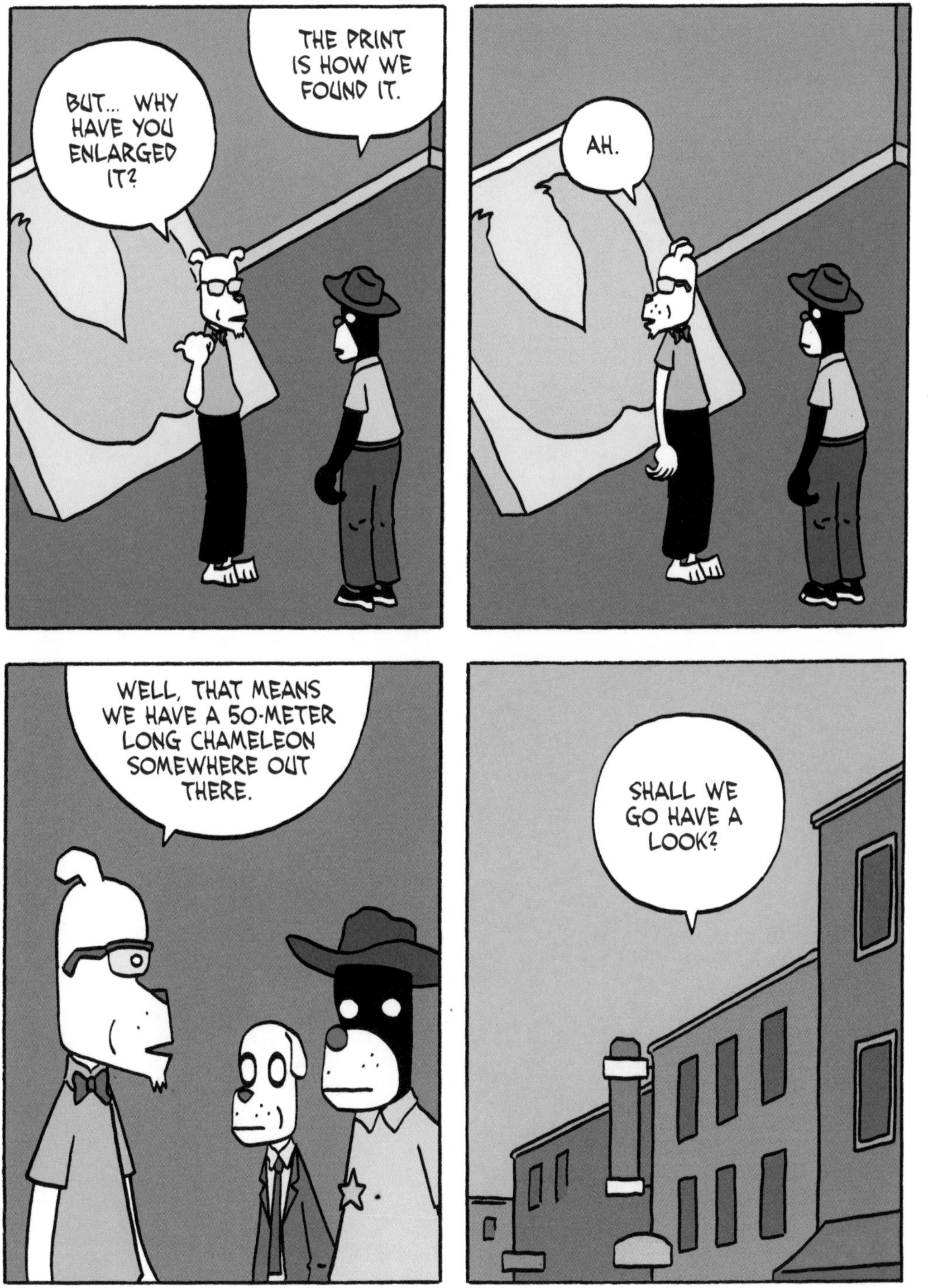
BUT... WHY HAVE YOU ENLARGED IT?
THE PRINT IS HOW WE FOUND IT.
AH.
WELL, THAT MEANS WE HAVE A 50-METER LONG CHAMELEON SOMEWHERE OUT THERE.
SHALL WE GO HAVE A LOOK?

DOC, WHY DON'T YOU AND MISS JONES GO TO THE FIRST CRIME SCENE, AND ME AND THE PROFESSOR TAKE THE SECOND ONE.

SO, HOW LONG HAVE YOU WORKED AS A ZOOLOGIST ASSISTANT?

A COUPLE OF MONTHS. I'M MORE OF A SECRETARY, ACTUALLY.

WHAT KIND OF ANIMAL IS THAT?

WHAT?

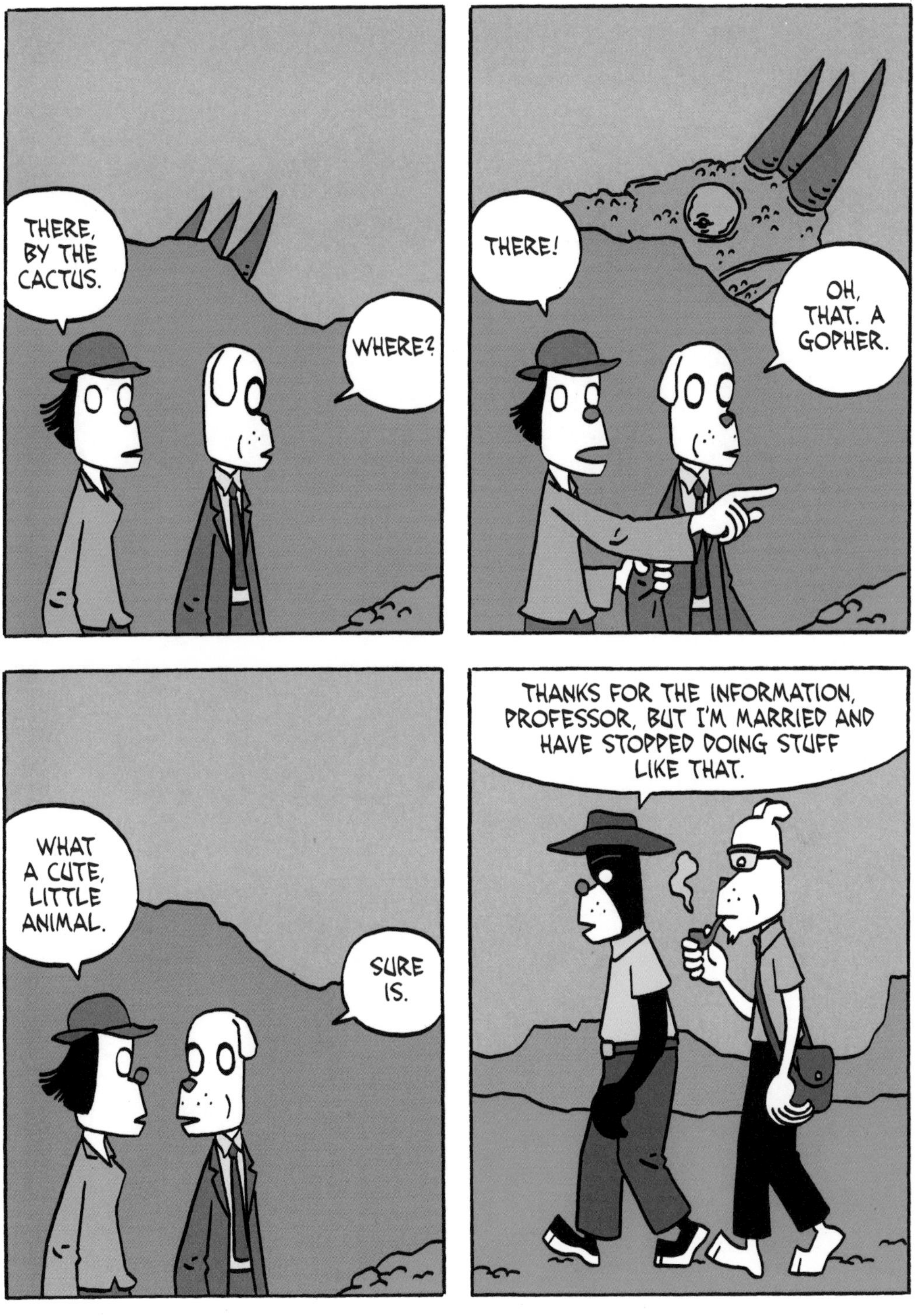
THERE, BY THE CACTUS.
WHERE?
THERE!
OH, THAT. A GOPHER.
WHAT A CUTE, LITTLE ANIMAL.
SURE IS.
THANKS FOR THE INFORMATION, PROFESSOR, BUT I'M MARRIED AND HAVE STOPPED DOING STUFF LIKE THAT.

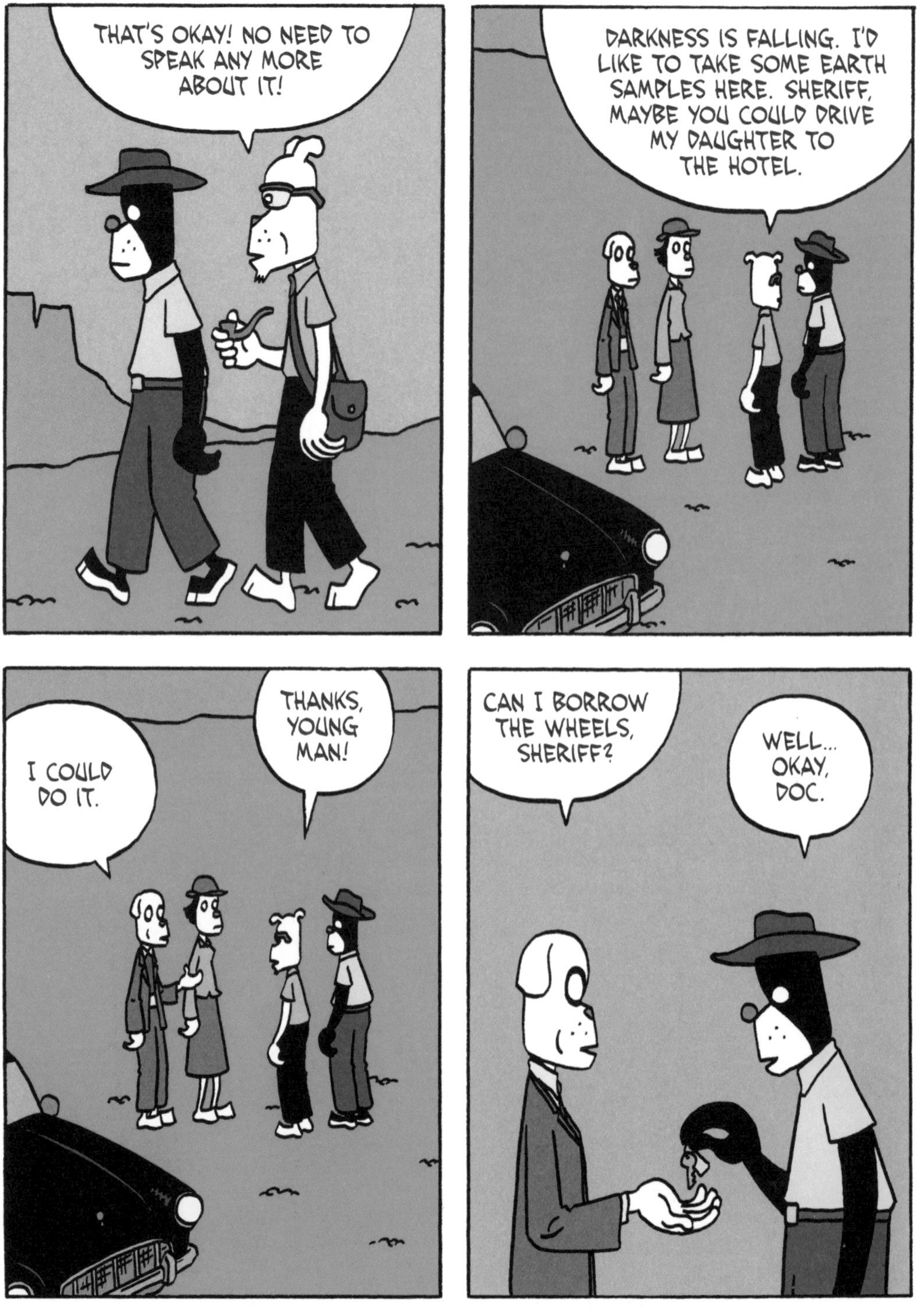
THAT'S OKAY! NO NEED TO SPEAK ANY MORE ABOUT IT!
DARKNESS IS FALLING. I'D LIKE TO TAKE SOME EARTH SAMPLES HERE. SHERIFF, MAYBE YOU COULD DRIVE MY DAUGHTER TO THE HOTEL.
I COULD DO IT.
THANKS, YOUNG MAN!
CAN I BORROW THE WHEELS, SHERIFF?
WELL... OKAY, DOC.

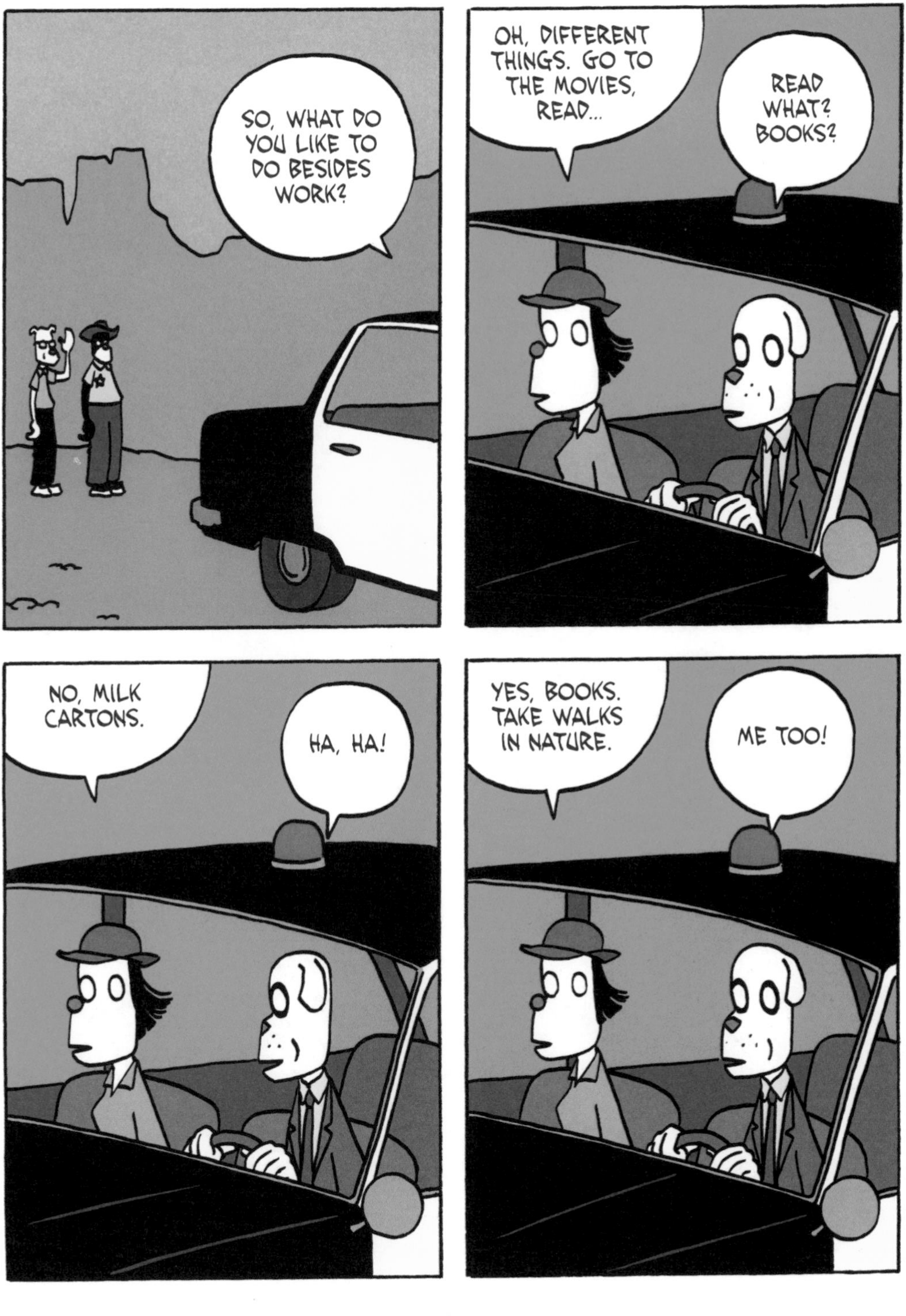
SO, WHAT DO YOU LIKE TO DO BESIDES WORK?
OH, DIFFERENT THINGS. GO TO THE MOVIES, READ...
READ WHAT? BOOKS?
NO, MILK CARTONS.
HA, HA!
YES, BOOKS. TAKE WALKS IN NATURE.
ME TOO!

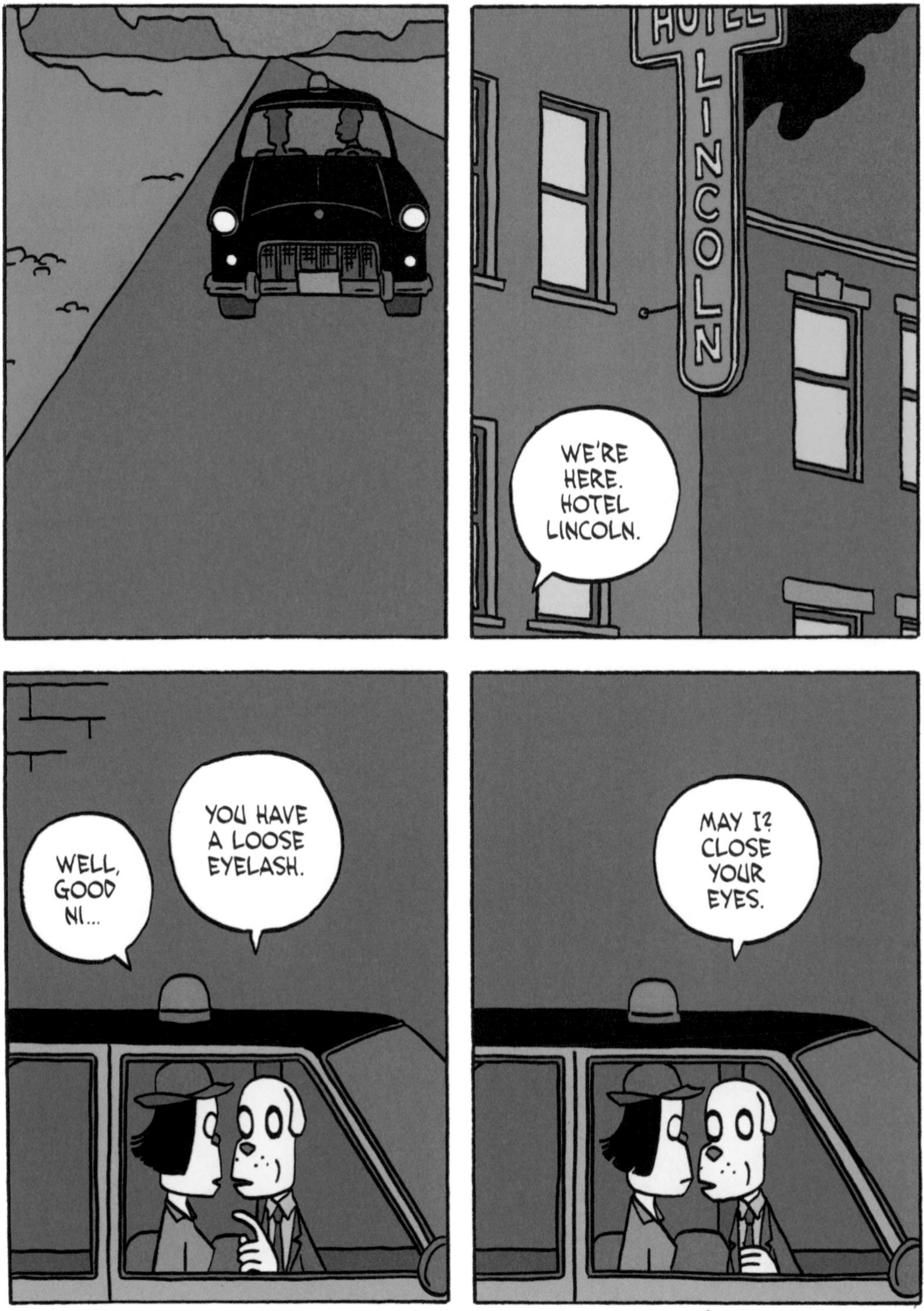
HOTEL LINCOLN
WE'RE HERE. HOTEL LINCOLN.
WELL, GOOD NI...
YOU HAVE A LOOSE EYELASH.
MAY I? CLOSE YOUR EYES.

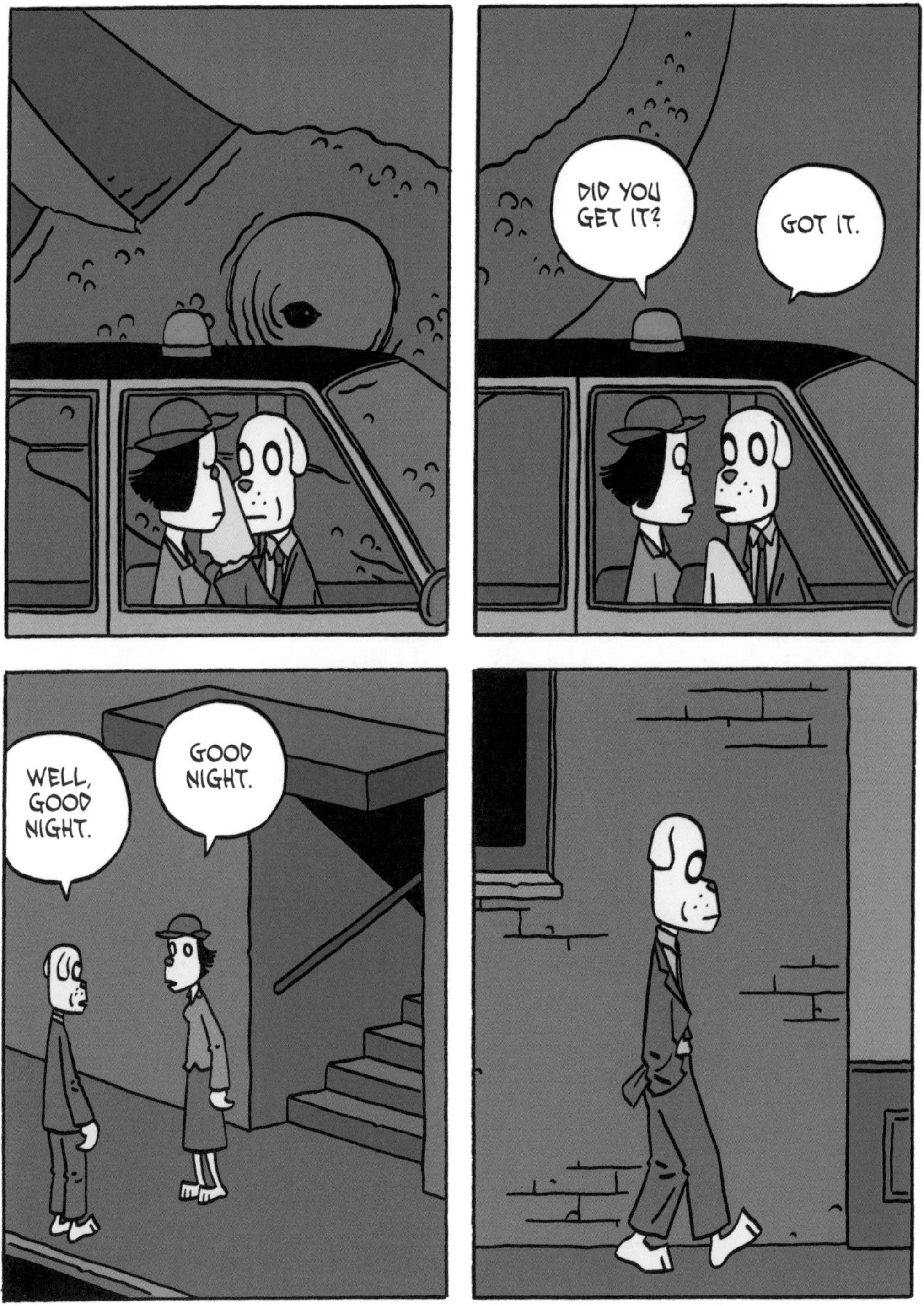
DID YOU GET IT?
GOT IT.
WELL, GOOD NIGHT.
GOOD NIGHT.

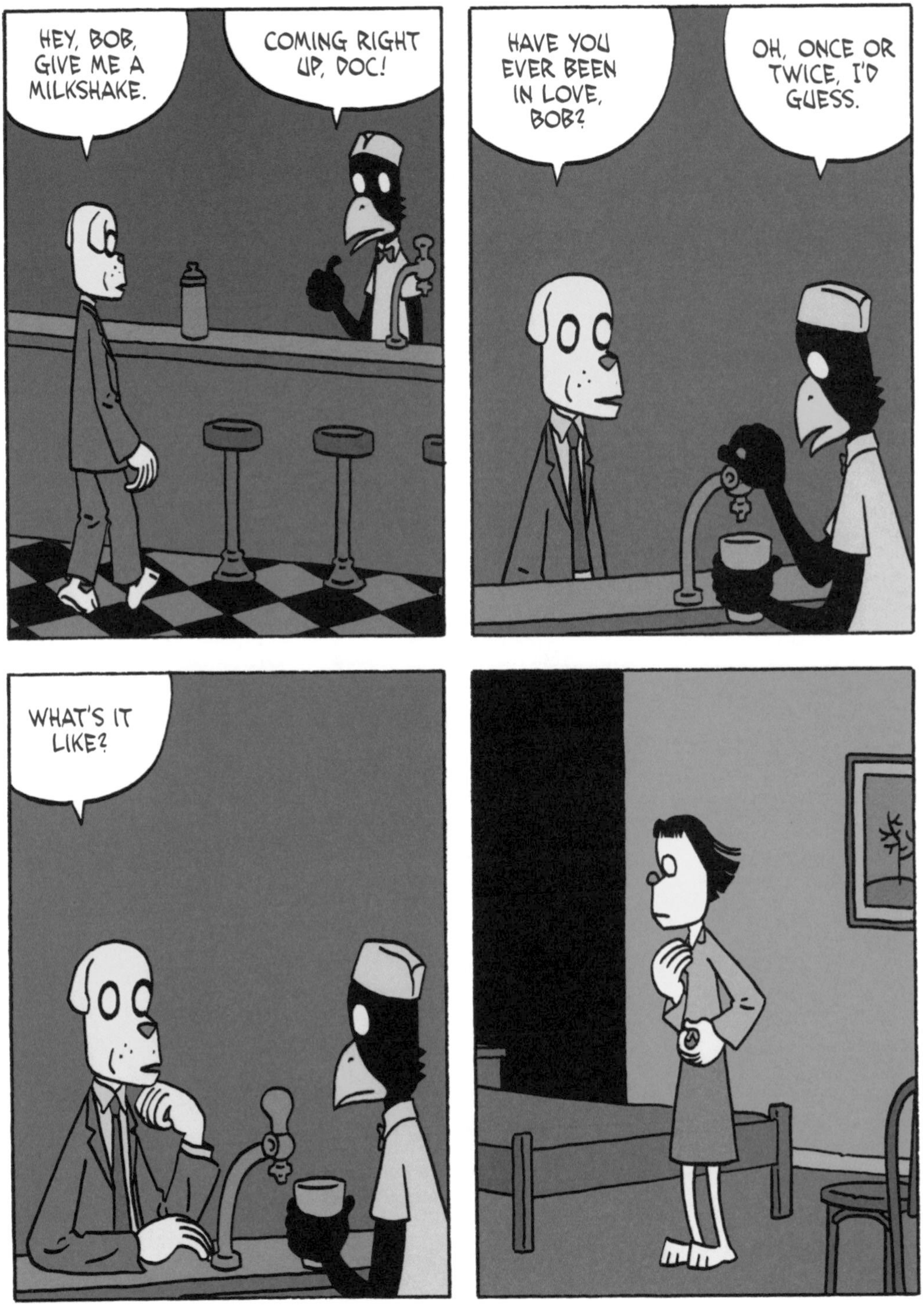
HEY, BOB, GIVE ME A MILKSHAKE.
COMING RIGHT UP, DOC!
HAVE YOU EVER BEEN IN LOVE, BOB?
OH, ONCE OR TWICE, I'D GUESS.
WHAT'S IT LIKE?

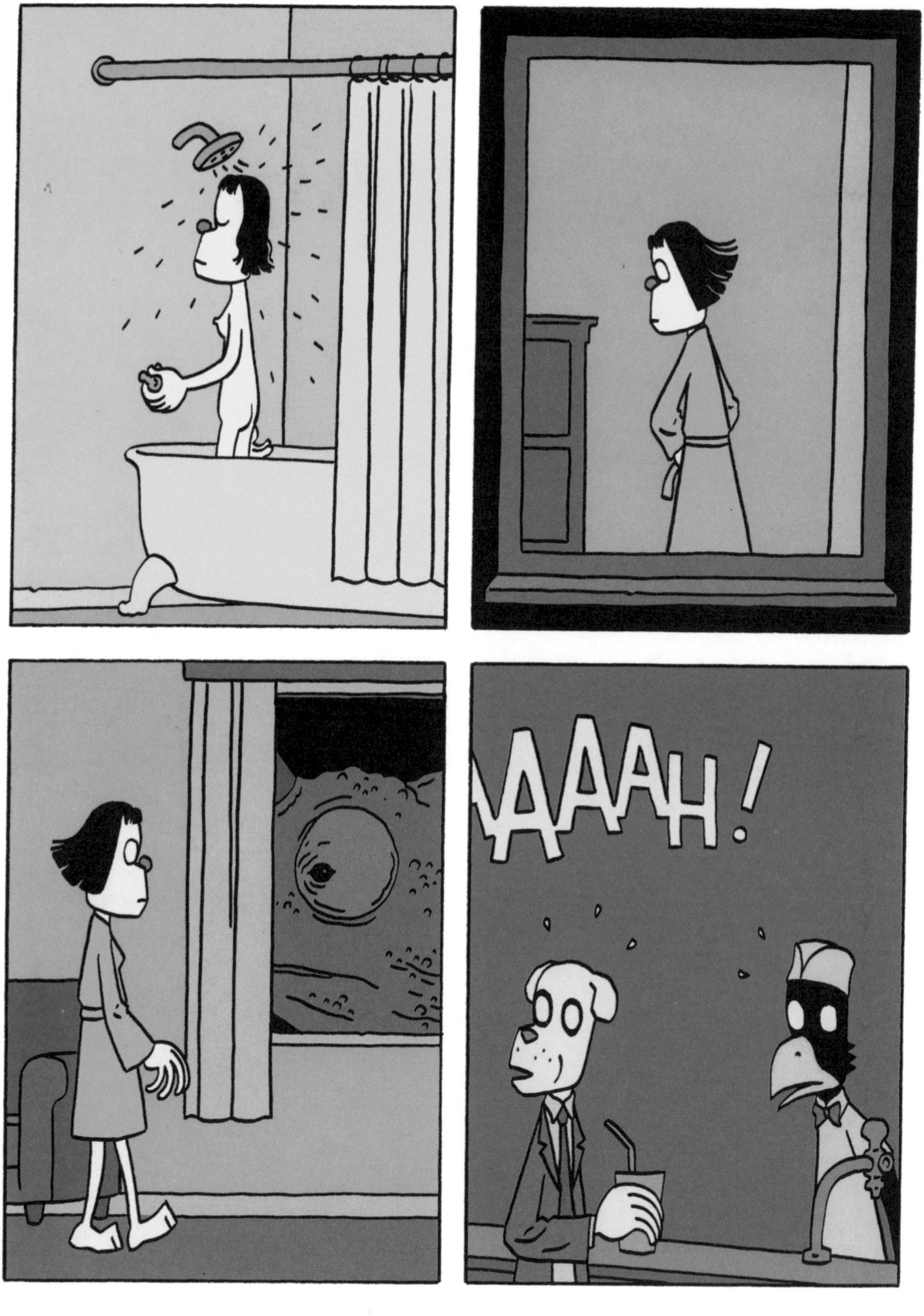
AAAAH!

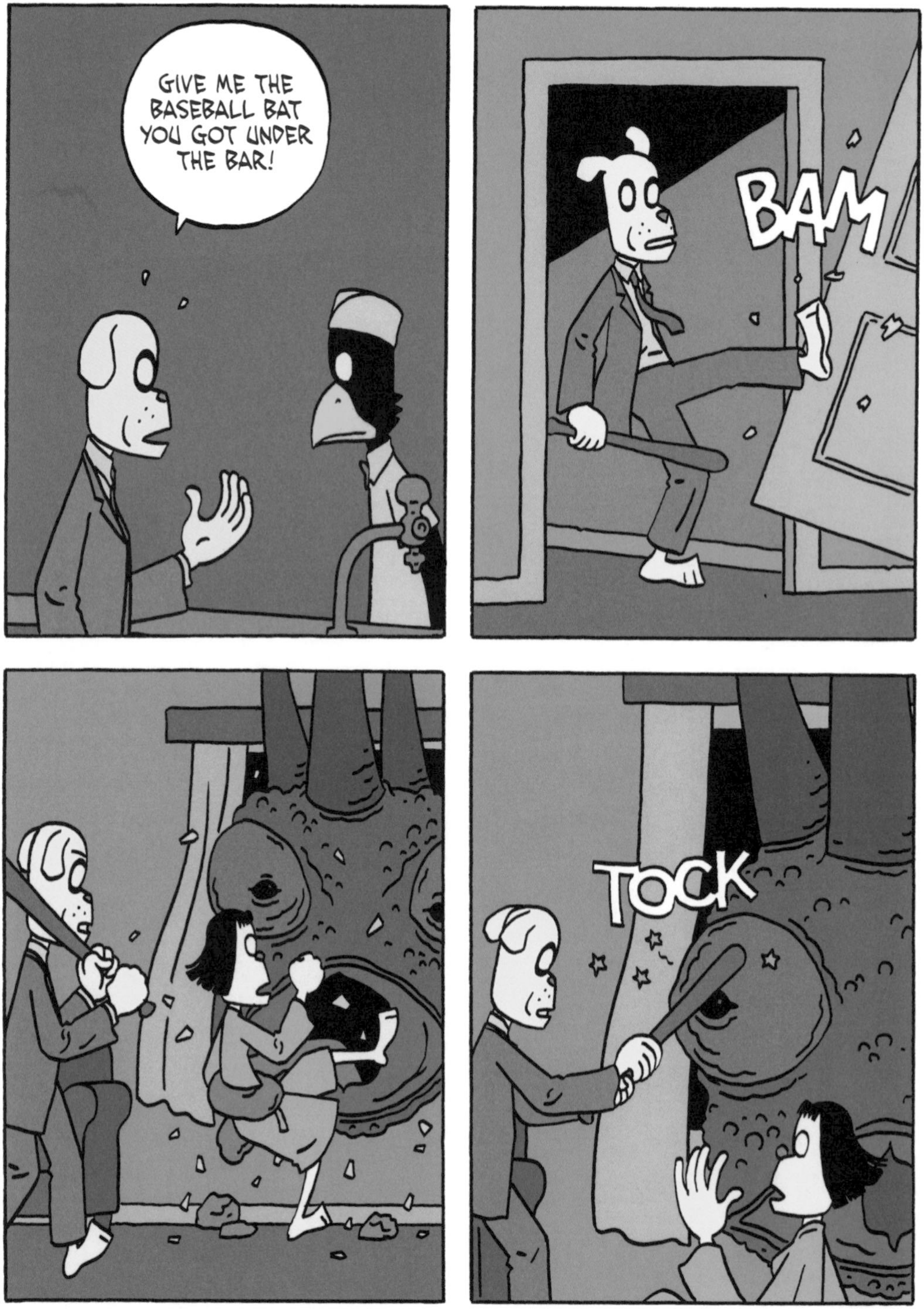
GIVE ME THE BASEBALL BAT YOU GOT UNDER THE BAR!
BAM
TOCK

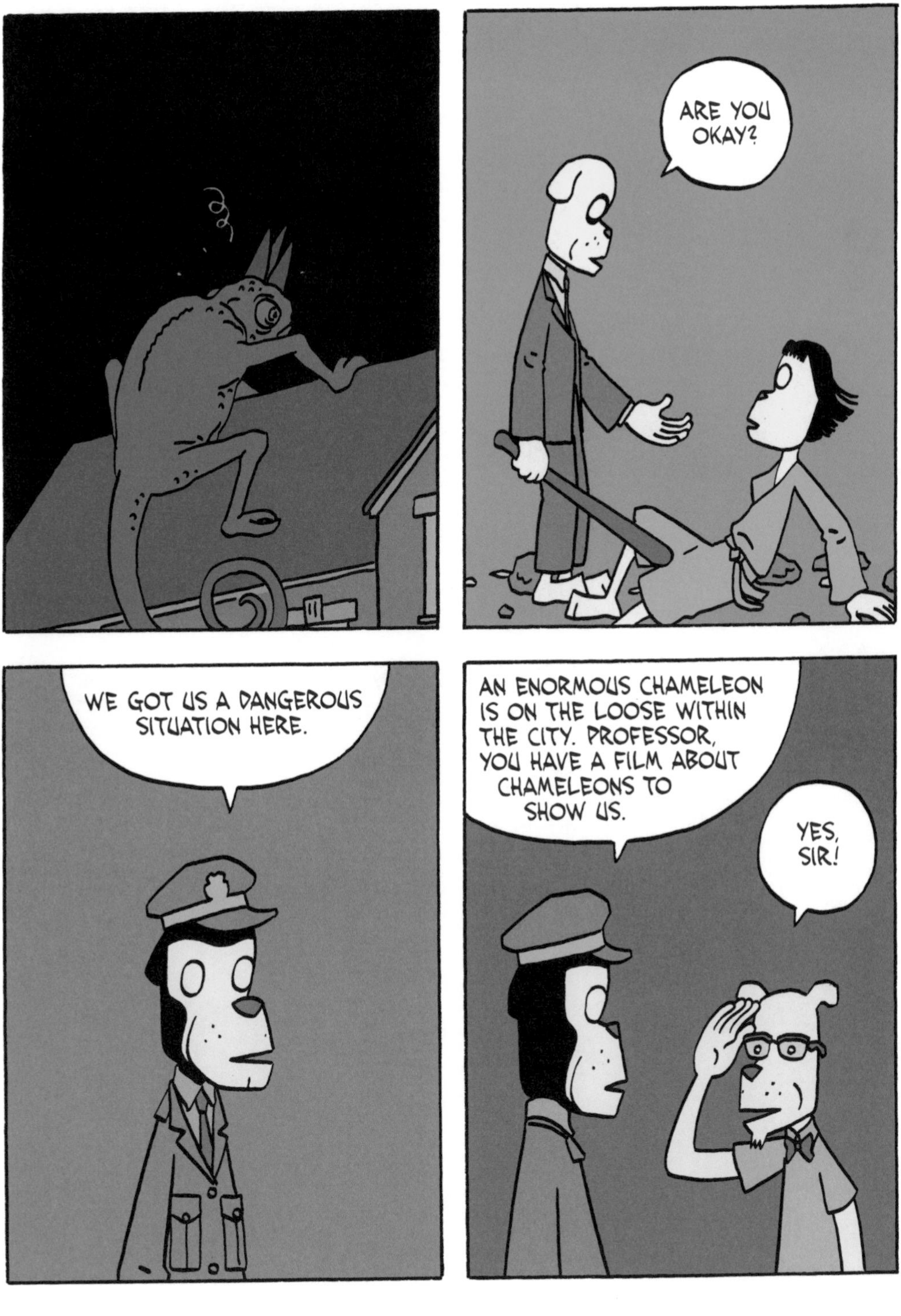
ARE YOU OKAY?
WE GOT US A DANGEROUS SITUATION HERE.
AN ENORMOUS CHAMELEON IS ON THE LOOSE WITHIN THE CITY. PROFESSOR, YOU HAVE A FILM ABOUT CHAMELEONS TO SHOW US.
YES, SIR!

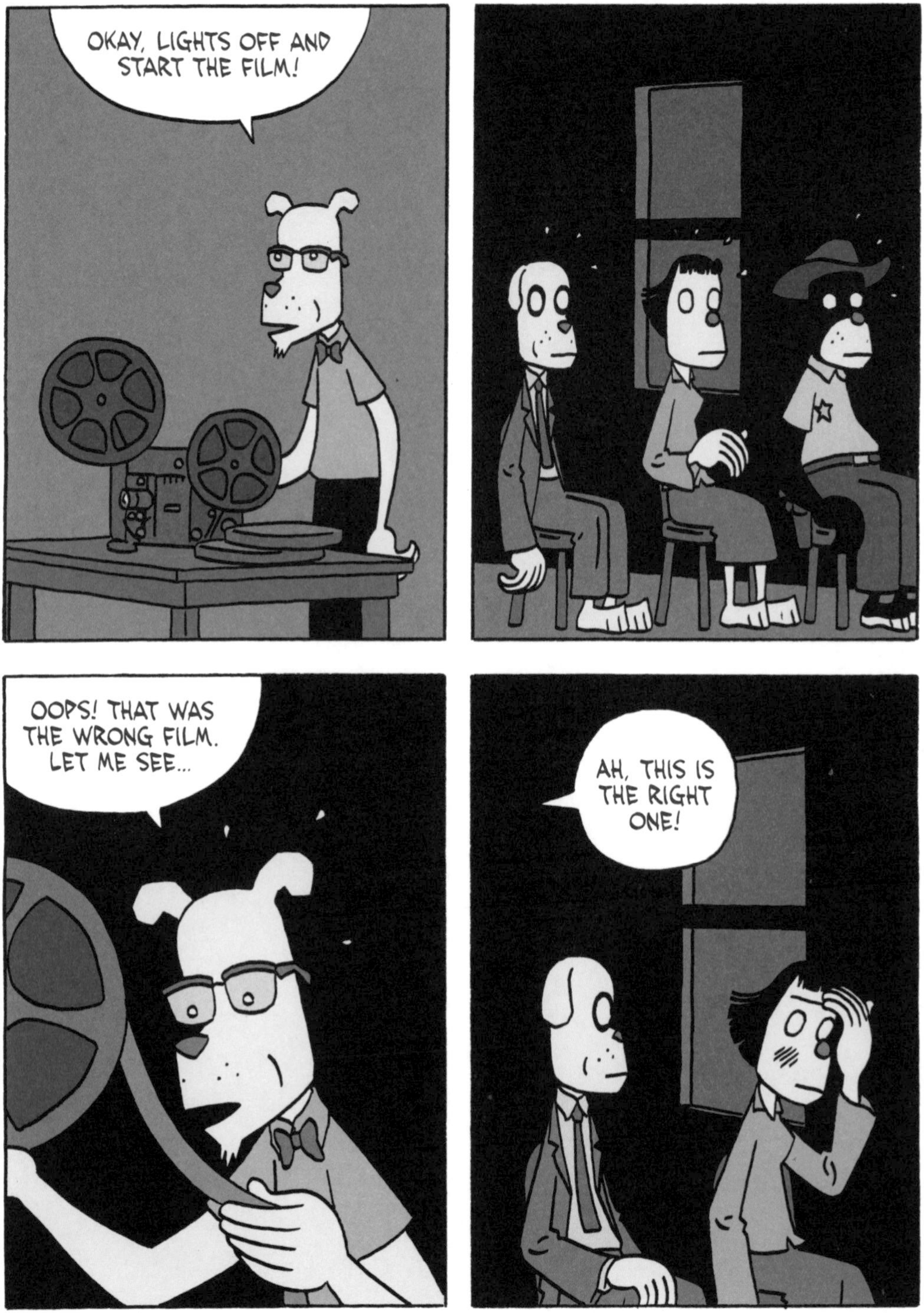
OKAY, LIGHTS OFF AND START THE FILM!
OOPS! THAT WAS THE WRONG FILM. LET ME SEE...
AH, THIS IS THE RIGHT ONE!

THE EYES OF THE CHAMELEON CAN MOVE INDEPENDENTLY OF EACH OTHER. THE EYELIDS ARE GROWN TOGETHER SO THAT THERE'S ONLY A SMALL OPENING FOR THE PUPIL. EACH EYE CAN SEE 180° HORIZONTALLY AND 90° VERTICALLY.

CHAMELEONS LACK THE OUTER EAR AND THE MIDDLE EAR. THEIR EARS ARE THEREFORE NOT SENSITIVE TO SOUND WAVES IN THE AIR. WHEN A CHAMELEON SHOOTS OUT ITS TONGUE, IT CAN BE AS LONG AS ITS BODY.

MAXIMUM ACCELERATION OF THE TONGUE IS ALMOST 500 METERS PER SECOND AND SPEED CAN BE OVER 12 MILES AN HOUR. WITH THE TONGUE THE CHAMELEON CAN LIFT A PREY WITH A WEIGHT OF 10% OF ITS OWN BODY WEIGHT.

THE CHAMELEON IS ABLE TO CHANGE COLOR. THIS ABILITY IS DEVELOPED FOR USE IN SOCIAL INTERACTION BETWEEN CHAMELEONS. THE MALE SHOWS PATTERNS TYPICAL FOR THAT SPECIES TO SCARE MALES AND ATTRACT FEMALES.

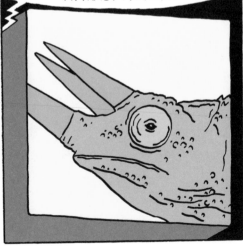

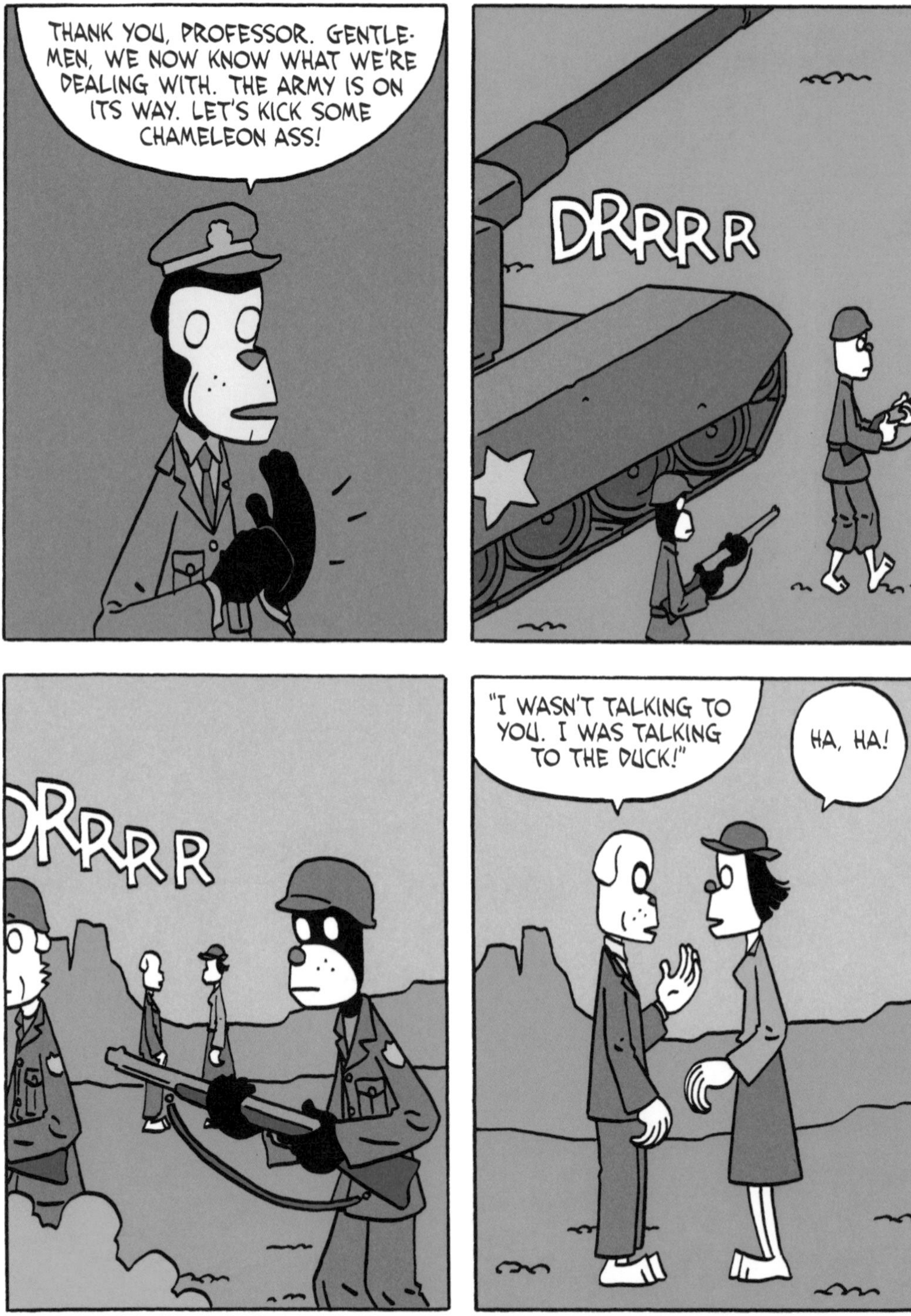
THANK YOU, PROFESSOR. GENTLEMEN, WE NOW KNOW WHAT WE'RE DEALING WITH. THE ARMY IS ON ITS WAY. LET'S KICK SOME CHAMELEON ASS!
DRRRR
DRRRR
"I WASN'T TALKING TO YOU. I WAS TALKING TO THE DUCK!"
HA, HA!

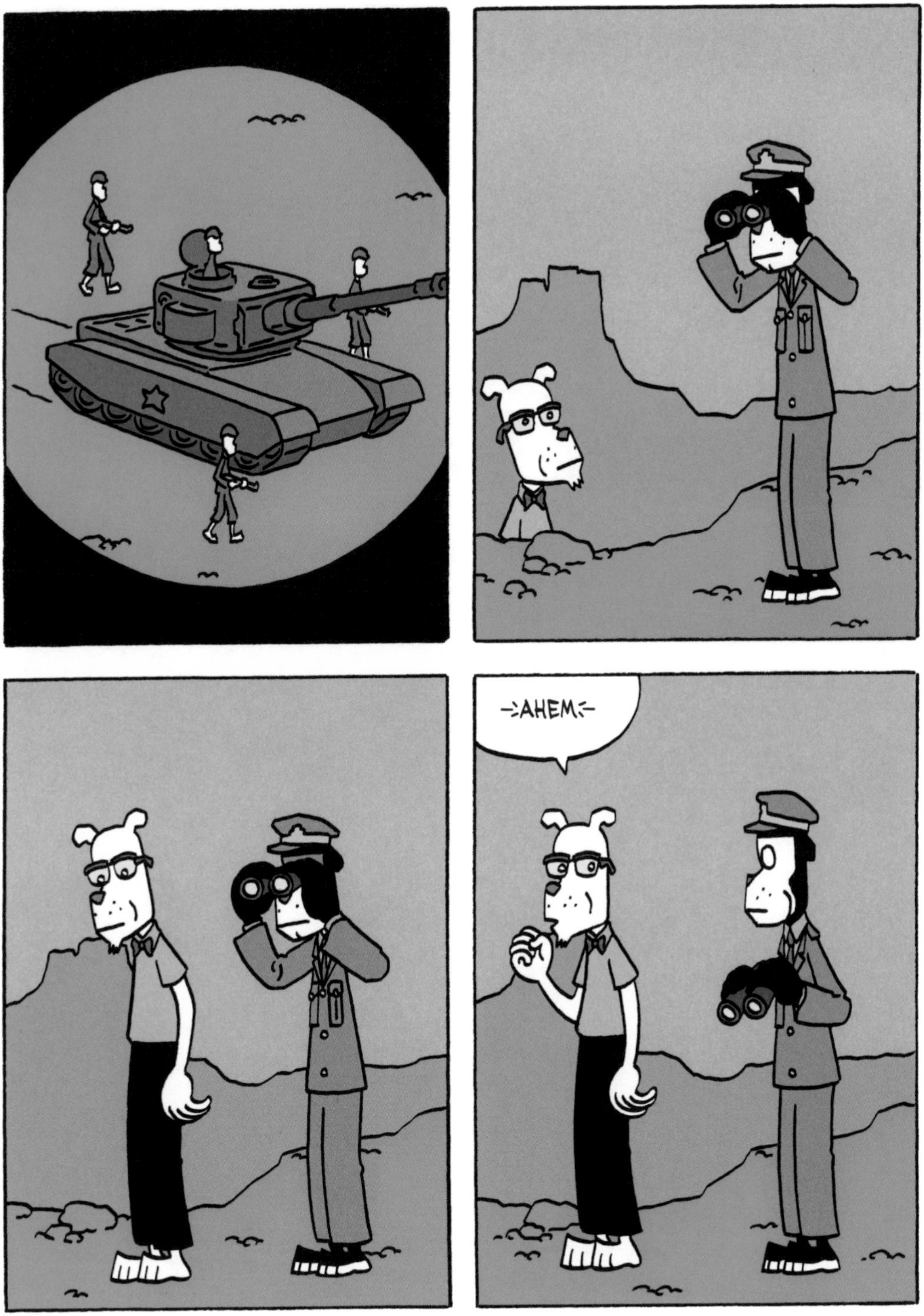
AHEM

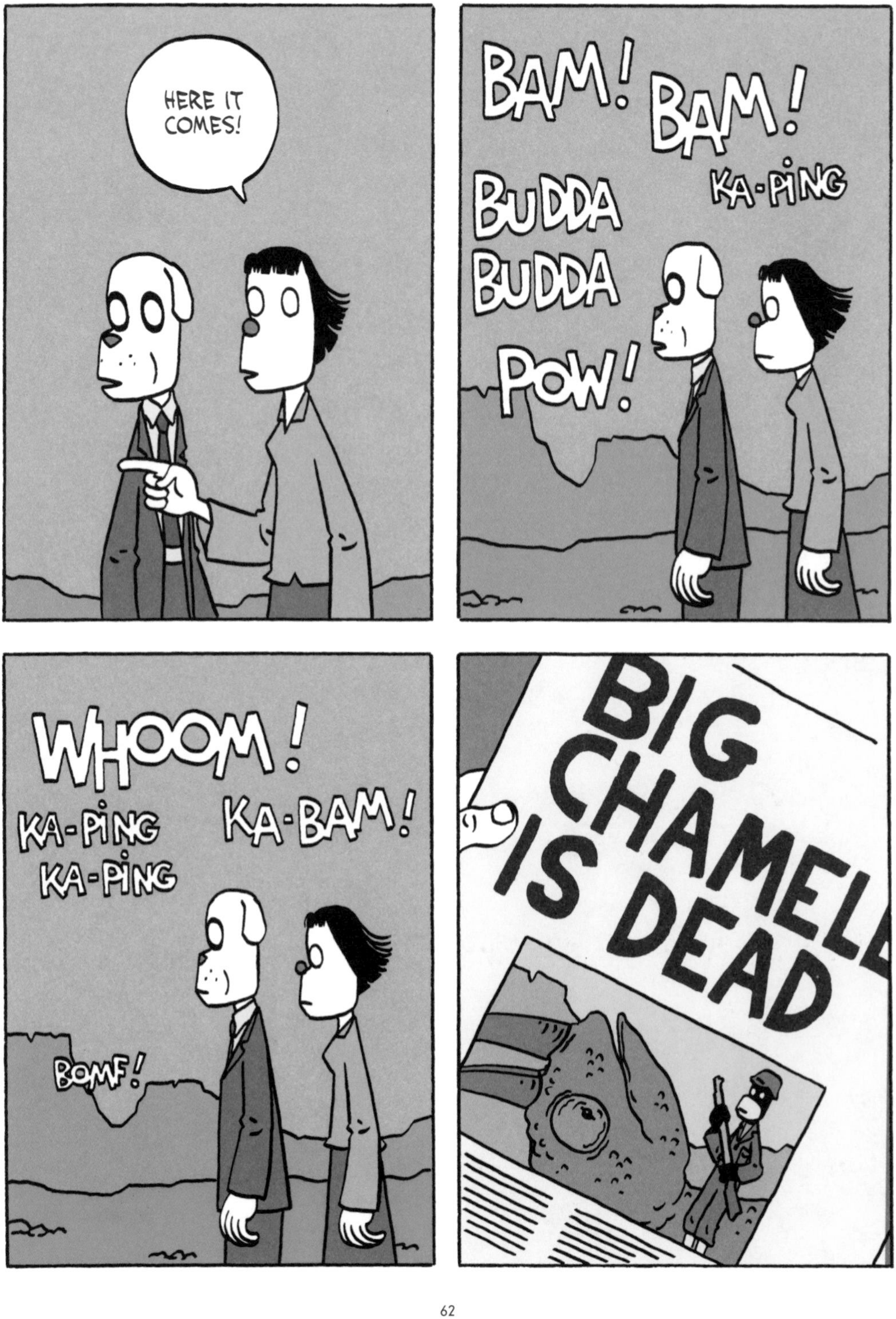
HERE IT COMES!
BAM! BAM!
BUDDA BUDDA
KA-PING
POW!
WHOOM!
KA-PING
KA-PING
KA-BAM!
BOMF!
BIG CHAMELE
IS DEAD

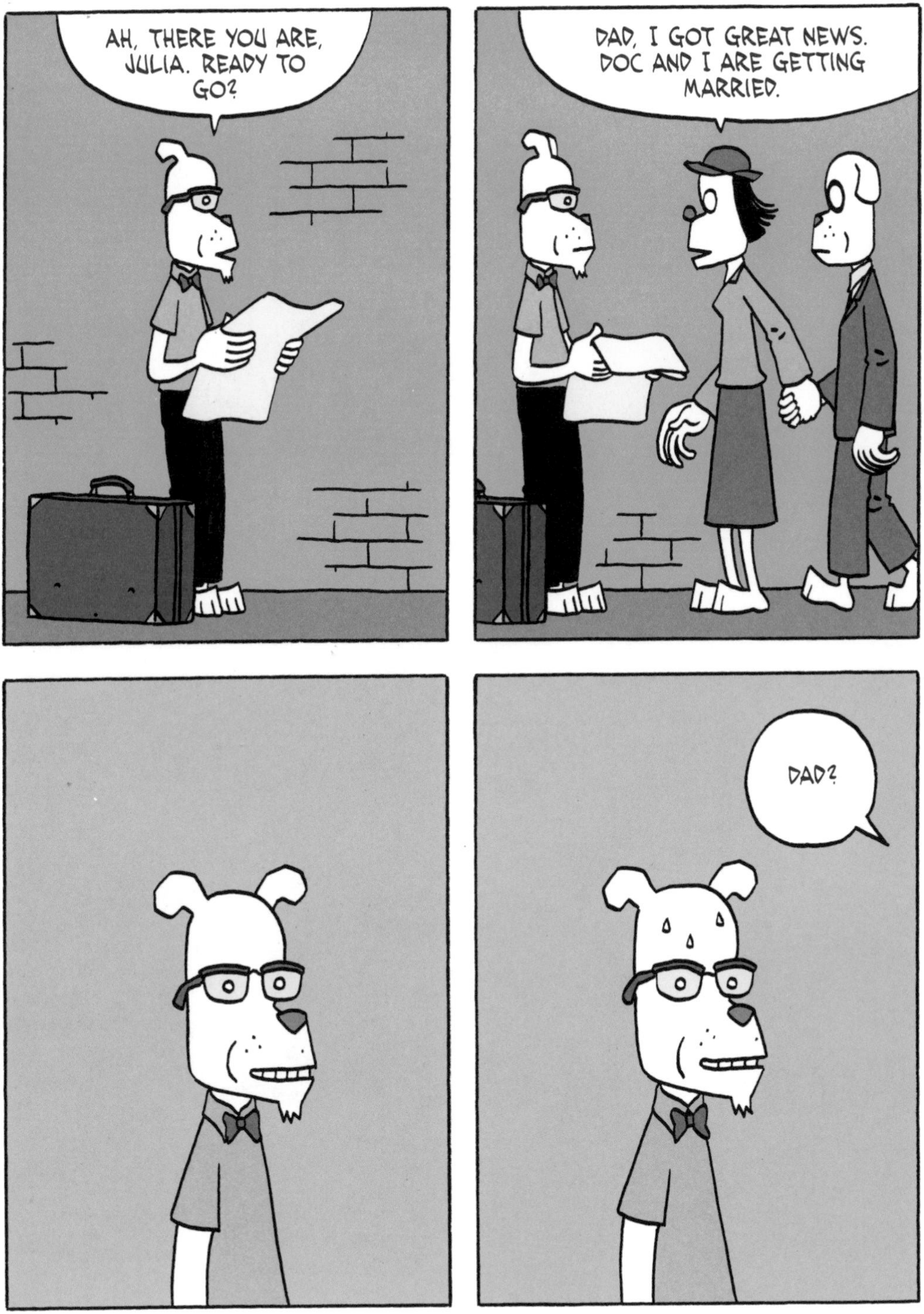
AH, THERE YOU ARE, JULIA. READY TO GO?
DAD, I GOT GREAT NEWS. DOC AND I ARE GETTING MARRIED.
DAD?

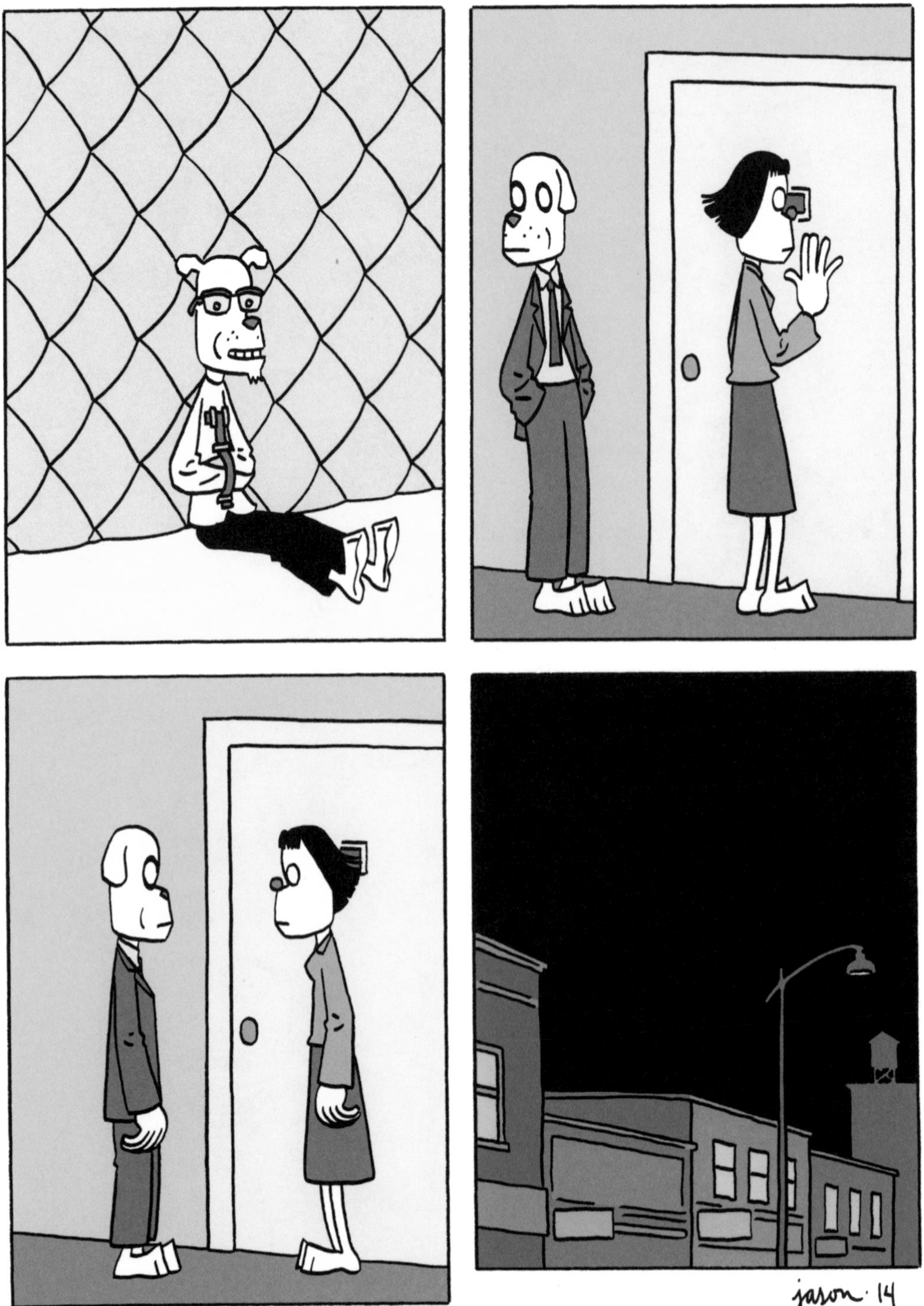

jason · 14

PRESENTING:

WAITING FOR BARDOT

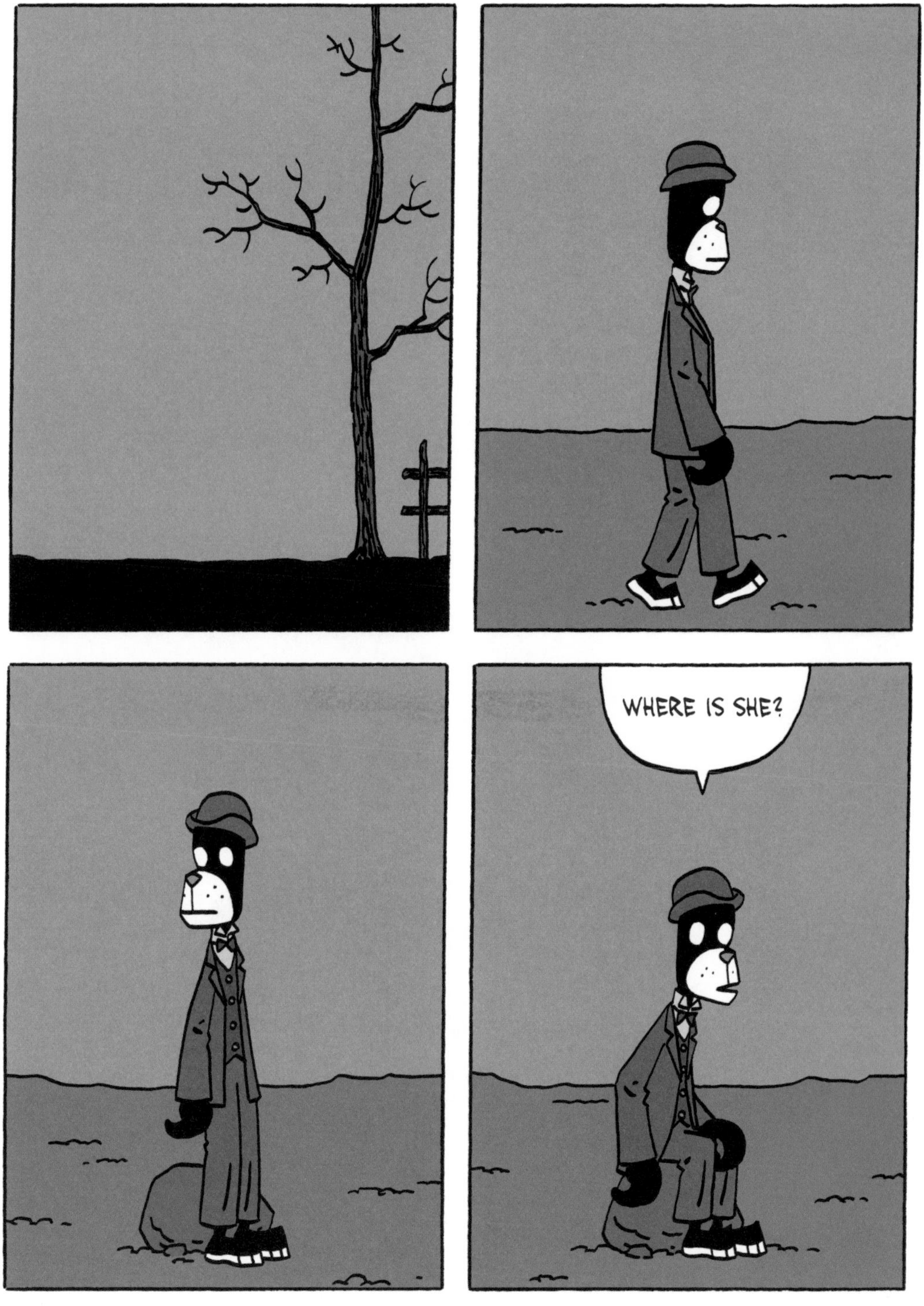
WHERE IS SHE?

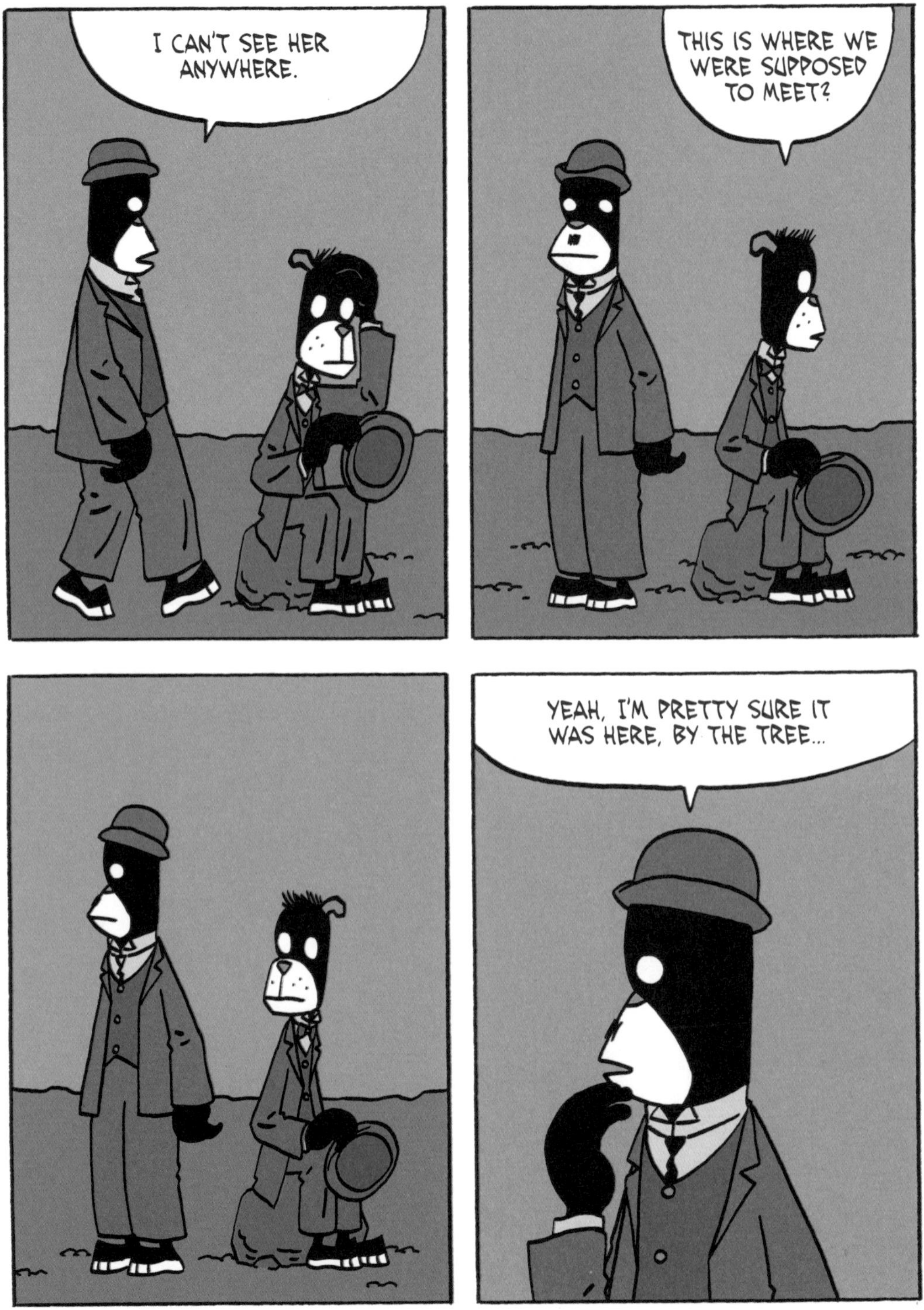
I CAN'T SEE HER ANYWHERE.
THIS IS WHERE WE WERE SUPPOSED TO MEET?
YEAH, I'M PRETTY SURE IT WAS HERE, BY THE TREE...

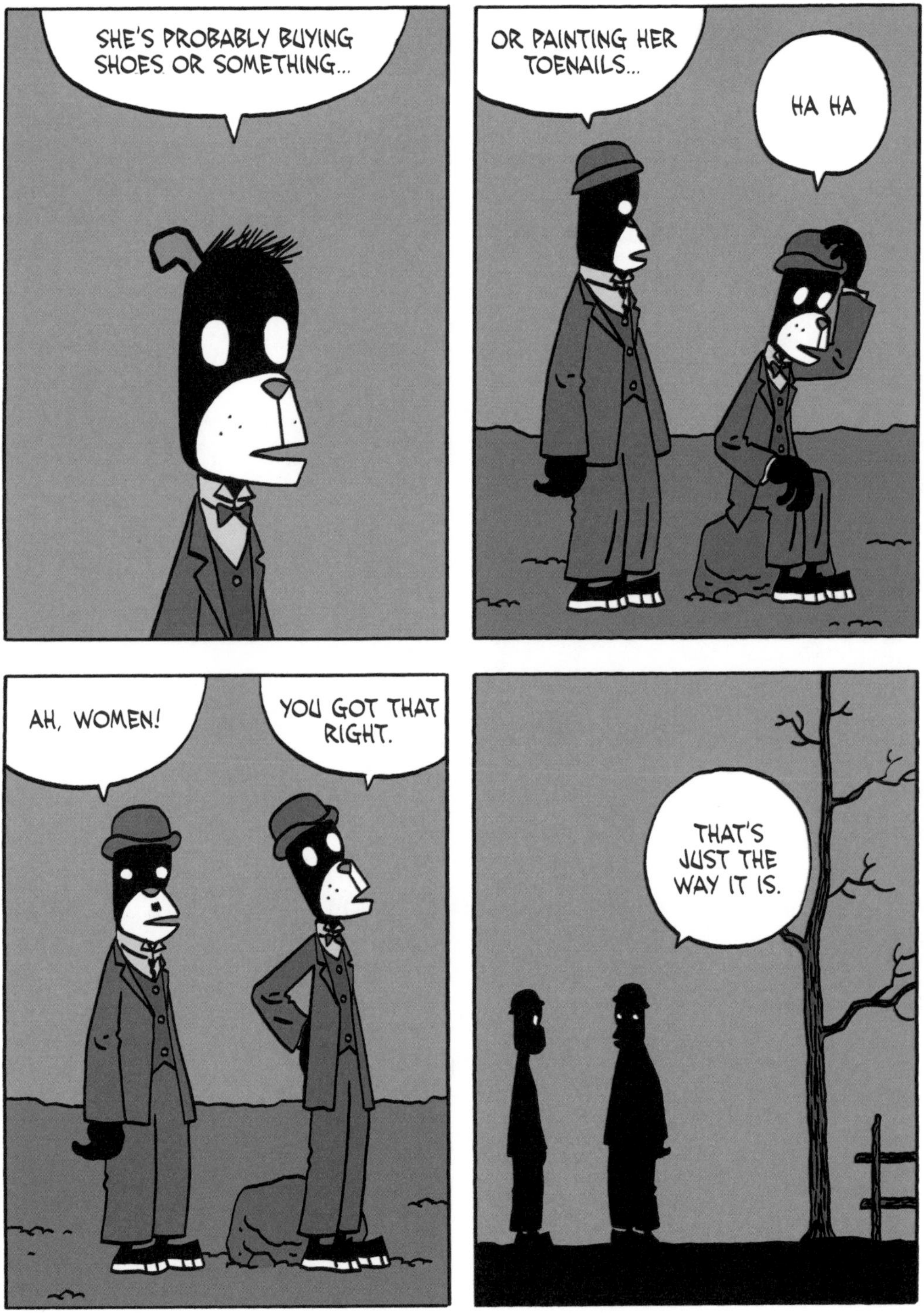
SHE'S PROBABLY BUYING SHOES OR SOMETHING...
OR PAINTING HER TOENAILS...
HA HA
AH, WOMEN!
YOU GOT THAT RIGHT.
THAT'S JUST THE WAY IT IS.

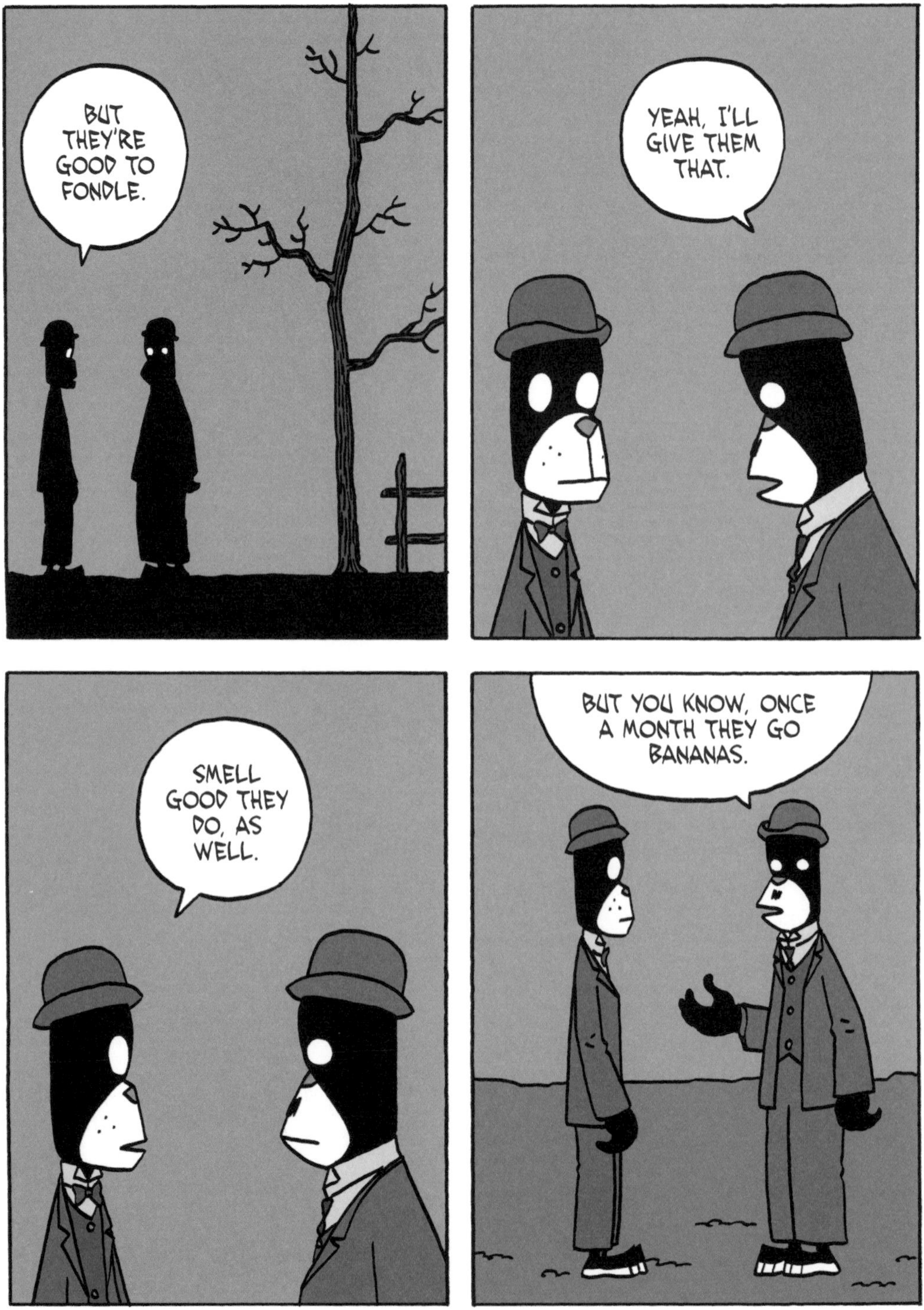
BUT THEY'RE GOOD TO FONDLE.
YEAH, I'LL GIVE THEM THAT.
SMELL GOOD THEY DO, AS WELL.
BUT YOU KNOW, ONCE A MONTH THEY GO BANANAS.

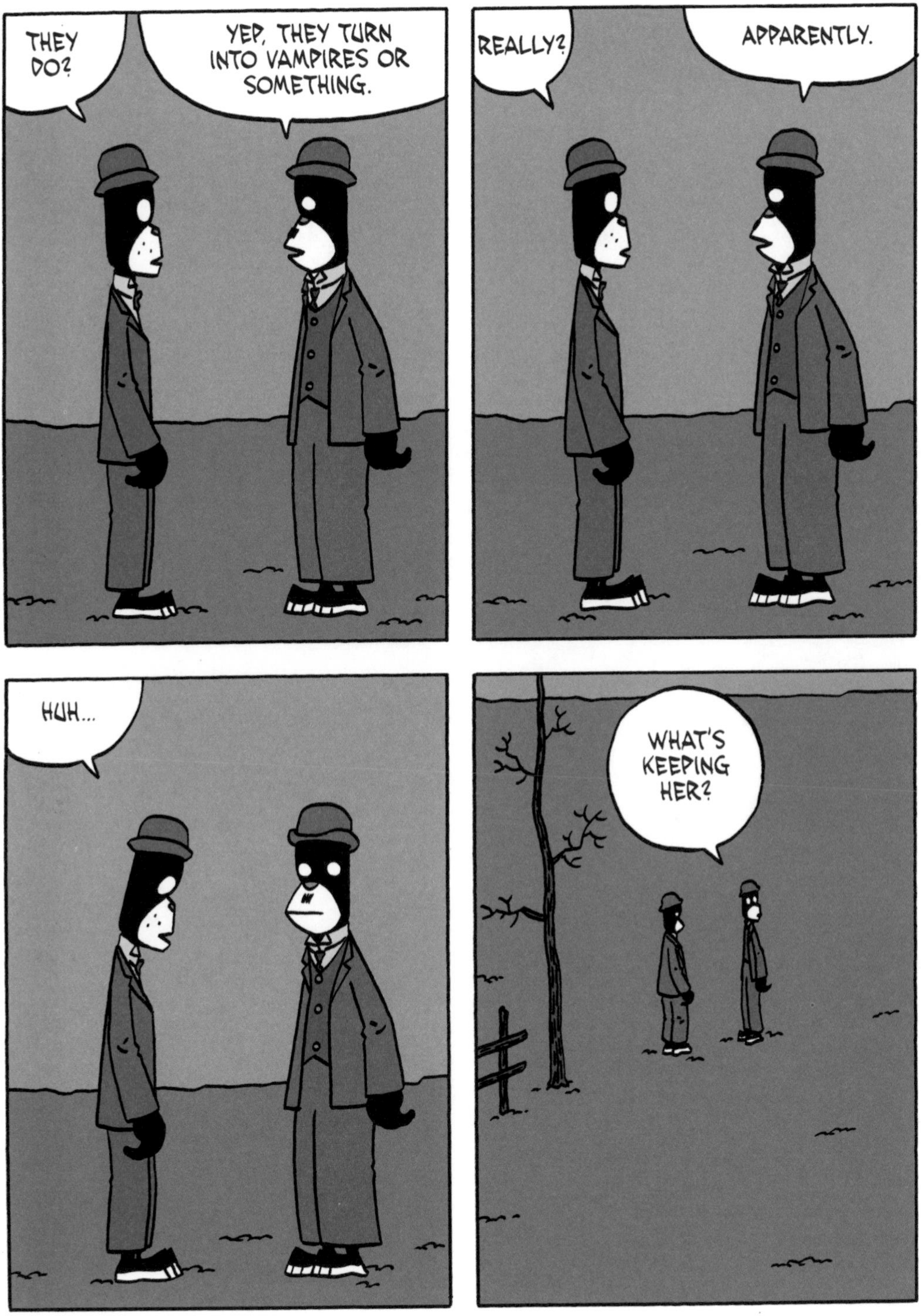
THEY DO?
YEP, THEY TURN INTO VAMPIRES OR SOMETHING.
REALLY?
APPARENTLY.
HUH...
WHAT'S KEEPING HER?

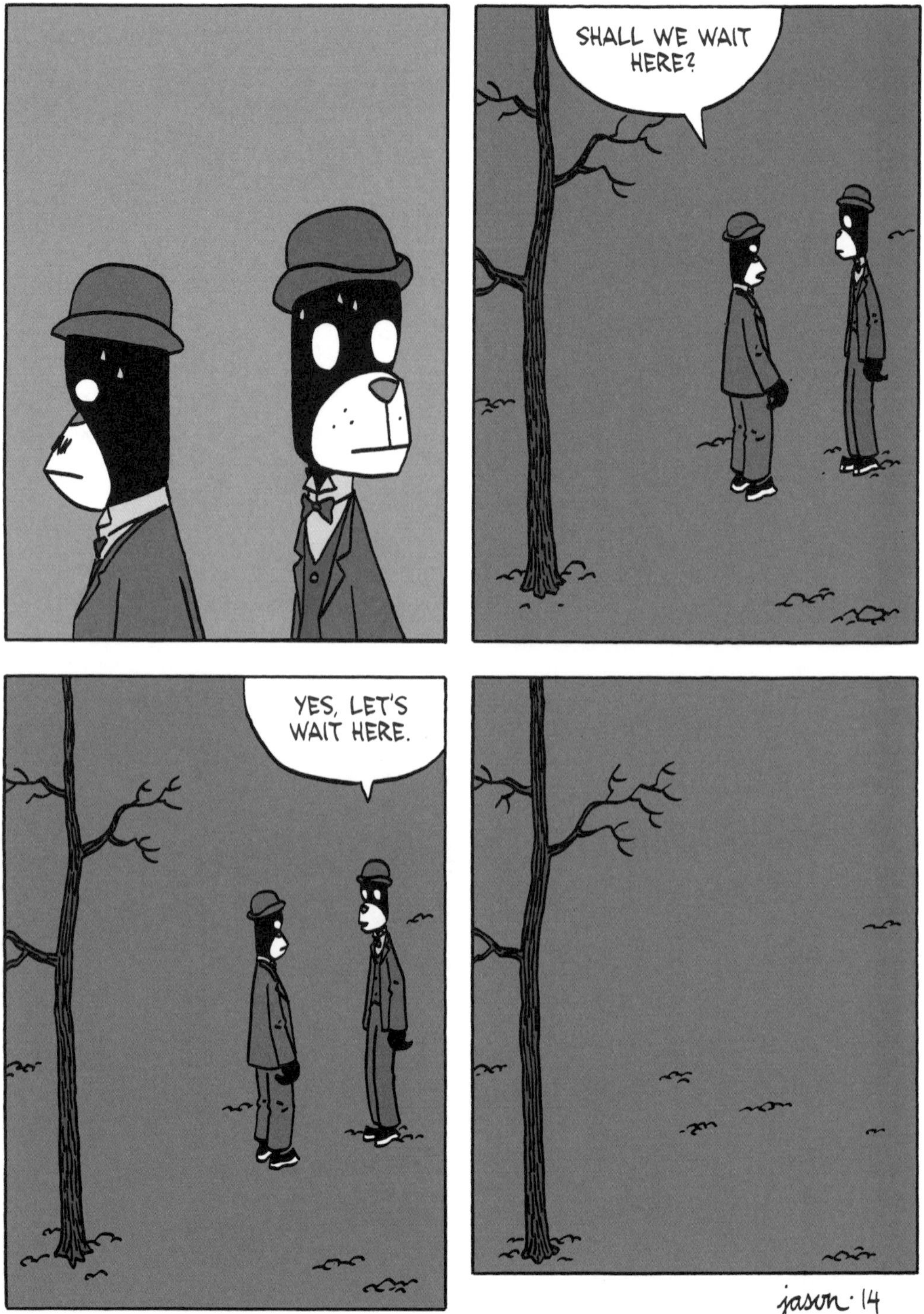
SHALL WE WAIT HERE?
YES, LET'S WAIT HERE.
jason · 14

PRESENTING:

LORENA VELAZQUEZ

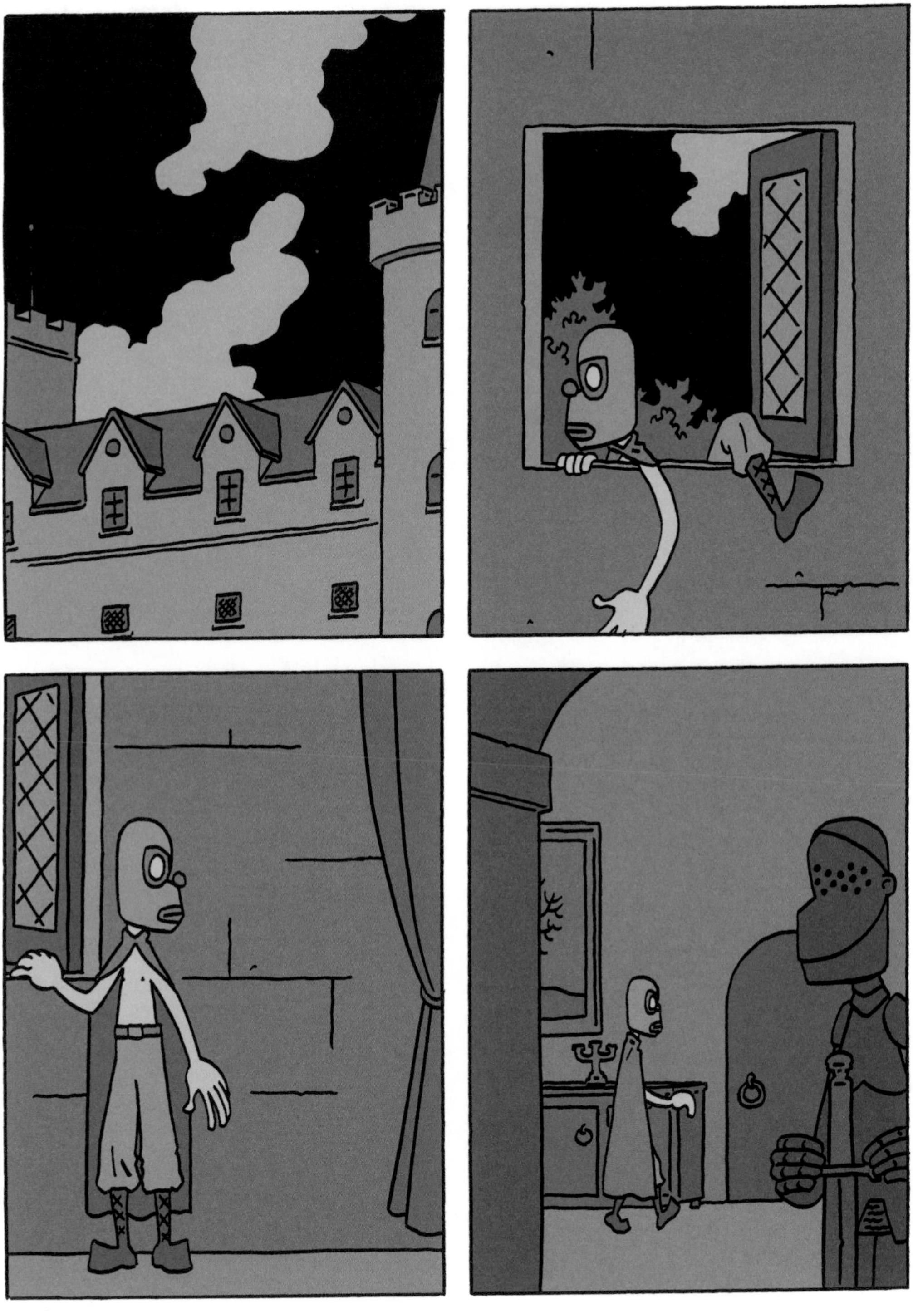

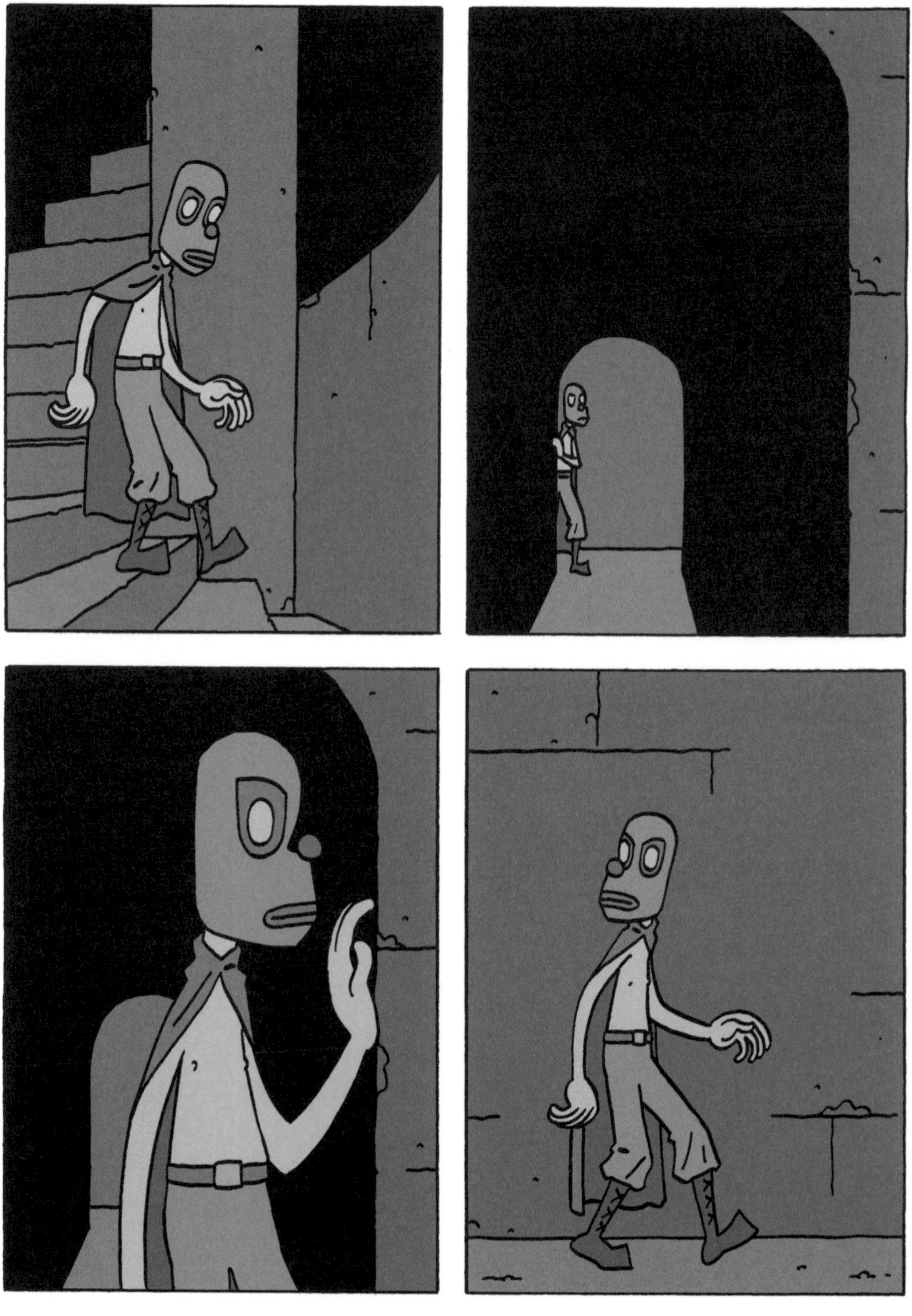

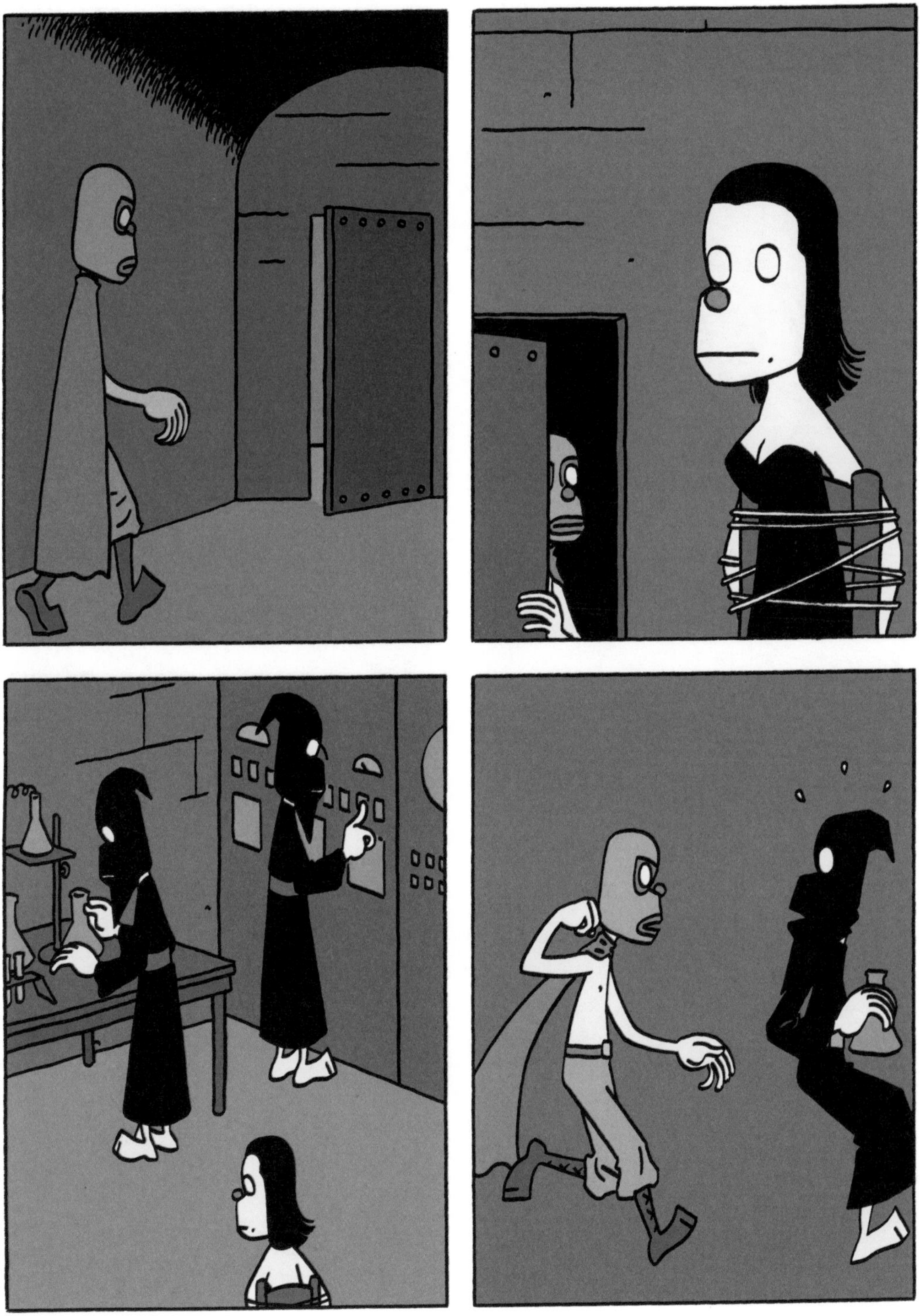

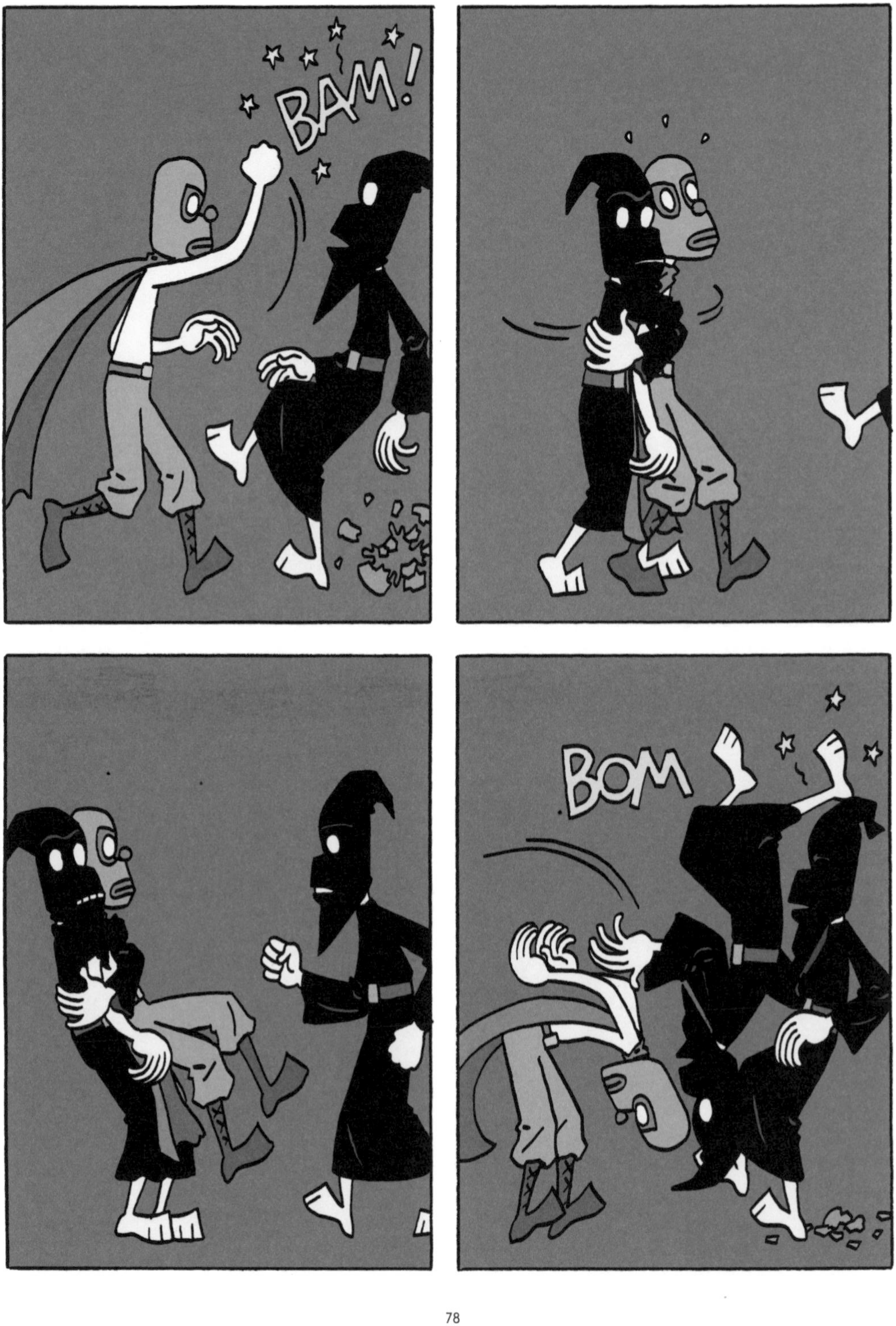
BAM!
BOM

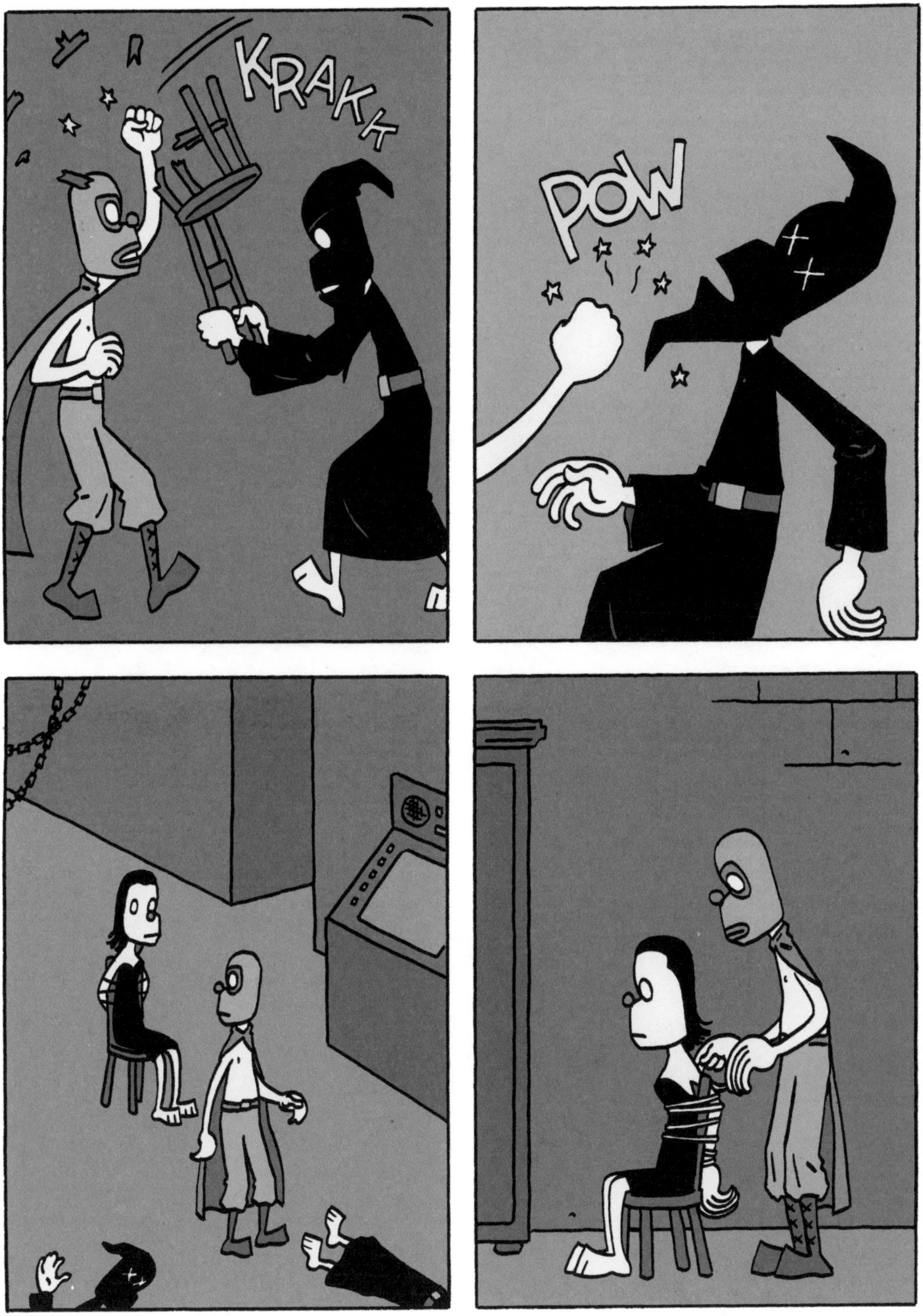
KRAKK
POW

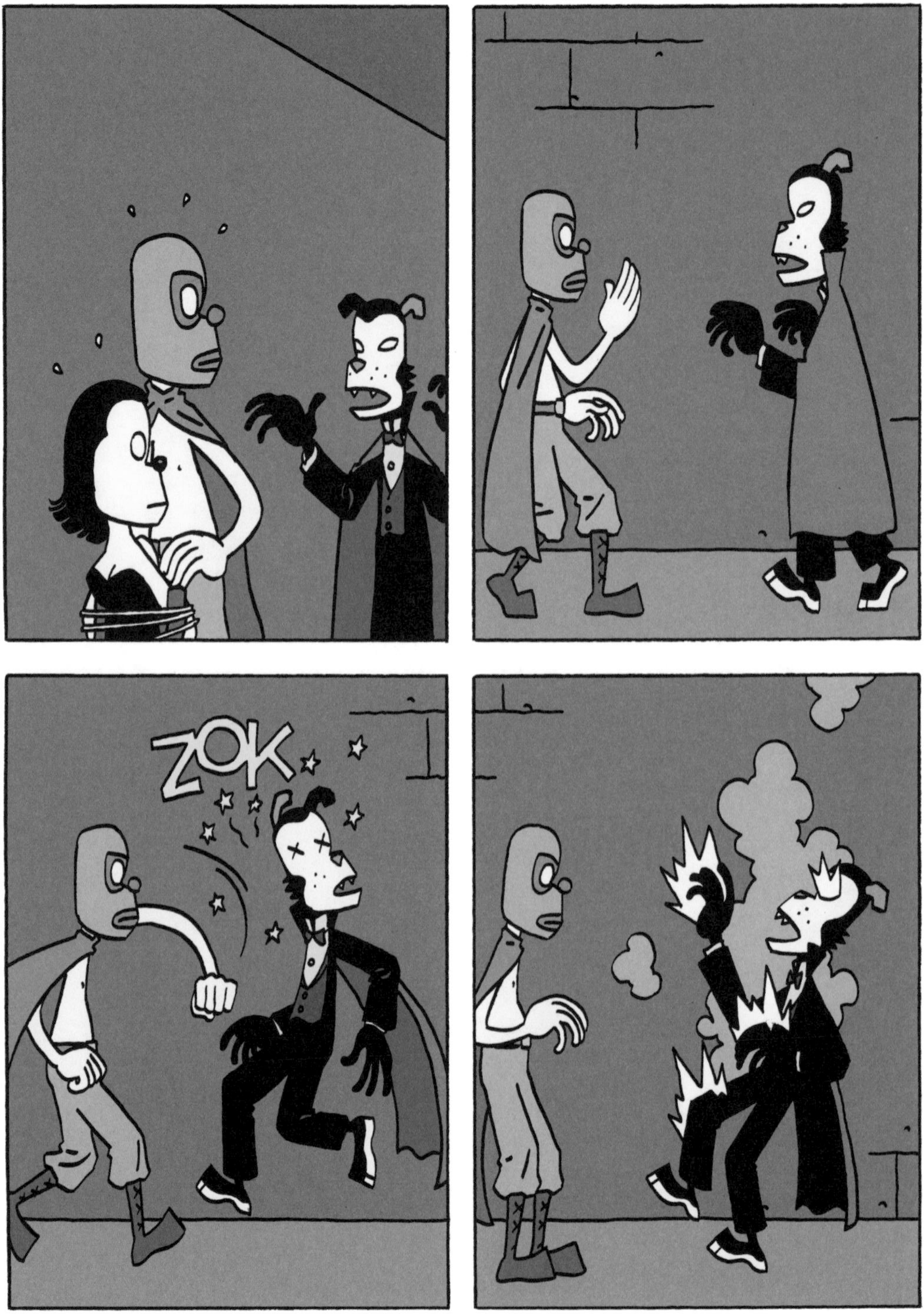
ZOK

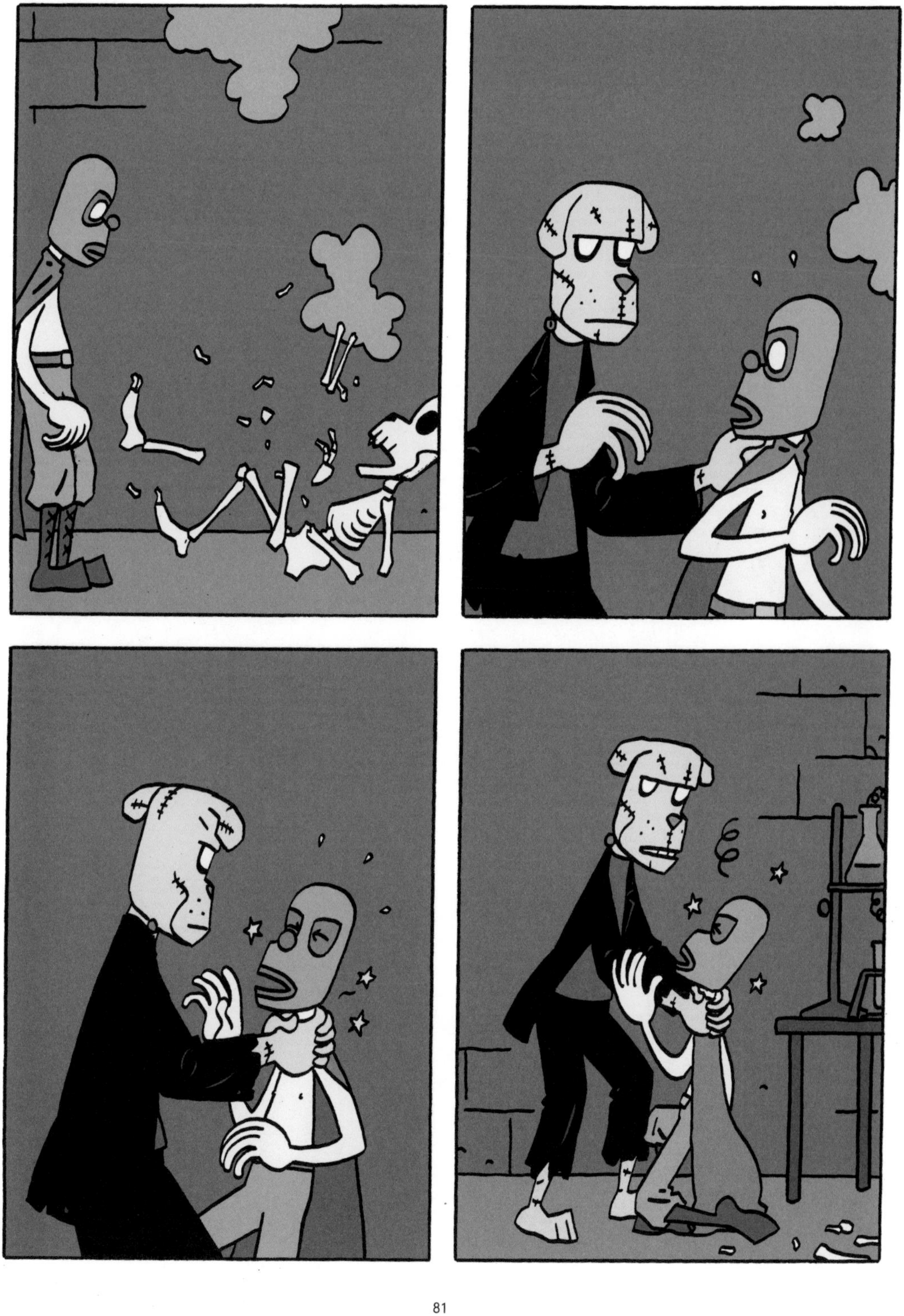

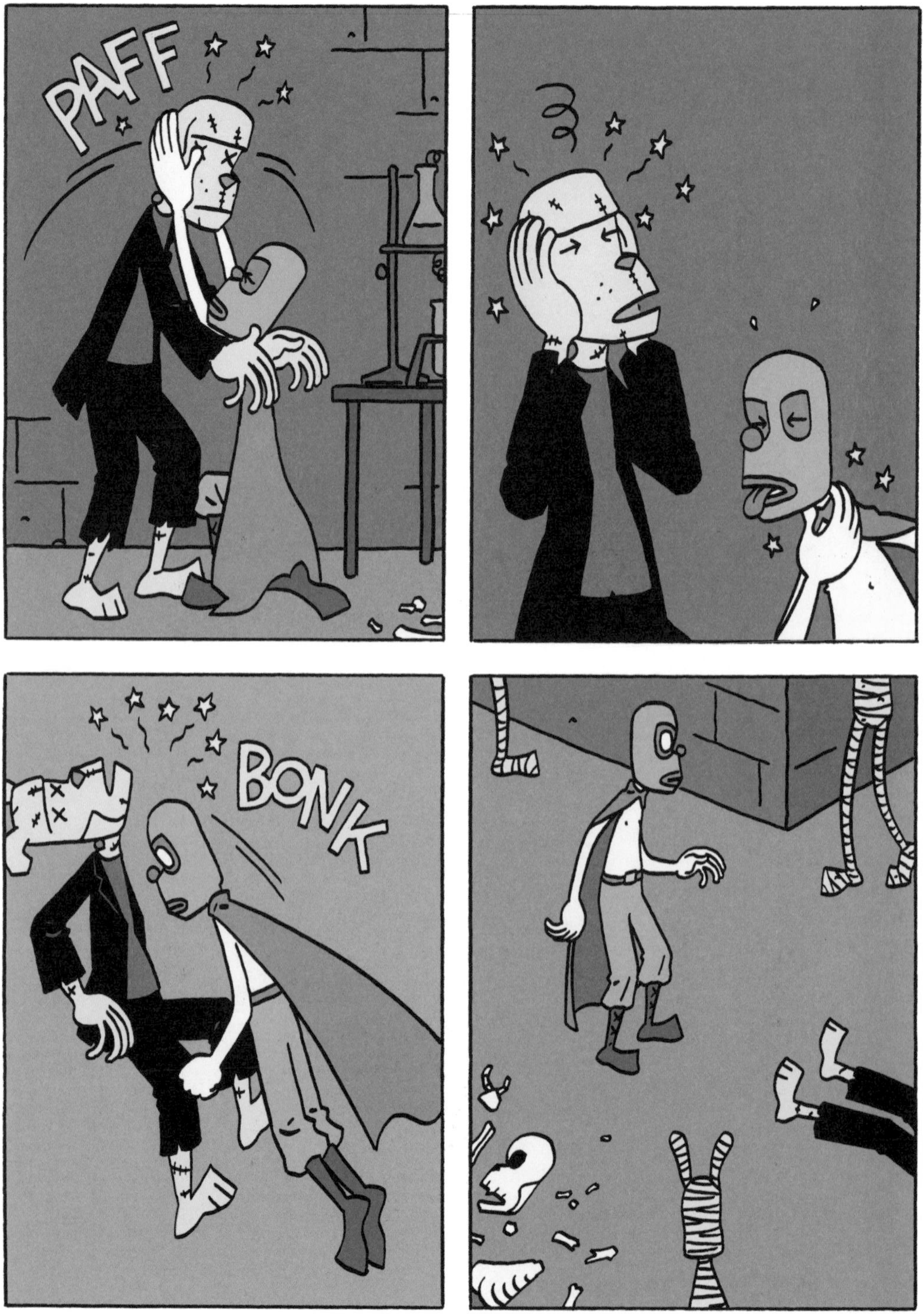
PAFF
BONK

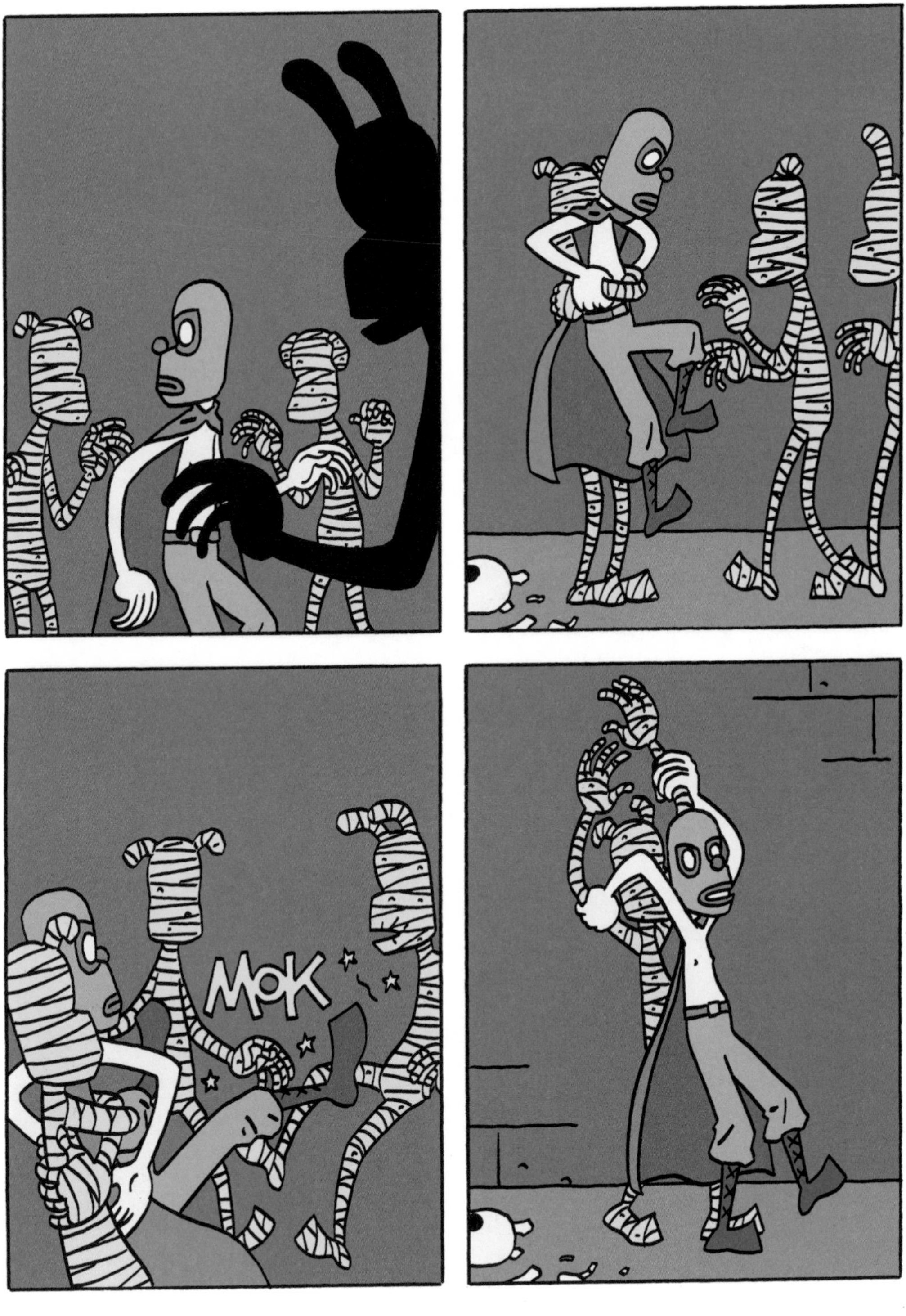
MOK

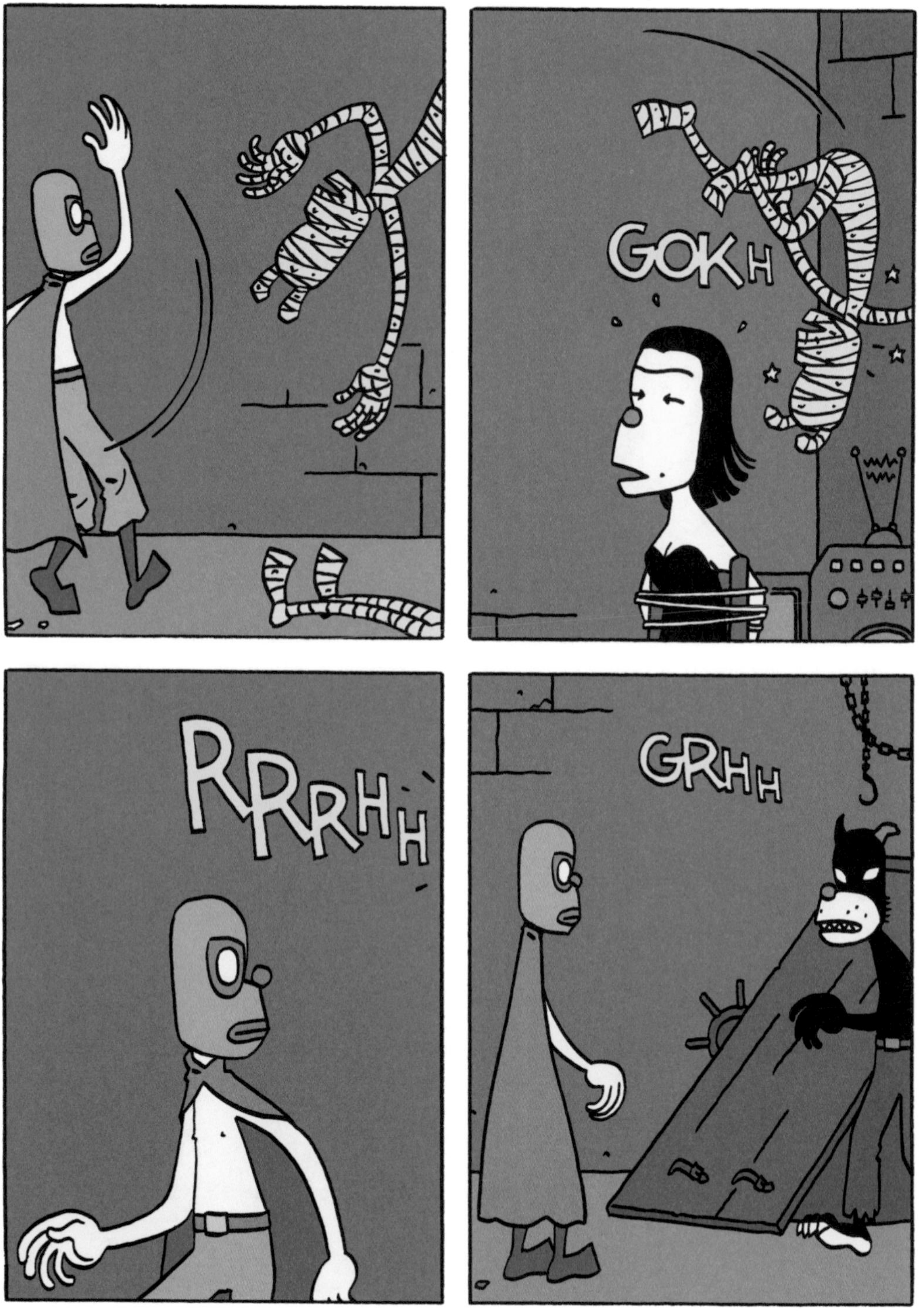
GOKH
RRRHHH
GRHH

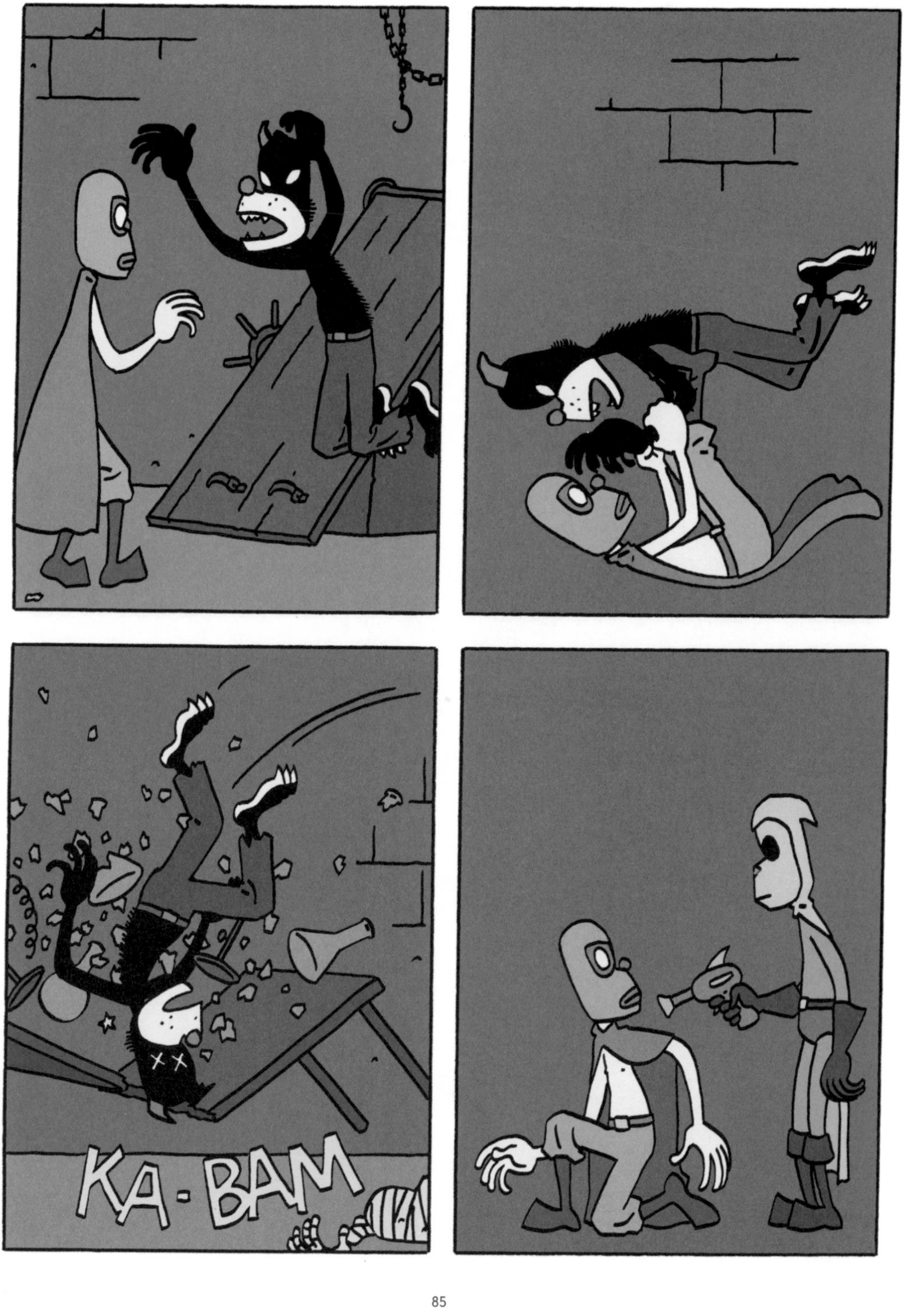
KA-BAM

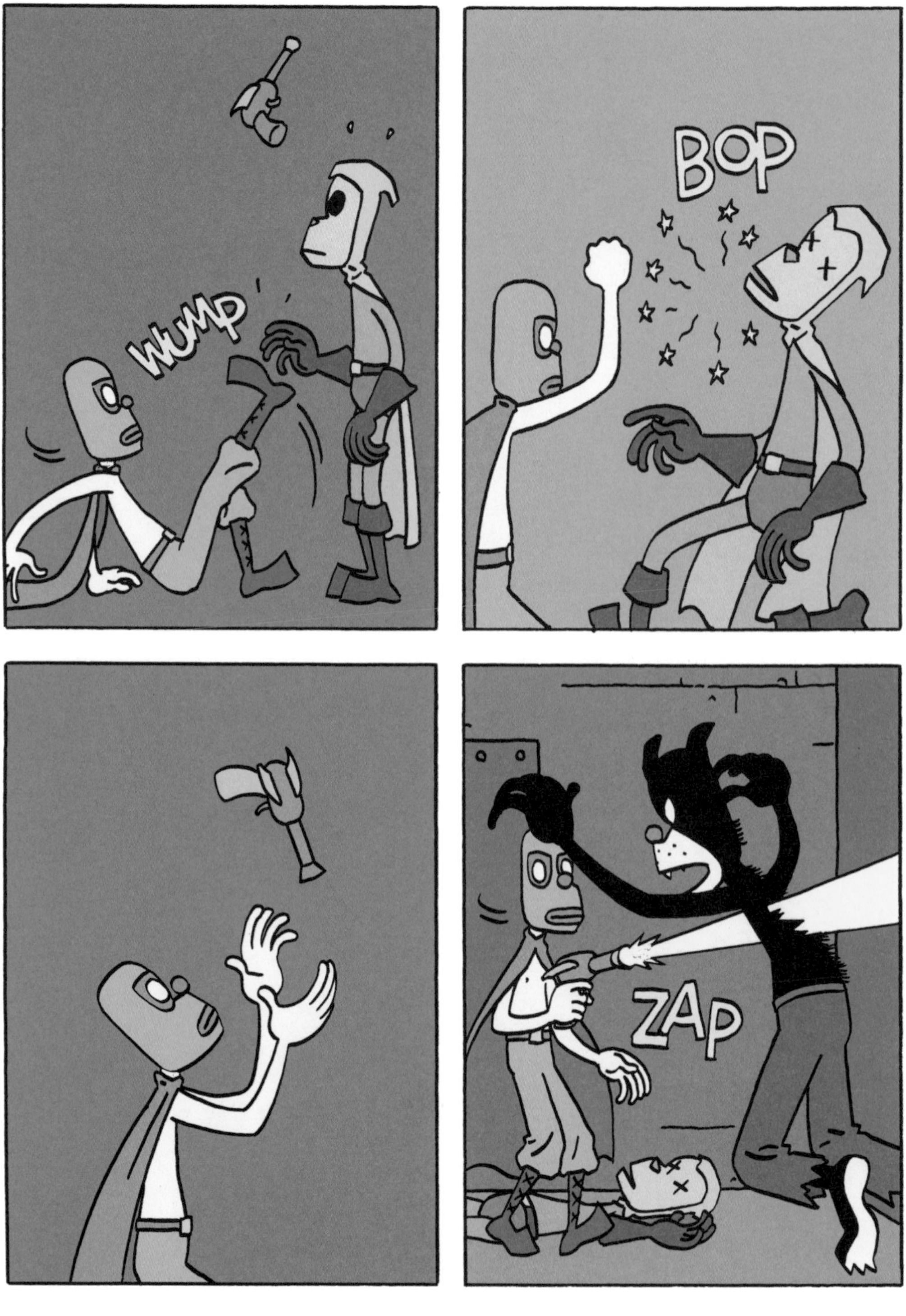
WUMP
BOP
ZAP

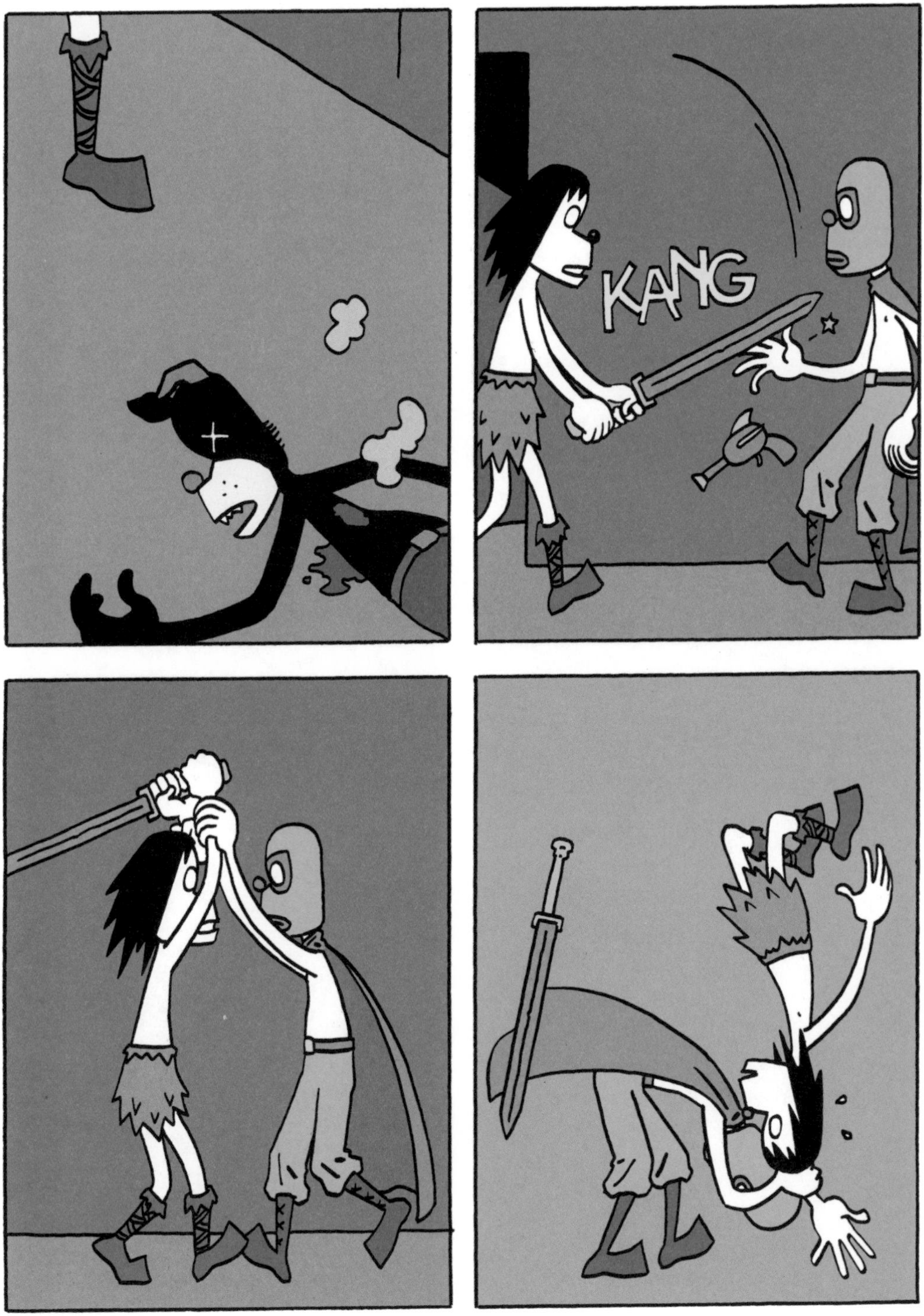
KANG

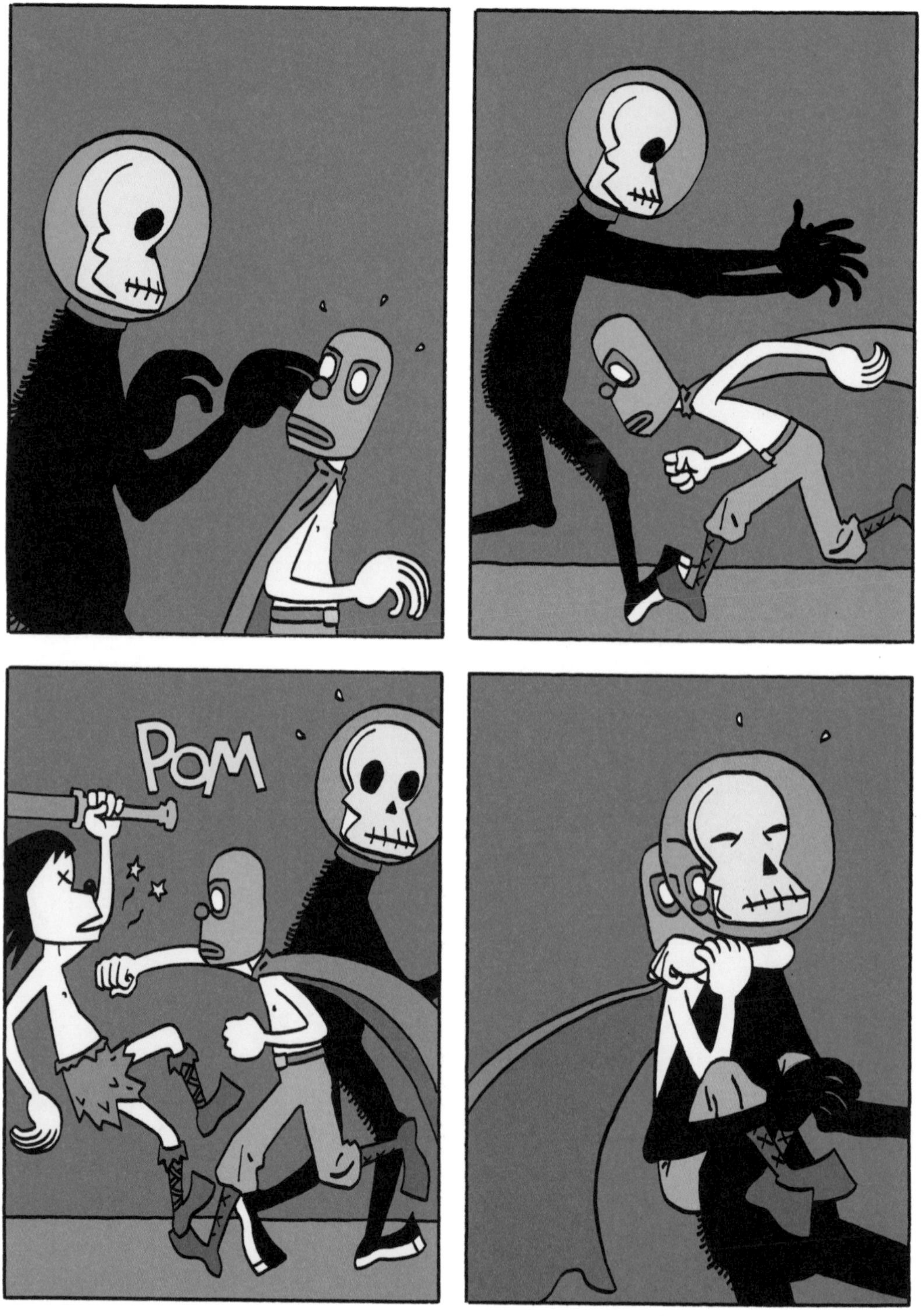
POM

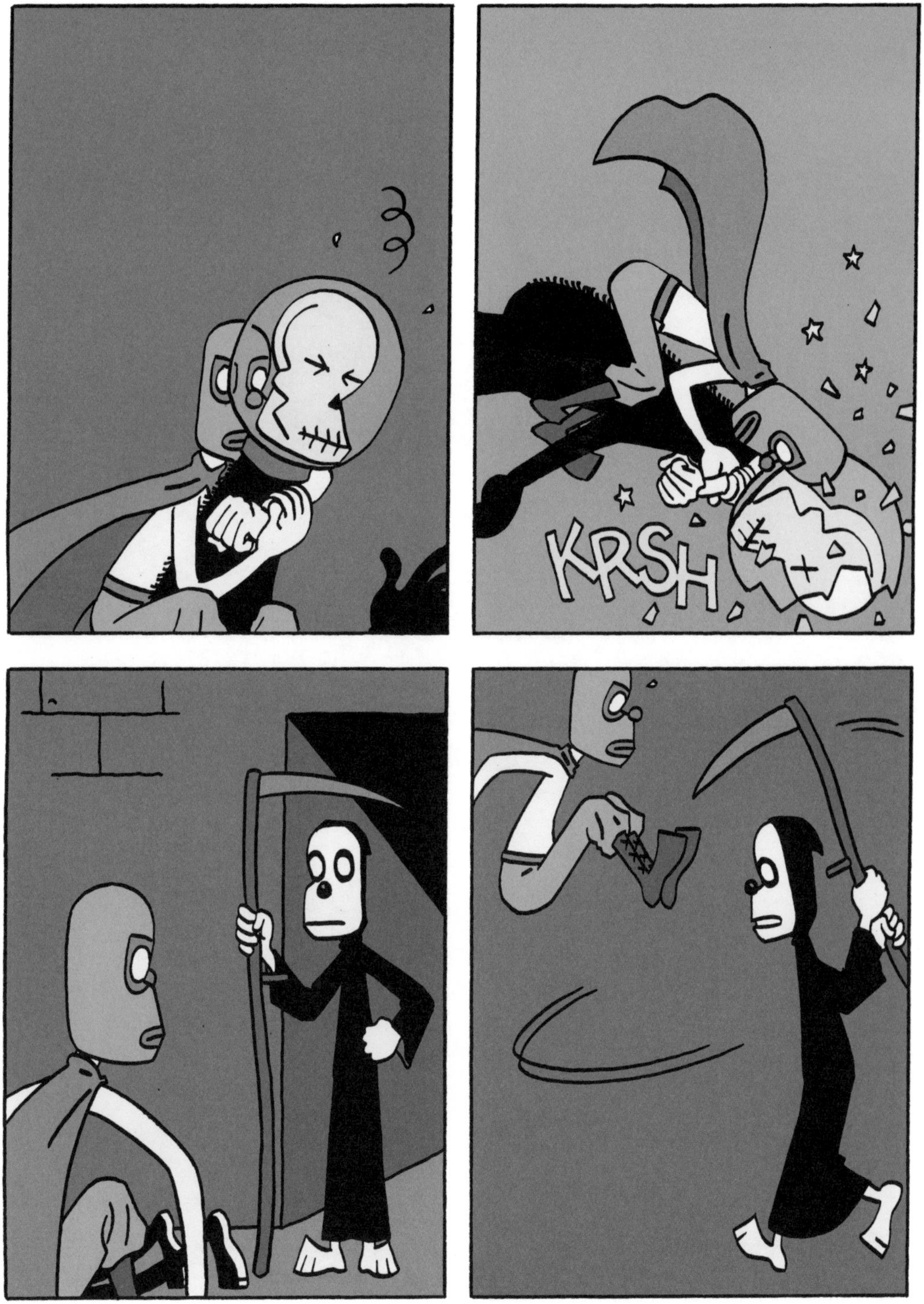
KRSH

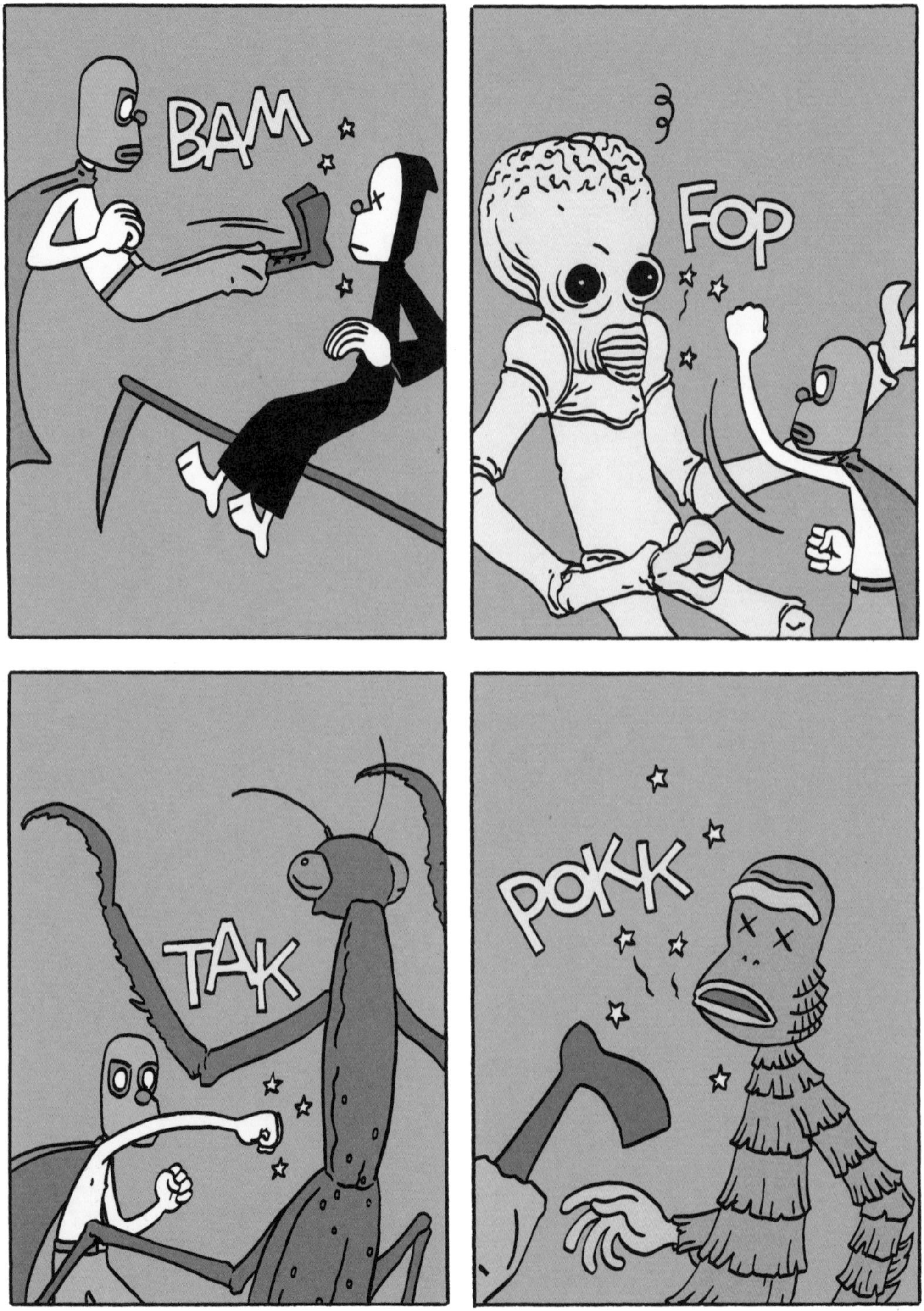
BAM
FOP
TAK
POKK

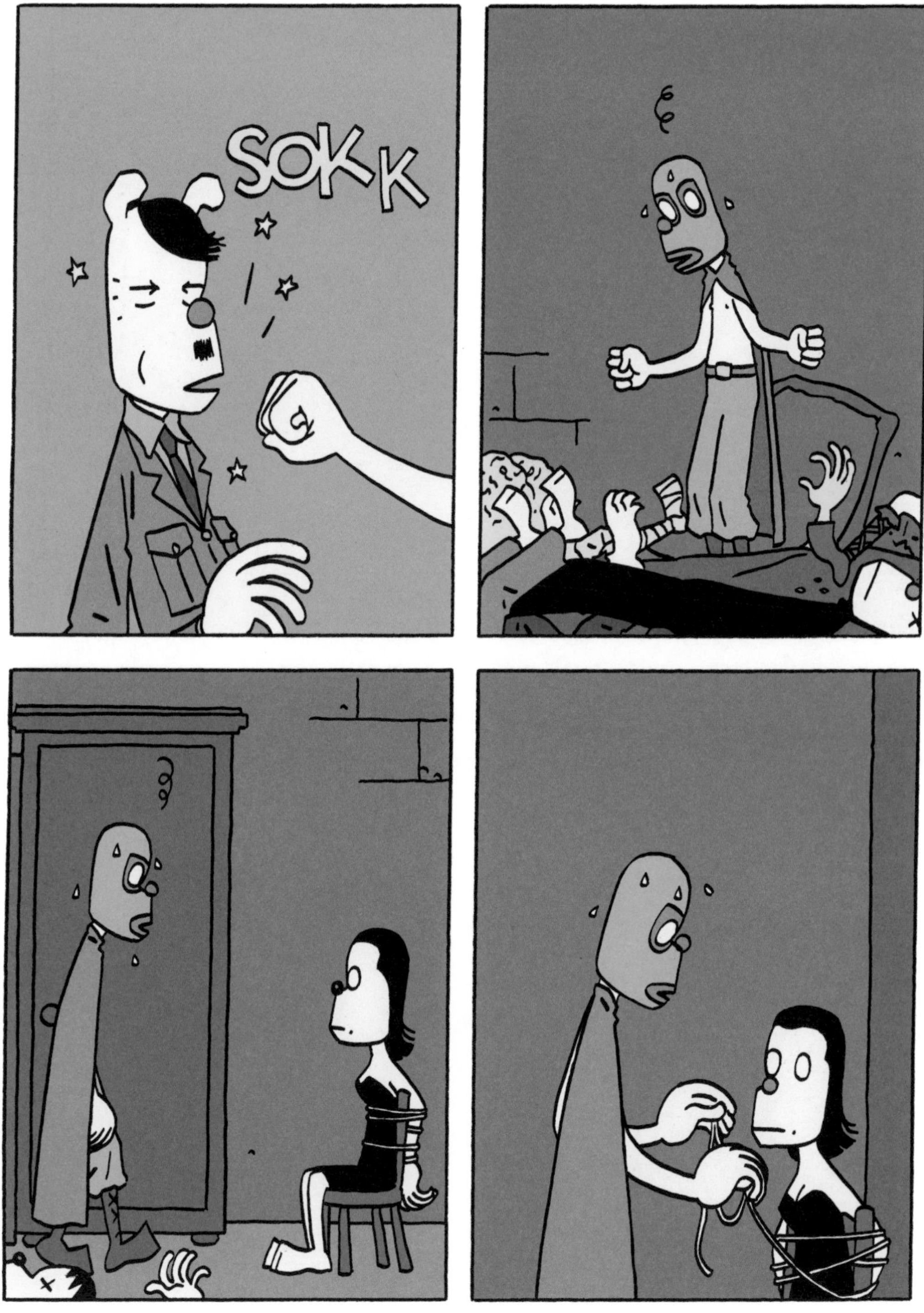
SOKK

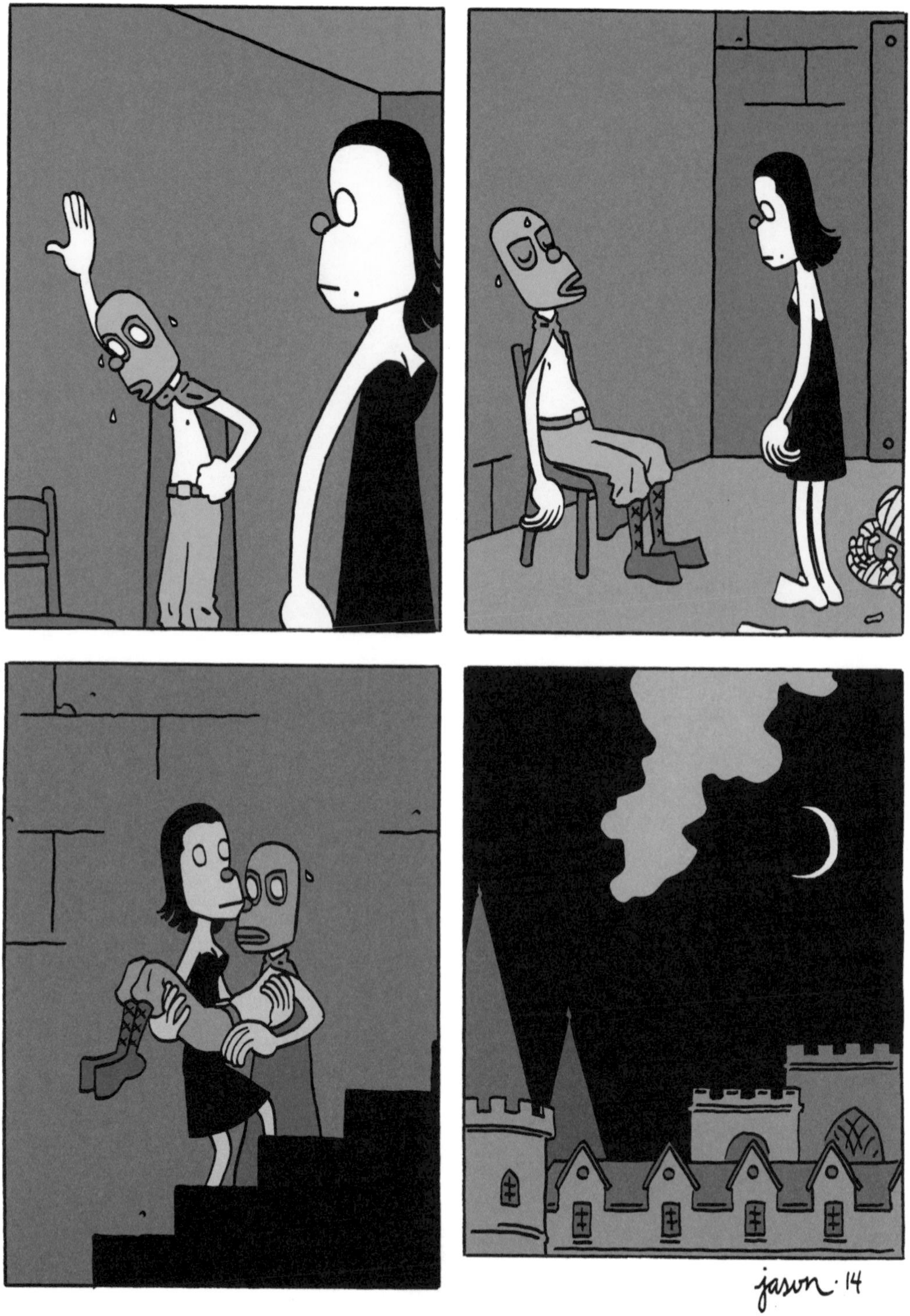
jason · 14

PRESENTING:

NEW FACE

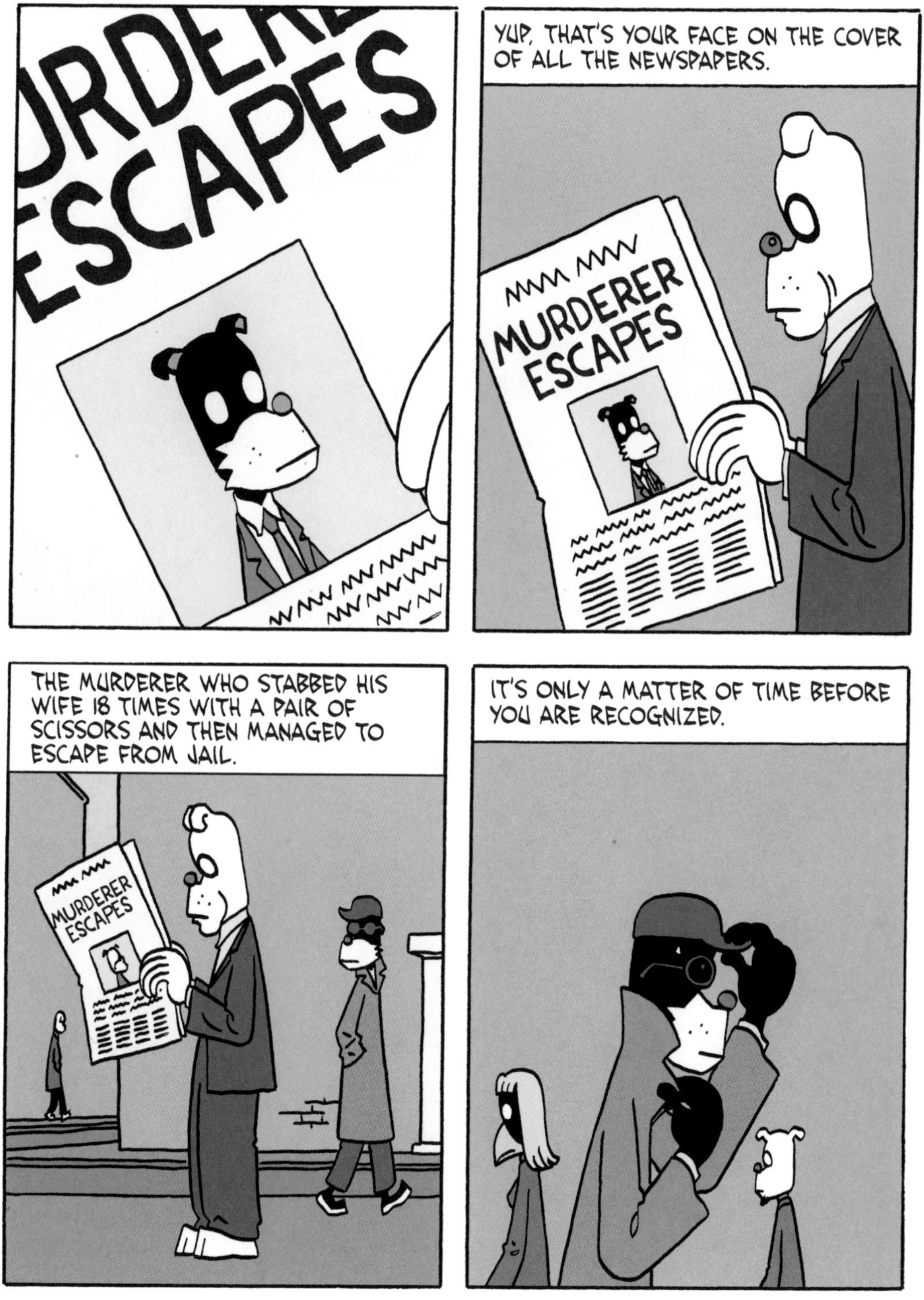

RDERE
ESCAPES
YUP, THAT'S YOUR FACE ON THE COVER OF ALL THE NEWSPAPERS.
MURDERER ESCAPES
THE MURDERER WHO STABBED HIS WIFE 18 TIMES WITH A PAIR OF SCISSORS AND THEN MANAGED TO ESCAPE FROM JAIL.
MURDERER ESCAPES
IT'S ONLY A MATTER OF TIME BEFORE YOU ARE RECOGNIZED.

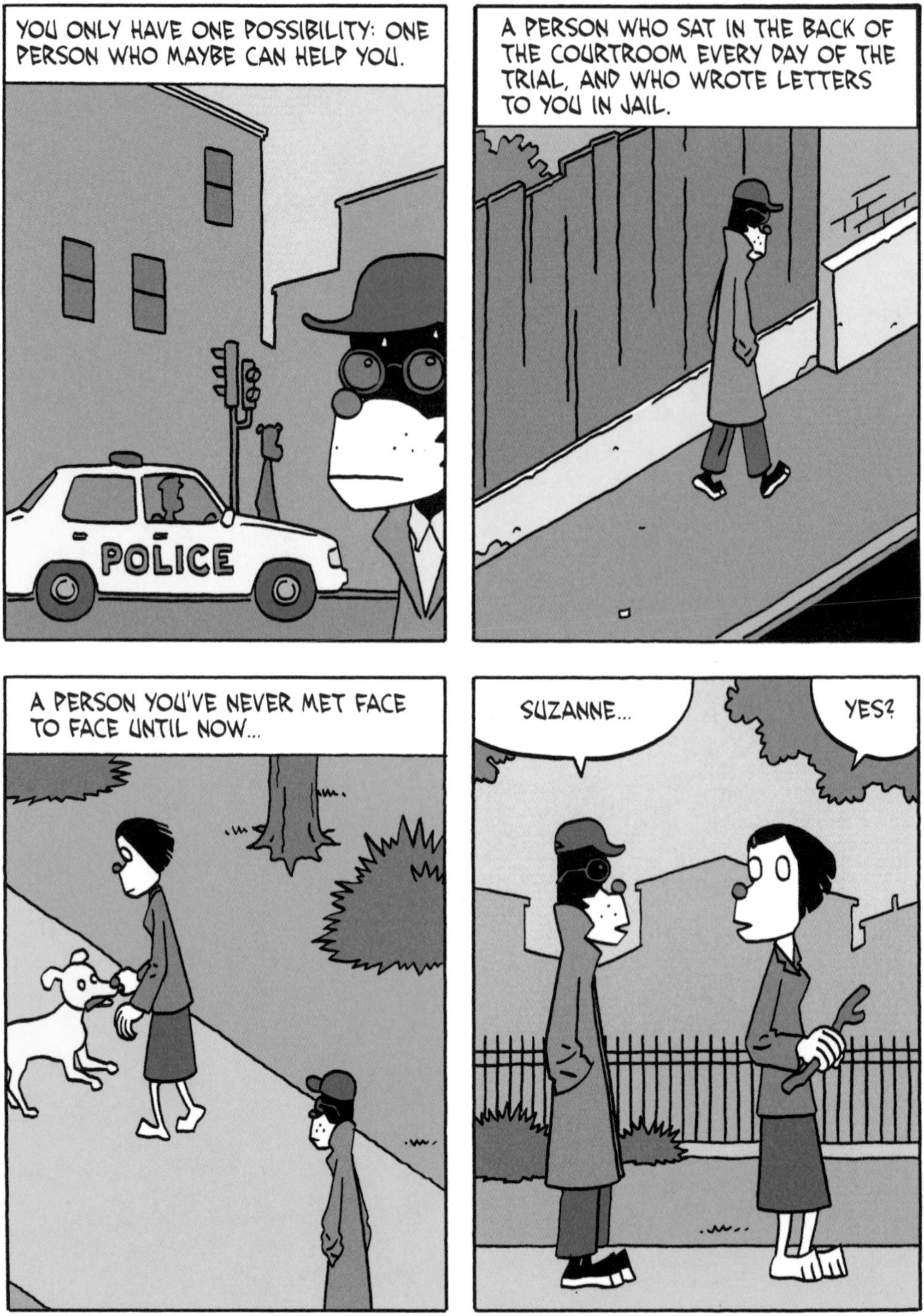
YOU ONLY HAVE ONE POSSIBILITY: ONE PERSON WHO MAYBE CAN HELP YOU.
POLICE
A PERSON WHO SAT IN THE BACK OF THE COURTROOM EVERY DAY OF THE TRIAL, AND WHO WROTE LETTERS TO YOU IN JAIL.
A PERSON YOU'VE NEVER MET FACE TO FACE UNTIL NOW...
SUZANNE...
YES?

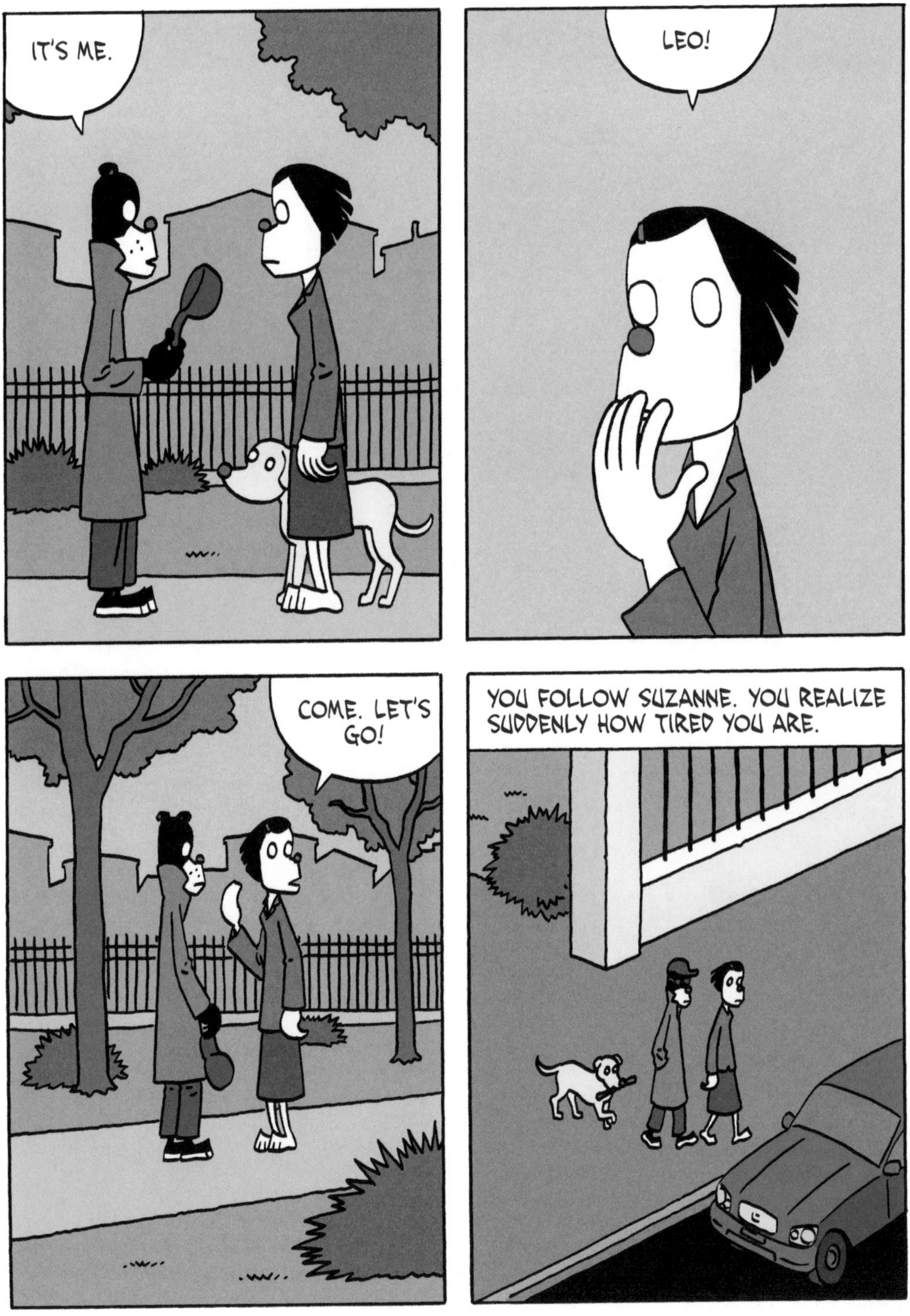
IT'S ME.
LEO!
COME. LET'S GO!
YOU FOLLOW SUZANNE. YOU REALIZE SUDDENLY HOW TIRED YOU ARE.

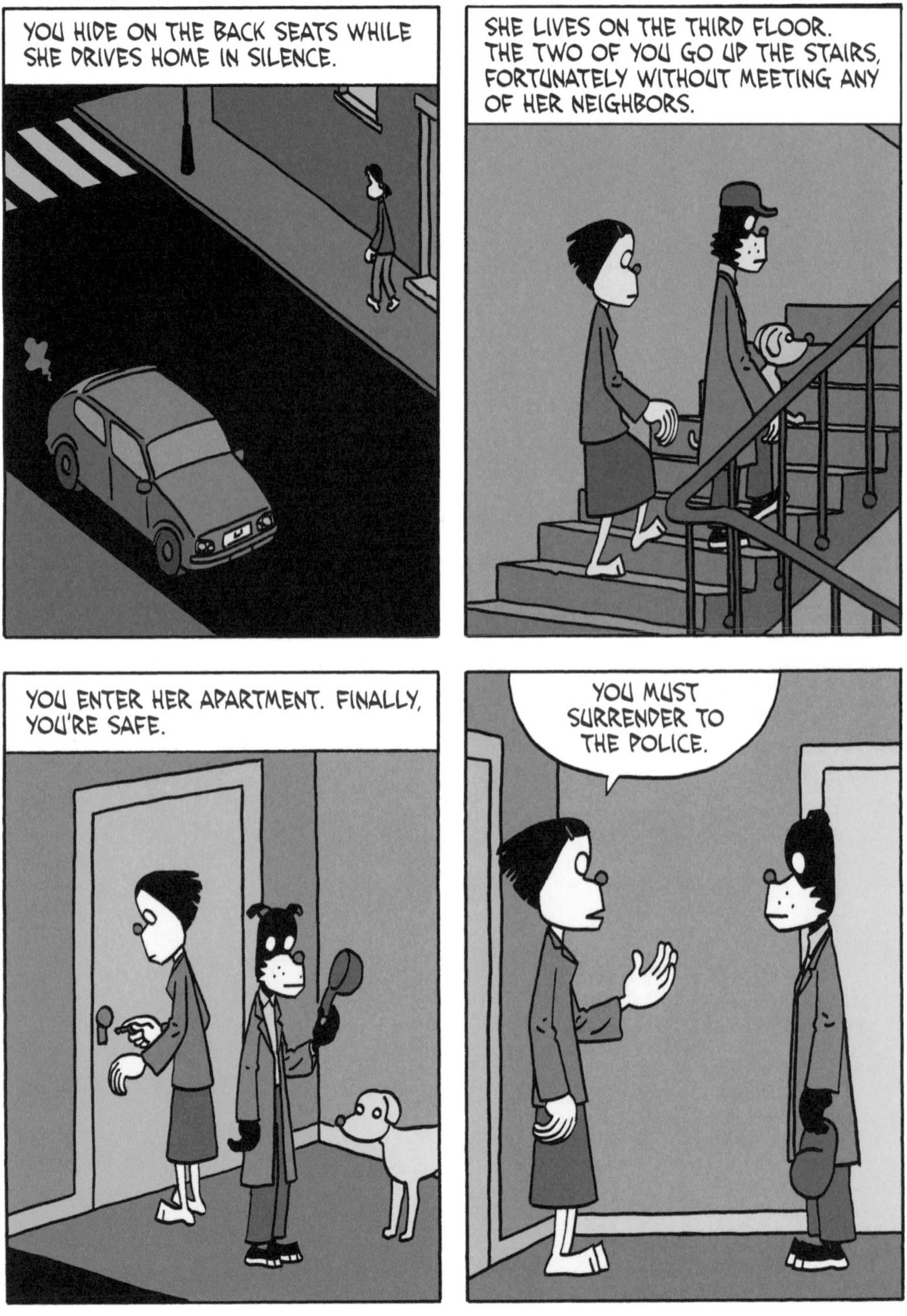
YOU HIDE ON THE BACK SEATS WHILE SHE DRIVES HOME IN SILENCE.
SHE LIVES ON THE THIRD FLOOR. THE TWO OF YOU GO UP THE STAIRS, FORTUNATELY WITHOUT MEETING ANY OF HER NEIGHBORS.
YOU ENTER HER APARTMENT. FINALLY, YOU'RE SAFE.
YOU MUST SURRENDER TO THE POLICE.

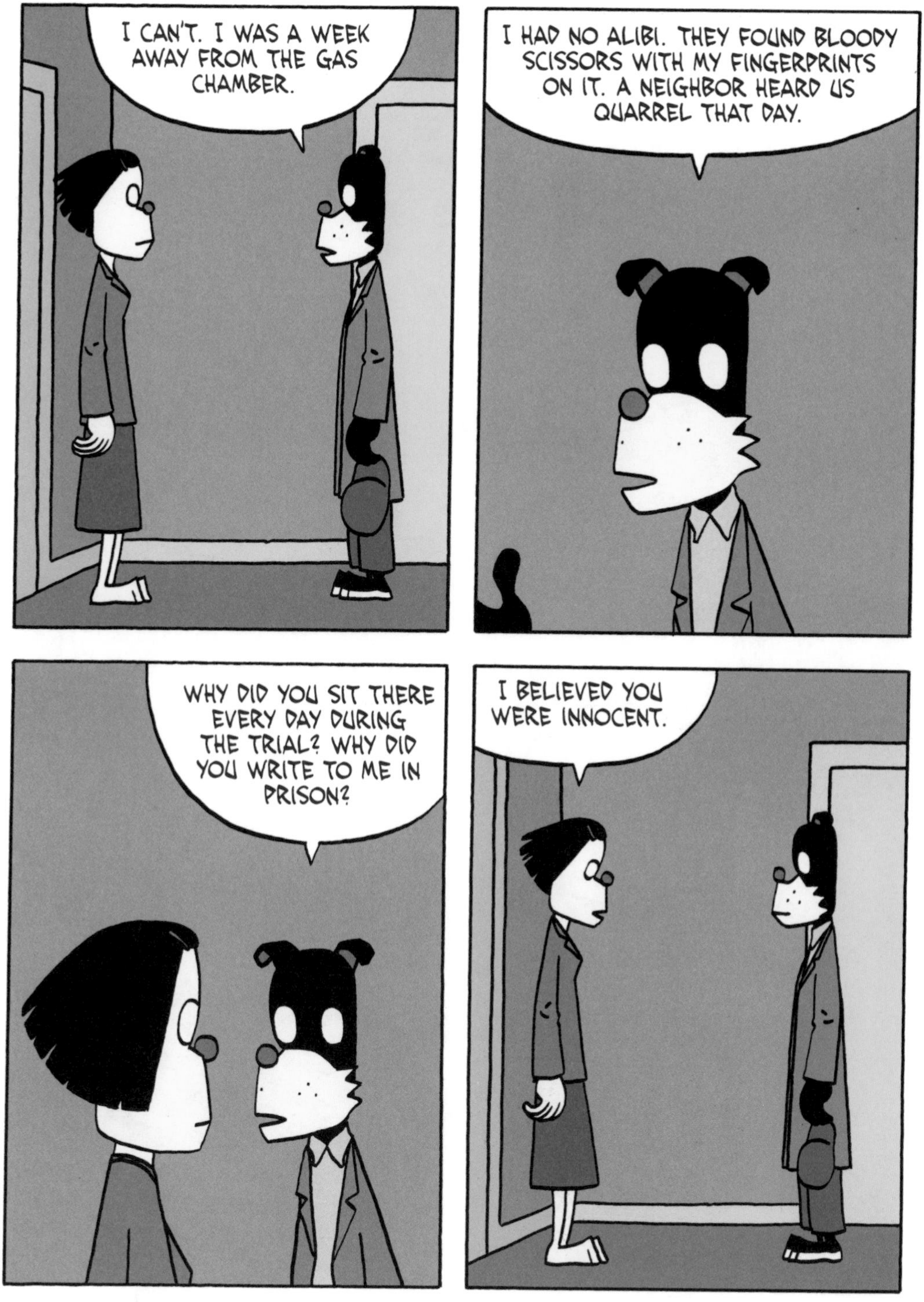
I CAN'T. I WAS A WEEK AWAY FROM THE GAS CHAMBER.
I HAD NO ALIBI. THEY FOUND BLOODY SCISSORS WITH MY FINGERPRINTS ON IT. A NEIGHBOR HEARD US QUARREL THAT DAY.
WHY DID YOU SIT THERE EVERY DAY DURING THE TRIAL? WHY DID YOU WRITE TO ME IN PRISON?
I BELIEVED YOU WERE INNOCENT.

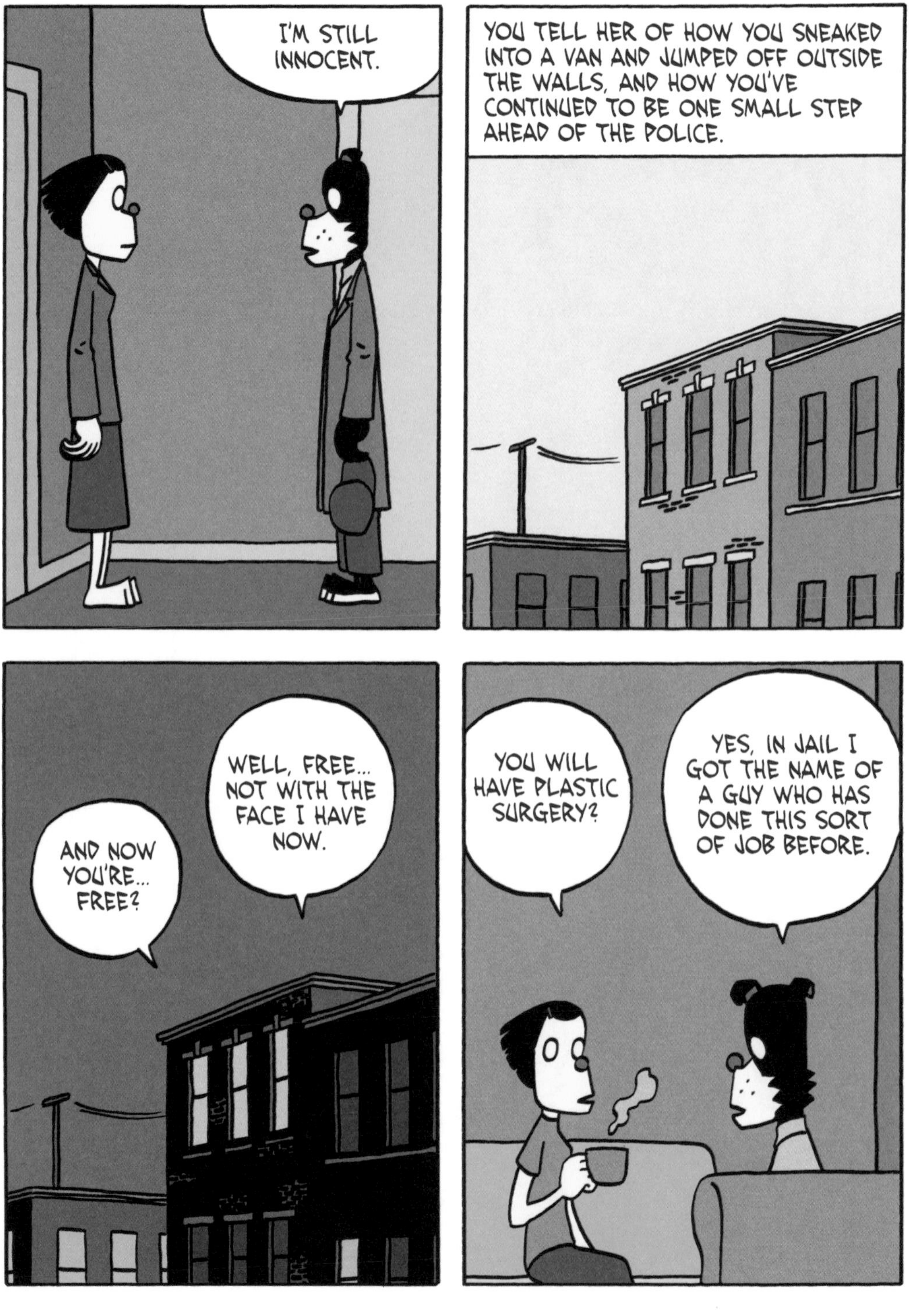
I'M STILL INNOCENT.
YOU TELL HER OF HOW YOU SNEAKED INTO A VAN AND JUMPED OFF OUTSIDE THE WALLS, AND HOW YOU'VE CONTINUED TO BE ONE SMALL STEP AHEAD OF THE POLICE.
AND NOW YOU'RE... FREE?
WELL, FREE... NOT WITH THE FACE I HAVE NOW.
YOU WILL HAVE PLASTIC SURGERY?
YES, IN JAIL I GOT THE NAME OF A GUY WHO HAS DONE THIS SORT OF JOB BEFORE.

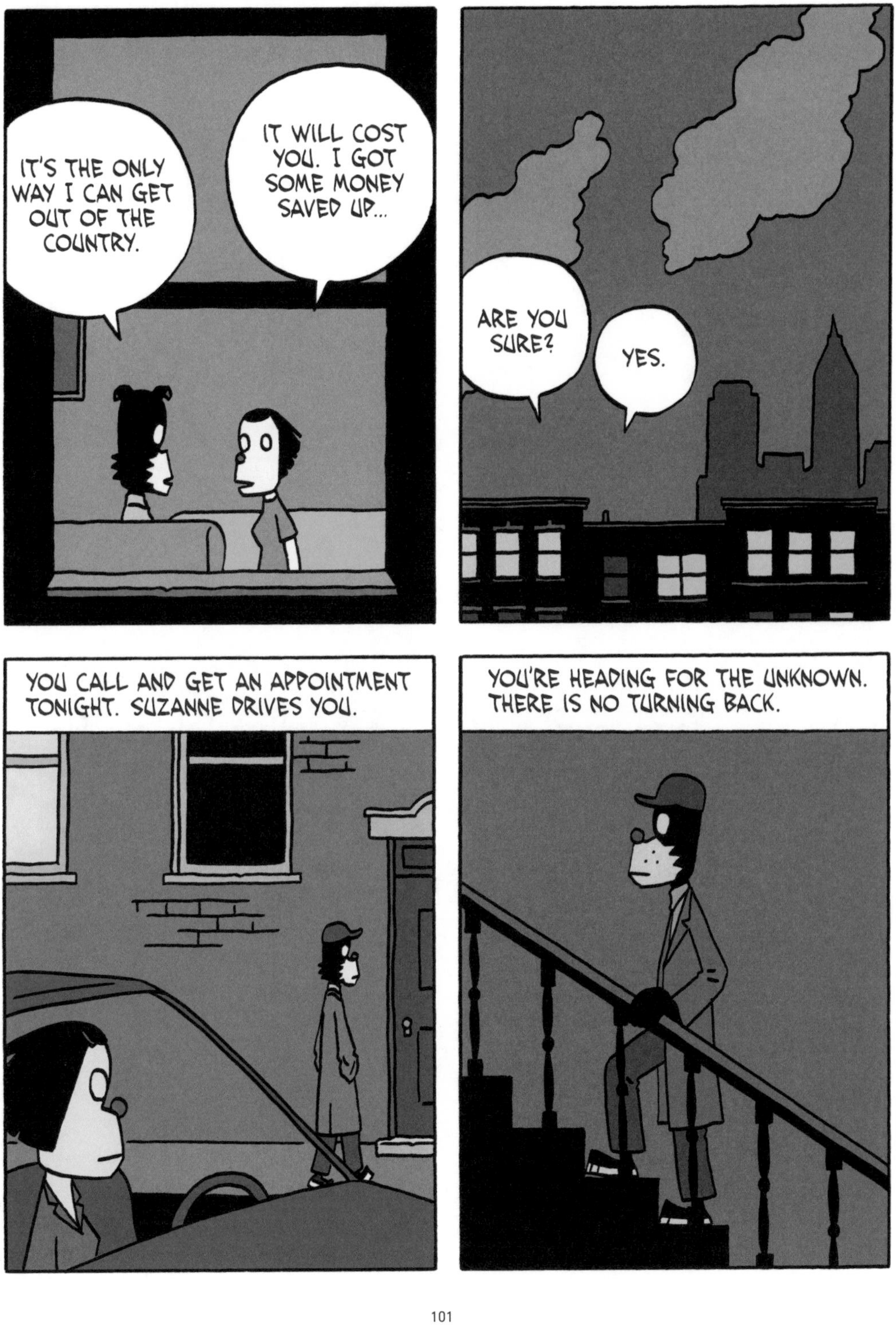
IT'S THE ONLY WAY I CAN GET OUT OF THE COUNTRY.
IT WILL COST YOU. I GOT SOME MONEY SAVED UP...
ARE YOU SURE?
YES.
YOU CALL AND GET AN APPOINTMENT TONIGHT. SUZANNE DRIVES YOU.
YOU'RE HEADING FOR THE UNKNOWN. THERE IS NO TURNING BACK.

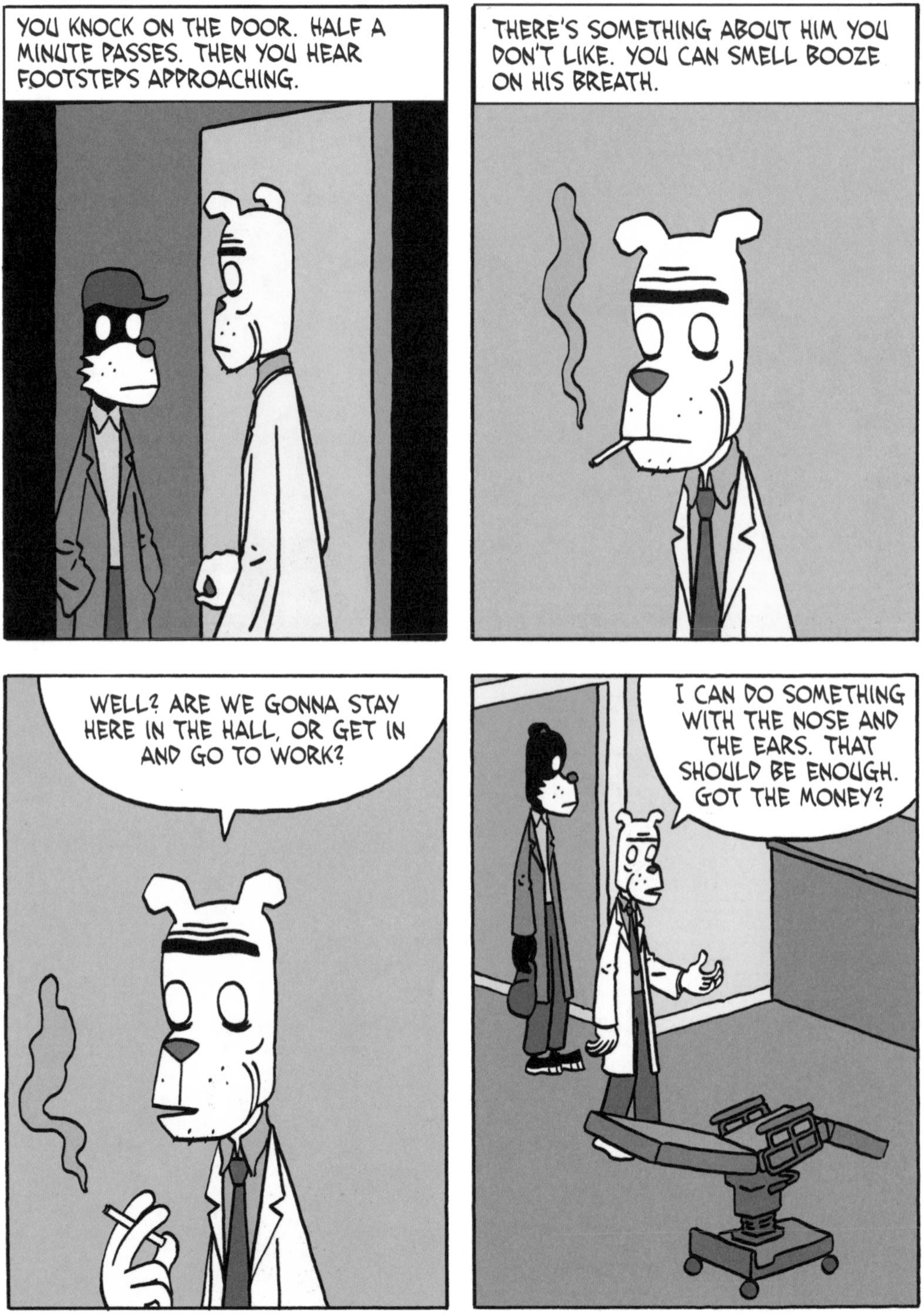
YOU KNOCK ON THE DOOR. HALF A MINUTE PASSES. THEN YOU HEAR FOOTSTEPS APPROACHING.
THERE'S SOMETHING ABOUT HIM YOU DON'T LIKE. YOU CAN SMELL BOOZE ON HIS BREATH.
WELL? ARE WE GONNA STAY HERE IN THE HALL, OR GET IN AND GO TO WORK?
I CAN DO SOMETHING WITH THE NOSE AND THE EARS. THAT SHOULD BE ENOUGH. GOT THE MONEY?

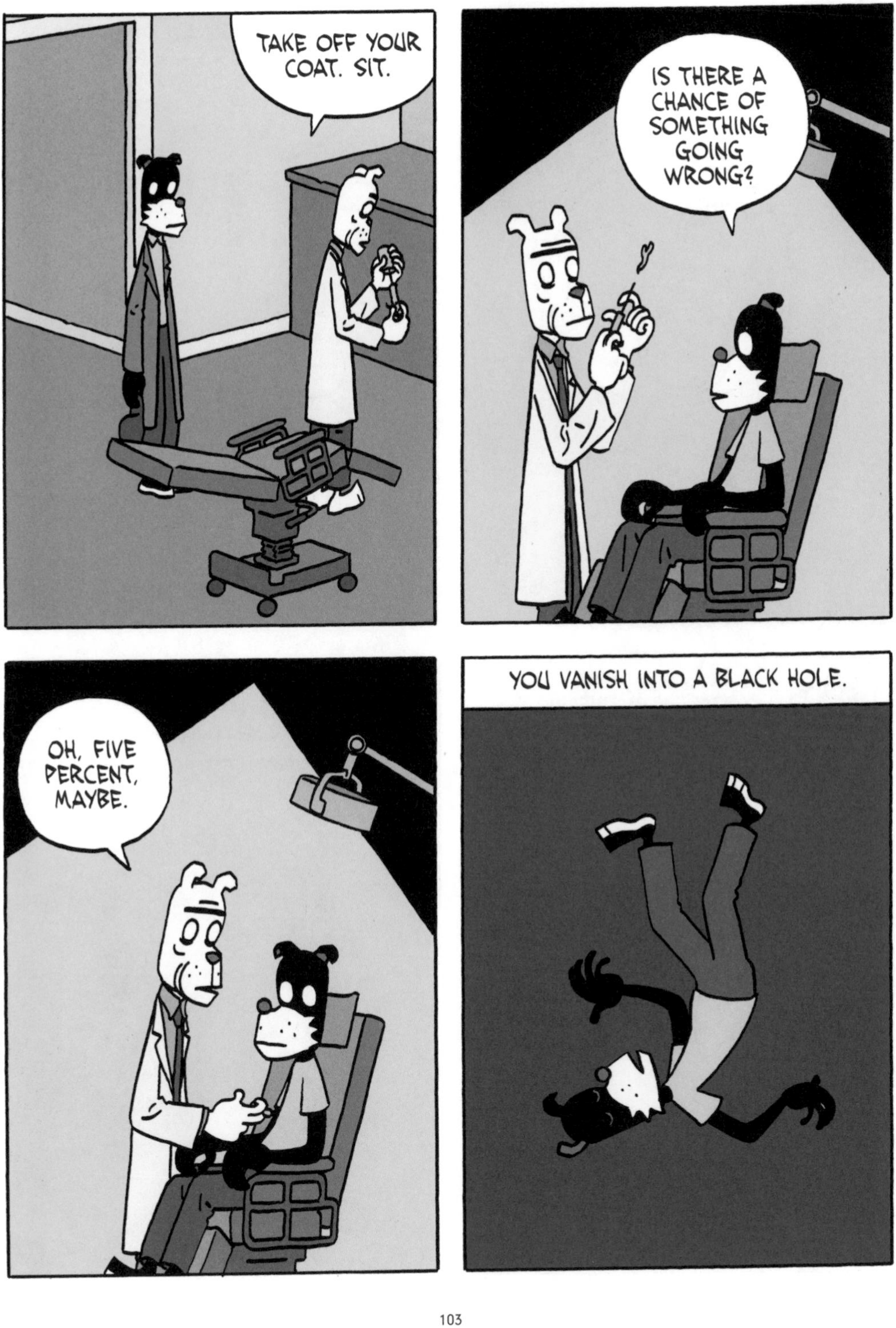
TAKE OFF YOUR COAT. SIT.
IS THERE A CHANCE OF SOMETHING GOING WRONG?
OH, FIVE PERCENT, MAYBE.
YOU VANISH INTO A BLACK HOLE.

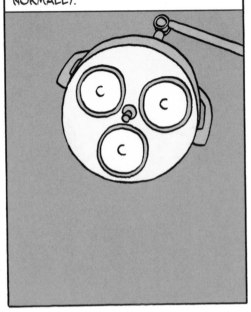

YOU OPEN YOUR EYES TO A BLINDING LIGHT. YOU BLINK UNTIL YOU CAN SEE NORMALLY.

YOU WILL BE ABLE TO TALK A BIT, BUT DON'T HOLD ANY LONG SPEECHES, OKAY? TAKE YOUR NUTRITION IN FLUIDS, THROUGH A STRAW.

YOU CAN REMOVE THE BANDAGES IN FIVE DAYS. THERE WILL BE NO STITCHES.

SUZANNE IS WAITING FOR YOU. A SMALL PART OF YOU WAS AFRAID HER CAR WOULDN'T BE THERE.

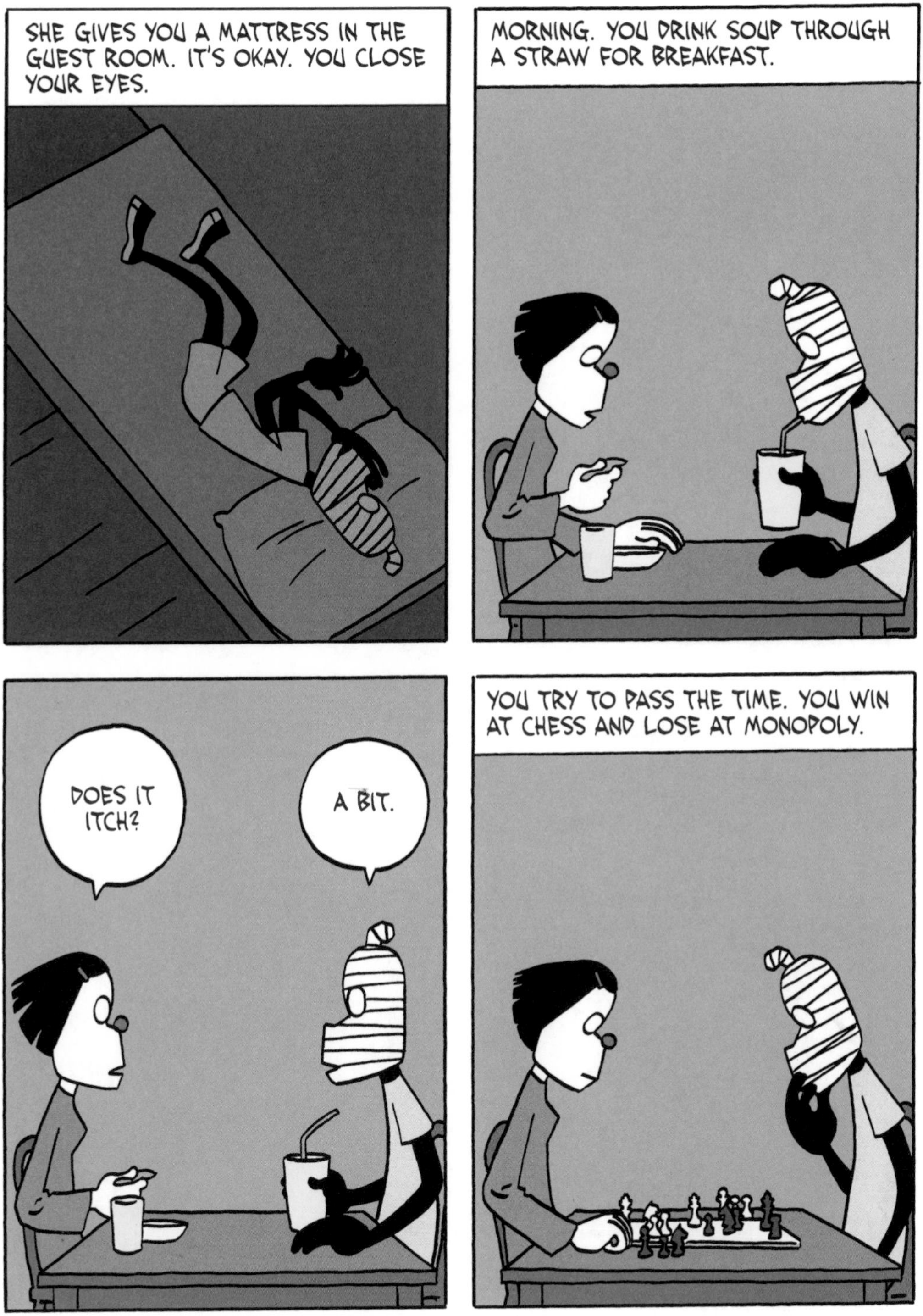
SHE GIVES YOU A MATTRESS IN THE GUEST ROOM. IT'S OKAY. YOU CLOSE YOUR EYES.
MORNING. YOU DRINK SOUP THROUGH A STRAW FOR BREAKFAST.
DOES IT ITCH?
A BIT.
YOU TRY TO PASS THE TIME. YOU WIN AT CHESS AND LOSE AT MONOPOLY.

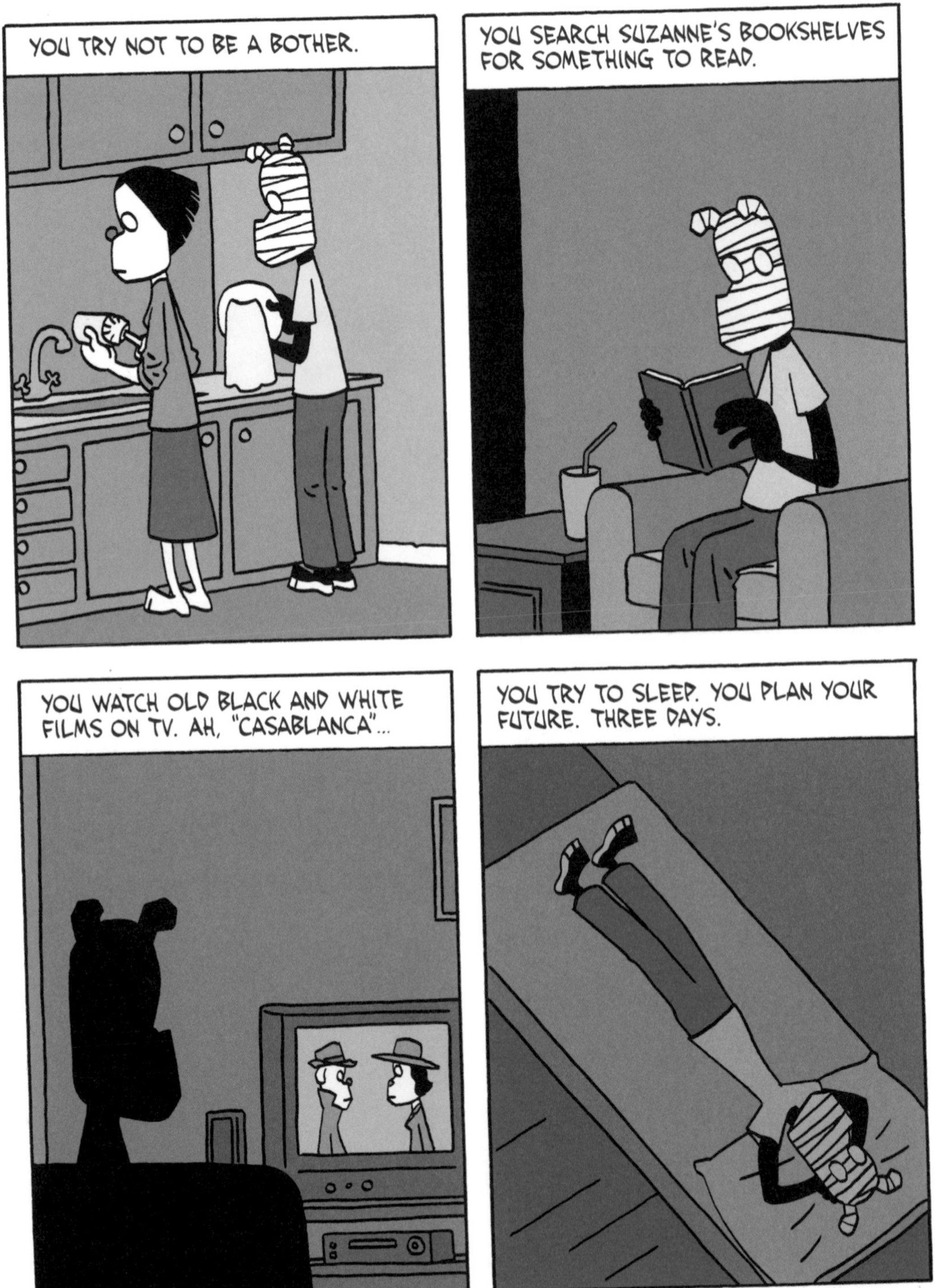
YOU TRY NOT TO BE A BOTHER.
YOU SEARCH SUZANNE'S BOOKSHELVES FOR SOMETHING TO READ.
YOU WATCH OLD BLACK AND WHITE FILMS ON TV. AH, "CASABLANCA"...
YOU TRY TO SLEEP. YOU PLAN YOUR FUTURE. THREE DAYS.

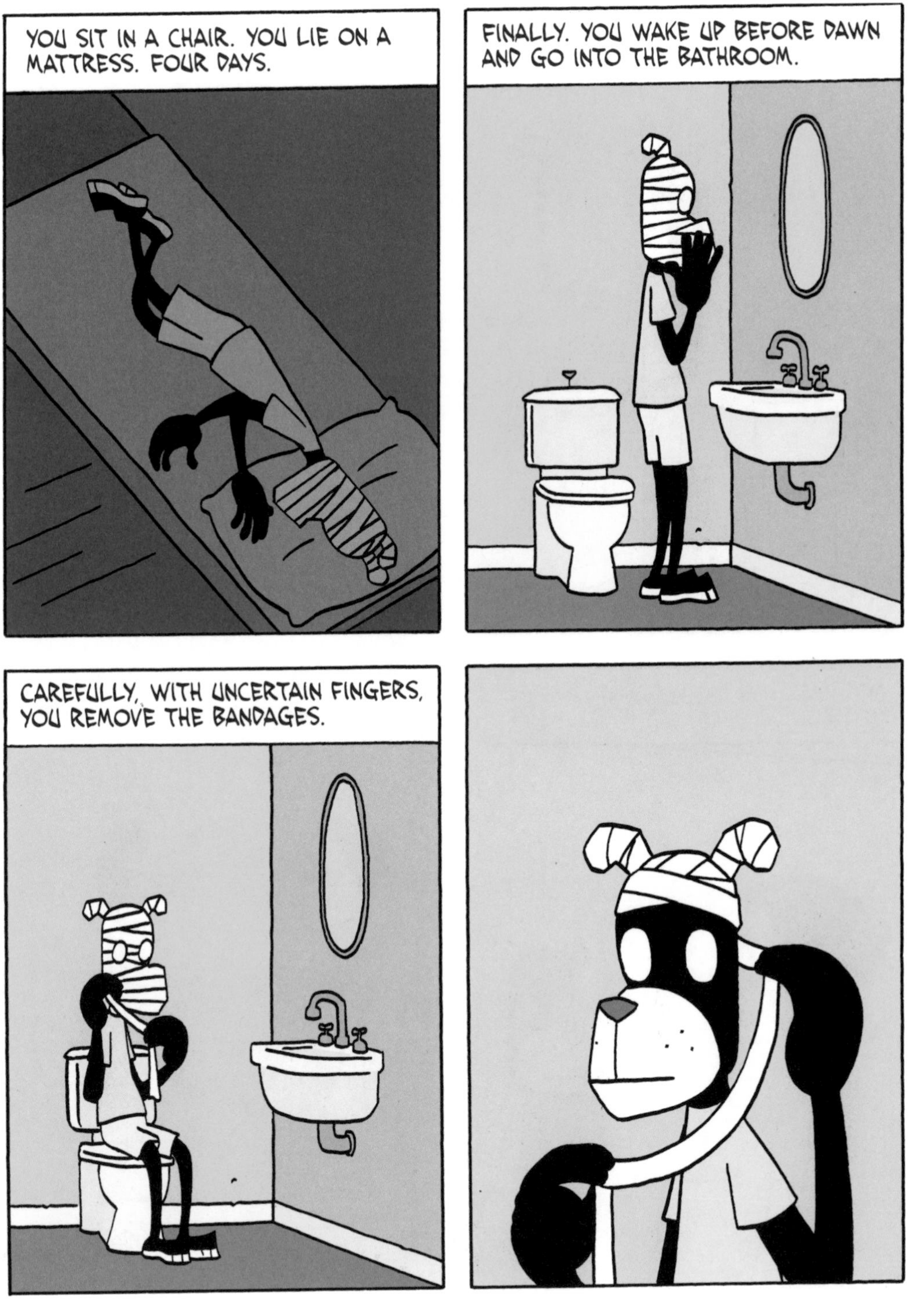
YOU SIT IN A CHAIR. YOU LIE ON A MATTRESS. FOUR DAYS.
FINALLY. YOU WAKE UP BEFORE DAWN AND GO INTO THE BATHROOM.
CAREFULLY, WITH UNCERTAIN FINGERS, YOU REMOVE THE BANDAGES.

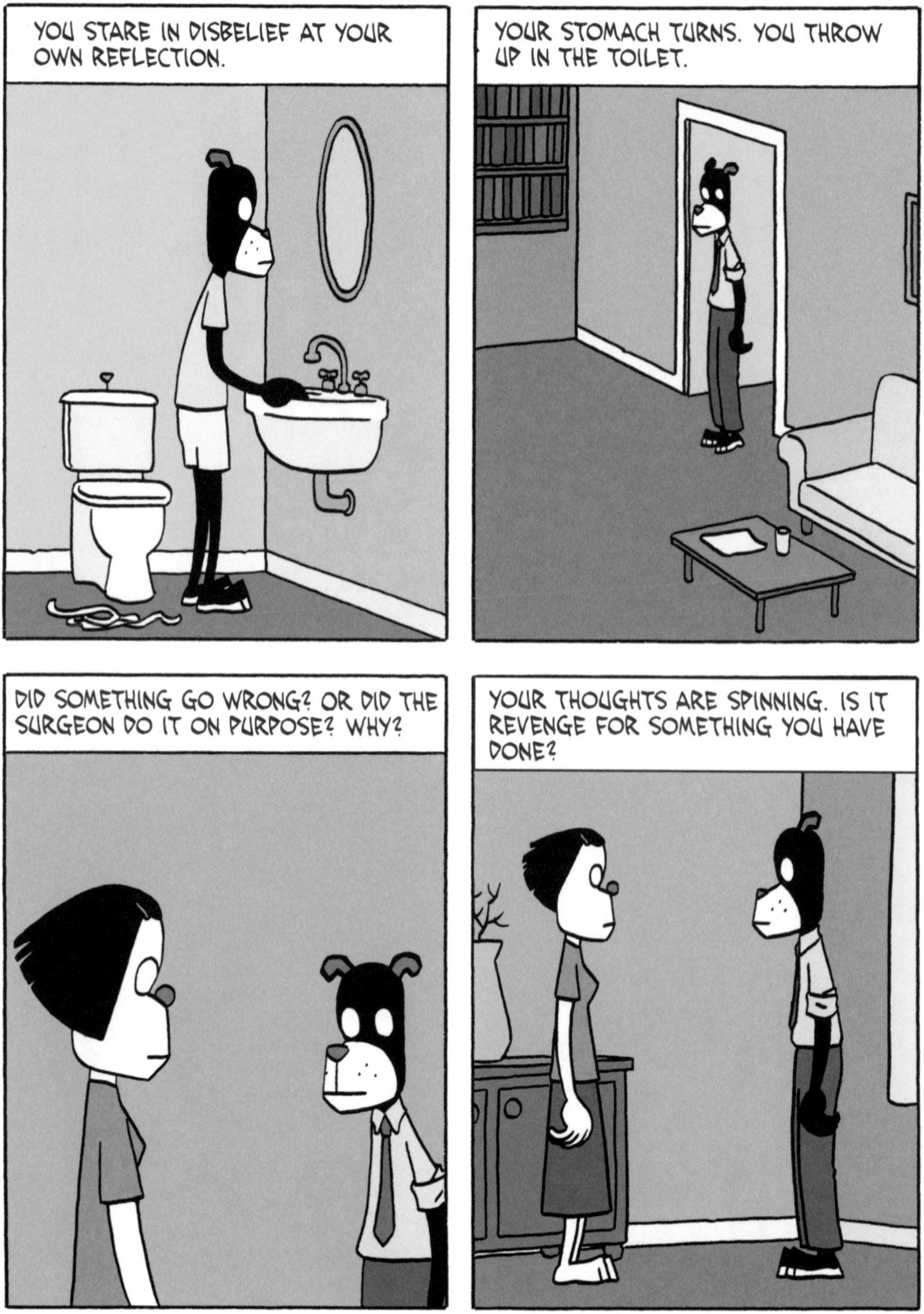
YOU STARE IN DISBELIEF AT YOUR OWN REFLECTION.
YOUR STOMACH TURNS. YOU THROW UP IN THE TOILET.
DID SOMETHING GO WRONG? OR DID THE SURGEON DO IT ON PURPOSE? WHY?
YOUR THOUGHTS ARE SPINNING. IS IT REVENGE FOR SOMETHING YOU HAVE DONE?

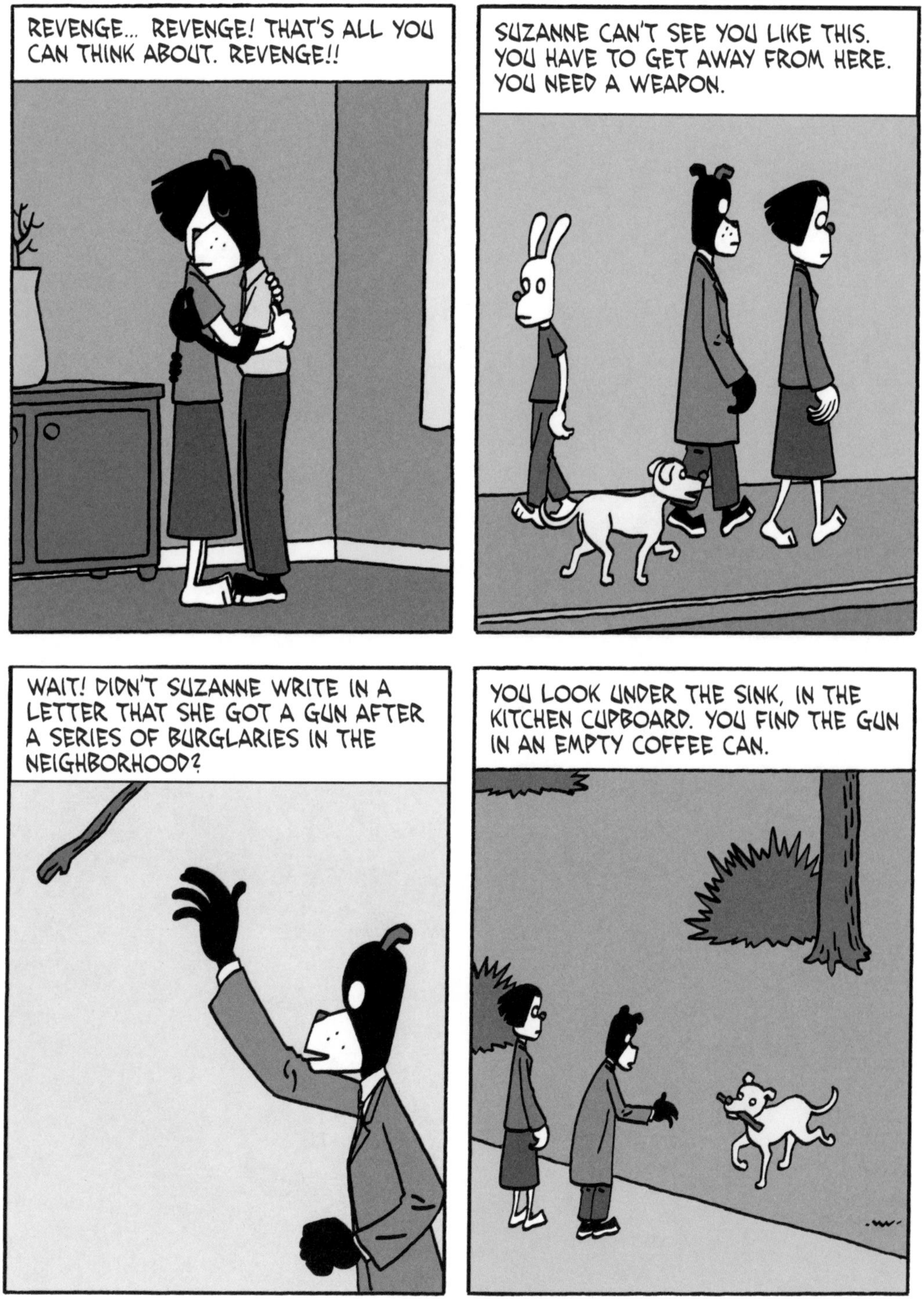
REVENGE... REVENGE! THAT'S ALL YOU CAN THINK ABOUT. REVENGE!!
SUZANNE CAN'T SEE YOU LIKE THIS. YOU HAVE TO GET AWAY FROM HERE. YOU NEED A WEAPON.
WAIT! DIDN'T SUZANNE WRITE IN A LETTER THAT SHE GOT A GUN AFTER A SERIES OF BURGLARIES IN THE NEIGHBORHOOD?
YOU LOOK UNDER THE SINK, IN THE KITCHEN CUPBOARD. YOU FIND THE GUN IN AN EMPTY COFFEE CAN.

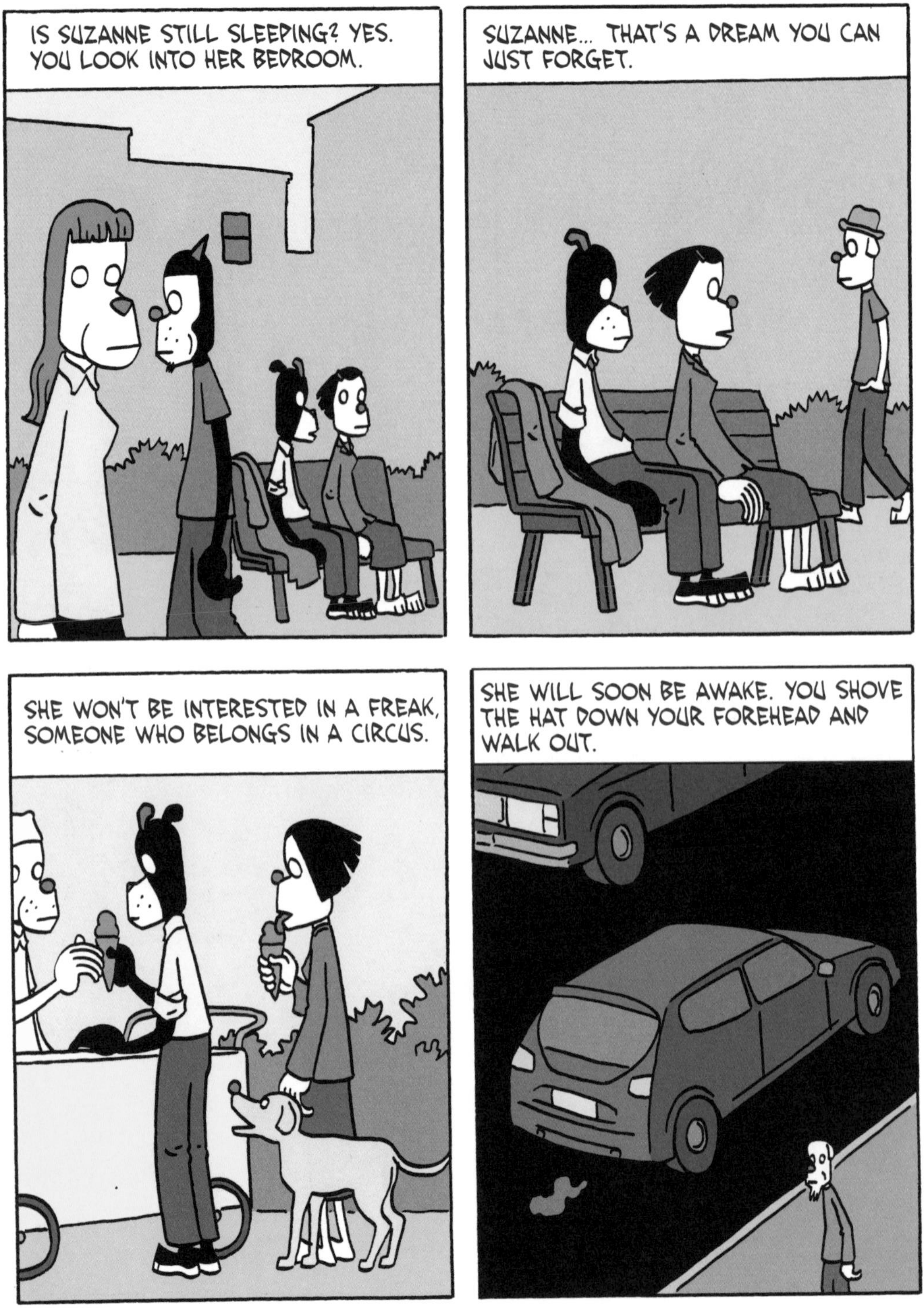
IS SUZANNE STILL SLEEPING? YES. YOU LOOK INTO HER BEDROOM.
SUZANNE... THAT'S A DREAM YOU CAN JUST FORGET.
SHE WON'T BE INTERESTED IN A FREAK, SOMEONE WHO BELONGS IN A CIRCUS.
SHE WILL SOON BE AWAKE. YOU SHOVE THE HAT DOWN YOUR FOREHEAD AND WALK OUT.

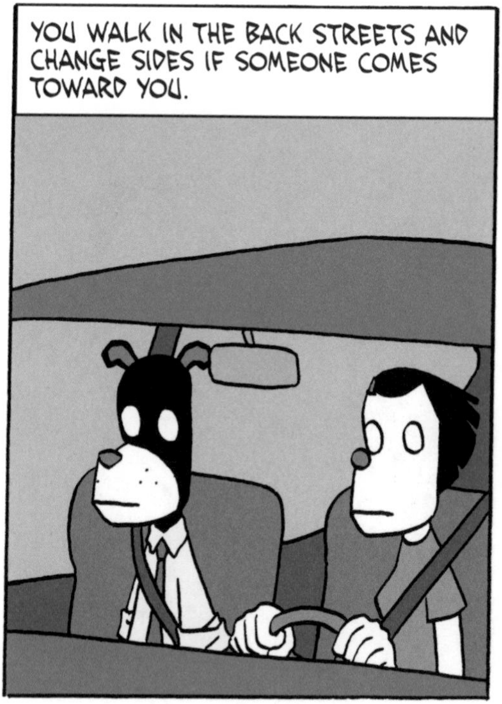
YOU WALK IN THE BACK STREETS AND CHANGE SIDES IF SOMEONE COMES TOWARD YOU.

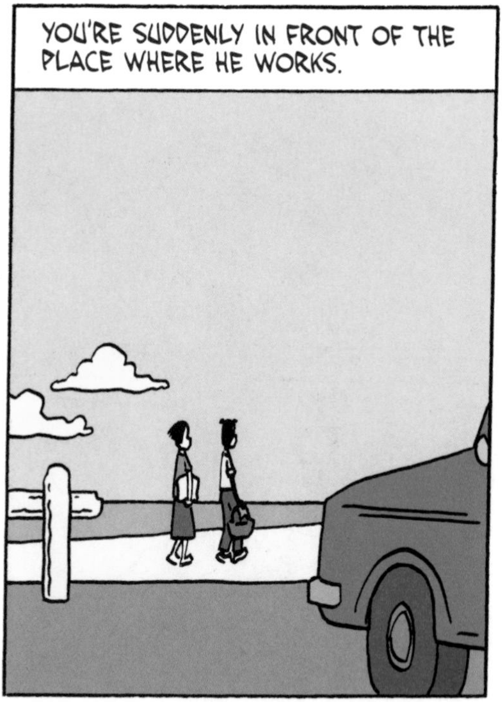
YOU'RE SUDDENLY IN FRONT OF THE PLACE WHERE HE WORKS.

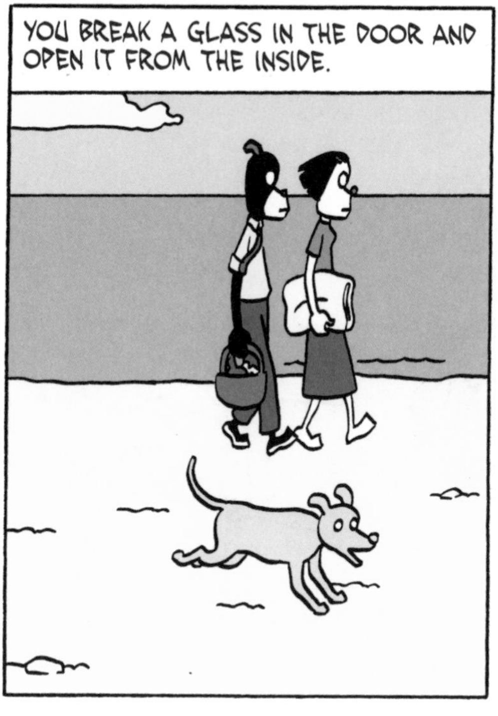
YOU BREAK A GLASS IN THE DOOR AND OPEN IT FROM THE INSIDE.

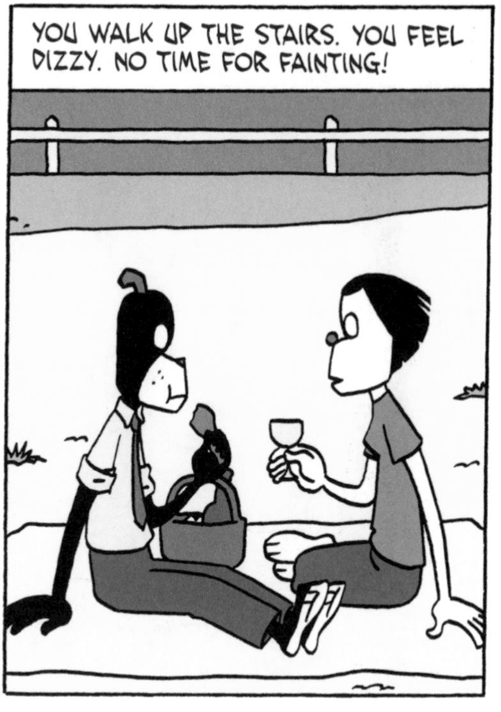
YOU WALK UP THE STAIRS. YOU FEEL DIZZY. NO TIME FOR FAINTING!

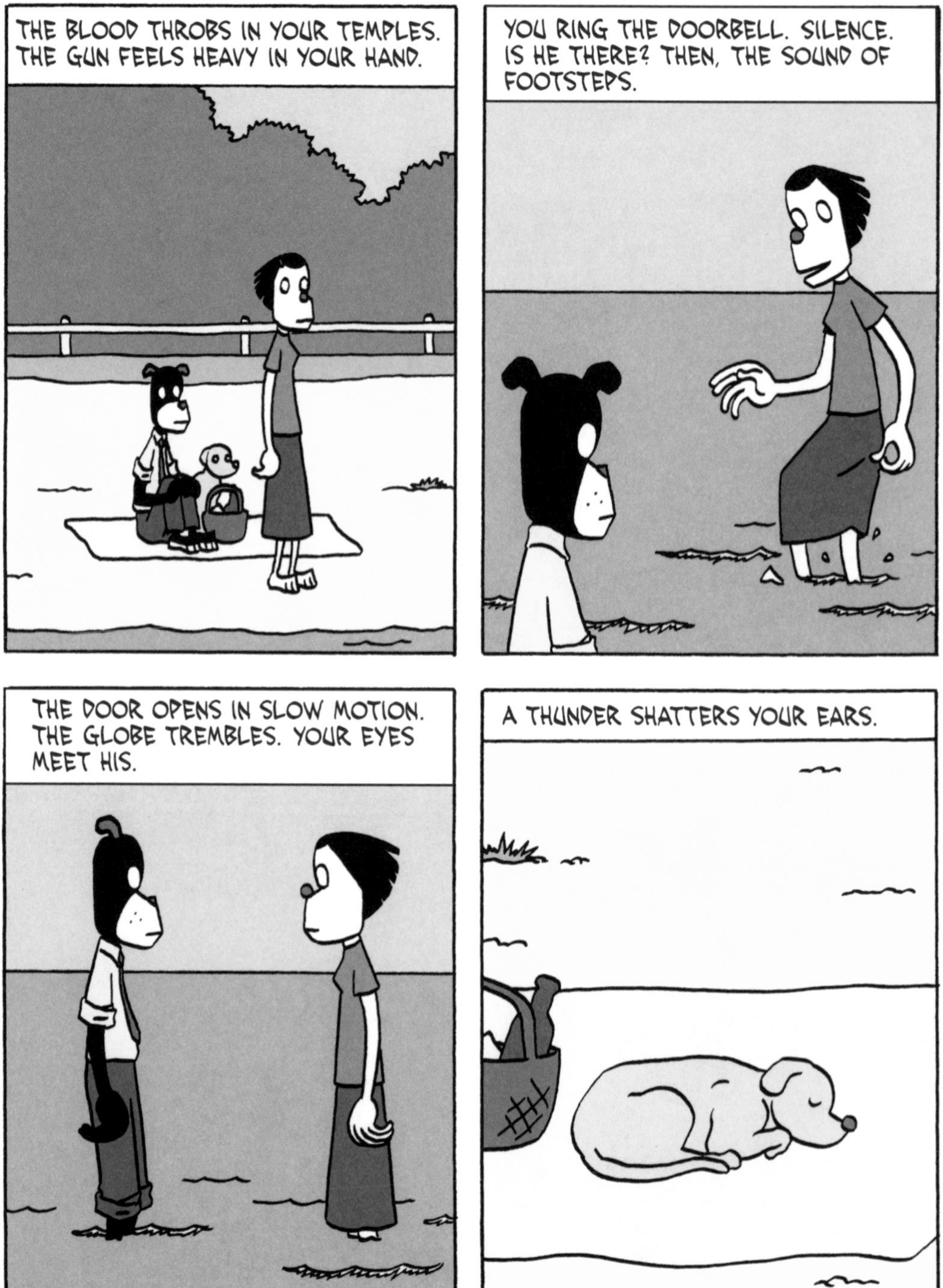
THE BLOOD THROBS IN YOUR TEMPLES. THE GUN FEELS HEAVY IN YOUR HAND.
YOU RING THE DOORBELL. SILENCE. IS HE THERE? THEN, THE SOUND OF FOOTSTEPS.
THE DOOR OPENS IN SLOW MOTION. THE GLOBE TREMBLES. YOUR EYES MEET HIS.
A THUNDER SHATTERS YOUR EARS.
jason · 14

PRESENTING:

―――――

MOONDANCE

―――――

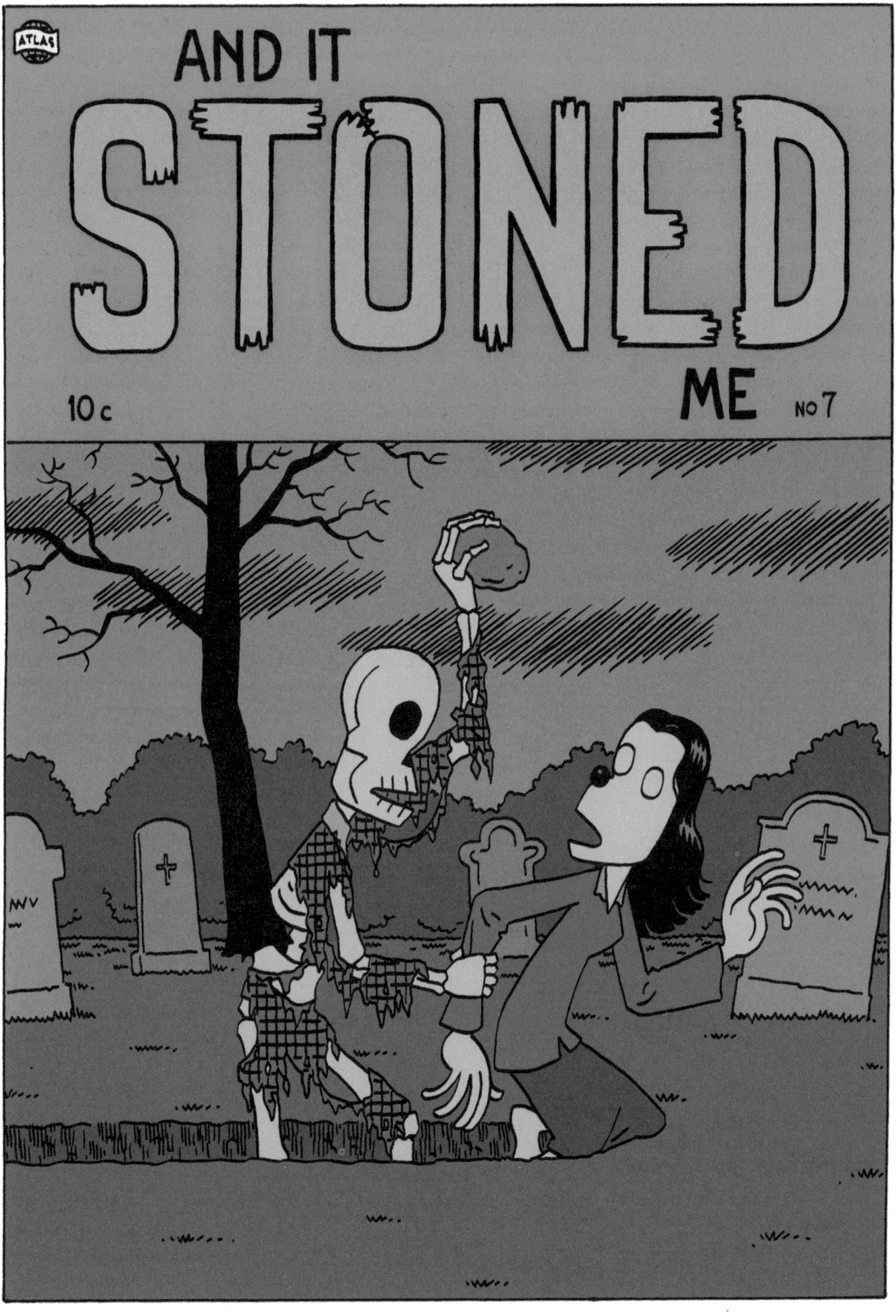
ATLAS
AND IT
STONED
ME
10c
NO 7

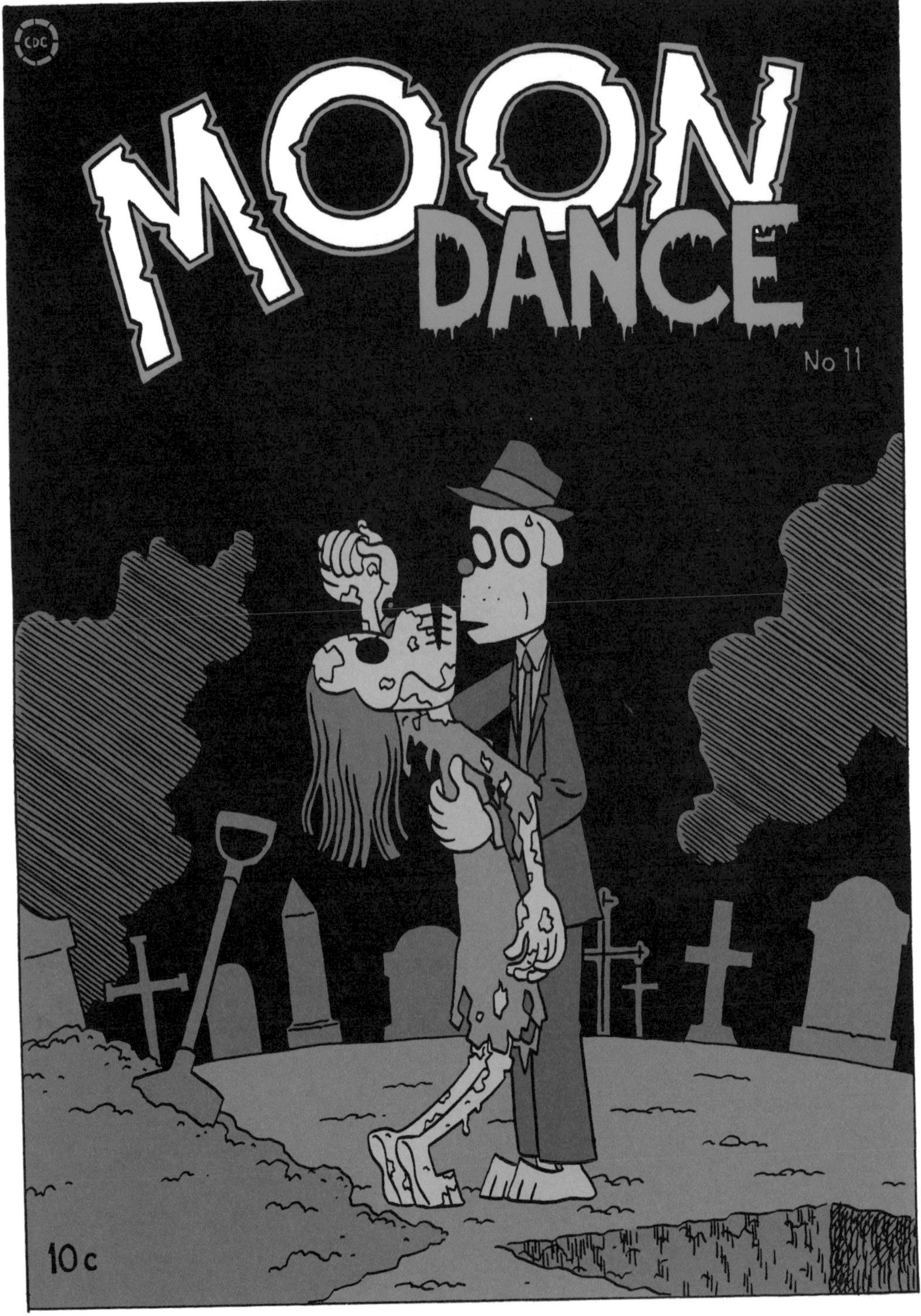
CDC
MOON DANCE
No 11
10c

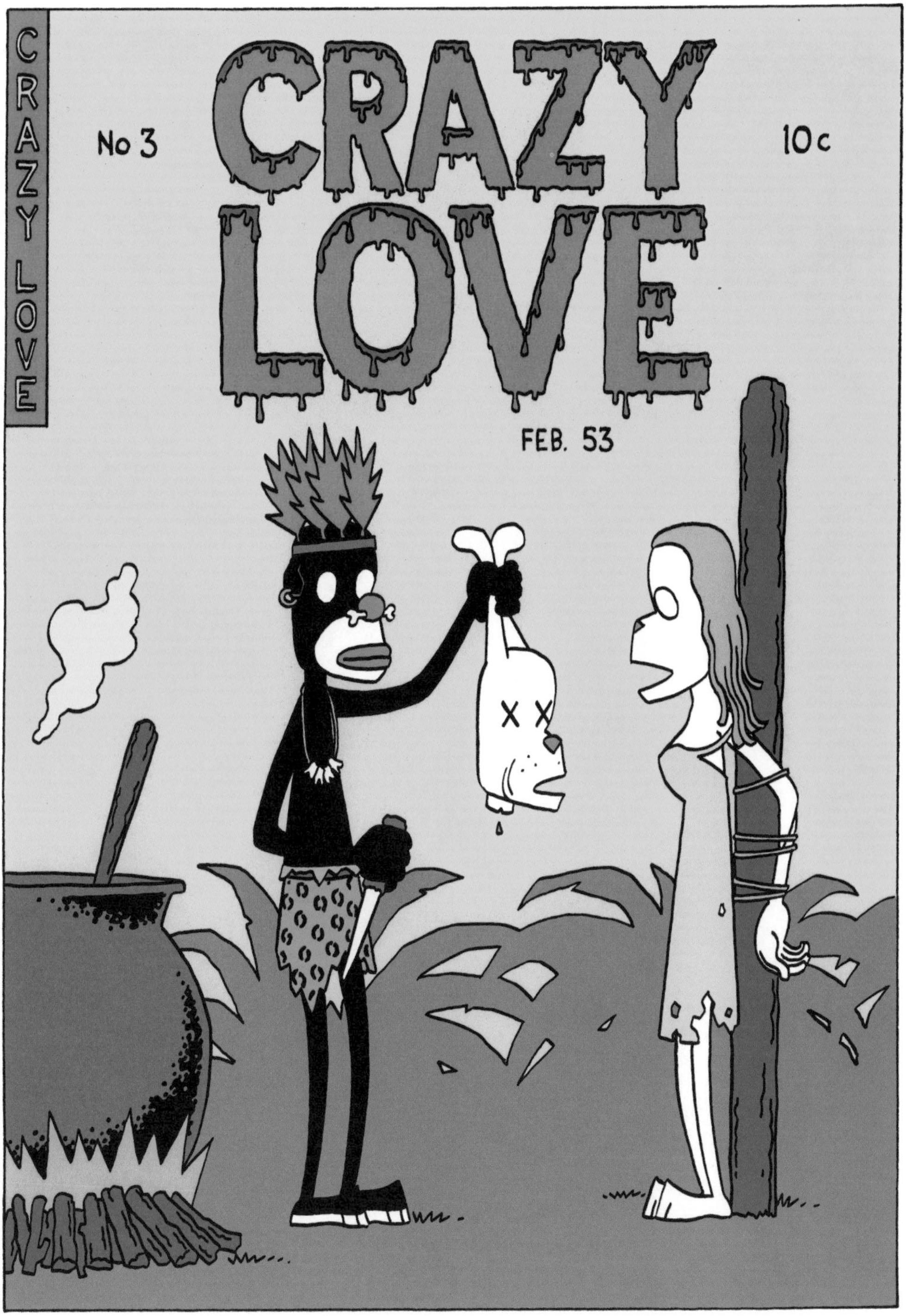
CRAZY LOVE
No 3
CRAZY LOVE
10c
FEB. 53

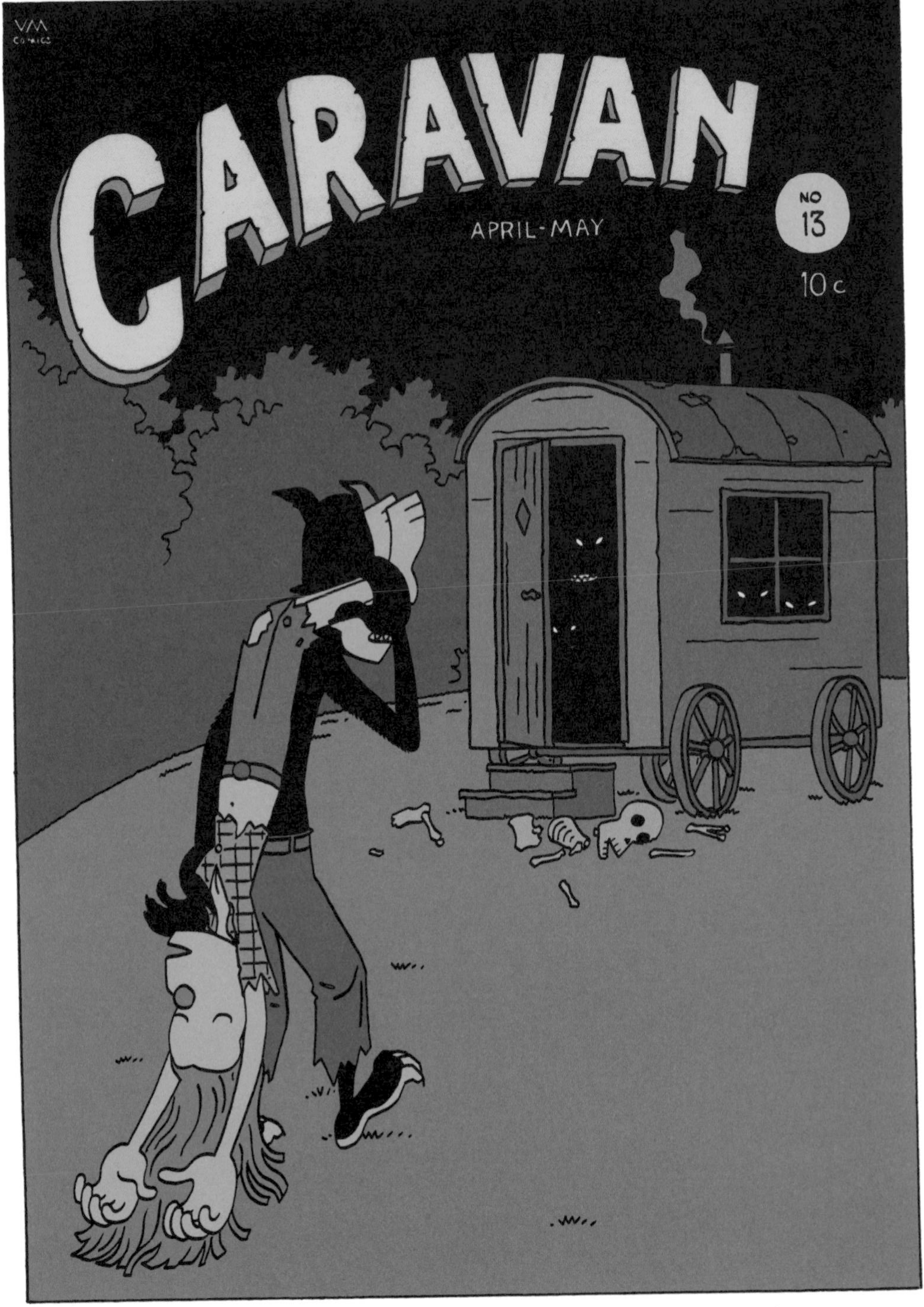
VM COMICS
CARAVAN
NO 13
APRIL-MAY
10c

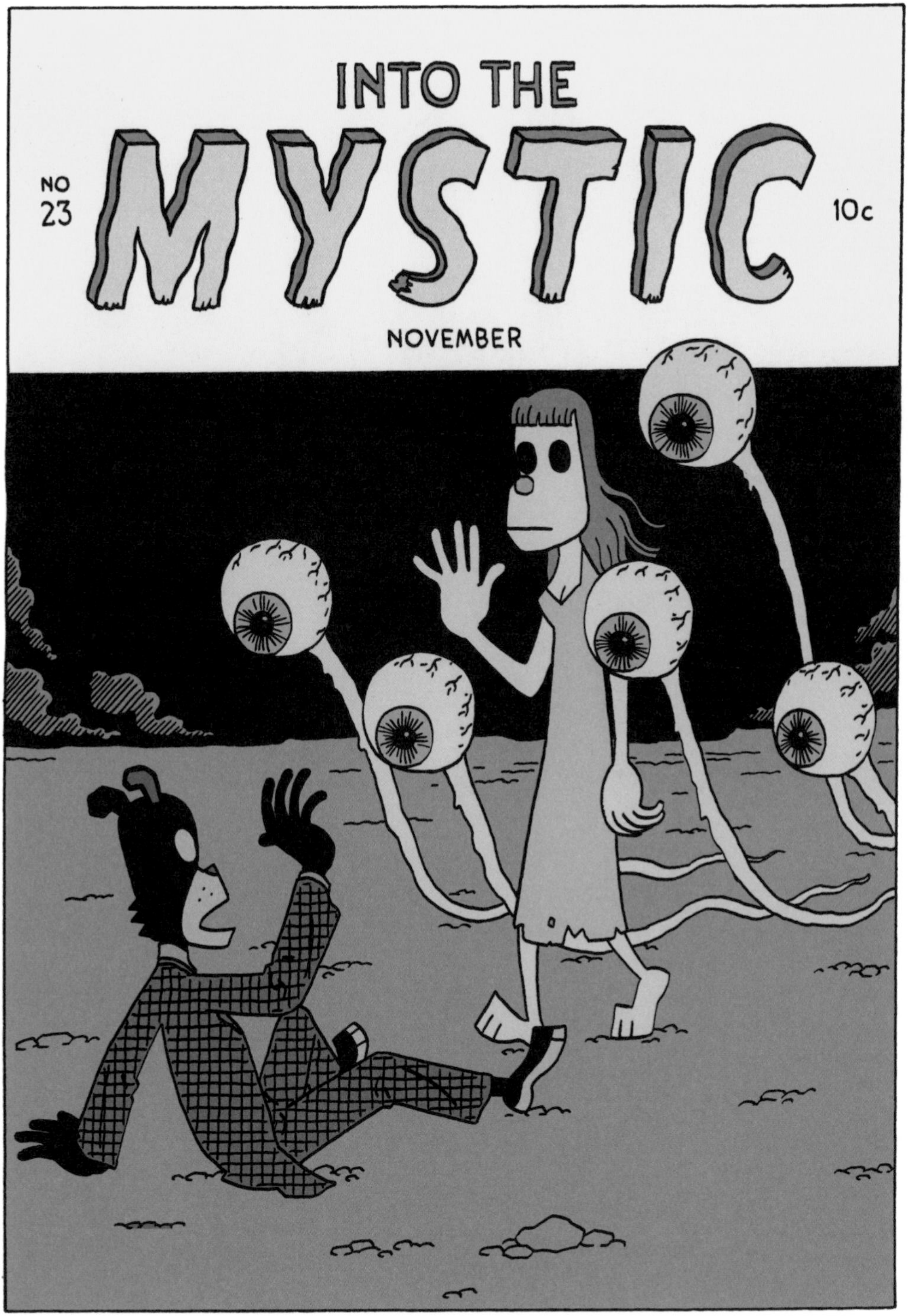
INTO THE
MYSTIC
NO 23
10c
NOVEMBER

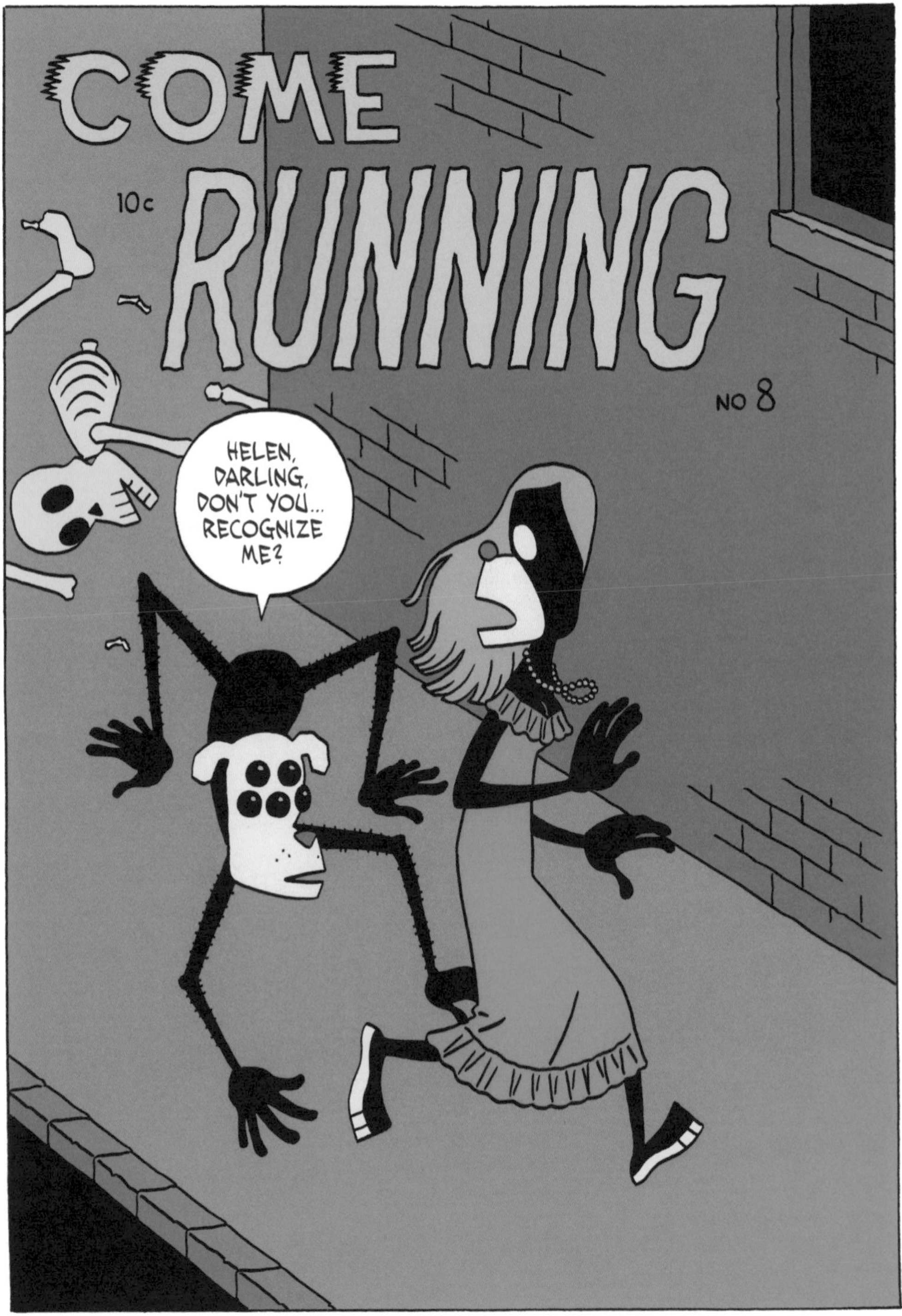
COME RUNNING
10c
NO 8
HELEN, DARLING, DON'T YOU... RECOGNIZE ME?

PRESENTING:

———

NIGHT OF THE

VAMPIRE HUNTER

———

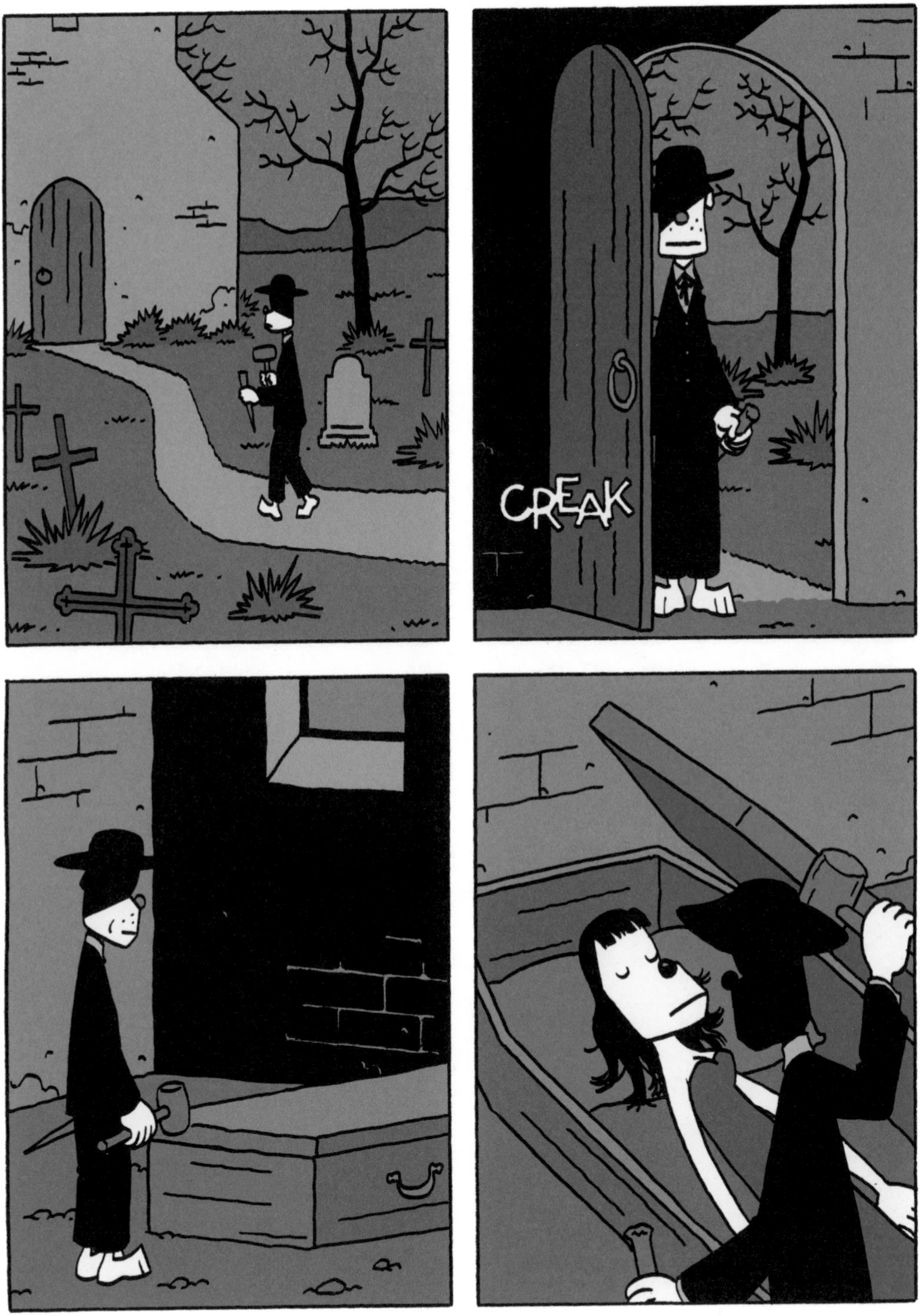
CREAK

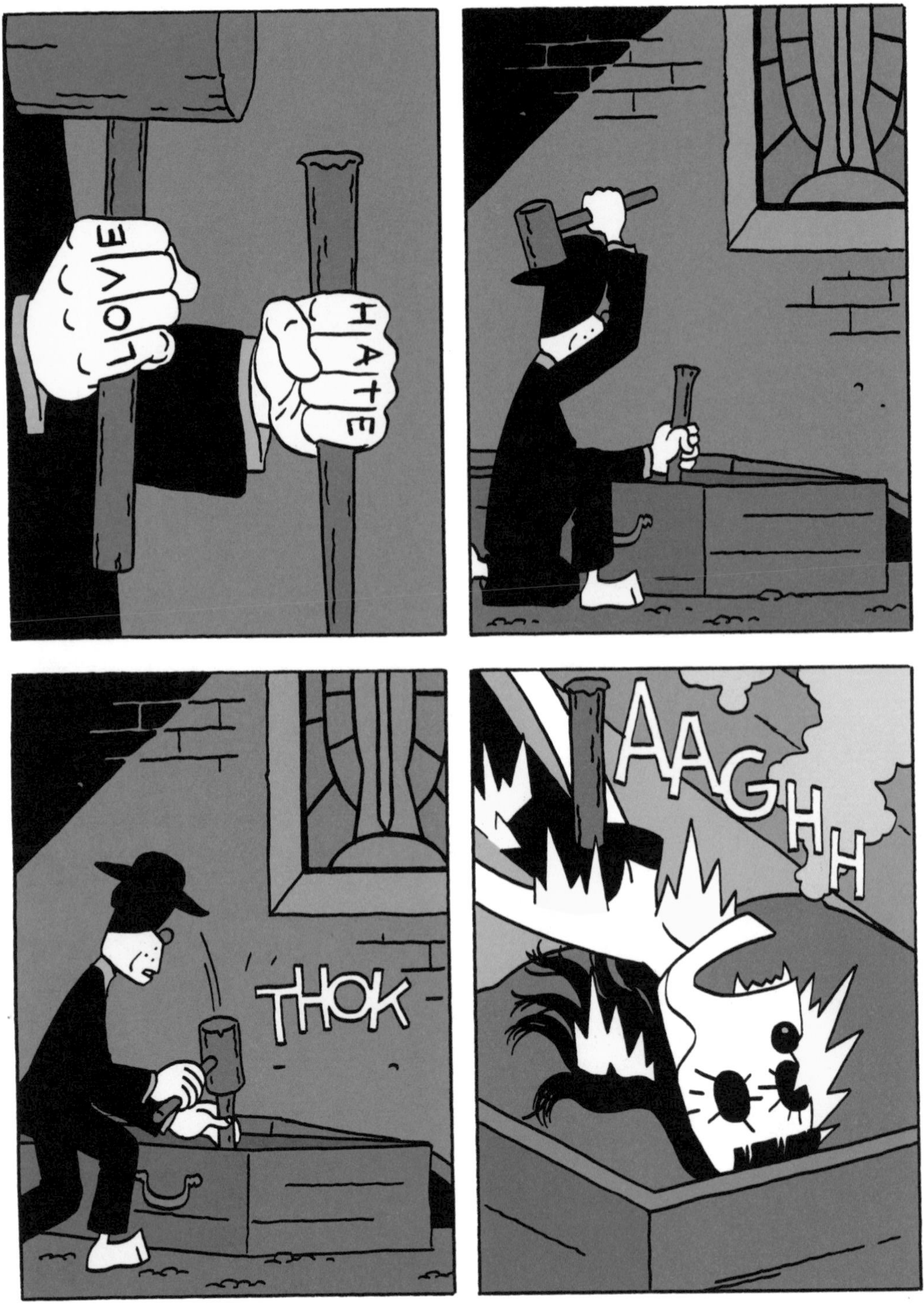
LOVE
HATE
THOK
AAGHHH

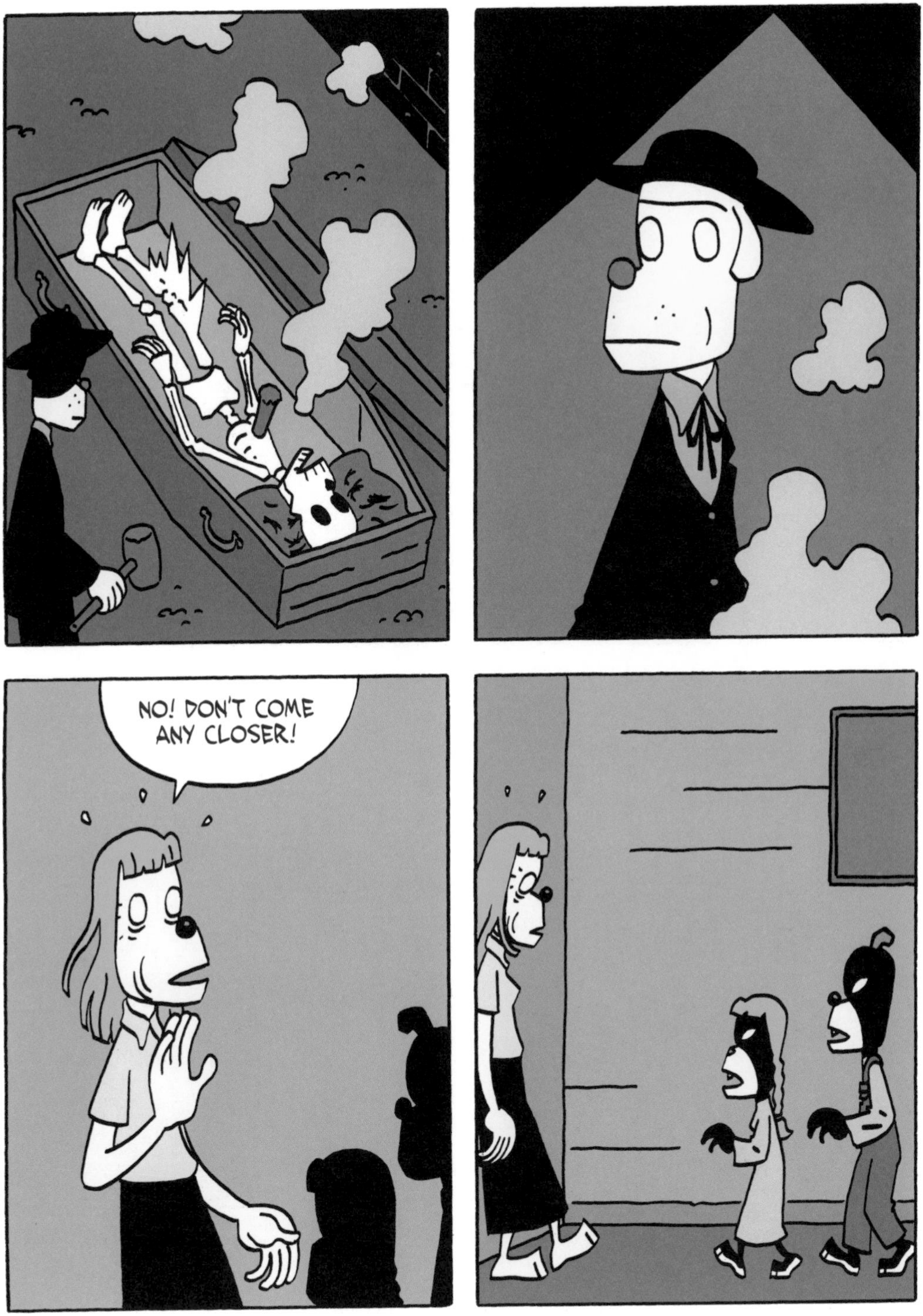
NO! DON'T COME ANY CLOSER!

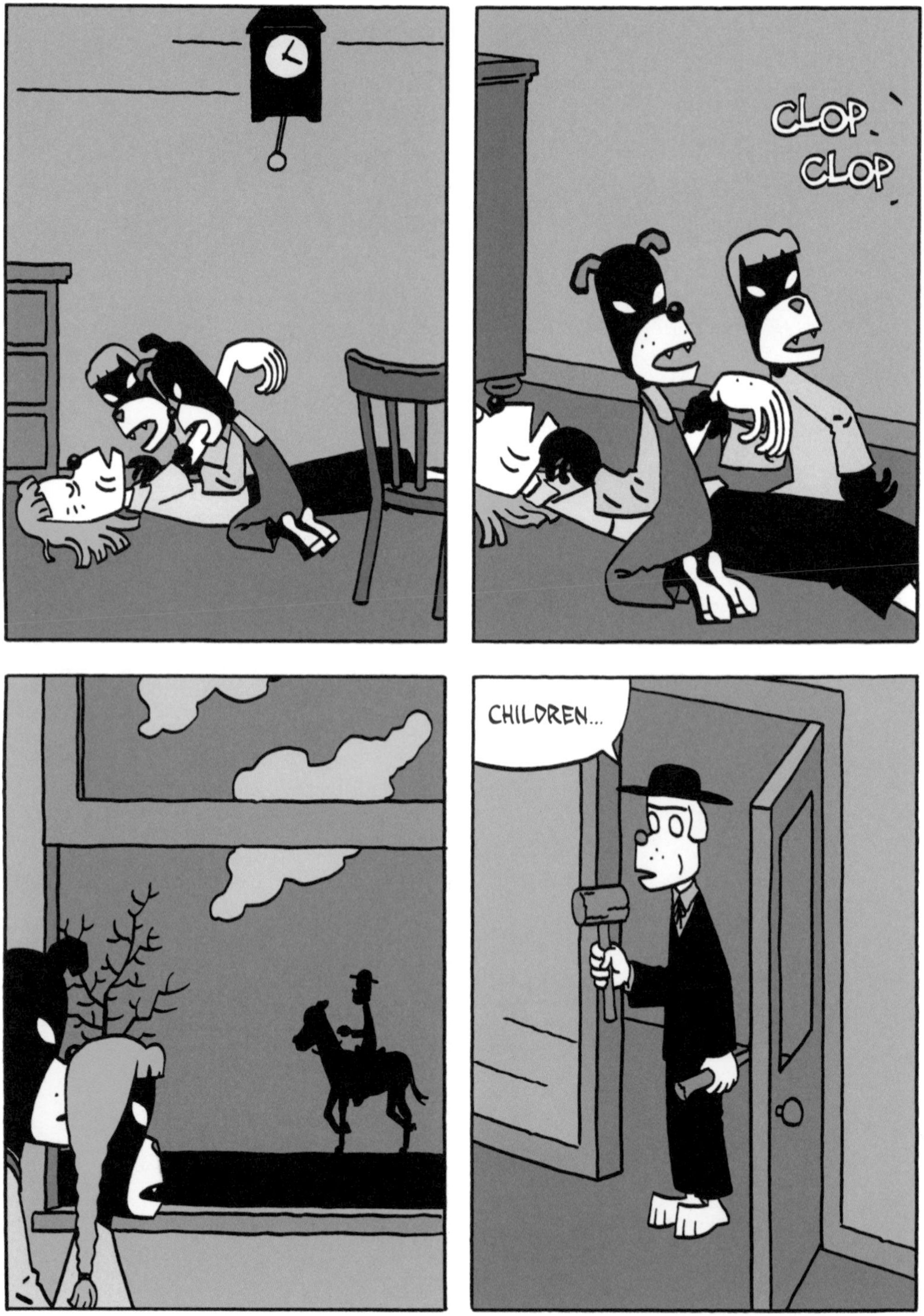
CLOP
CLOP
CHILDREN...

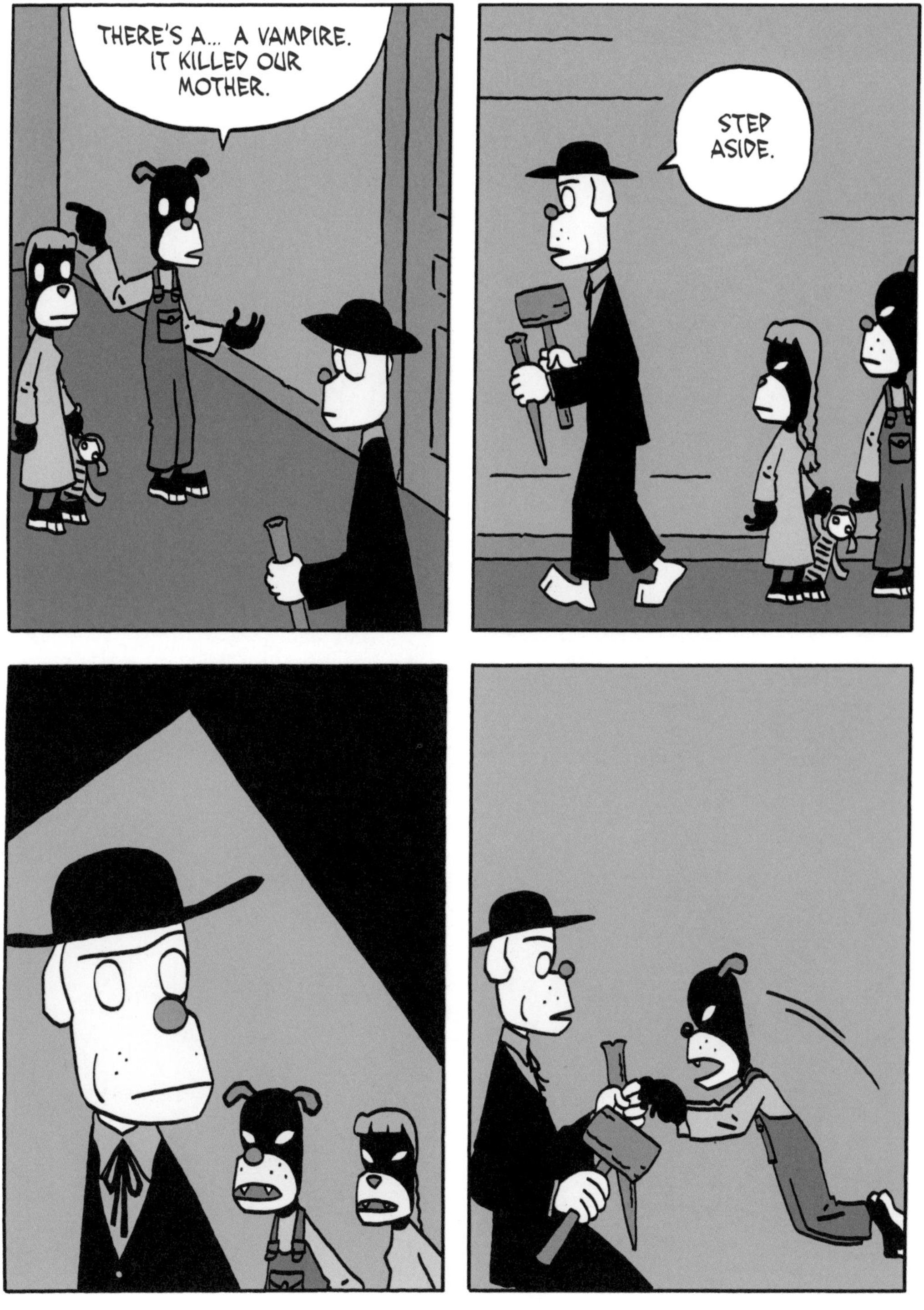
THERE'S A... A VAMPIRE. IT KILLED OUR MOTHER.
STEP ASIDE.

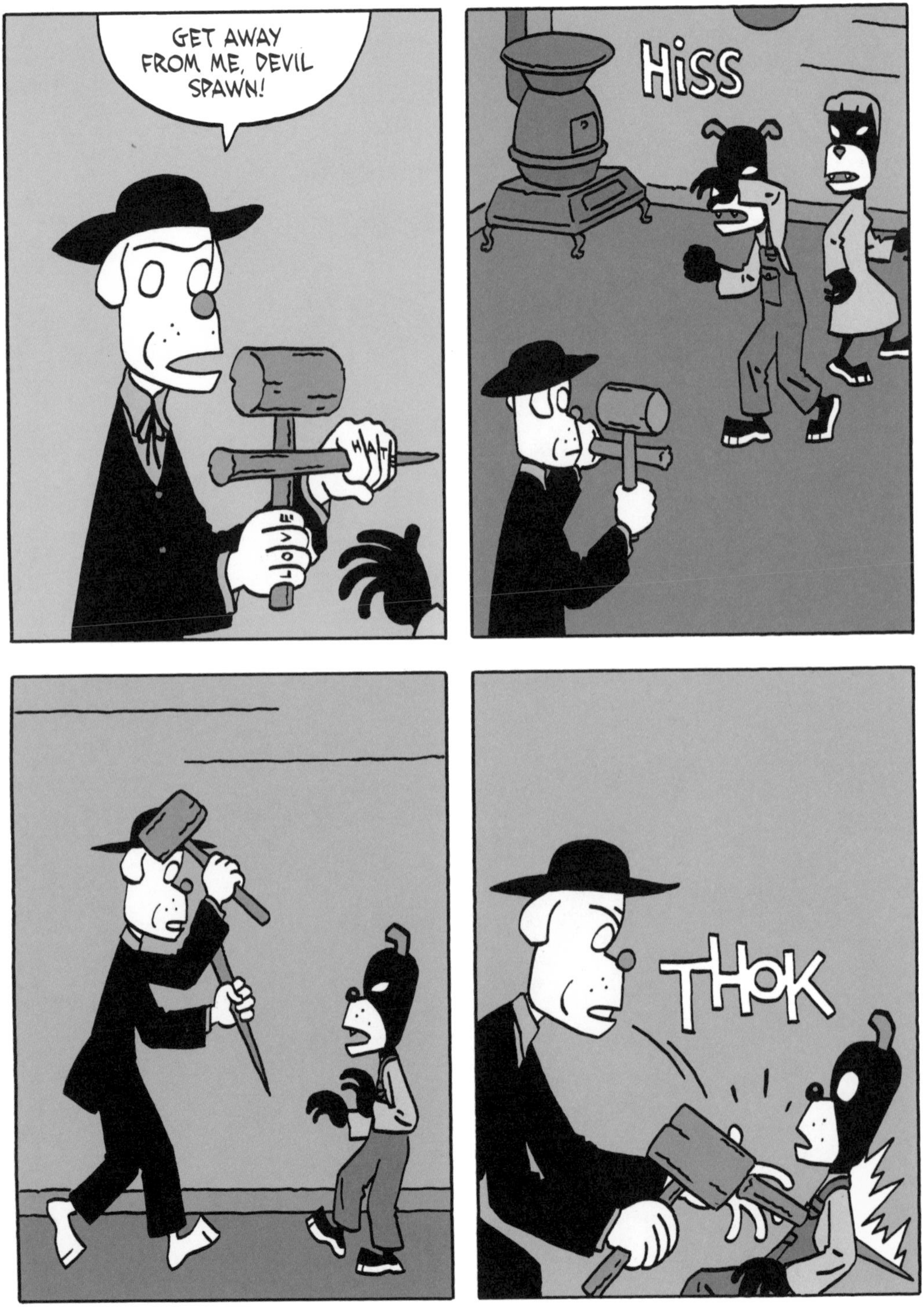
GET AWAY FROM ME, DEVIL SPAWN!
HAT
LOVE
HISS
THOK

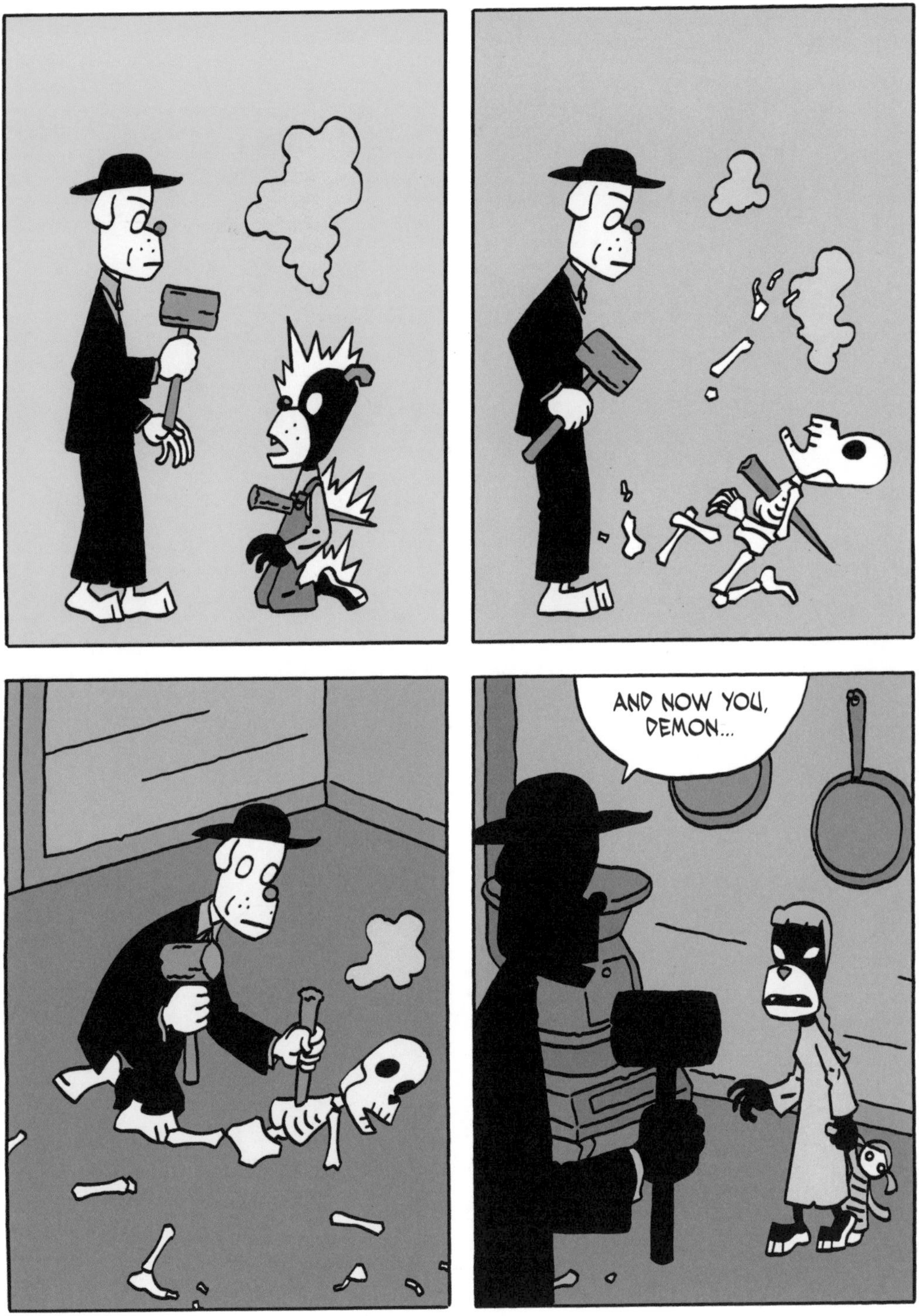
AND NOW YOU,
DEMON...

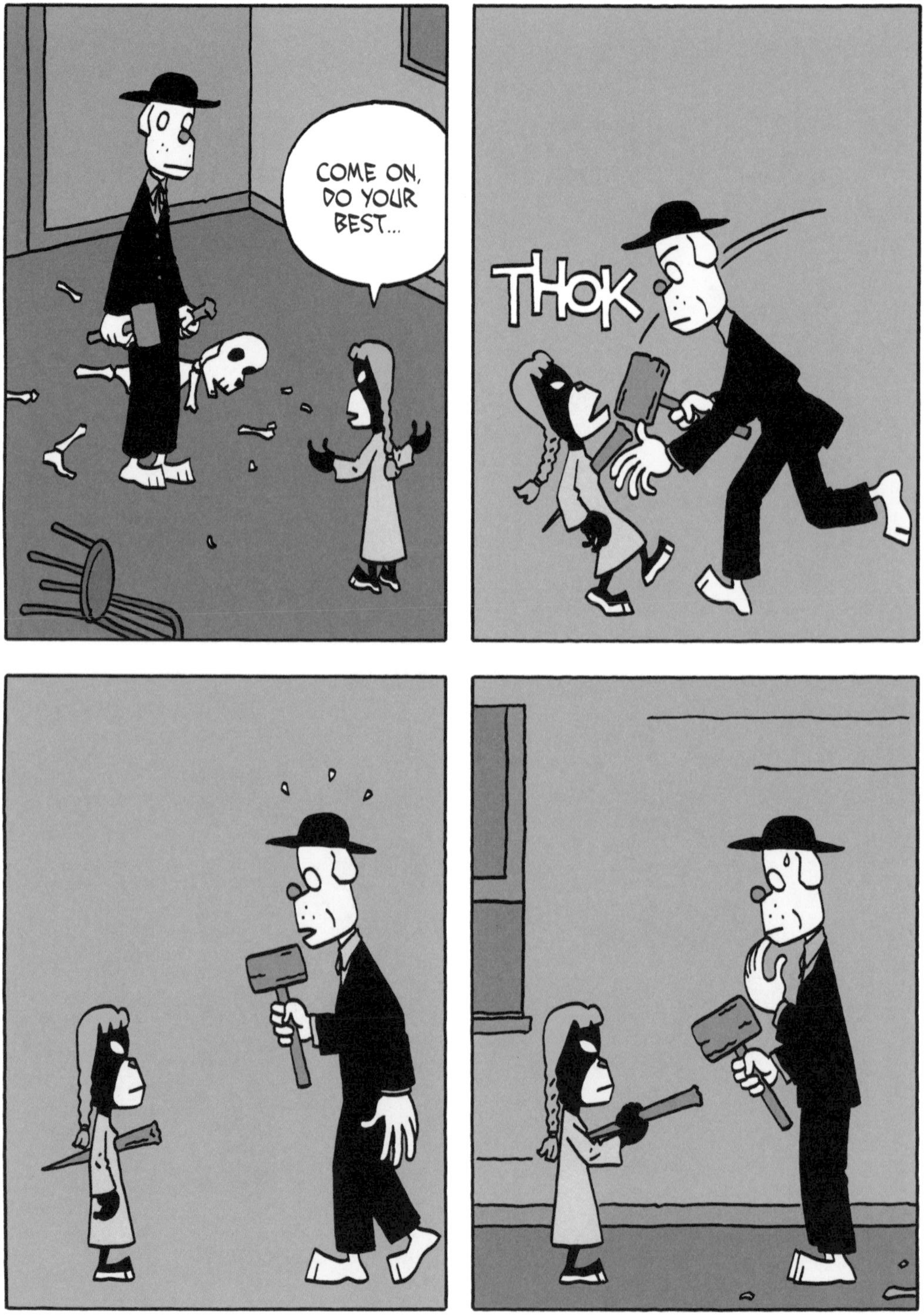
COME ON, DO YOUR BEST...
THOK

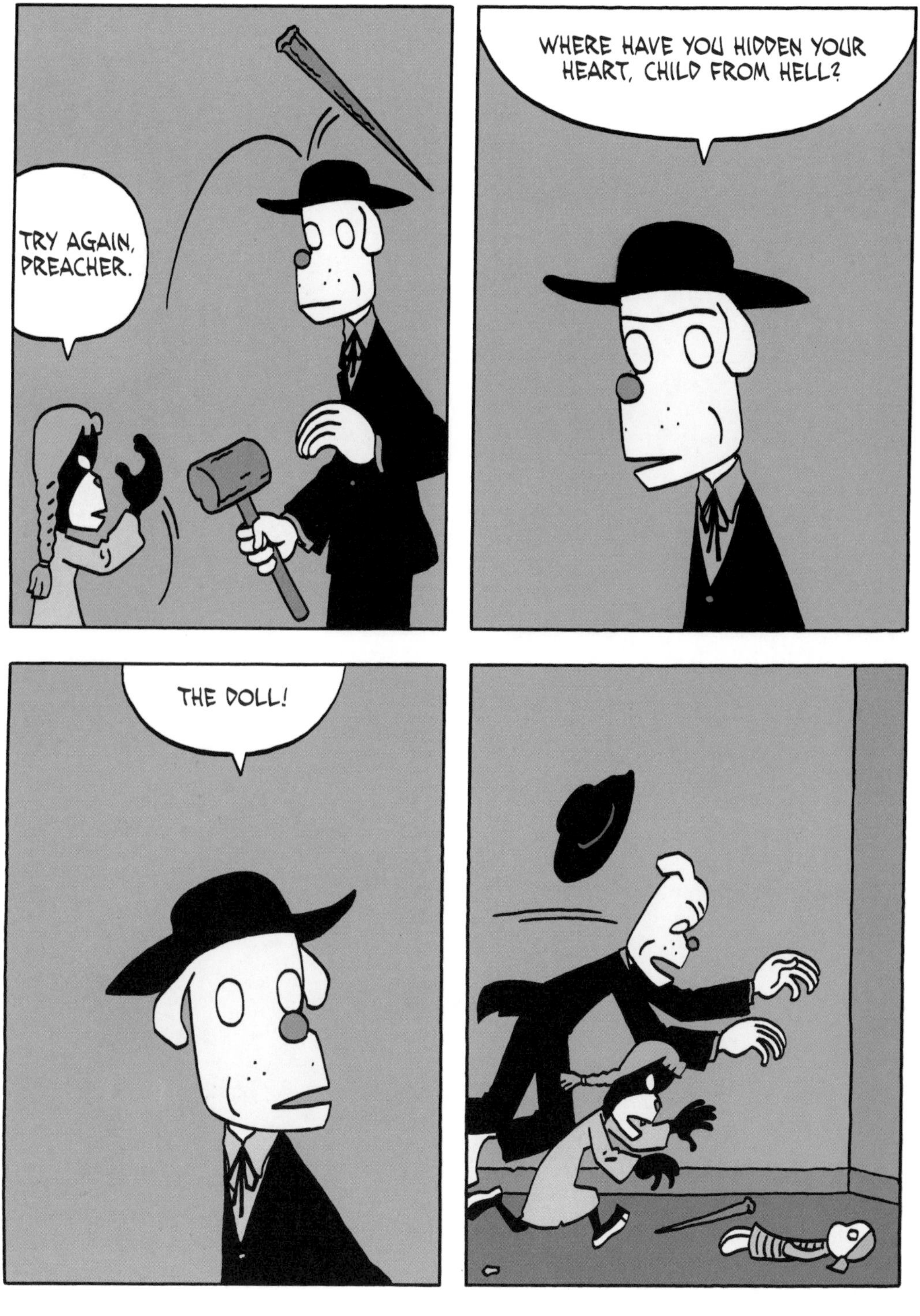
TRY AGAIN, PREACHER.
WHERE HAVE YOU HIDDEN YOUR HEART, CHILD FROM HELL?
THE DOLL!

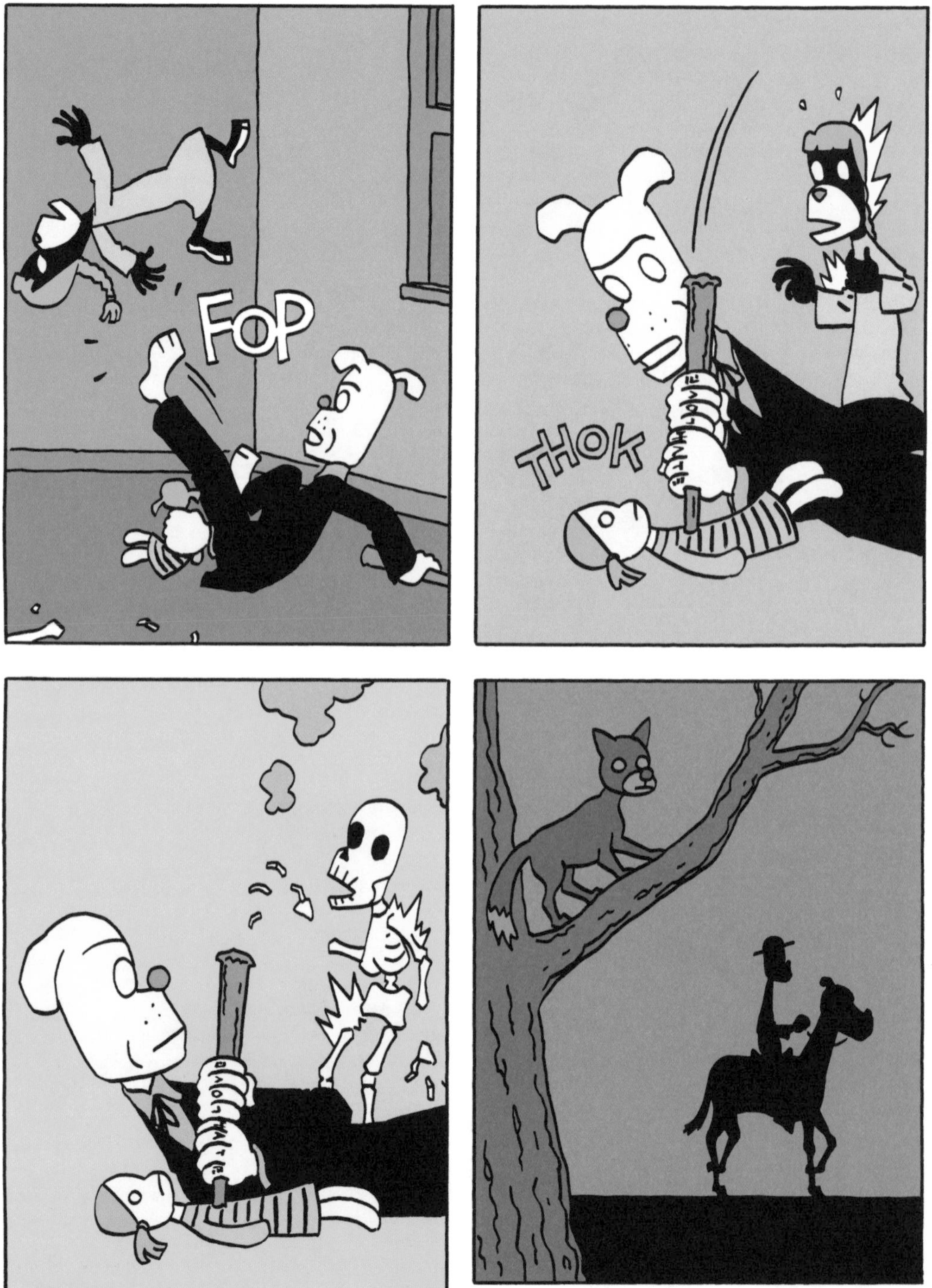
FOP
THOK

jason · 14

PRESENTING:

POLLY WANTS A CRACKER

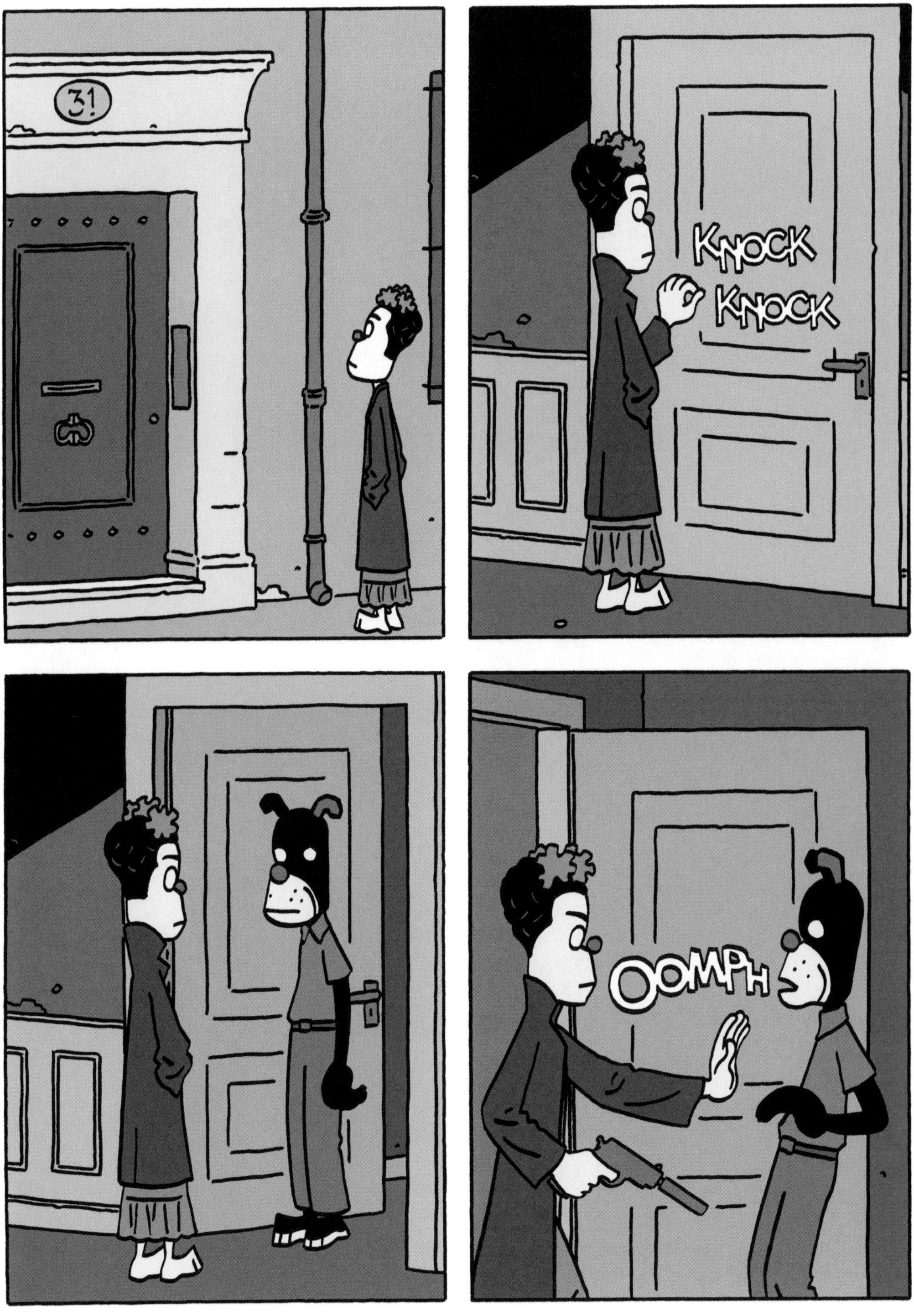
31
KNOCK
KNOCK
OOMPH

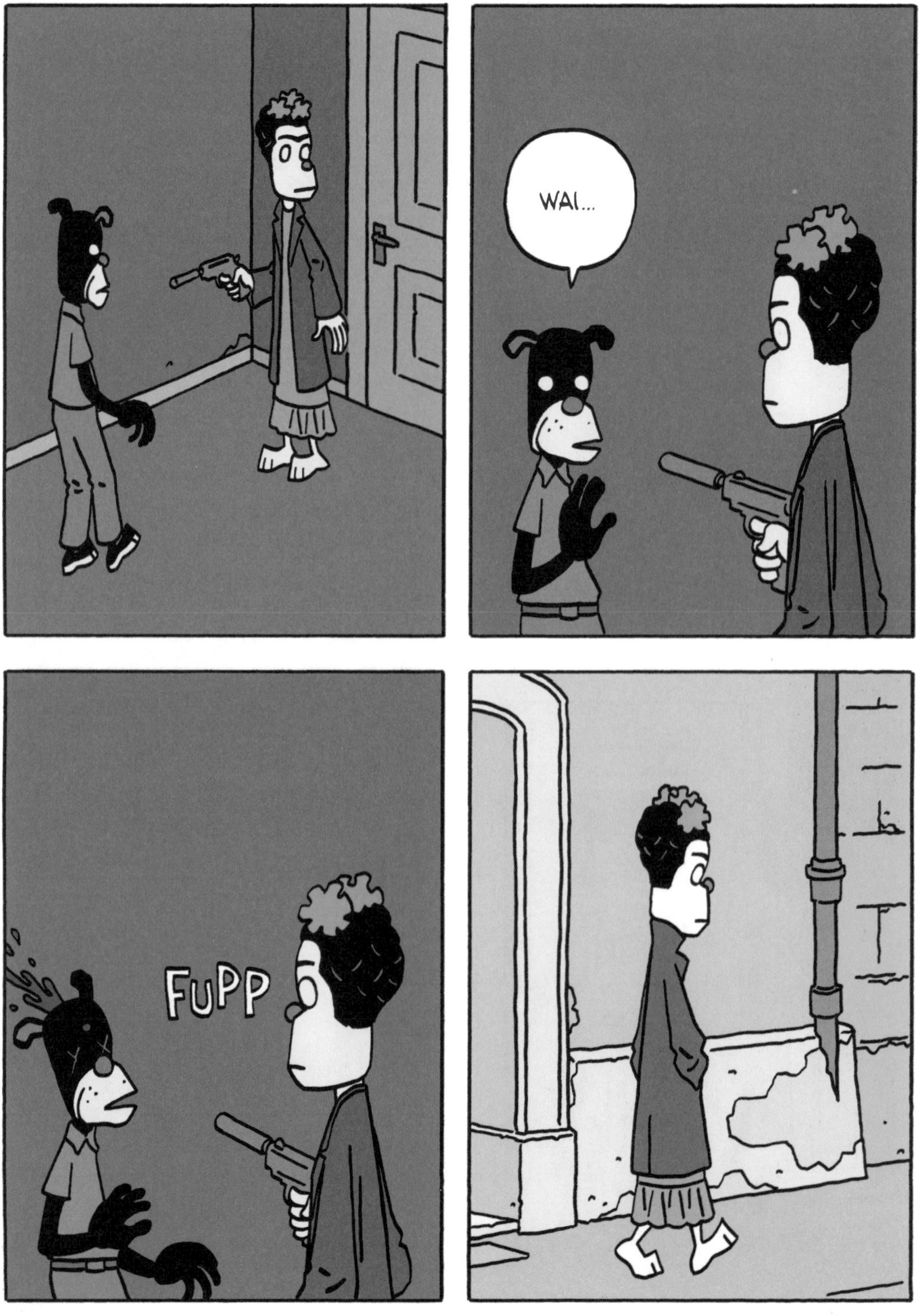
WAI...
FUPP

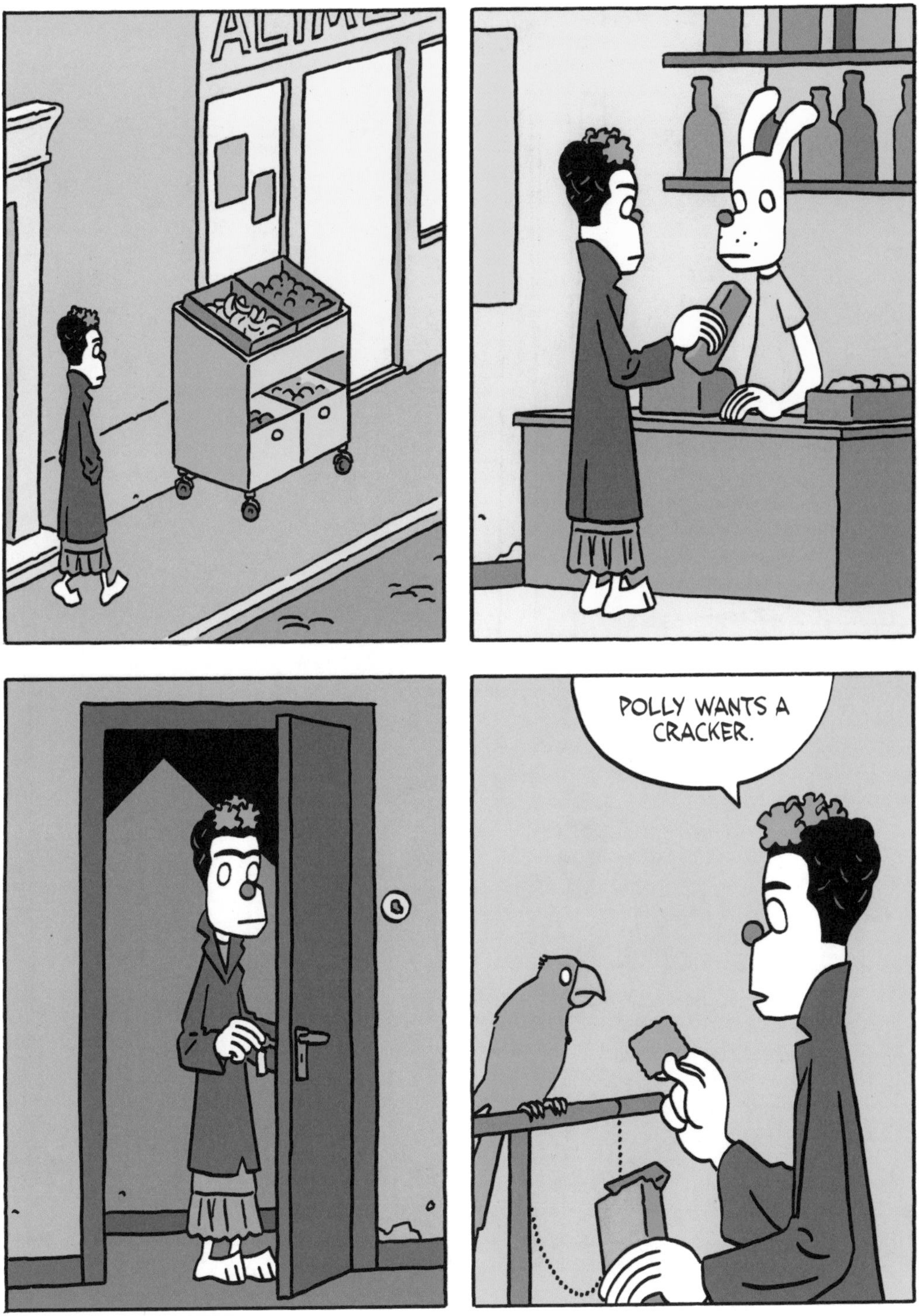
ALIME
POLLY WANTS A CRACKER.

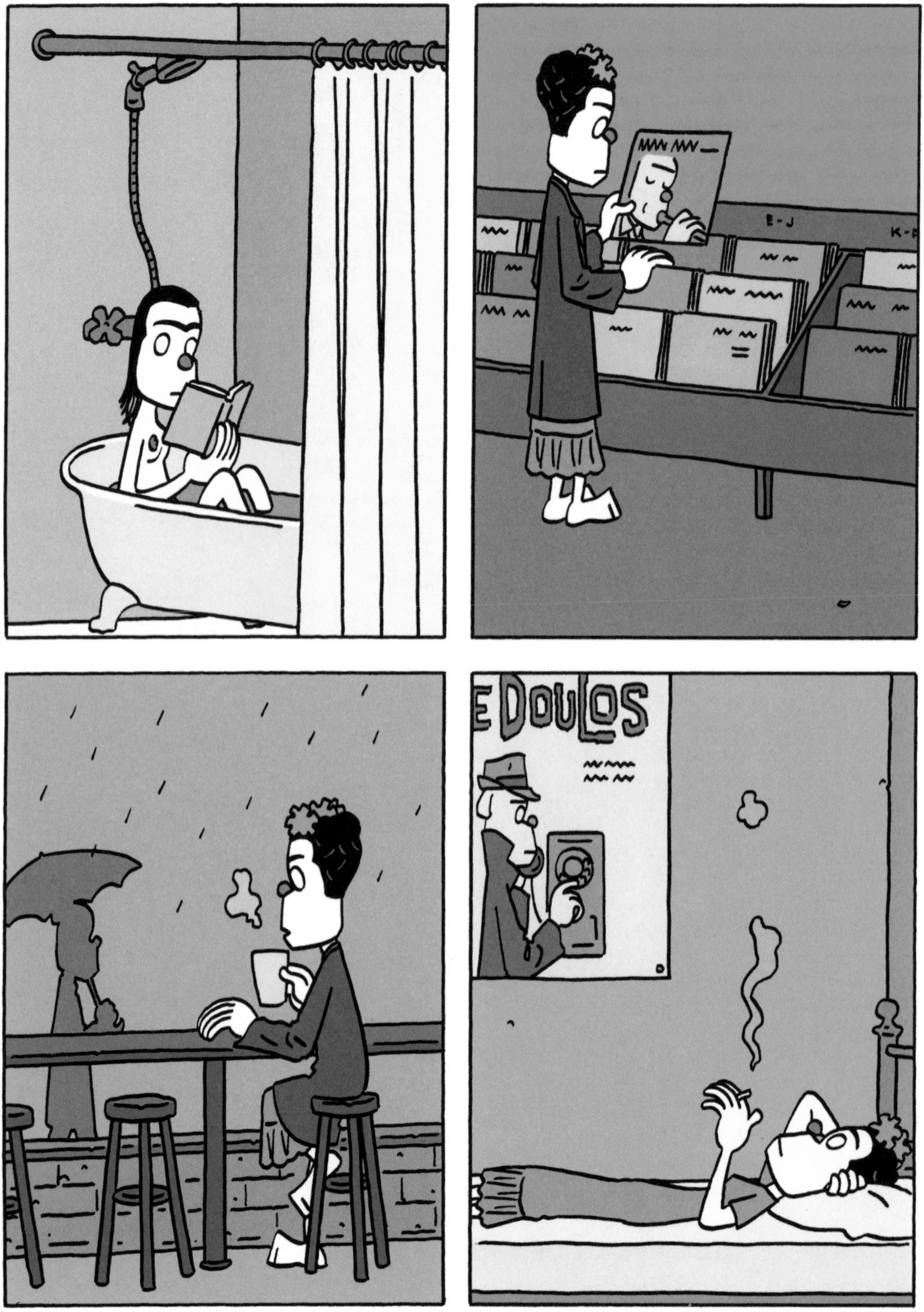
E-J
E DOULOS

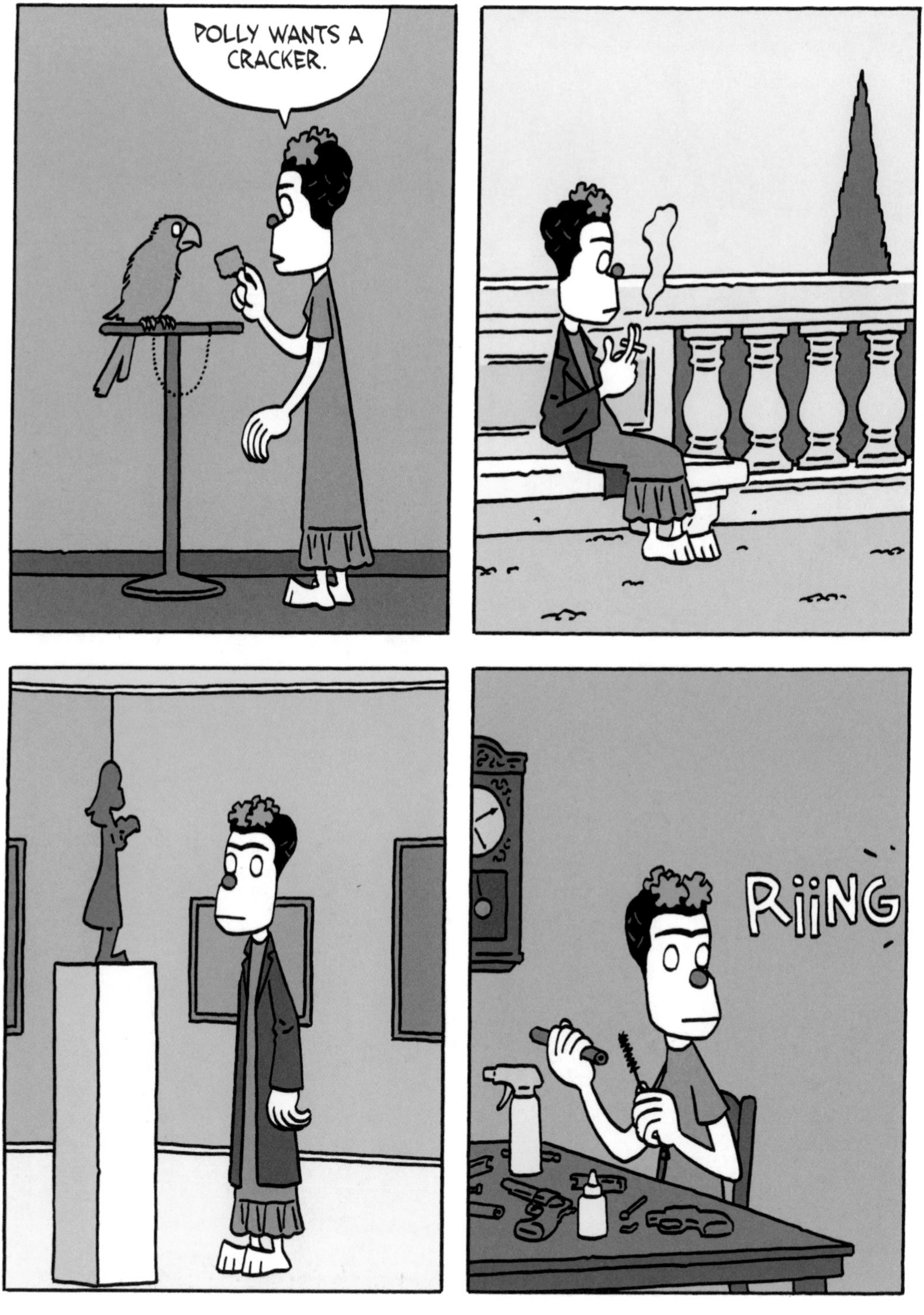
POLLY WANTS A CRACKER.
RIING

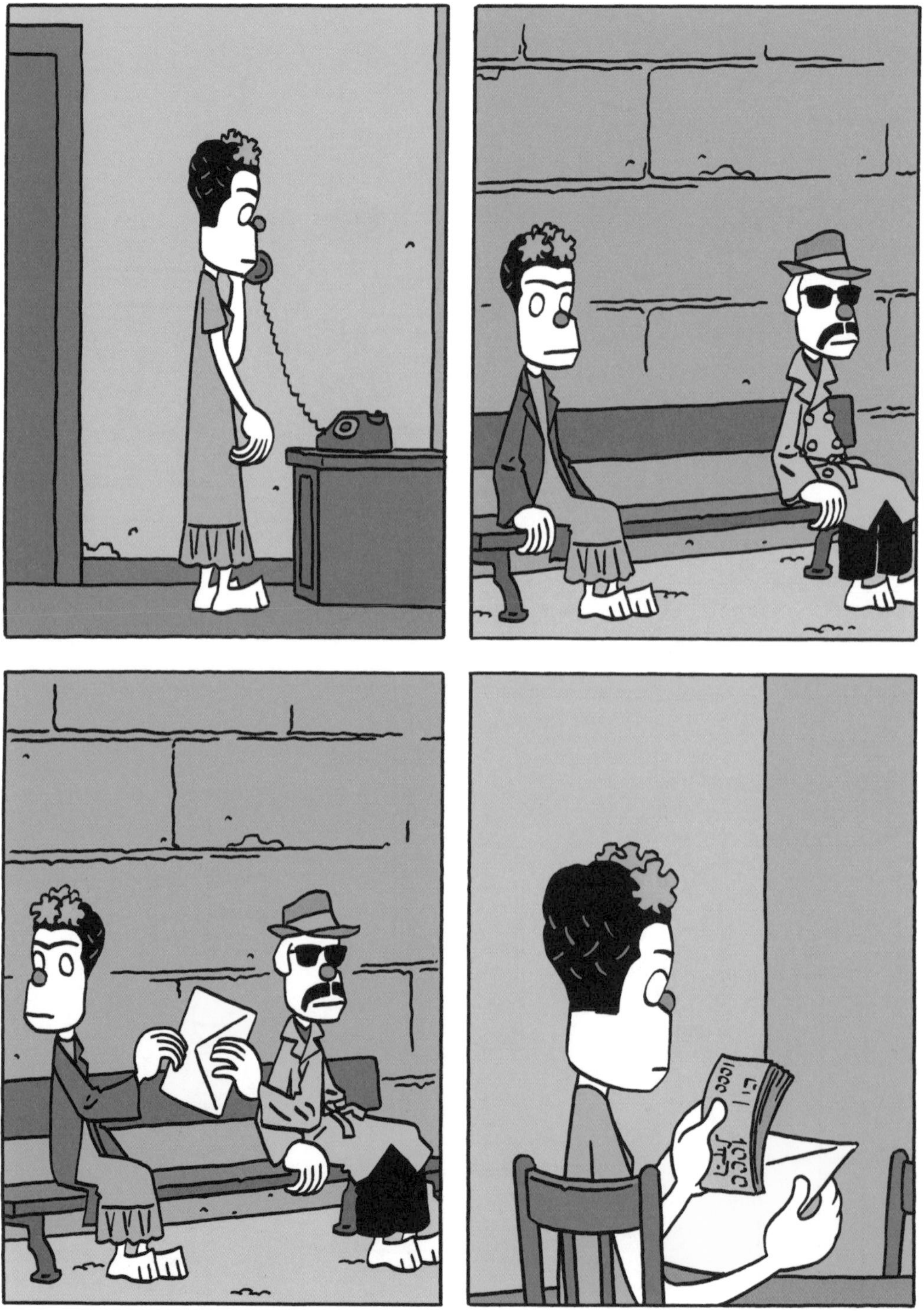

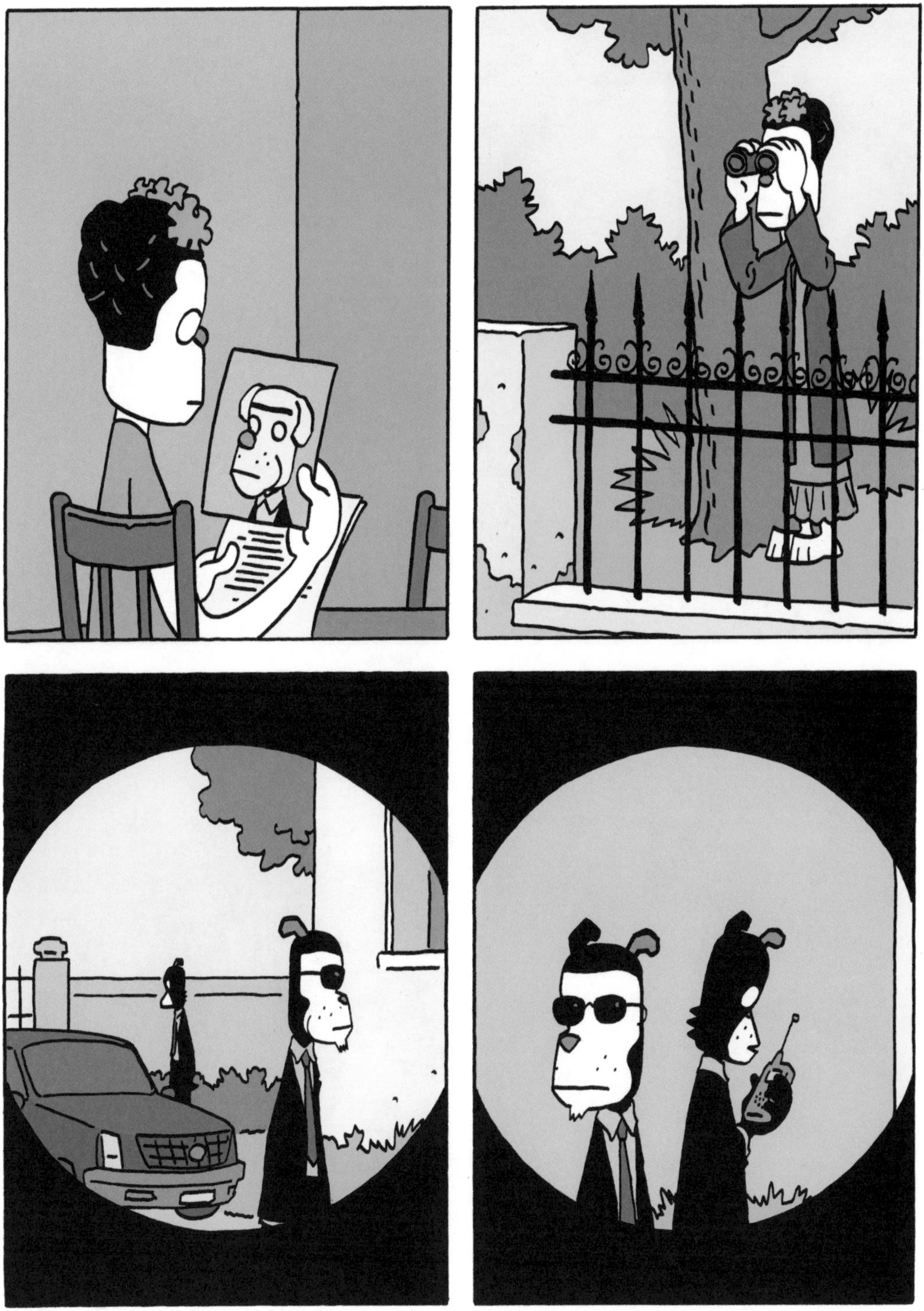

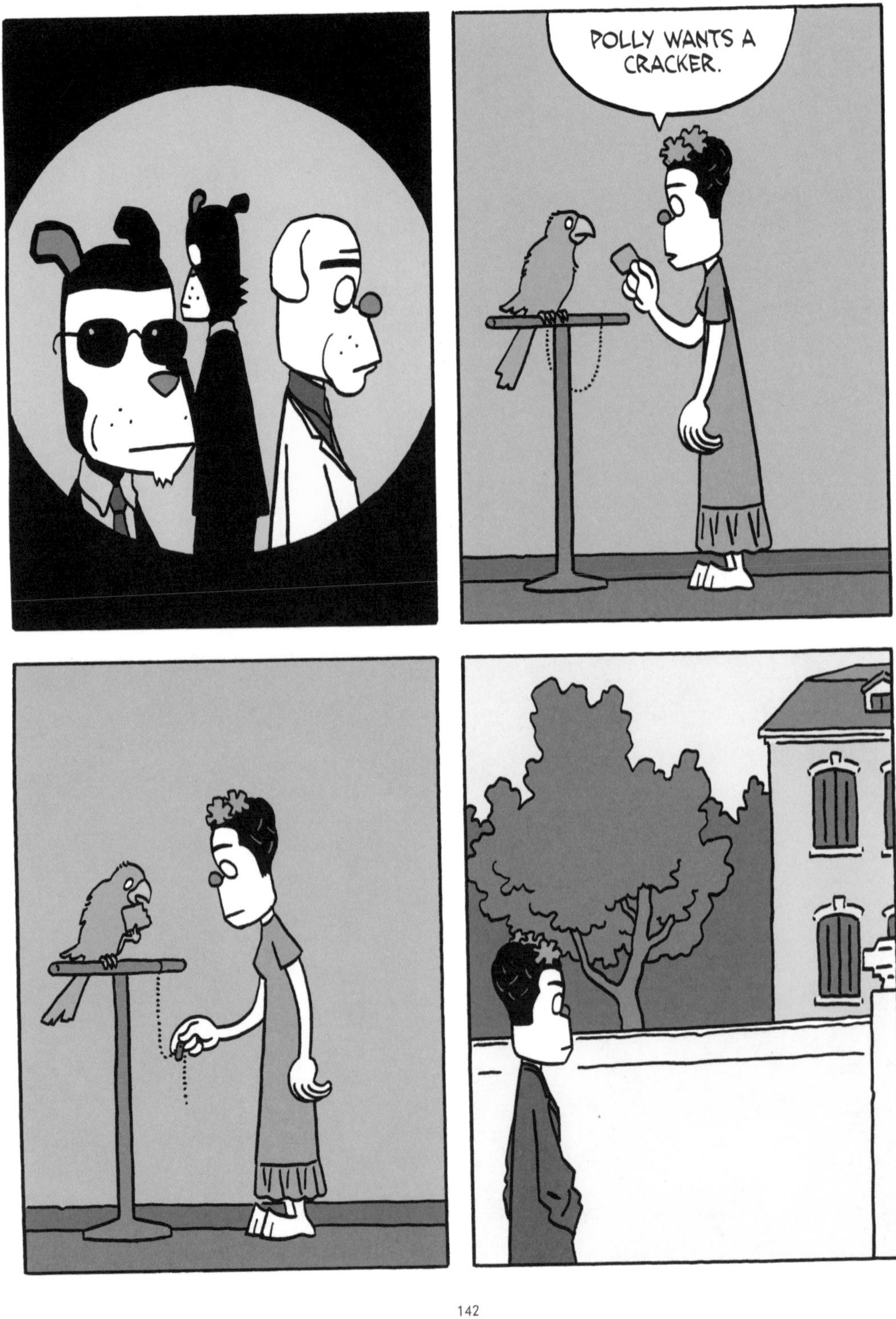
POLLY WANTS A
CRACKER.

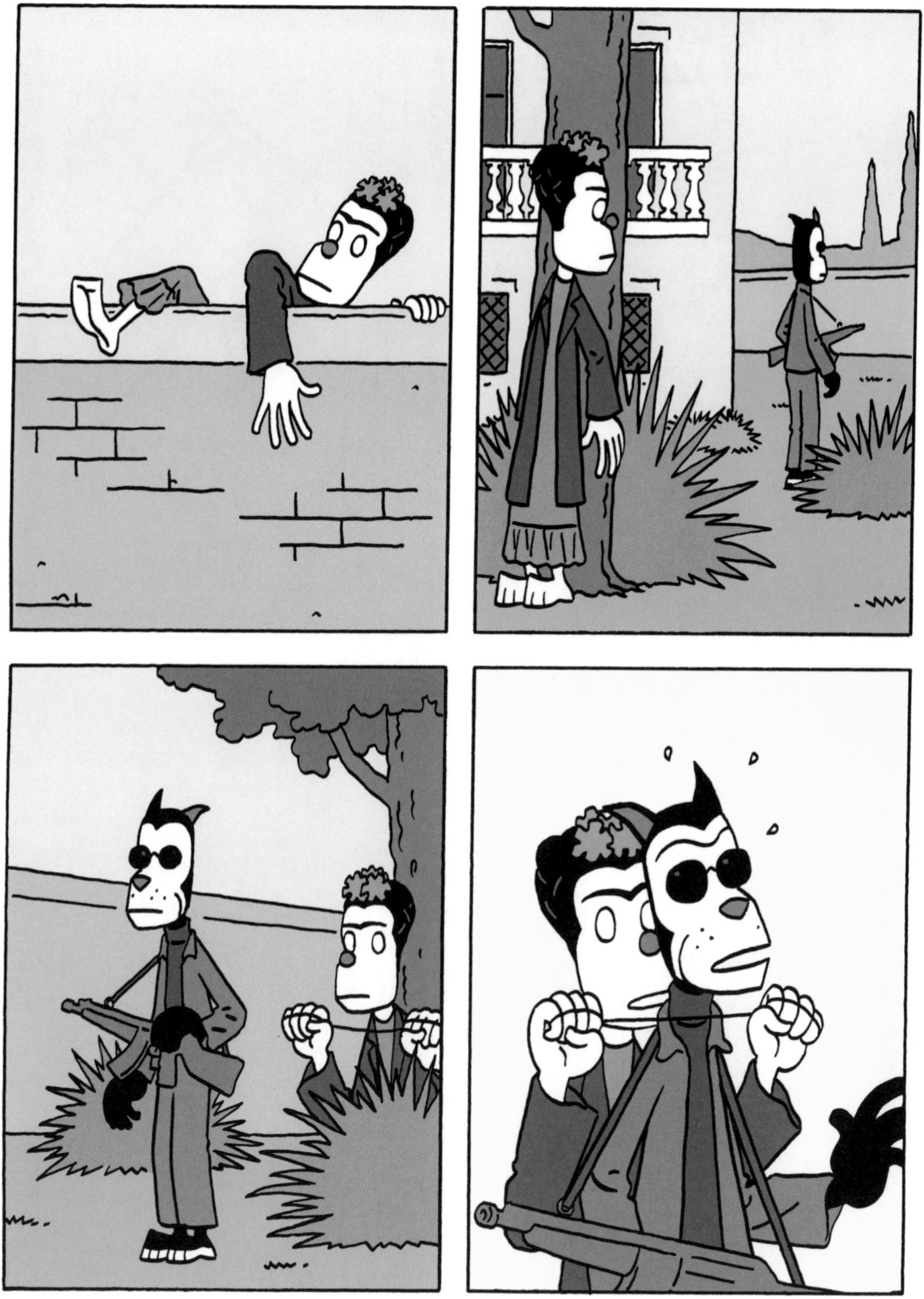

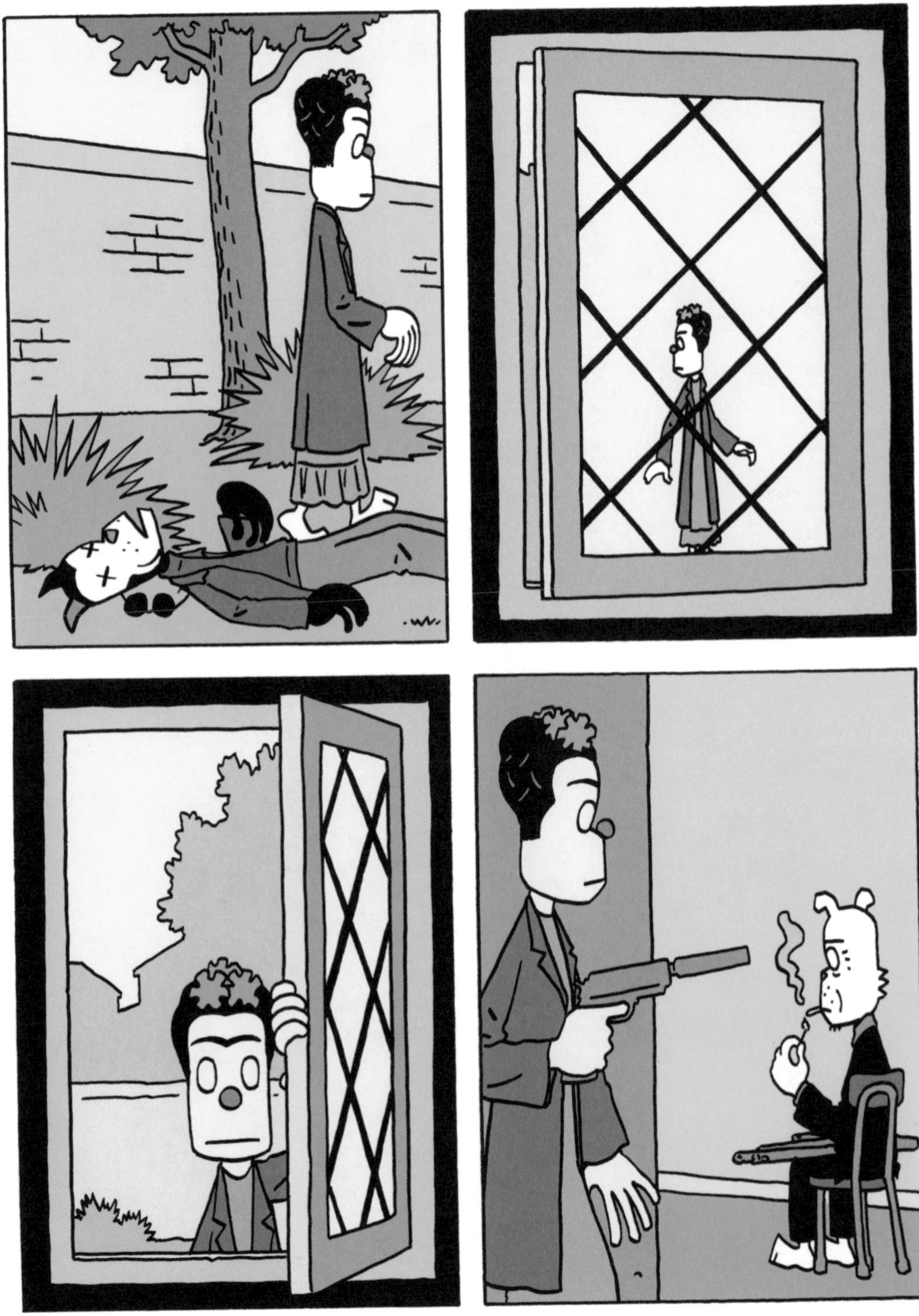

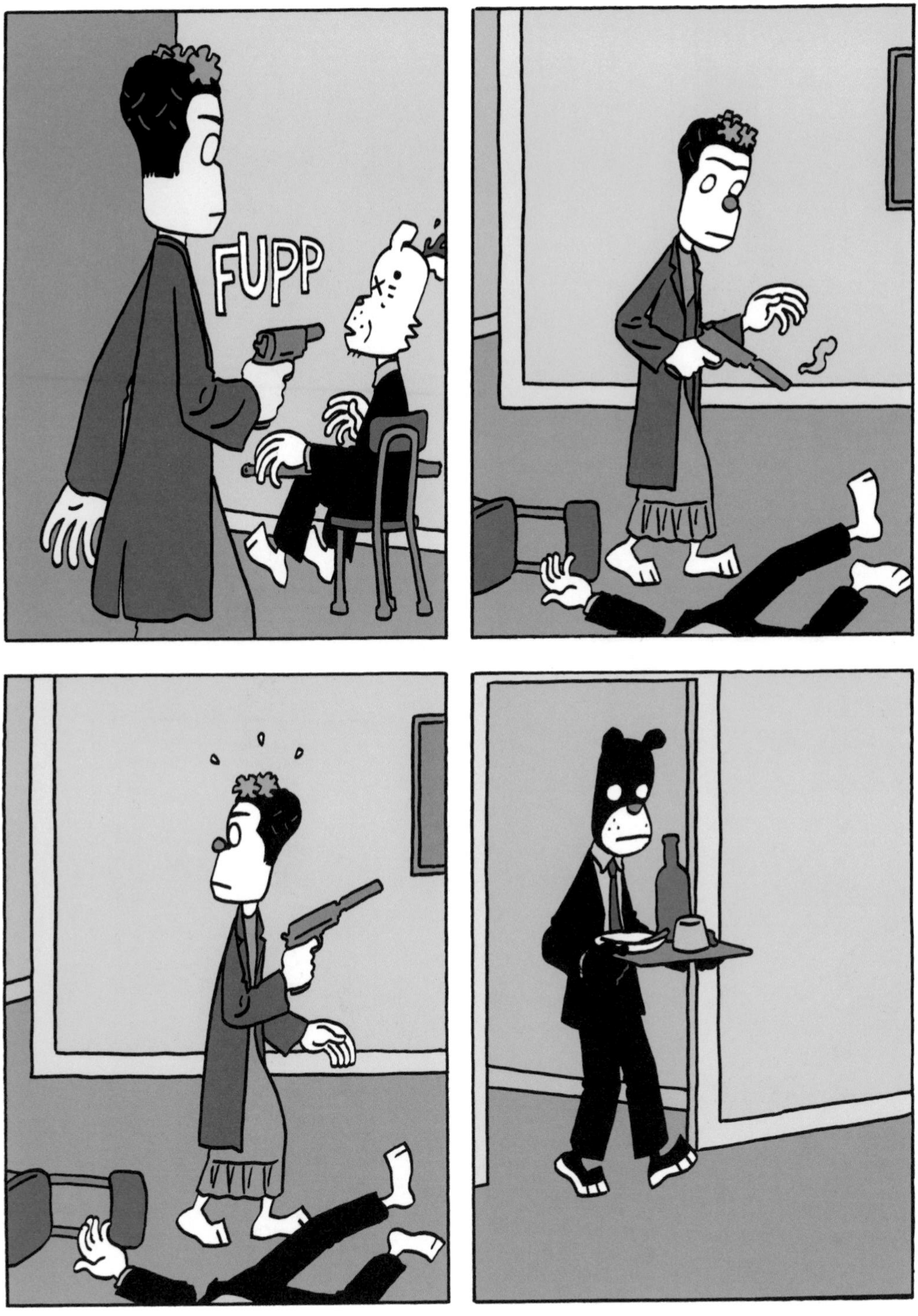
FUPP

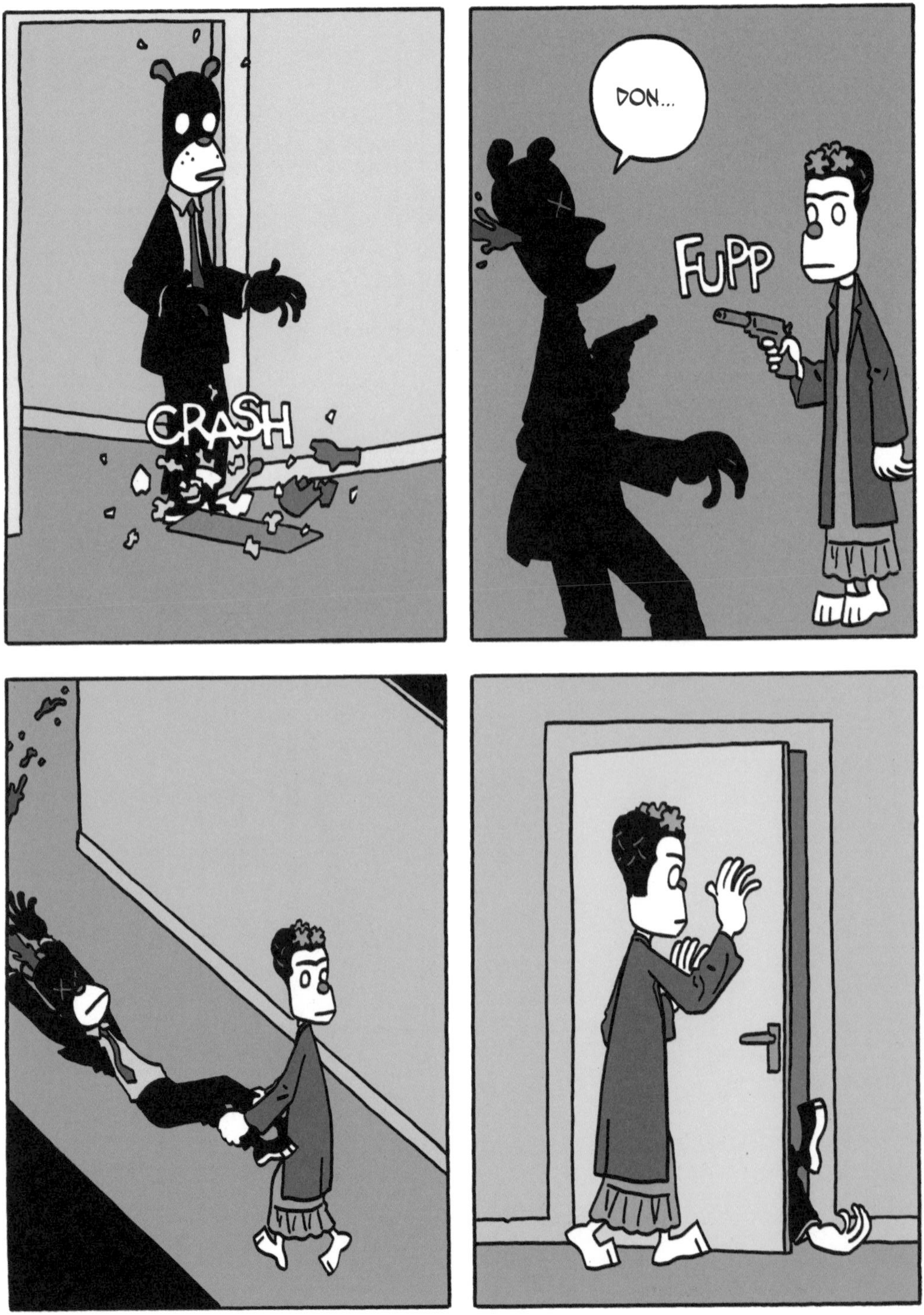
CRASH
DON...
FUPP

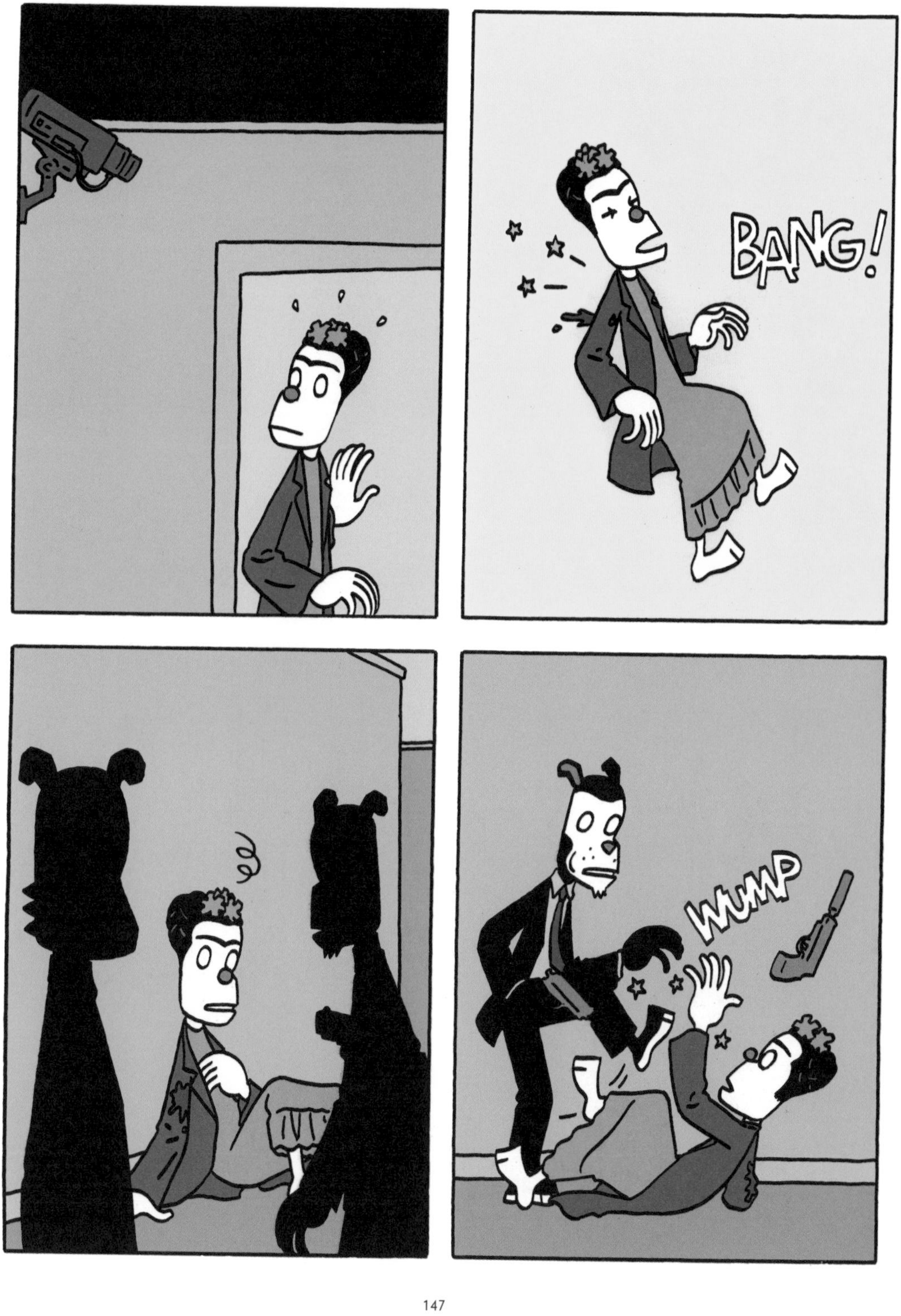
BANG!
WUMP

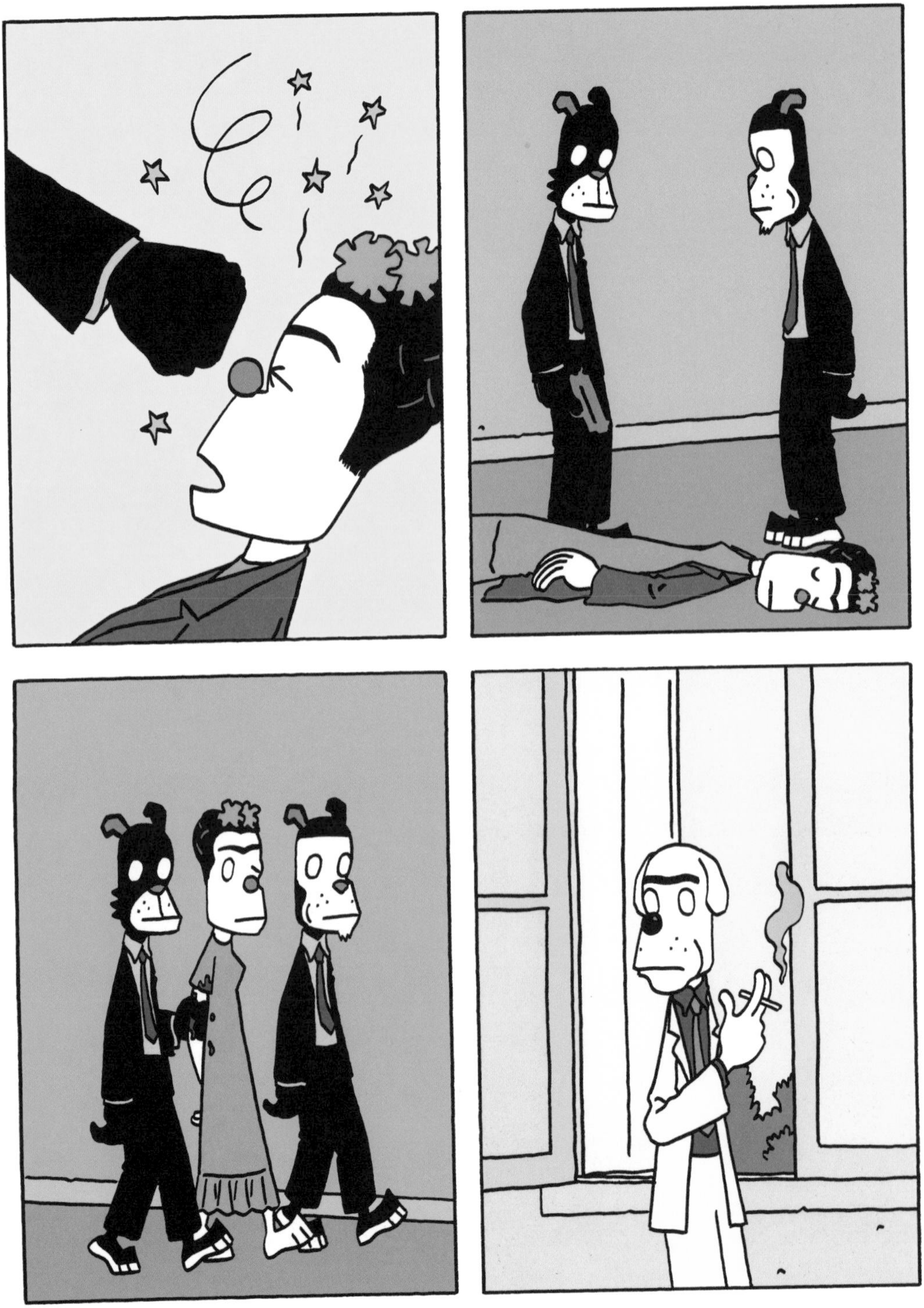

THOK
BONK

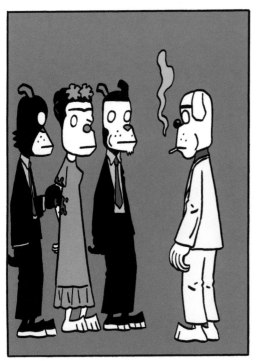

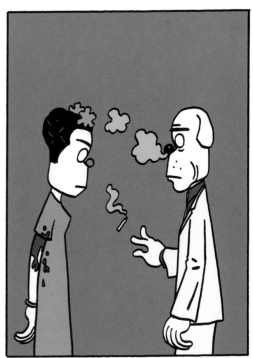

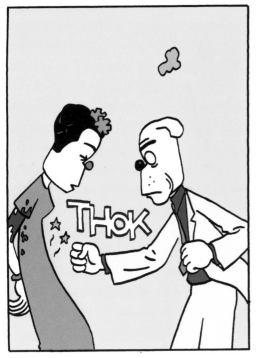

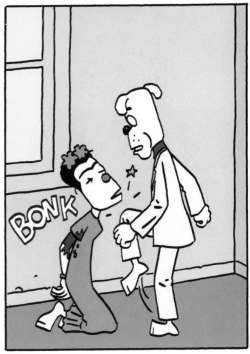

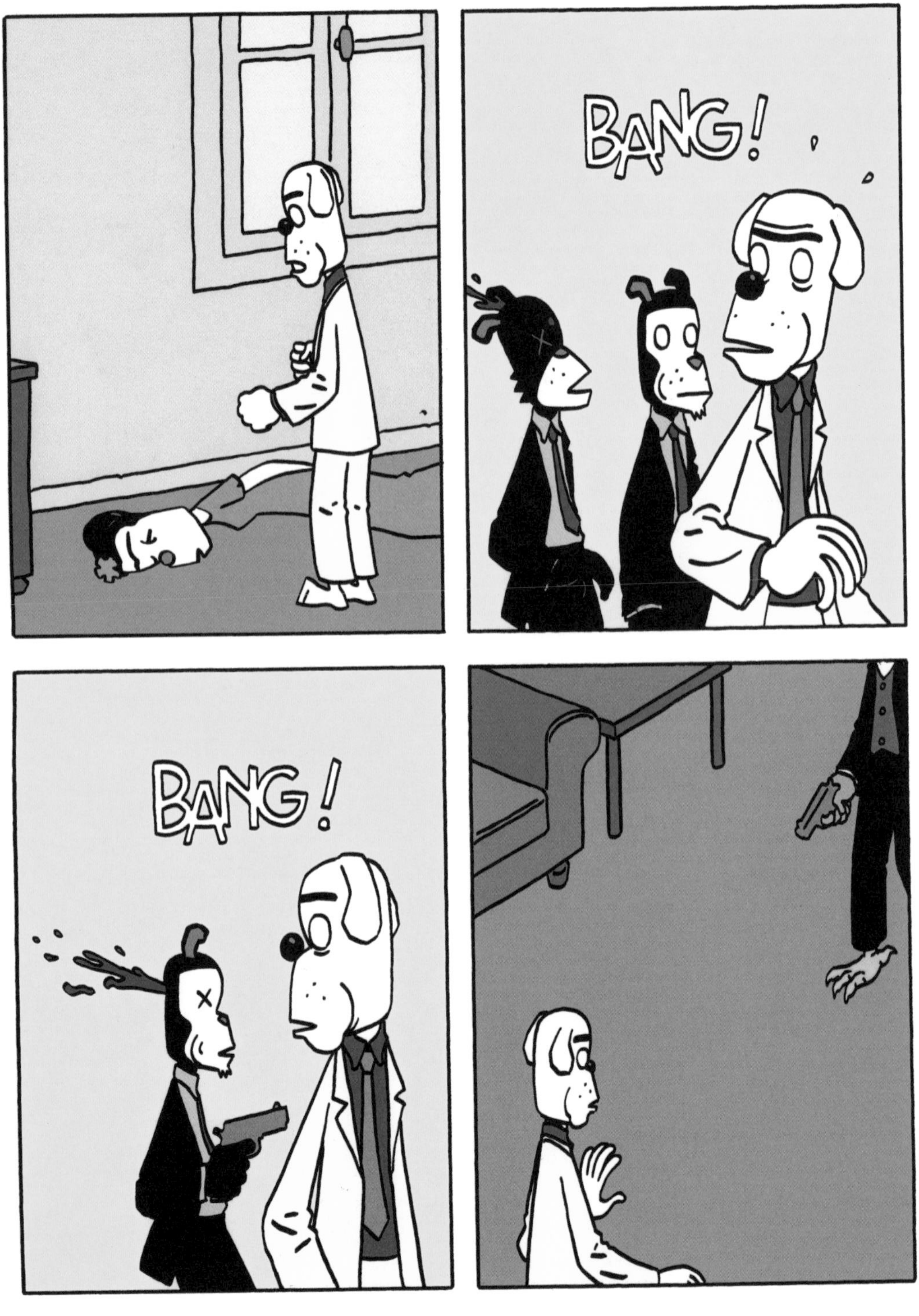
BANG!
BANG!

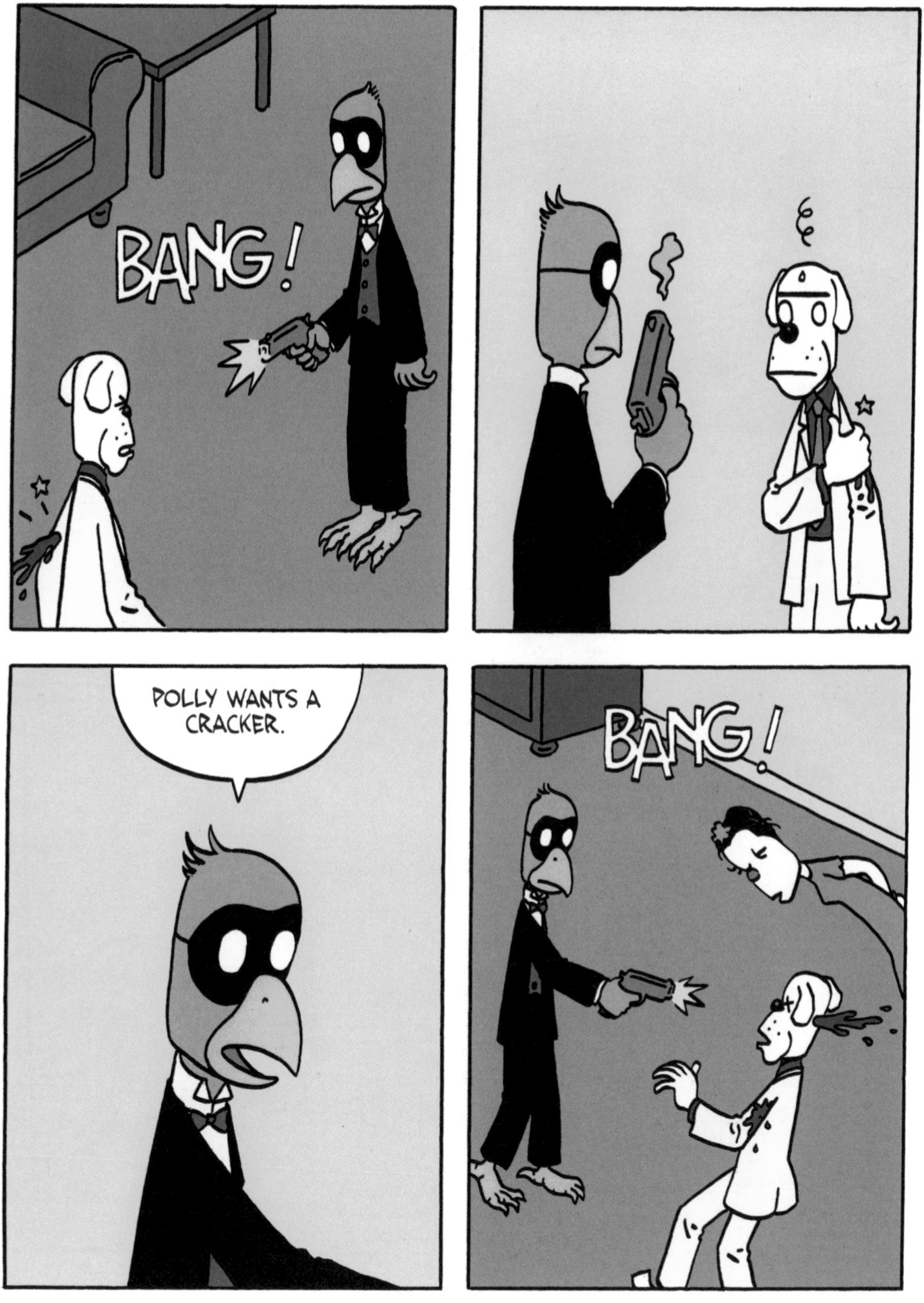
BANG!
POLLY WANTS A CRACKER.
BANG!

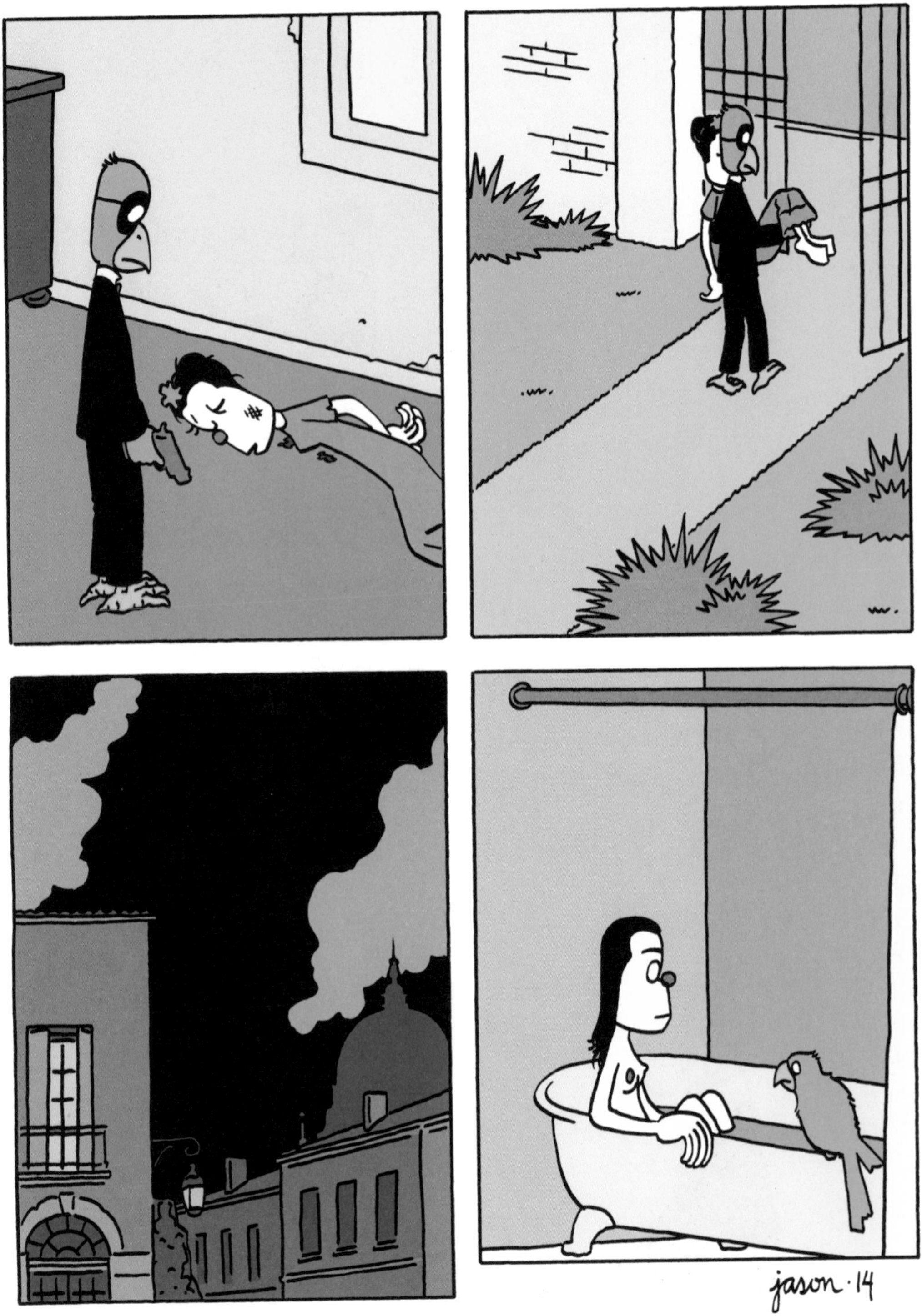
jason · 14

PRESENTING:

THE THRILL IS GONE

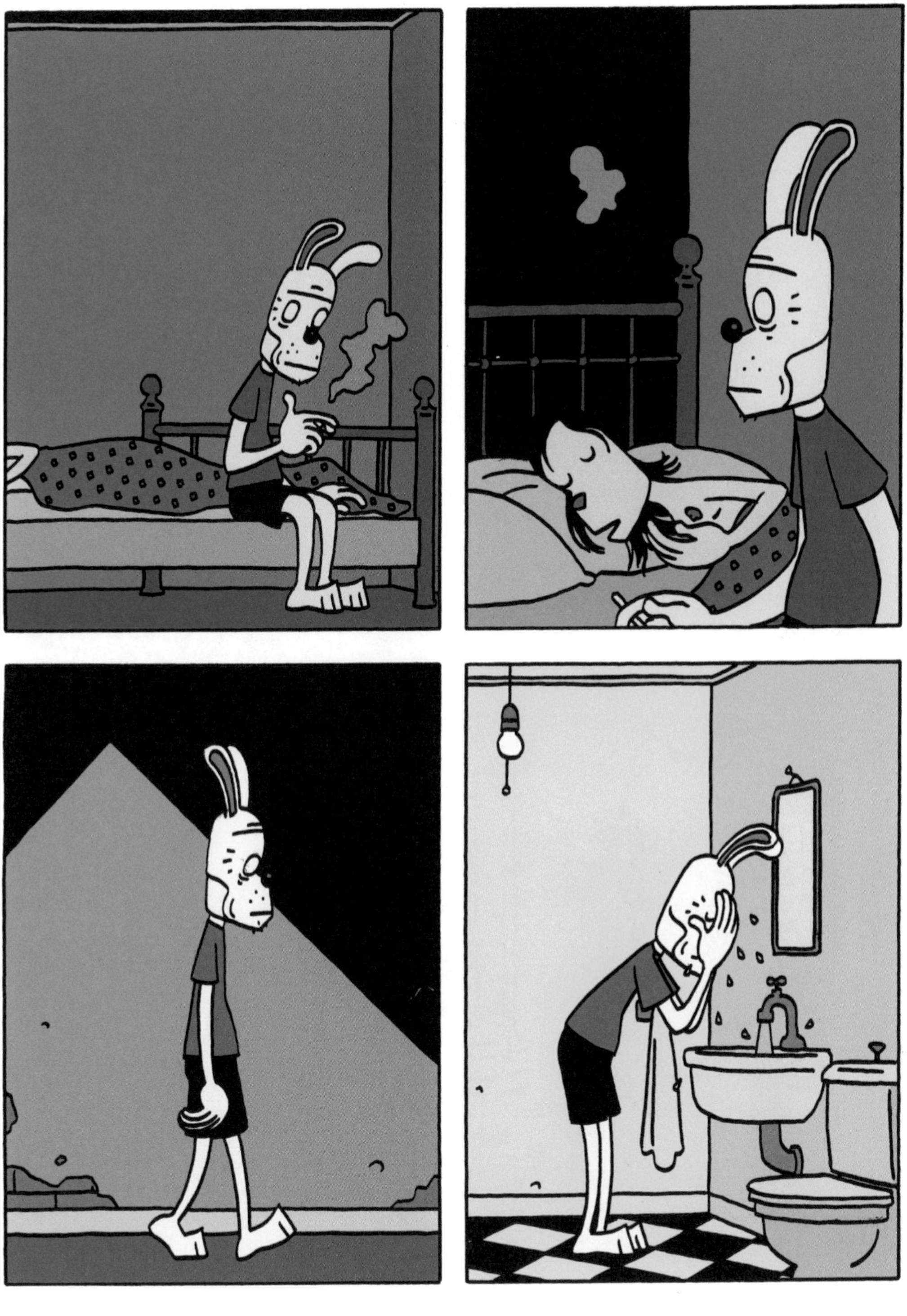

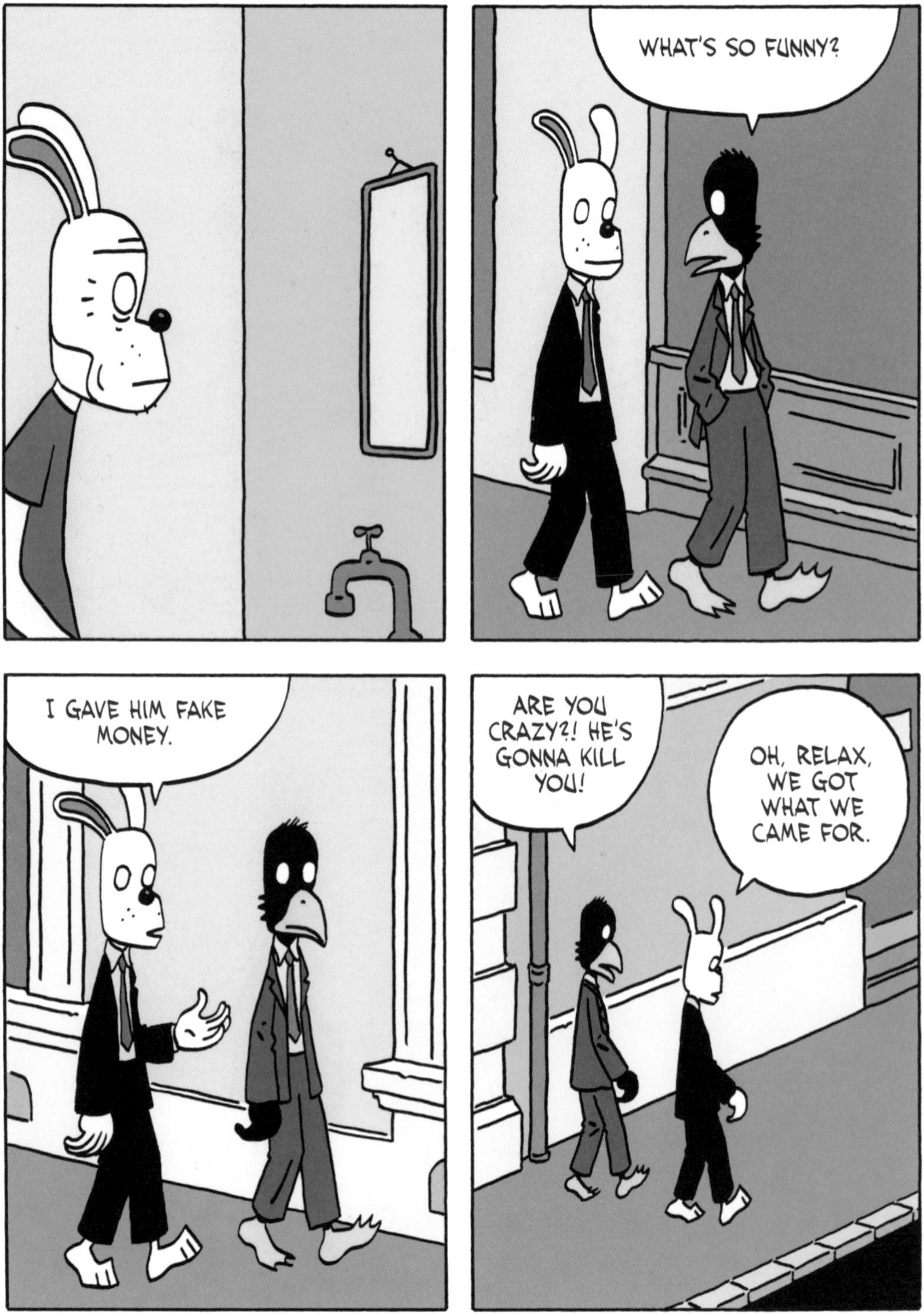
WHAT'S SO FUNNY?
I GAVE HIM FAKE MONEY.
ARE YOU CRAZY?! HE'S GONNA KILL YOU!
OH, RELAX, WE GOT WHAT WE CAME FOR.

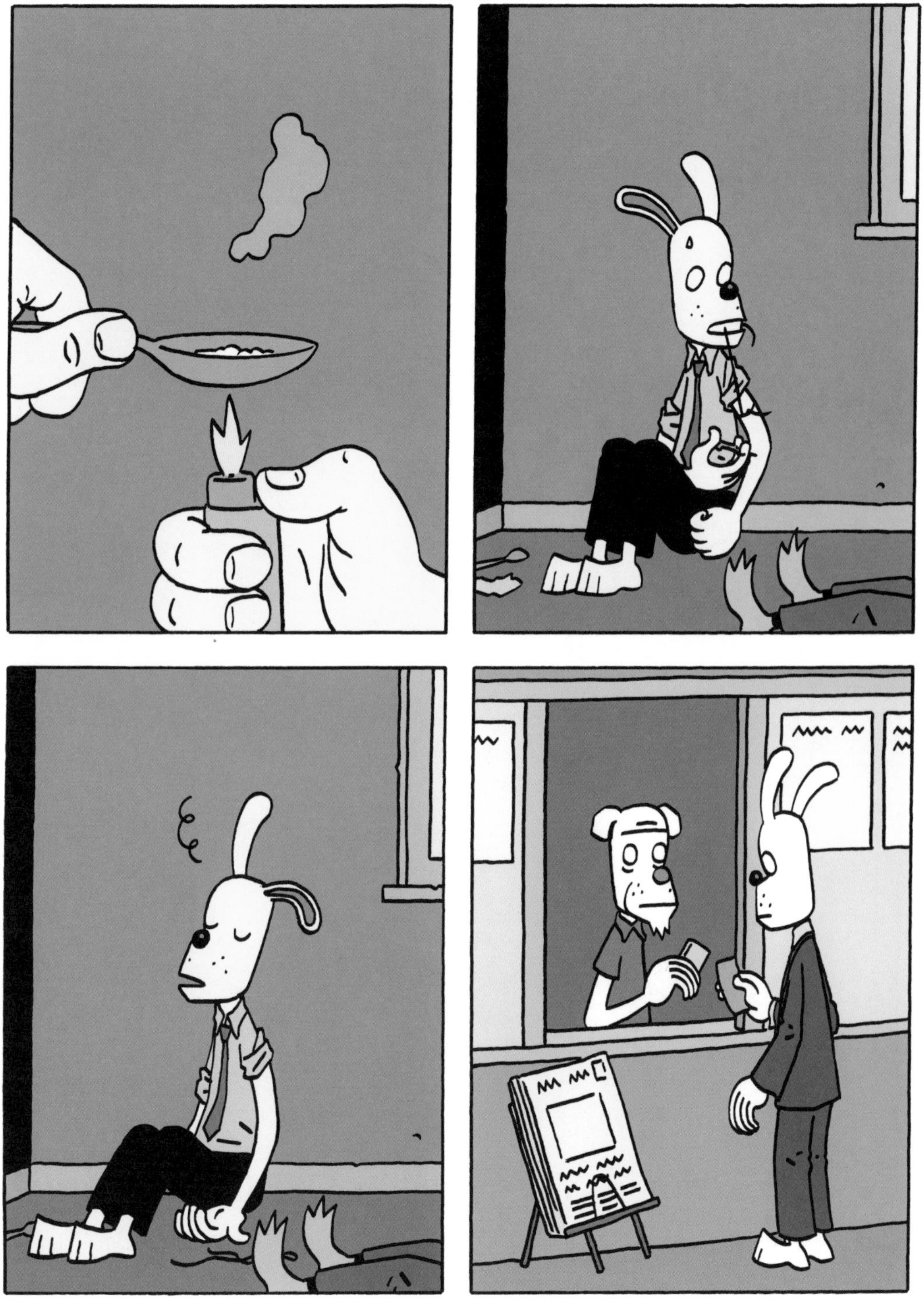

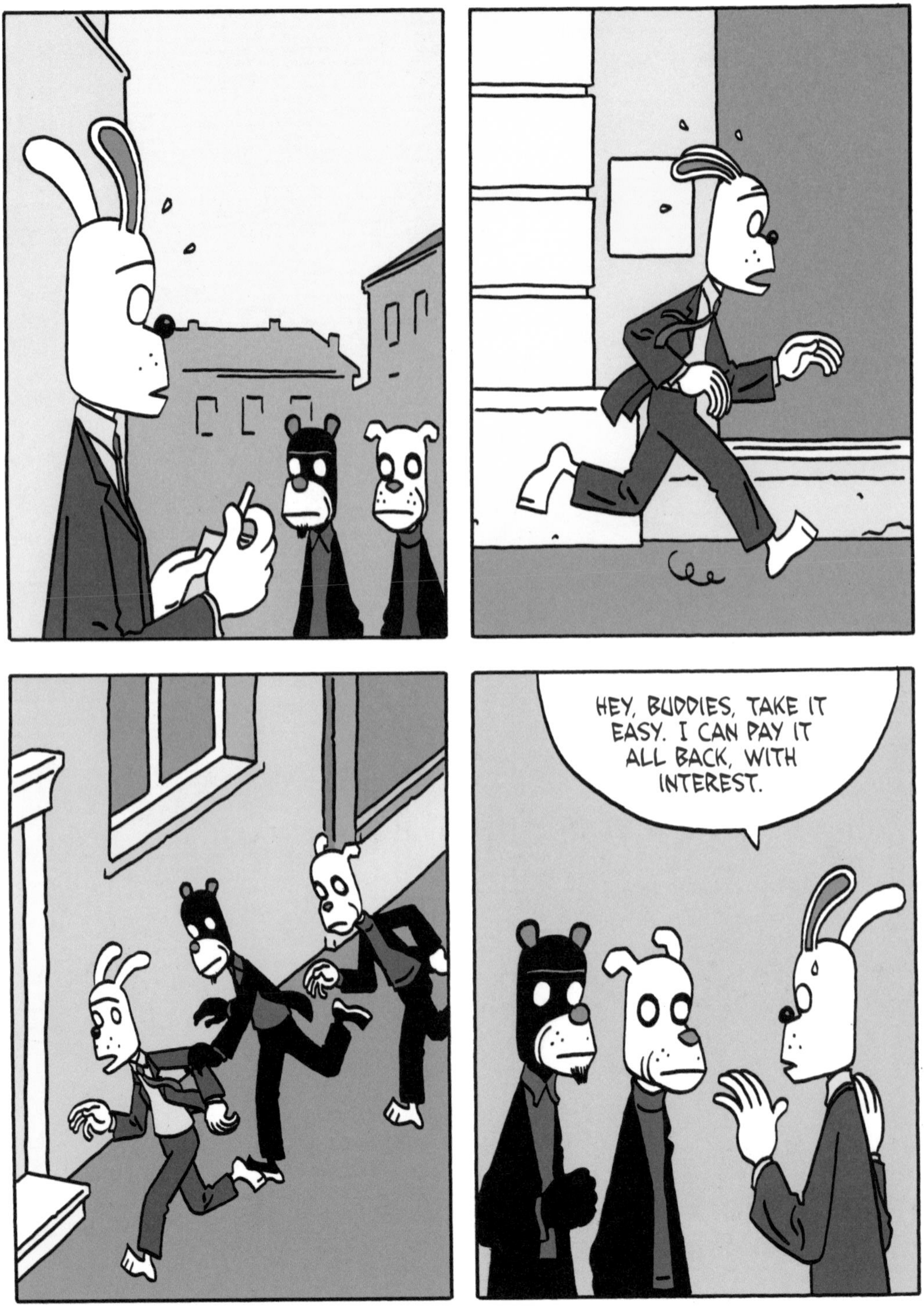
HEY, BUDDIES, TAKE IT EASY. I CAN PAY IT ALL BACK, WITH INTEREST.

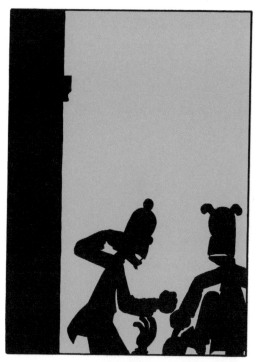

OH, JESUS
CHRIST!

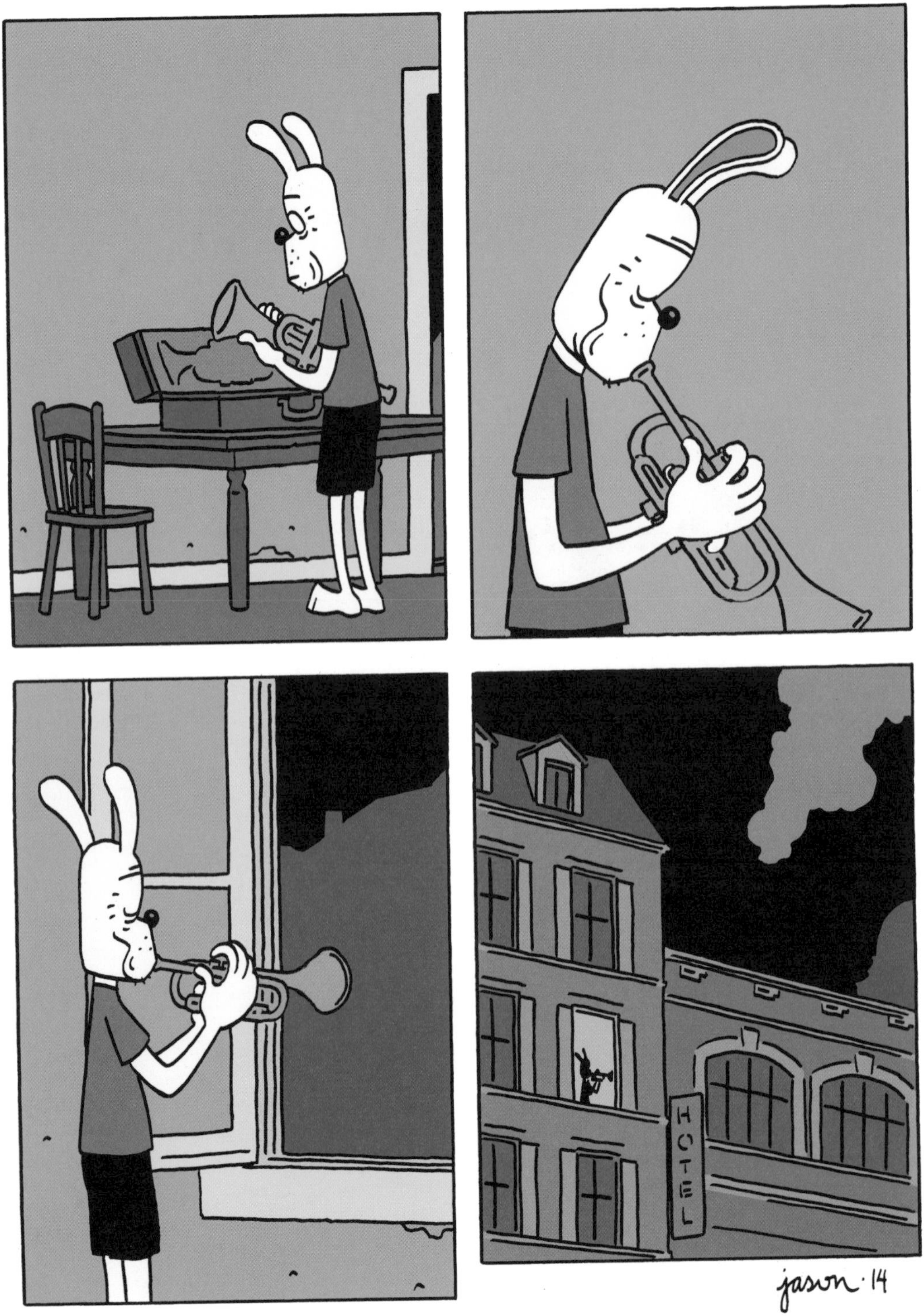
HOTEL
jason·14

PRESENTING:

———

ASK NOT

———

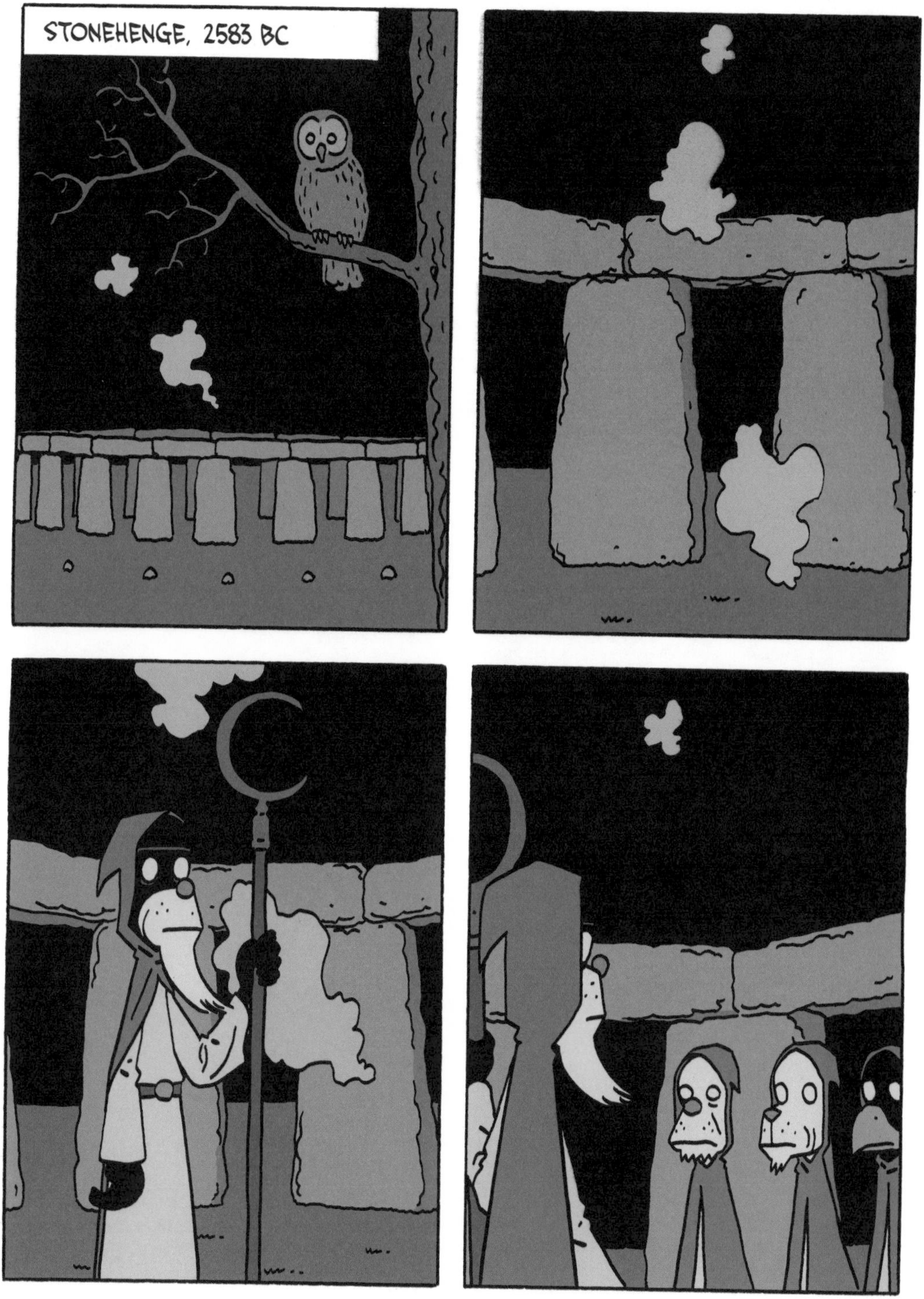
STONEHENGE, 2583 BC

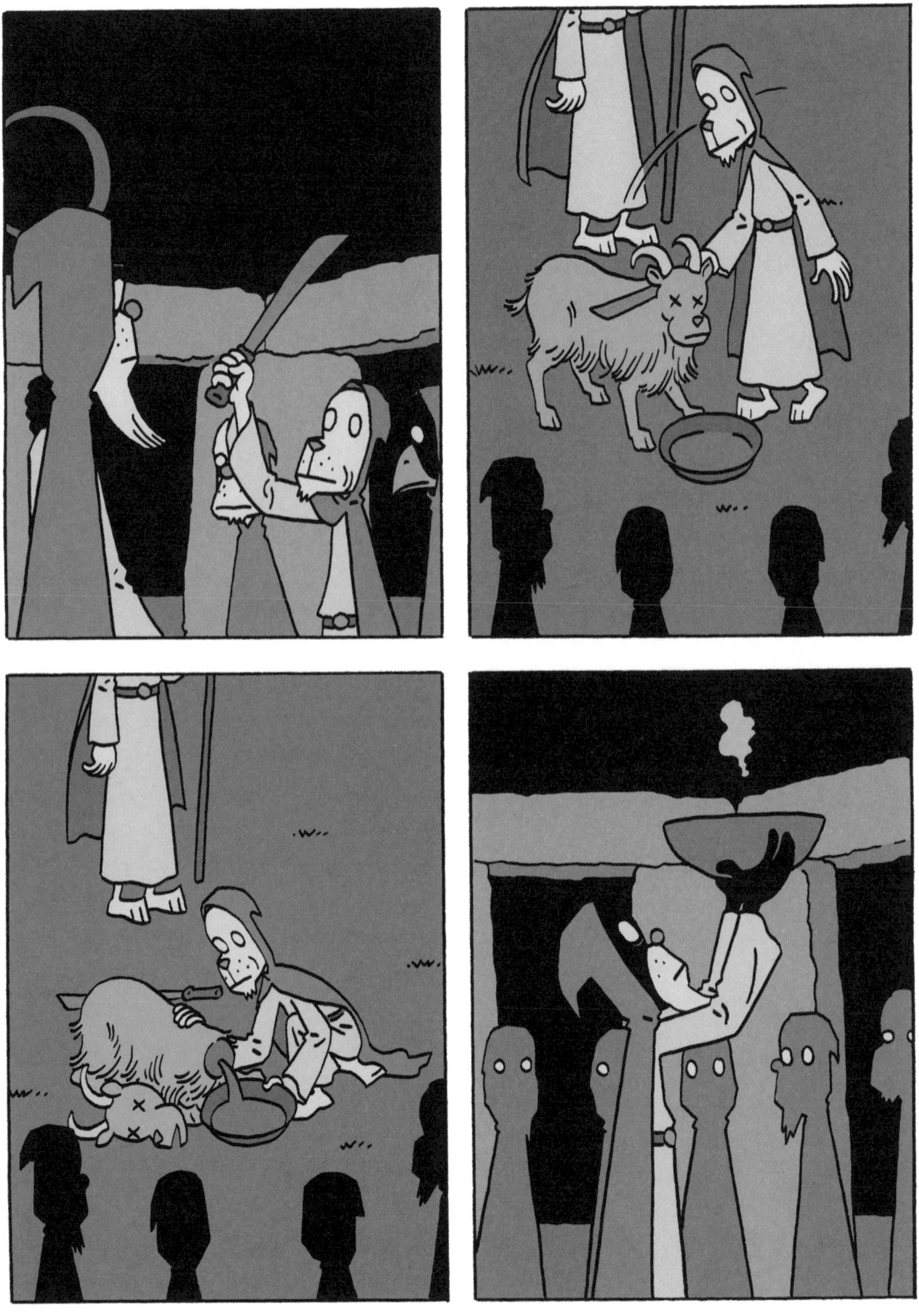

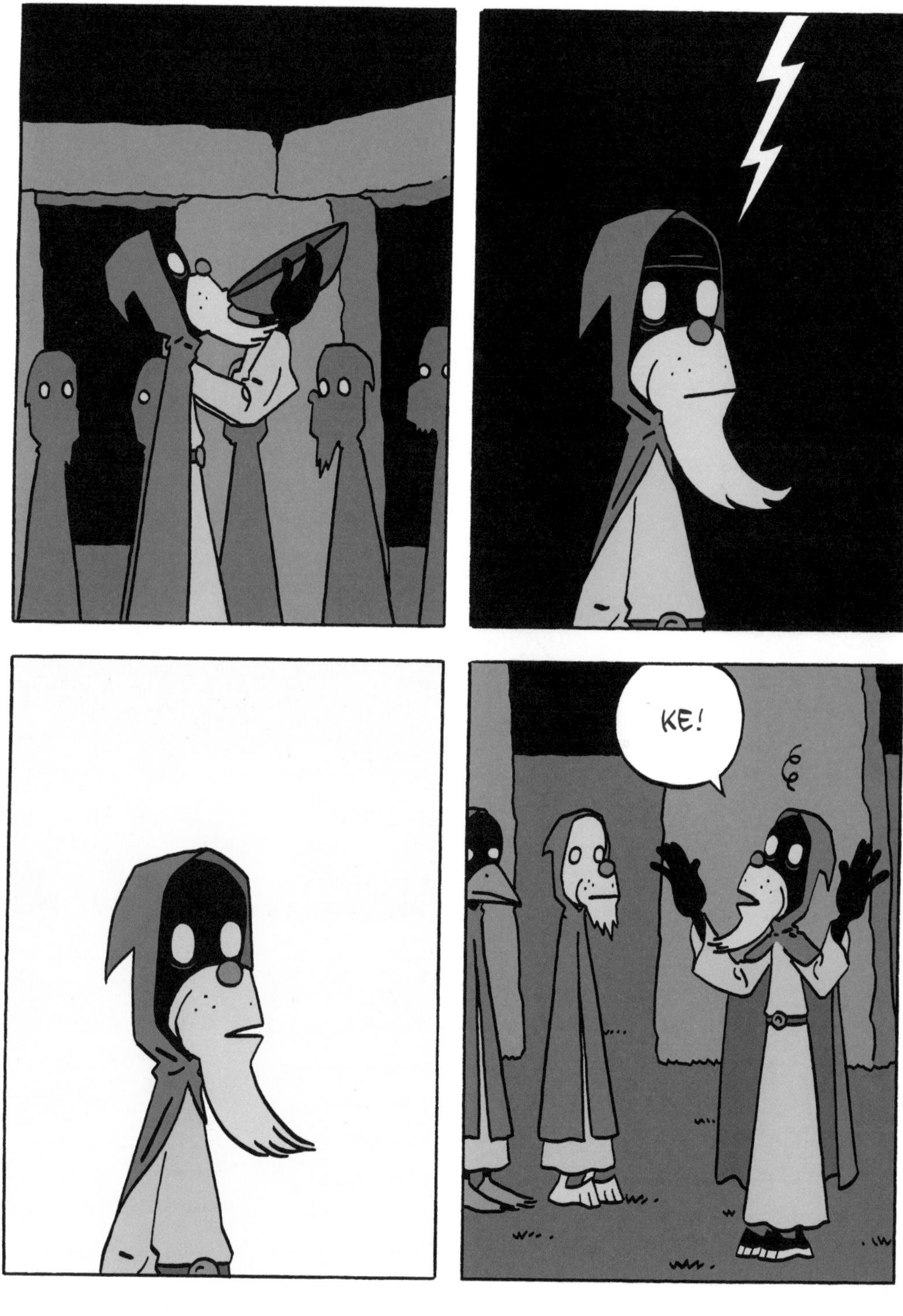
KE!

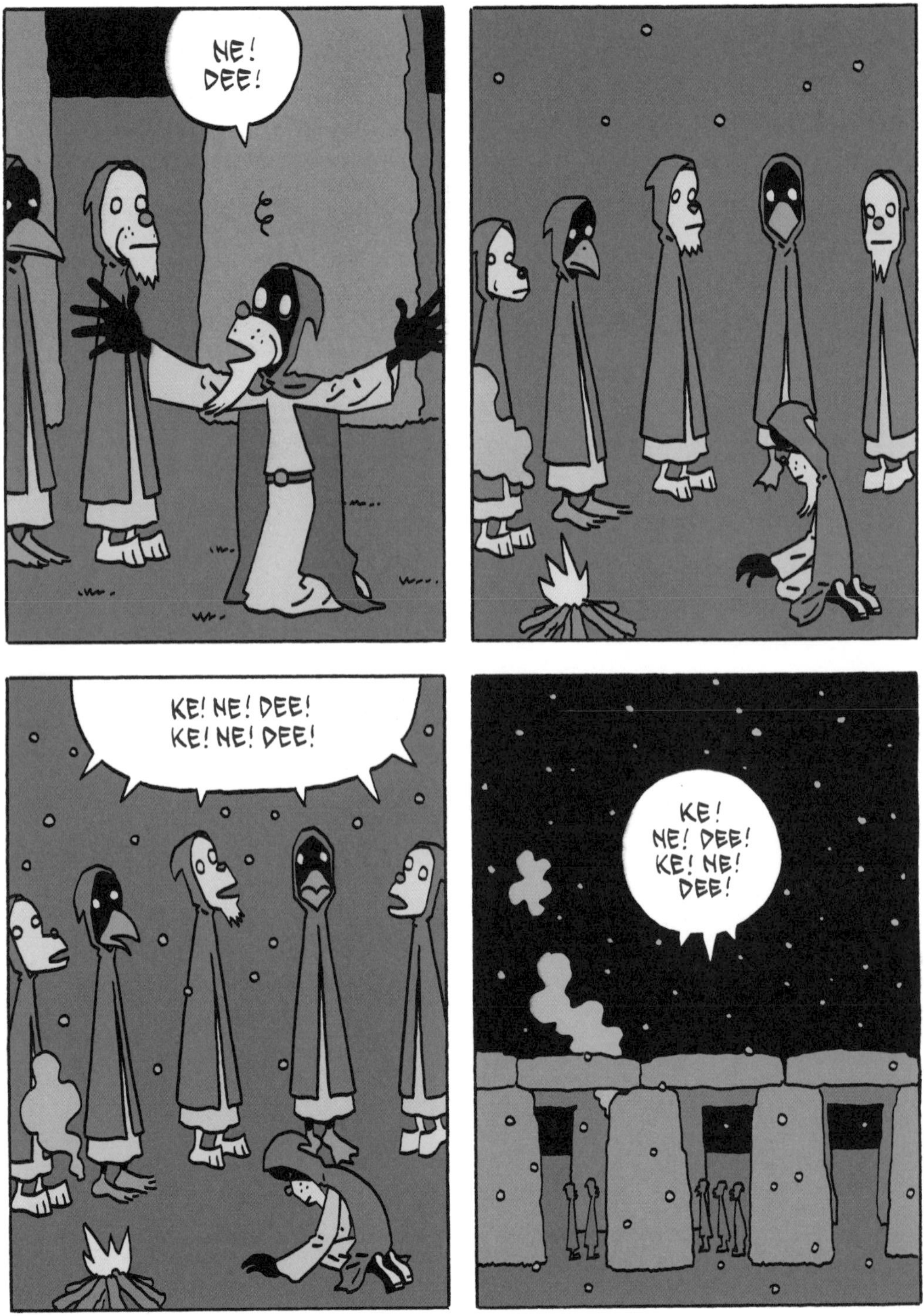
NE! DEE!
KE! NE! DEE! KE! NE! DEE!
KE! NE! DEE! KE! NE! DEE!

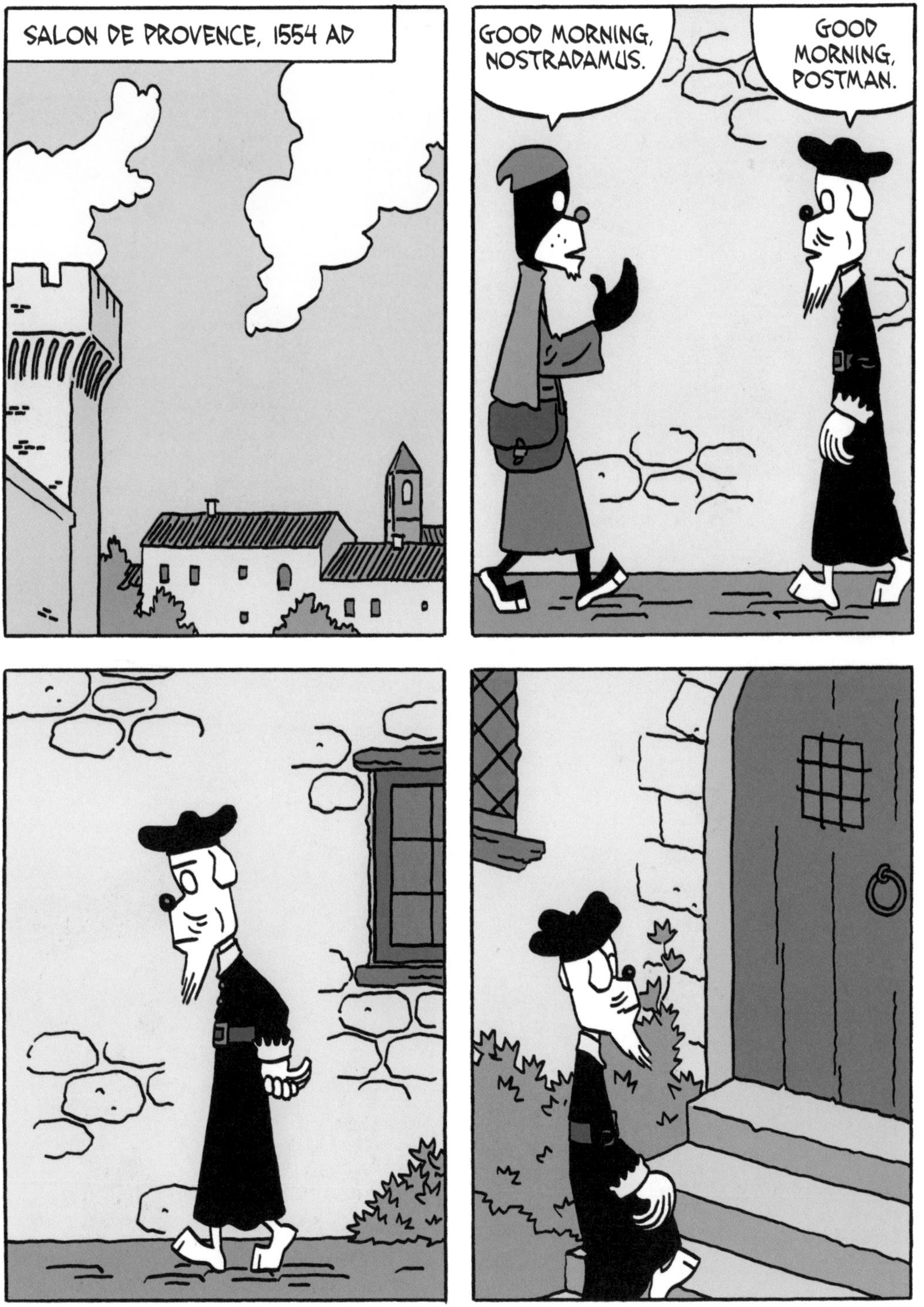
SALON DE PROVENCE, 1554 AD
GOOD MORNING, NOSTRADAMUS.
GOOD MORNING, POSTMAN.

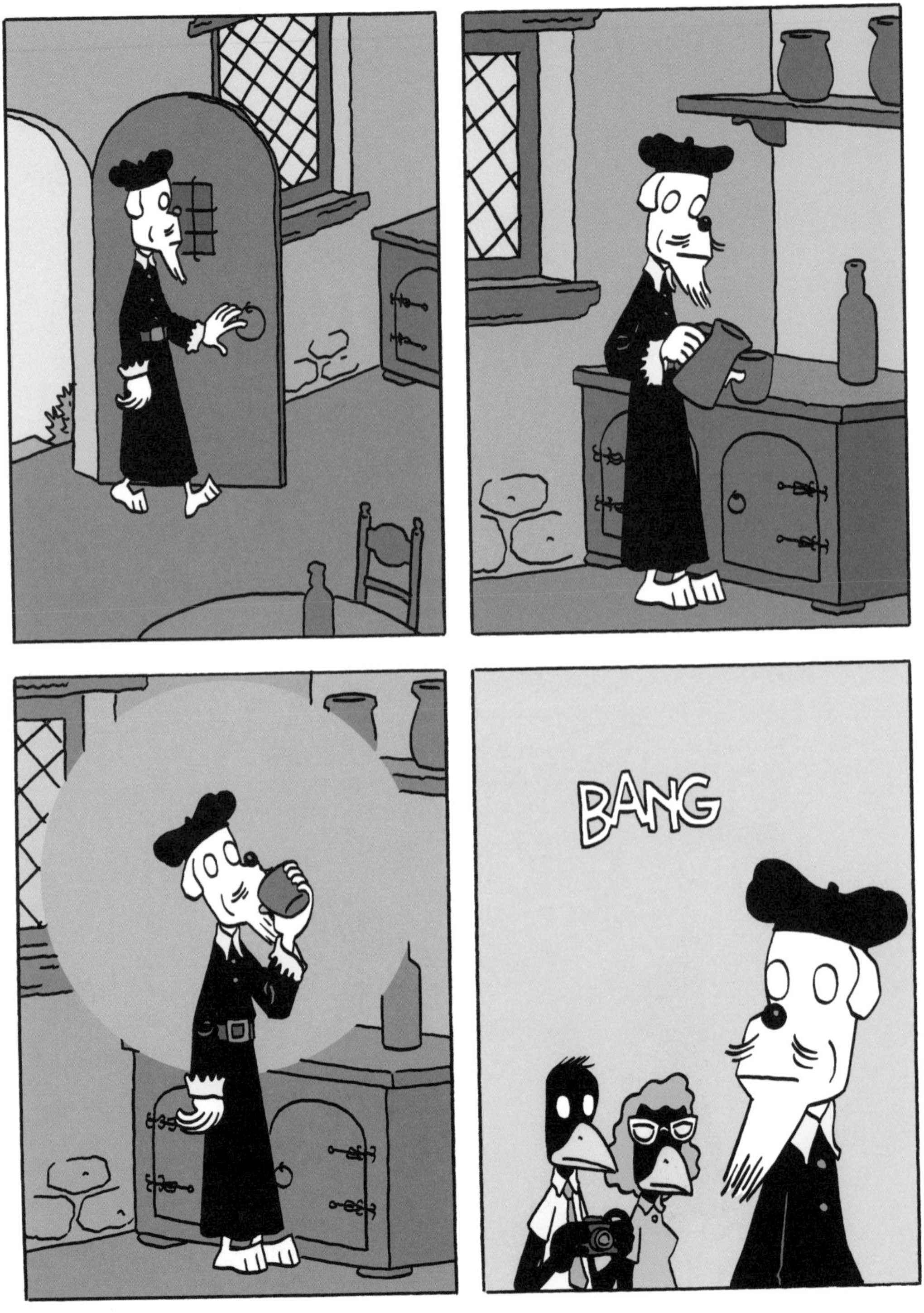
BANG

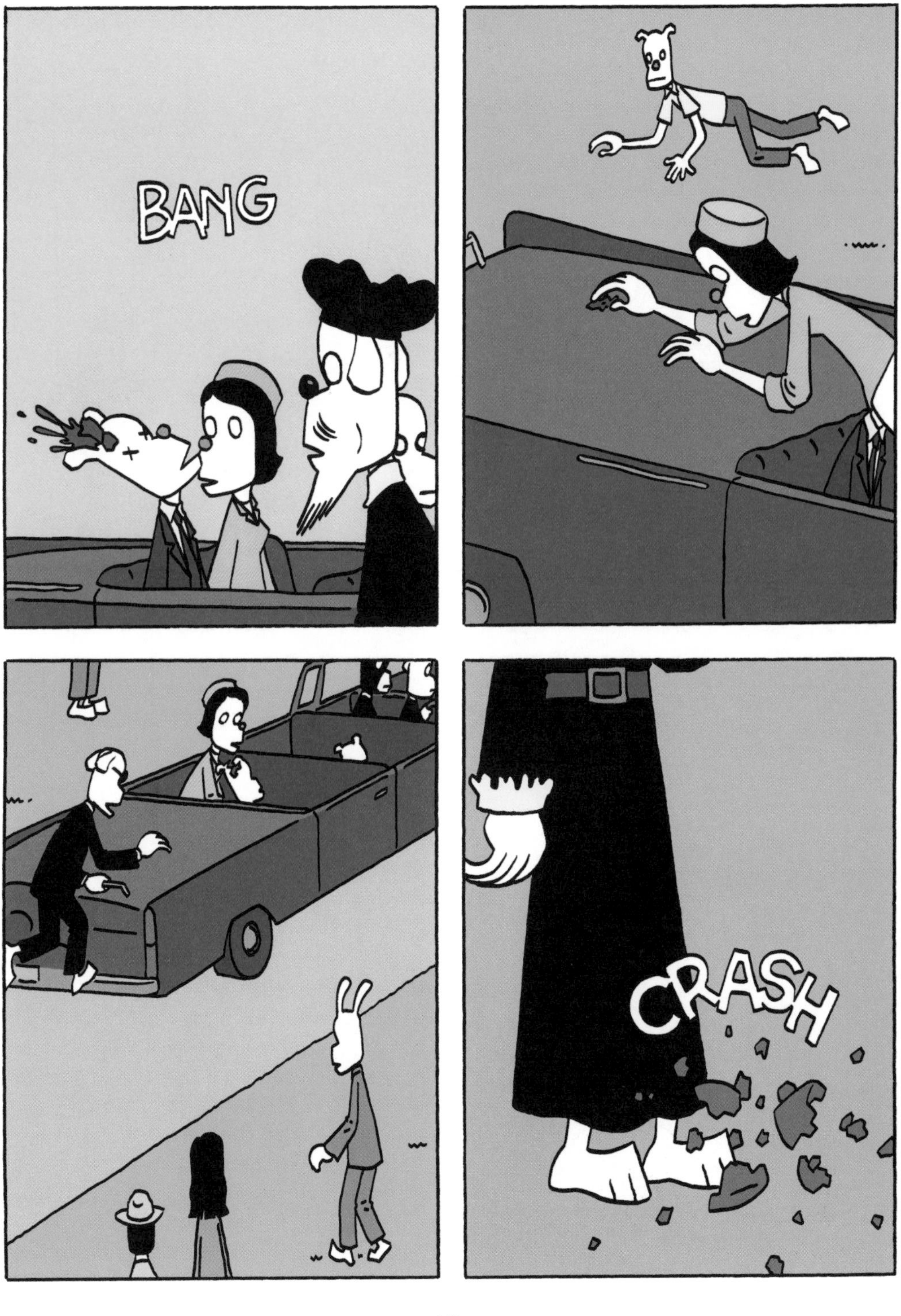
BANG
CRASH

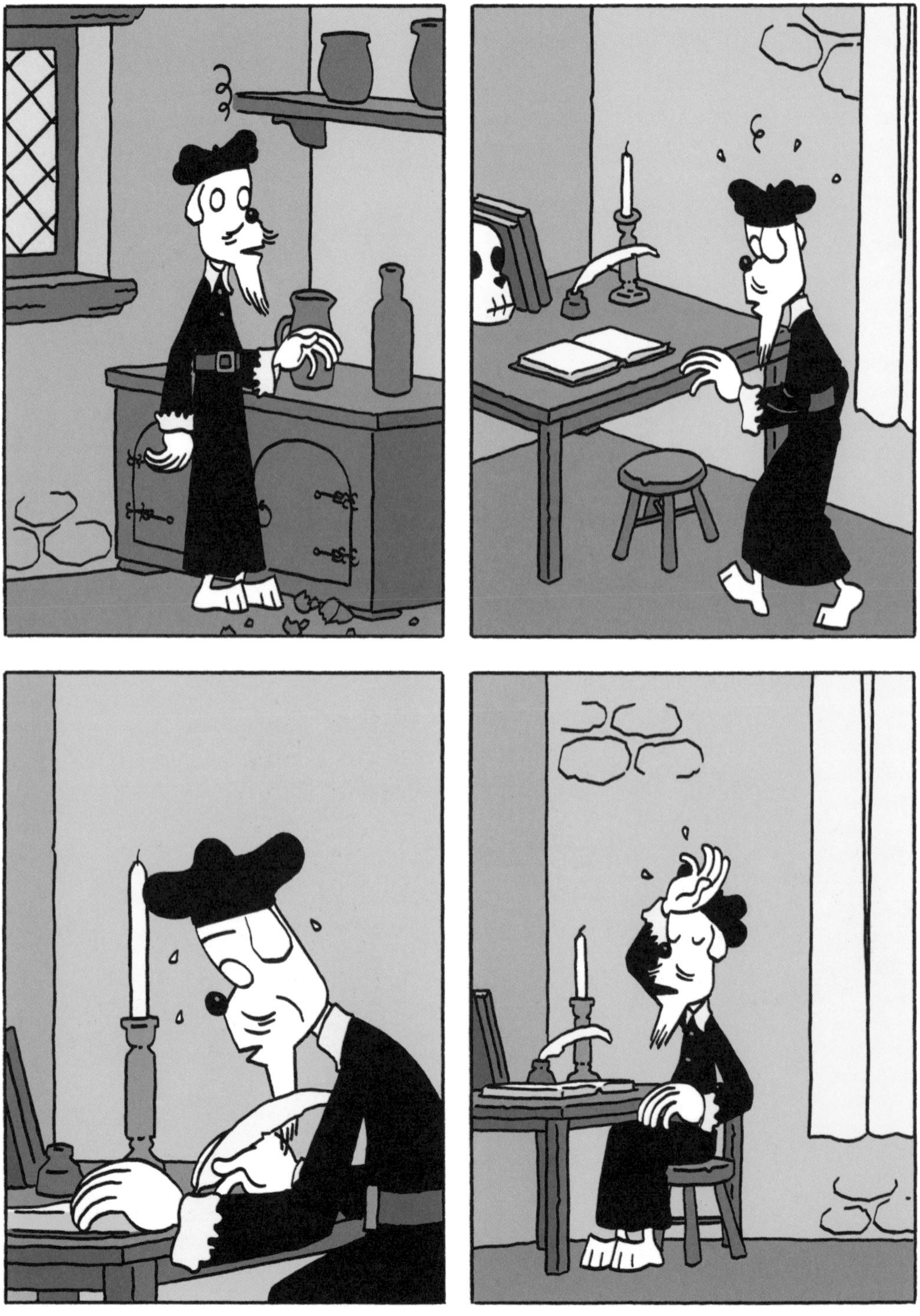

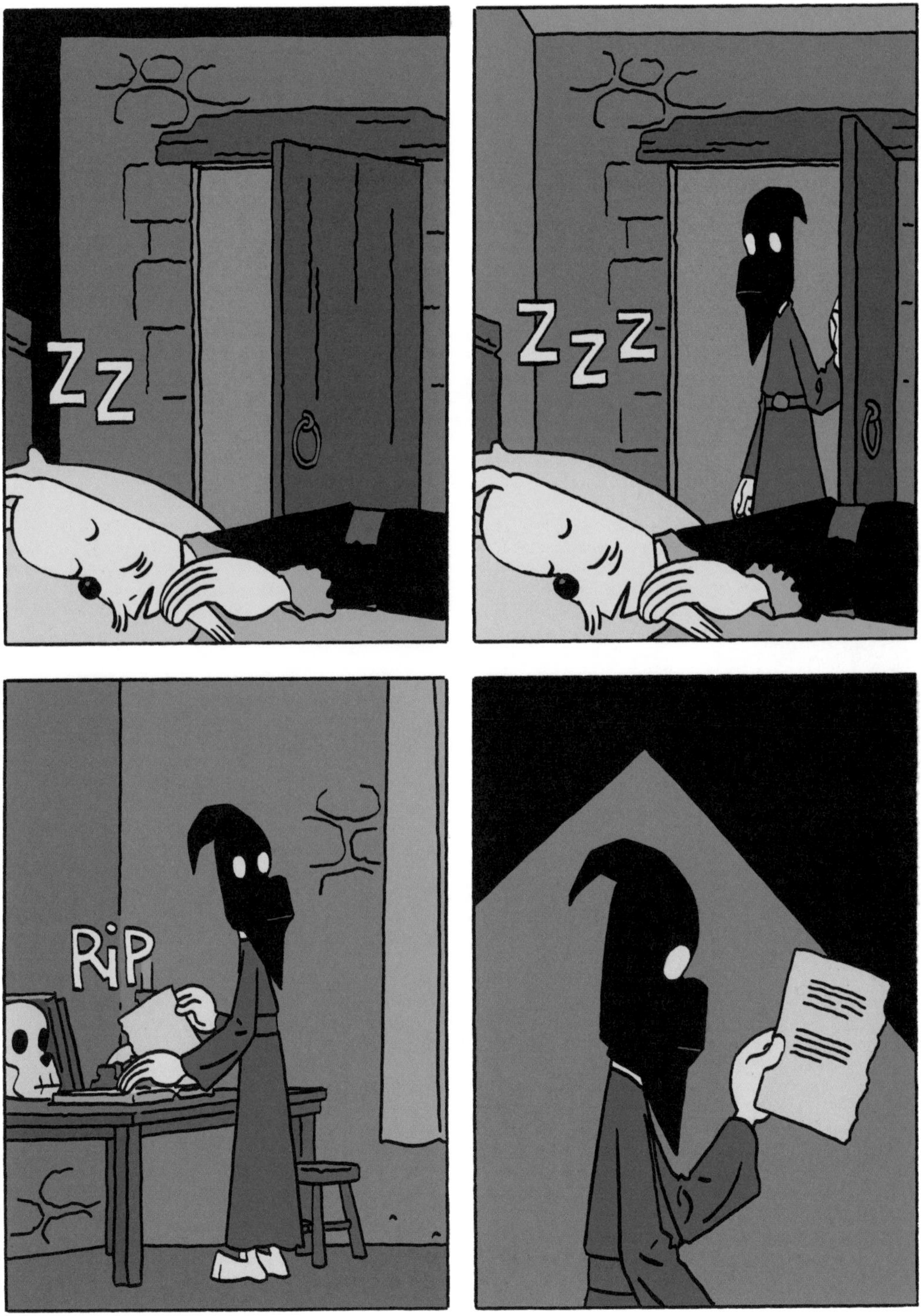
ZZ
ZZZ
RiP

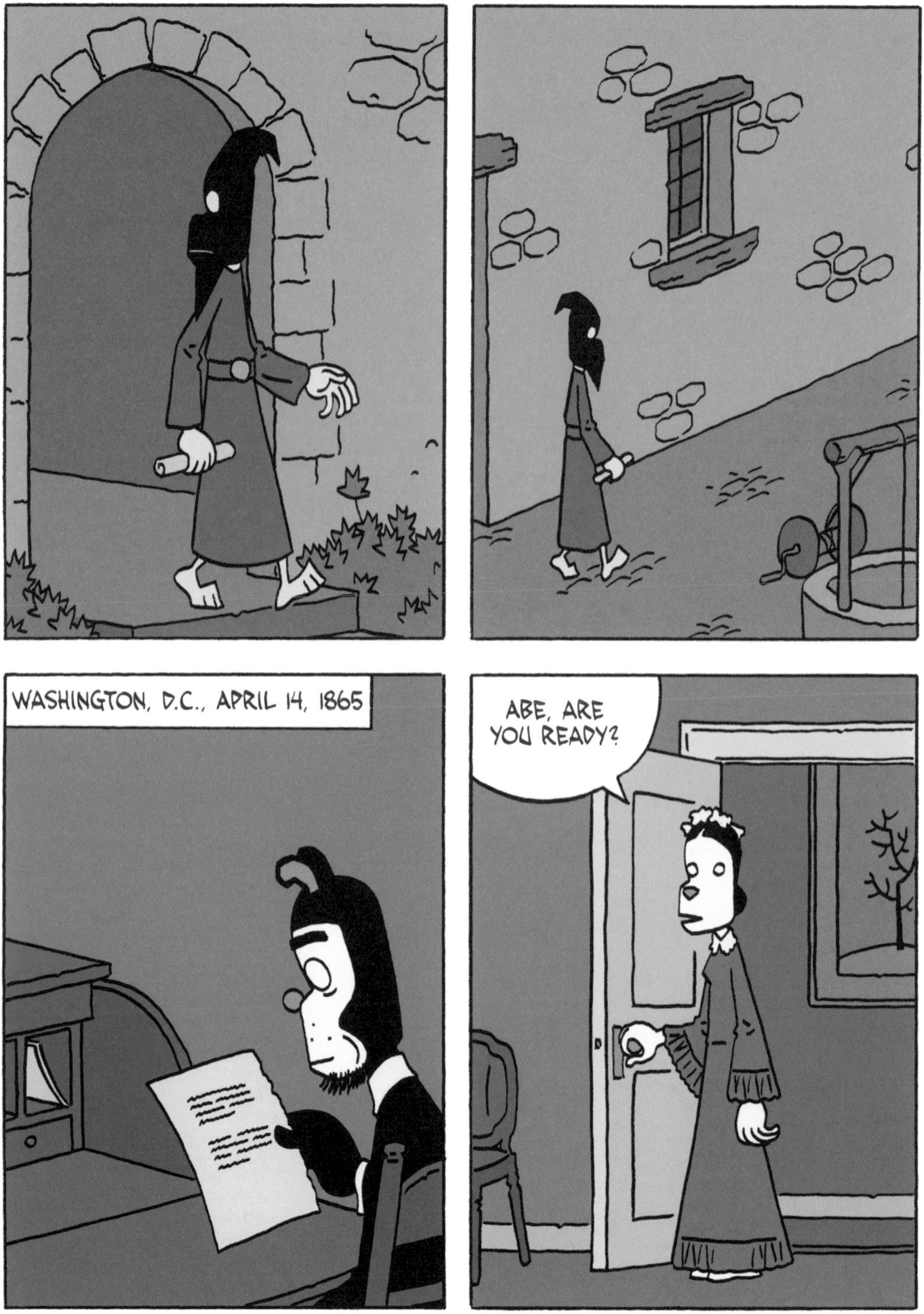
WASHINGTON, D.C., APRIL 14, 1865
ABE, ARE YOU READY?

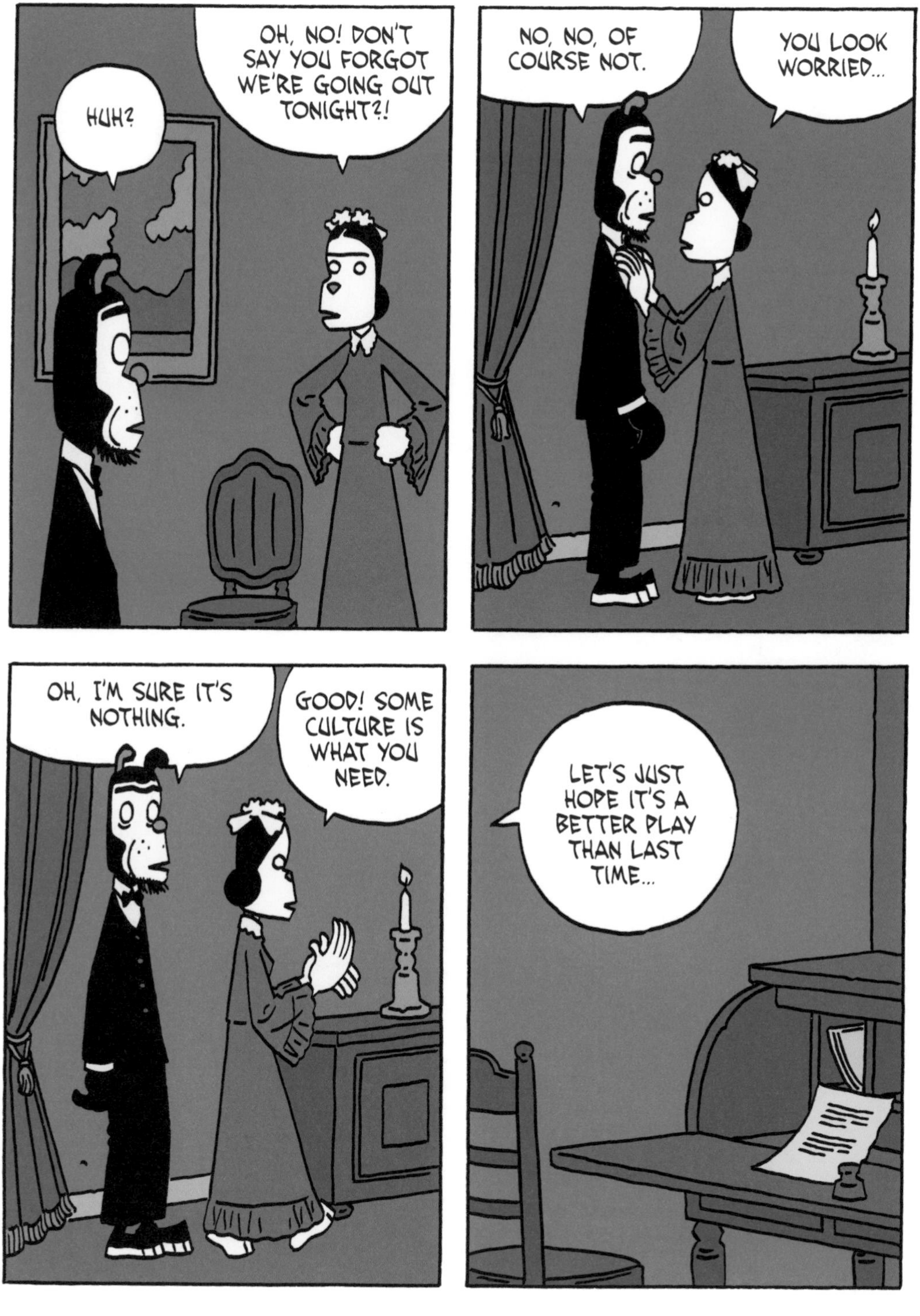

HUH?
OH, NO! DON'T SAY YOU FORGOT WE'RE GOING OUT TONIGHT?!
NO, NO, OF COURSE NOT.
YOU LOOK WORRIED...
OH, I'M SURE IT'S NOTHING.
GOOD! SOME CULTURE IS WHAT YOU NEED.
LET'S JUST HOPE IT'S A BETTER PLAY THAN LAST TIME...

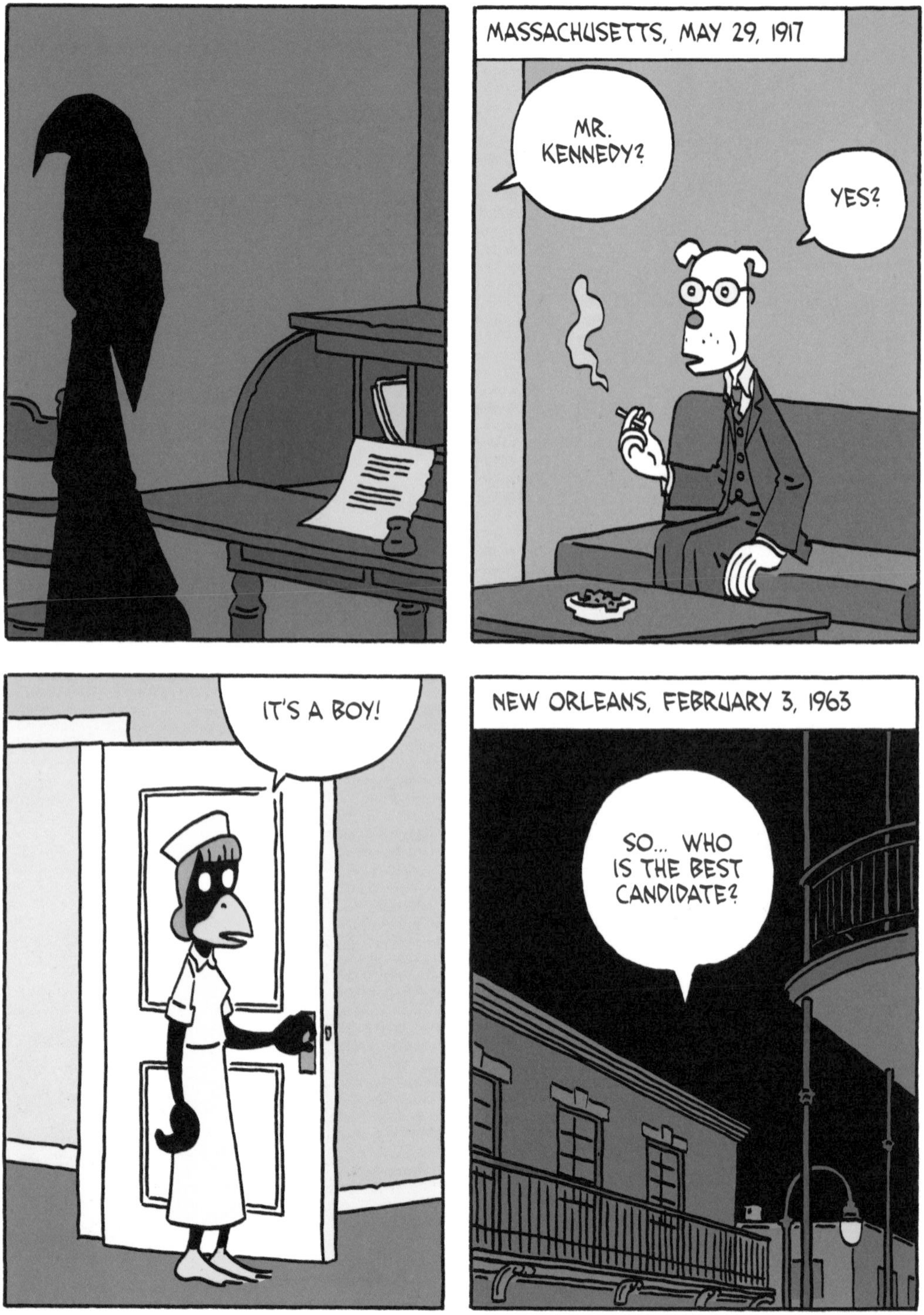
MASSACHUSETTS, MAY 29, 1917
MR. KENNEDY?
YES?
IT'S A BOY!
NEW ORLEANS, FEBRUARY 3, 1963
SO... WHO IS THE BEST CANDIDATE?

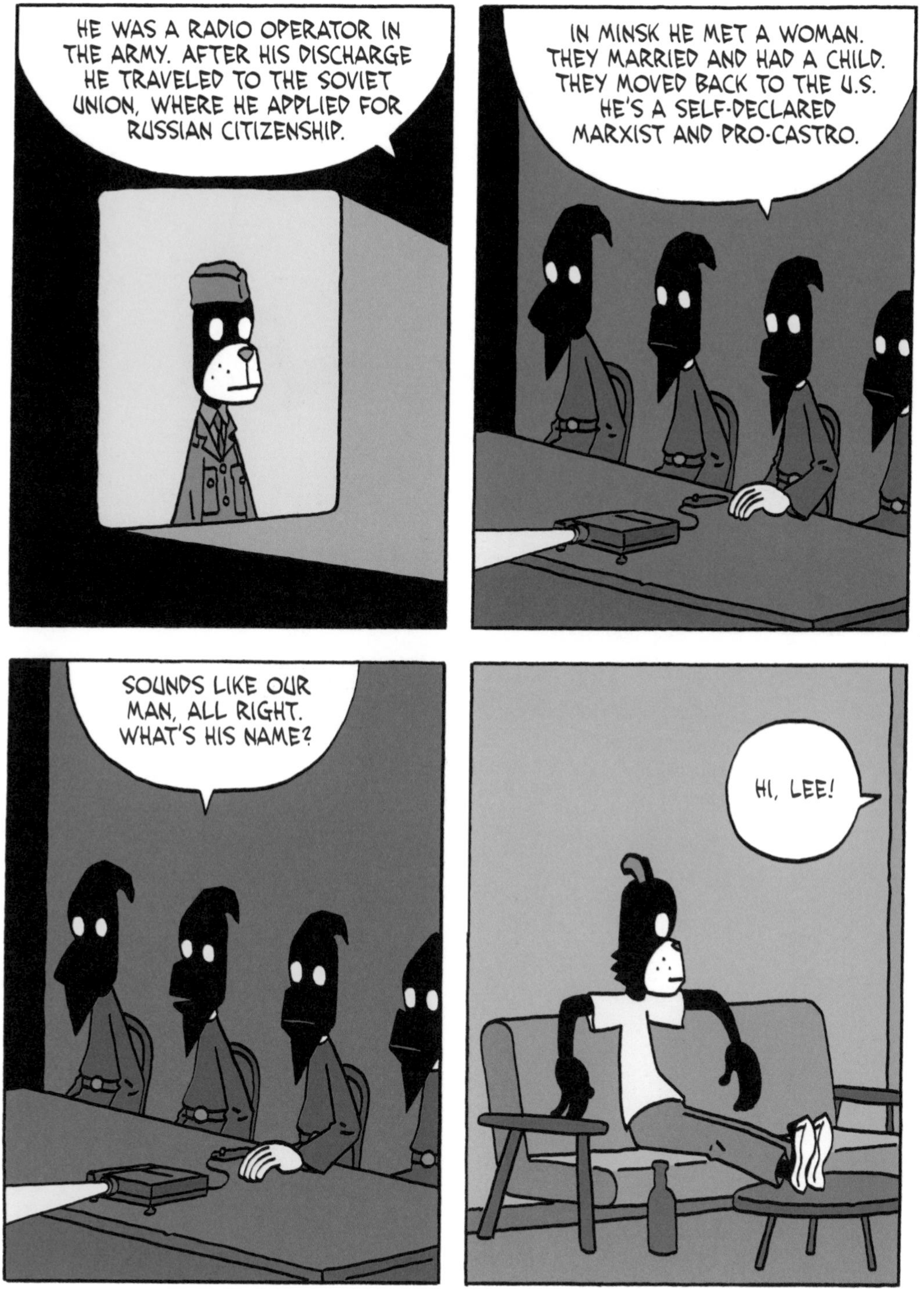
HE WAS A RADIO OPERATOR IN THE ARMY. AFTER HIS DISCHARGE HE TRAVELED TO THE SOVIET UNION, WHERE HE APPLIED FOR RUSSIAN CITIZENSHIP.
IN MINSK HE MET A WOMAN. THEY MARRIED AND HAD A CHILD. THEY MOVED BACK TO THE U.S. HE'S A SELF-DECLARED MARXIST AND PRO-CASTRO.
SOUNDS LIKE OUR MAN, ALL RIGHT. WHAT'S HIS NAME?
HI, LEE!

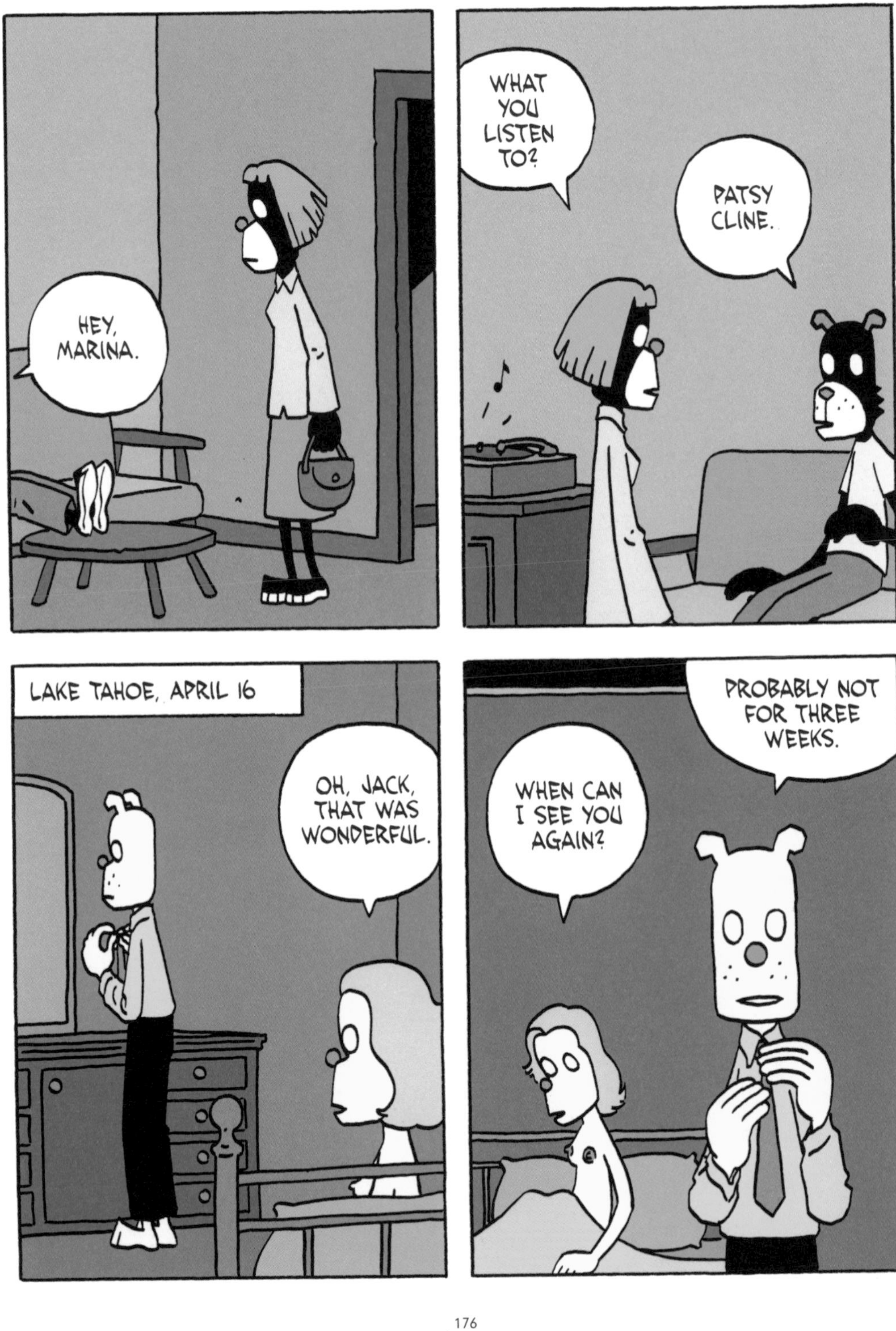
HEY, MARINA.
WHAT YOU LISTEN TO?
PATSY CLINE.
LAKE TAHOE, APRIL 16
OH, JACK, THAT WAS WONDERFUL.
WHEN CAN I SEE YOU AGAIN?
PROBABLY NOT FOR THREE WEEKS.

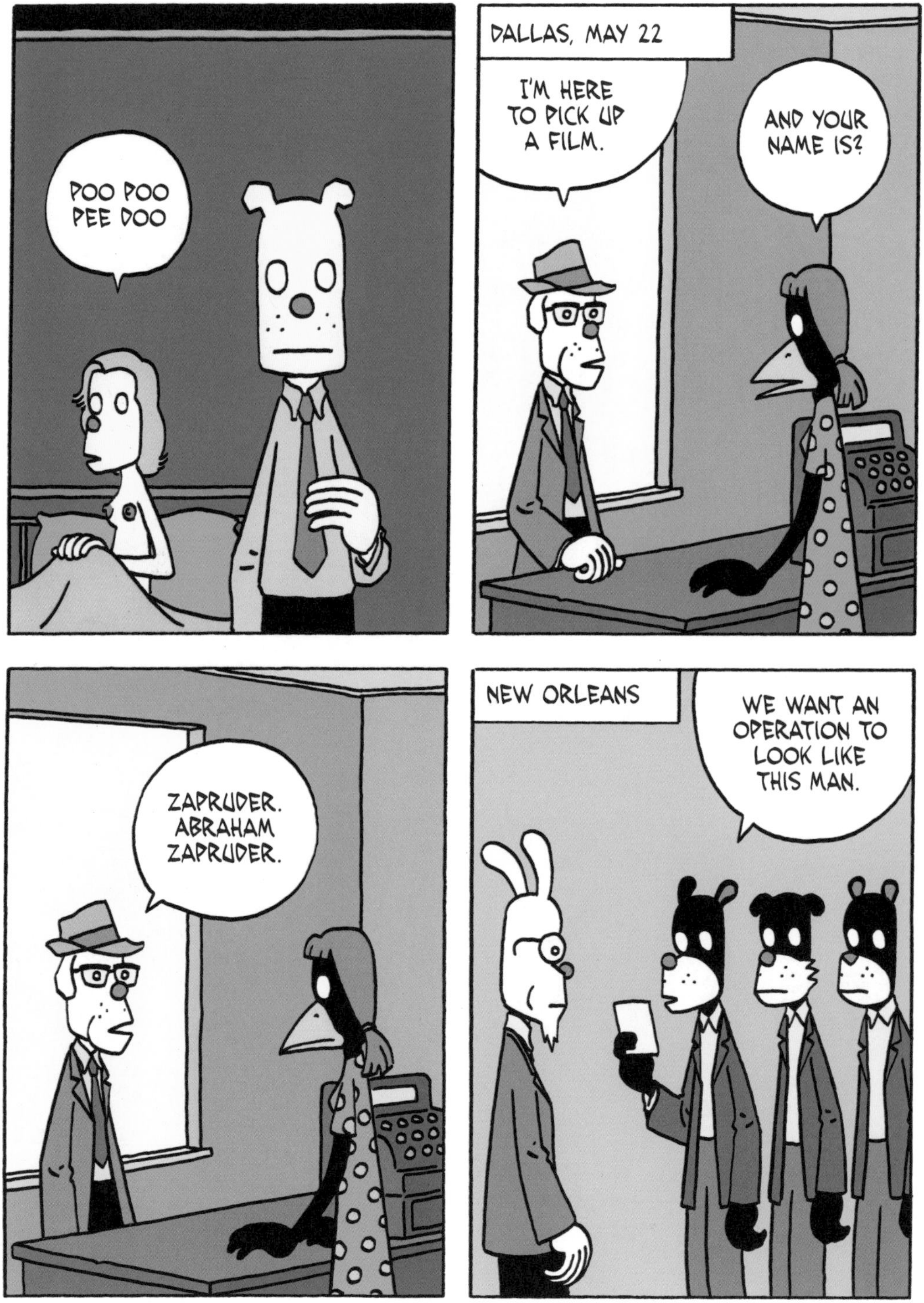
POO POO
PEE DOO
DALLAS, MAY 22
I'M HERE
TO PICK UP
A FILM.
AND YOUR
NAME IS?
ZAPRUDER.
ABRAHAM
ZAPRUDER.
NEW ORLEANS
WE WANT AN
OPERATION TO
LOOK LIKE
THIS MAN.

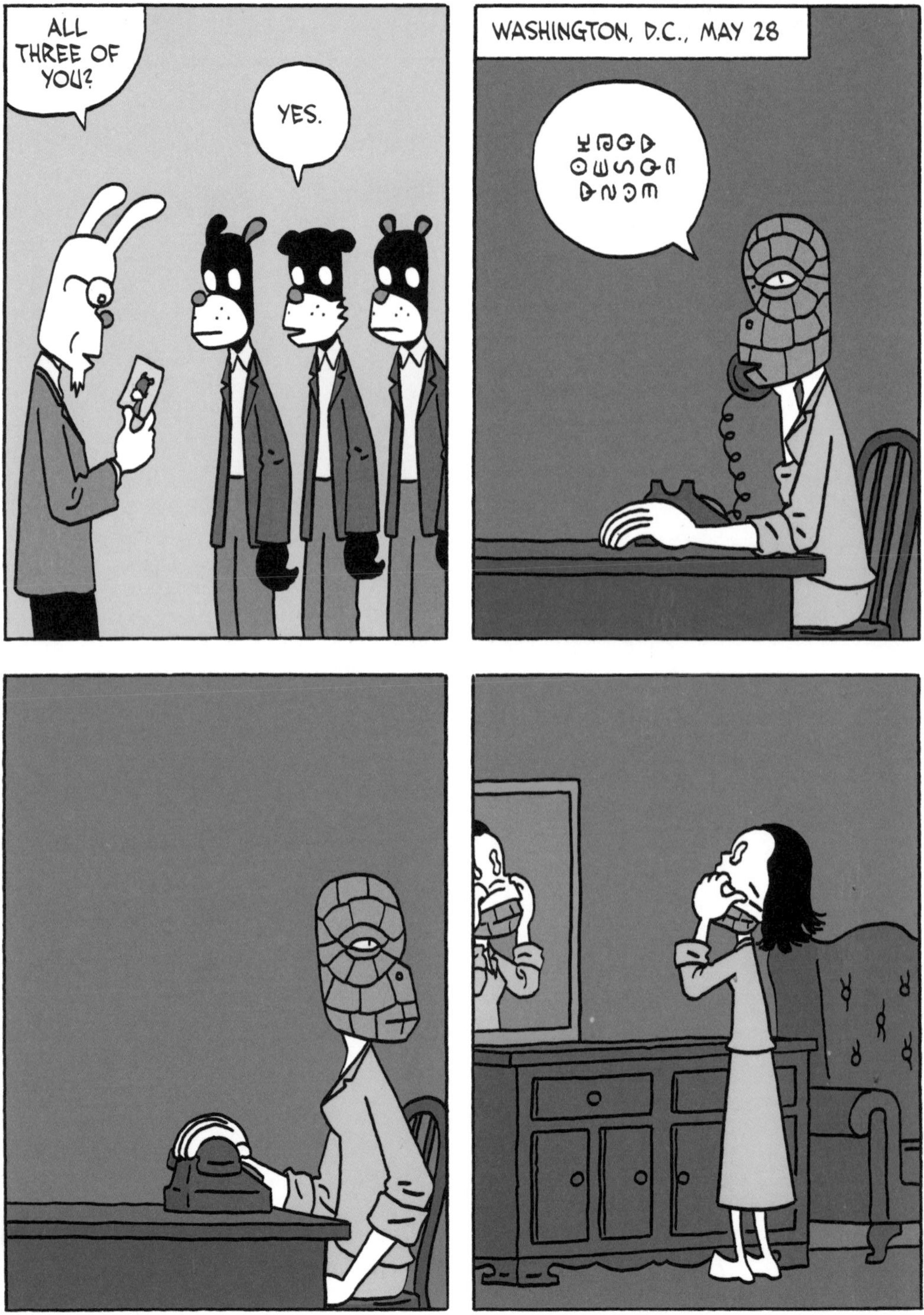
ALL THREE OF YOU?
YES.
WASHINGTON, D.C., MAY 28

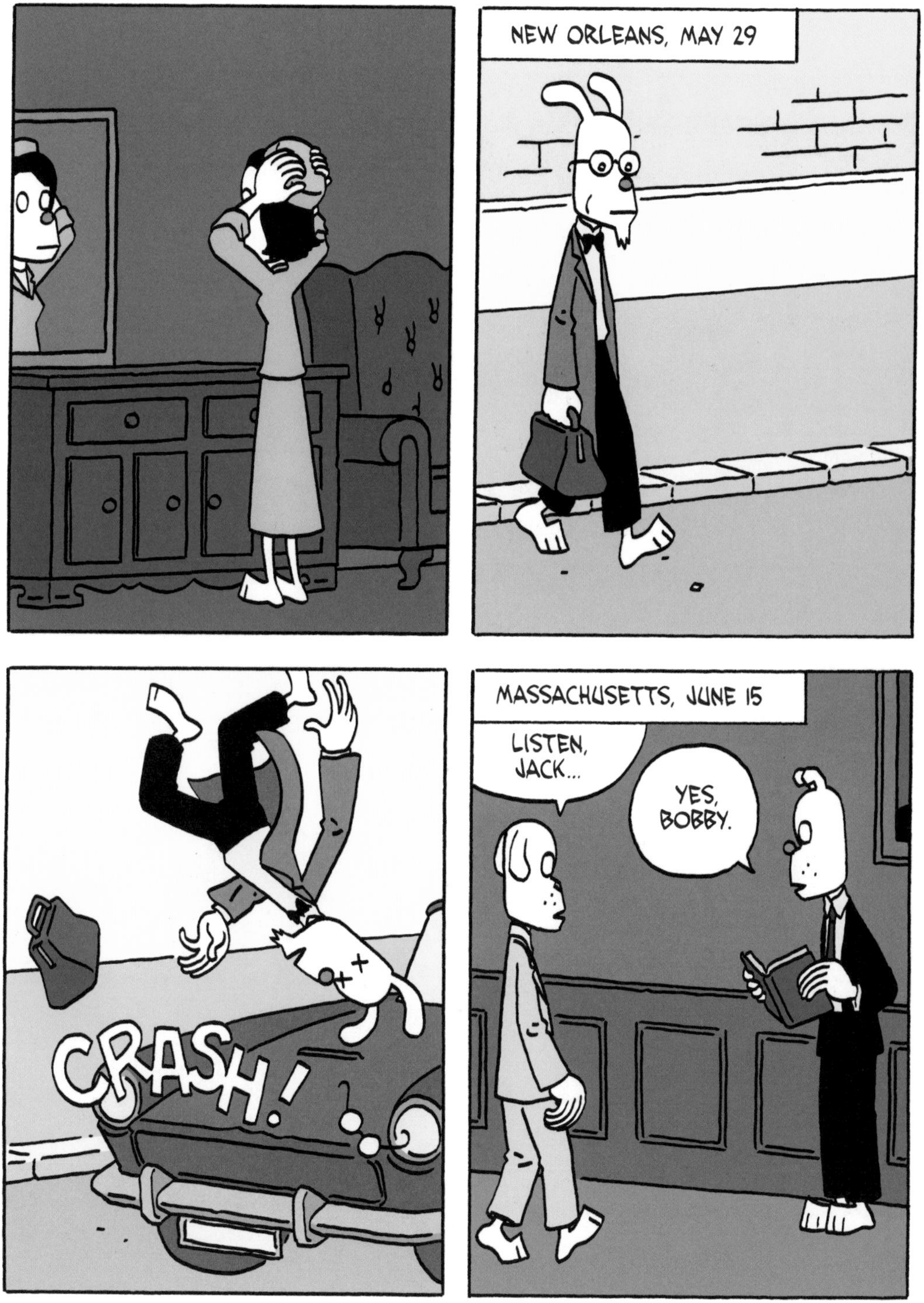
NEW ORLEANS, MAY 29
CRASH!
MASSACHUSETTS, JUNE 15
LISTEN, JACK...
YES, BOBBY.

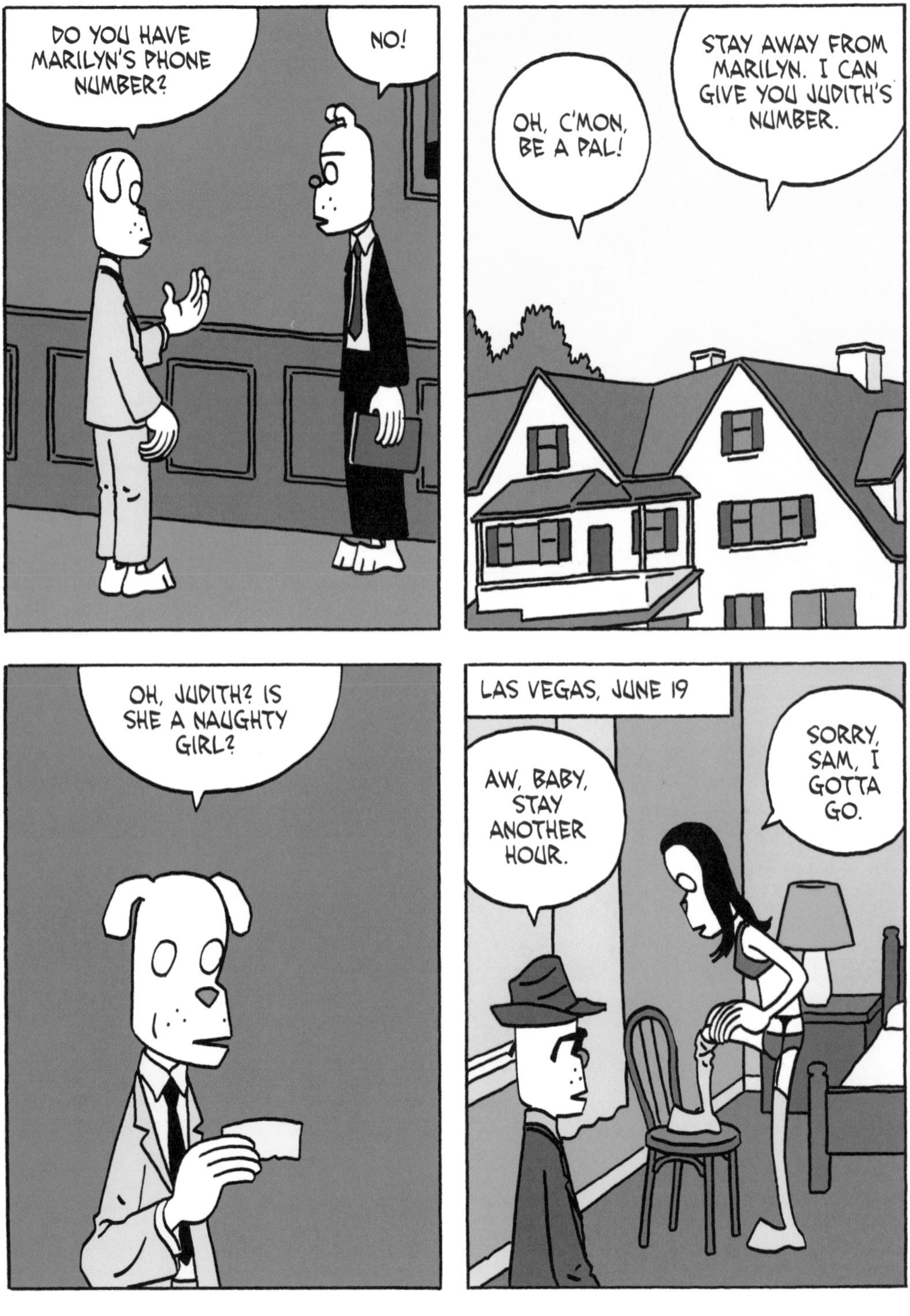
DO YOU HAVE MARILYN'S PHONE NUMBER?
NO!
OH, C'MON, BE A PAL!
STAY AWAY FROM MARILYN. I CAN GIVE YOU JUDITH'S NUMBER.
OH, JUDITH? IS SHE A NAUGHTY GIRL?
LAS VEGAS, JUNE 19
AW, BABY, STAY ANOTHER HOUR.
SORRY, SAM, I GOTTA GO.

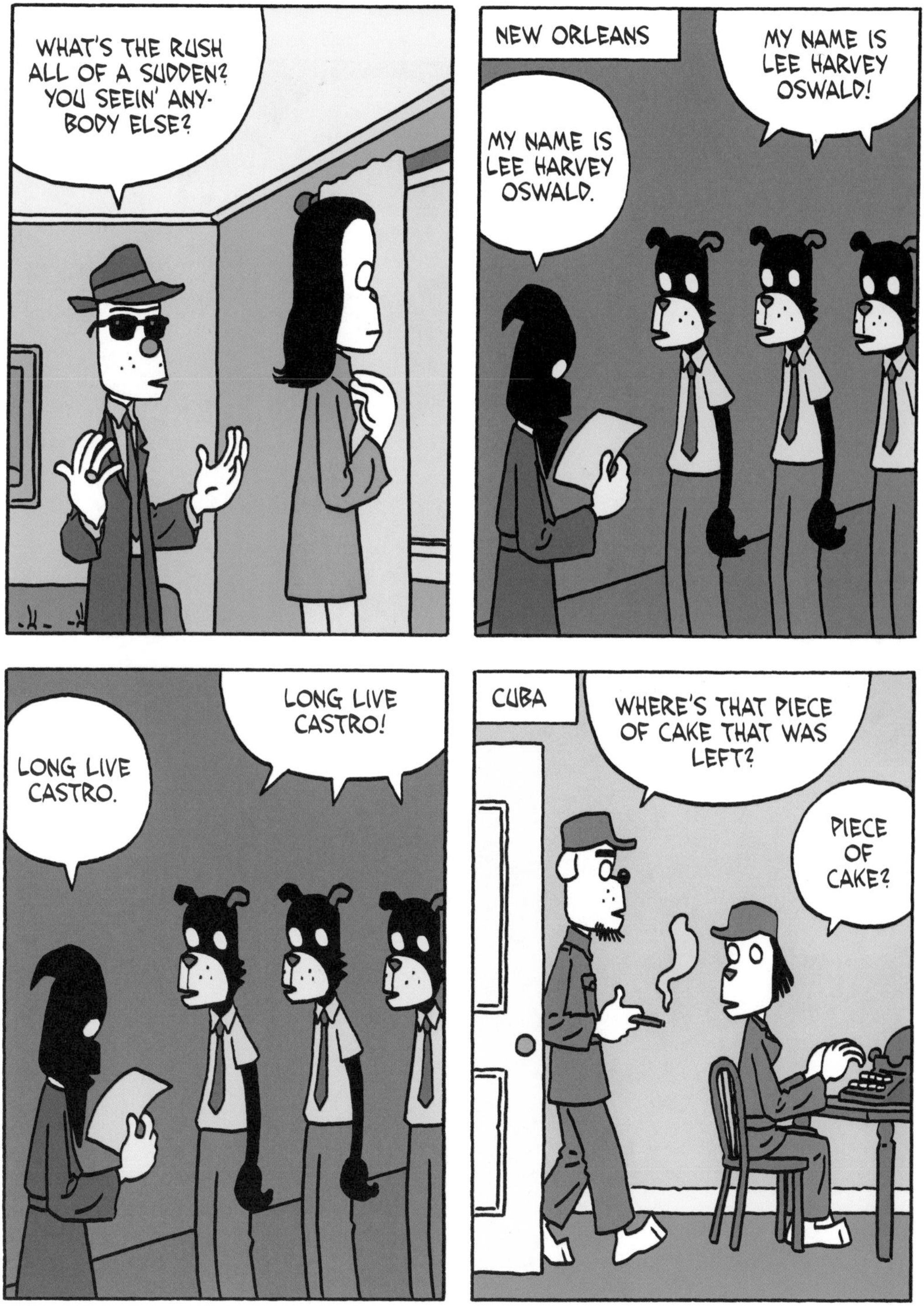
WHAT'S THE RUSH ALL OF A SUDDEN? YOU SEEIN' ANY-BODY ELSE?
NEW ORLEANS
MY NAME IS LEE HARVEY OSWALD.
MY NAME IS LEE HARVEY OSWALD!
LONG LIVE CASTRO.
LONG LIVE CASTRO!
CUBA
WHERE'S THAT PIECE OF CAKE THAT WAS LEFT?
PIECE OF CAKE?

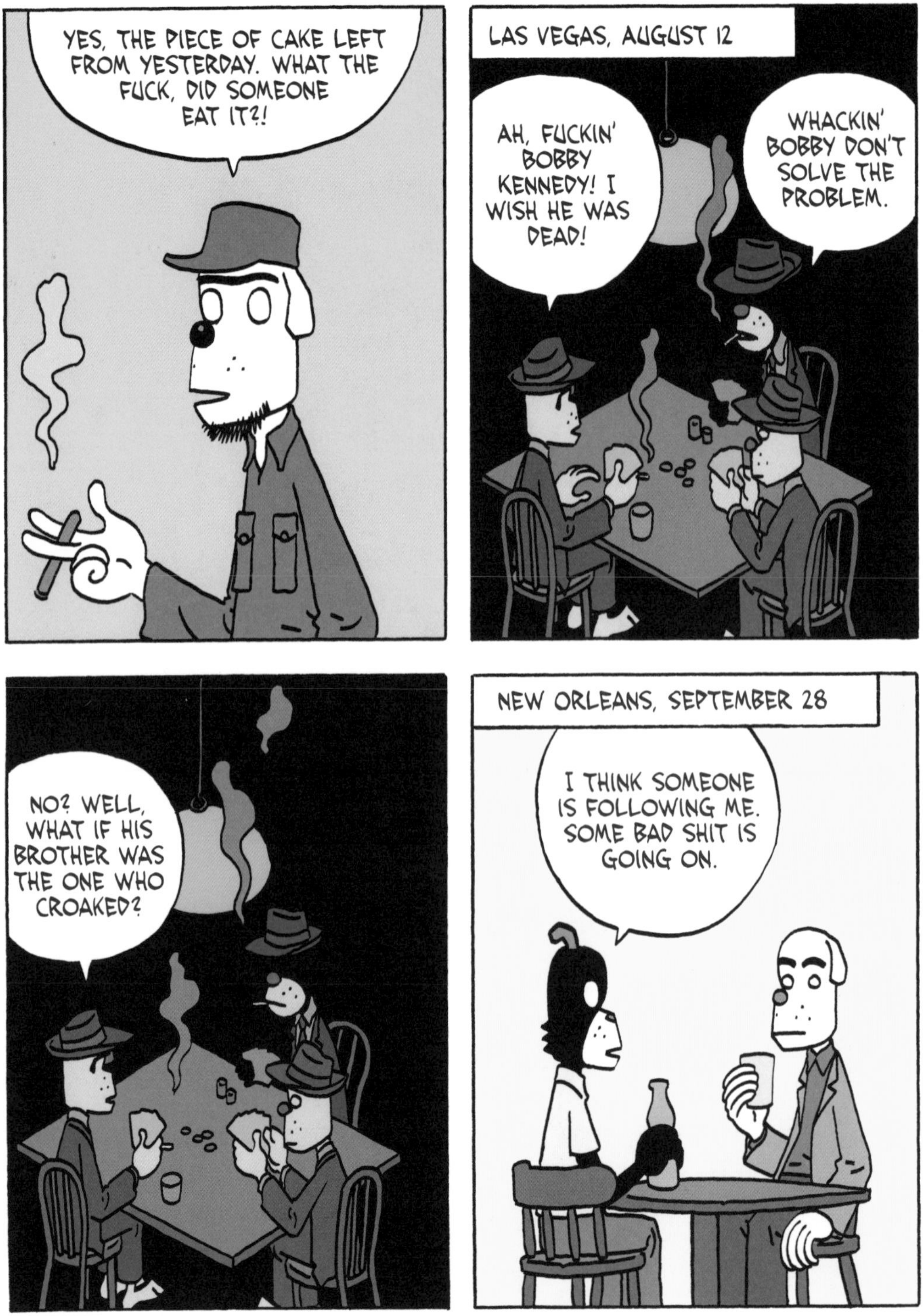
YES, THE PIECE OF CAKE LEFT FROM YESTERDAY. WHAT THE FUCK, DID SOMEONE EAT IT?!
LAS VEGAS, AUGUST 12
AH, FUCKIN' BOBBY KENNEDY! I WISH HE WAS DEAD!
WHACKIN' BOBBY DON'T SOLVE THE PROBLEM.
NO? WELL, WHAT IF HIS BROTHER WAS THE ONE WHO CROAKED?
NEW ORLEANS, SEPTEMBER 28
I THINK SOMEONE IS FOLLOWING ME. SOME BAD SHIT IS GOING ON.

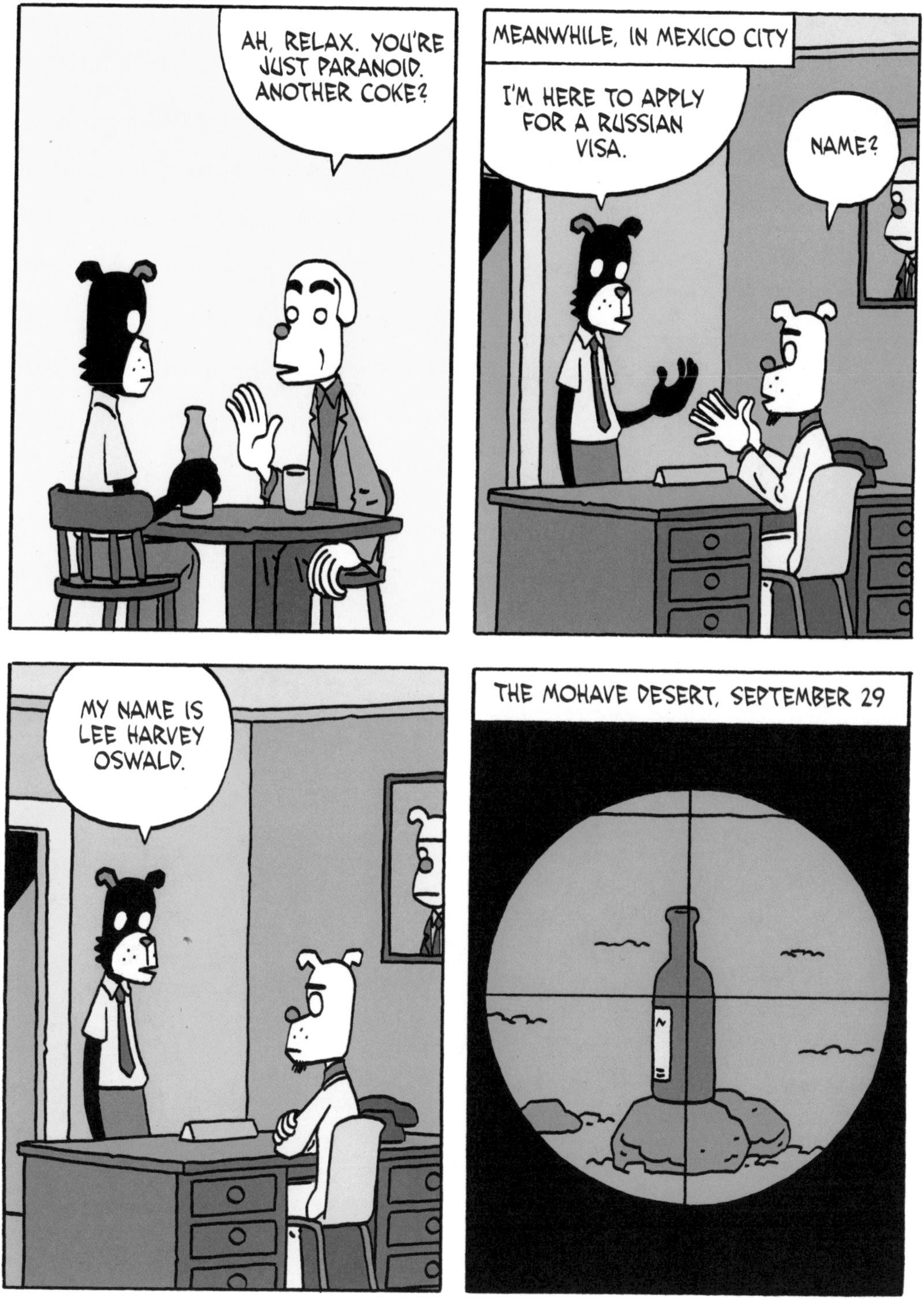
AH, RELAX. YOU'RE JUST PARANOID. ANOTHER COKE?
MEANWHILE, IN MEXICO CITY
I'M HERE TO APPLY FOR A RUSSIAN VISA.
NAME?
MY NAME IS LEE HARVEY OSWALD.
THE MOHAVE DESERT, SEPTEMBER 29

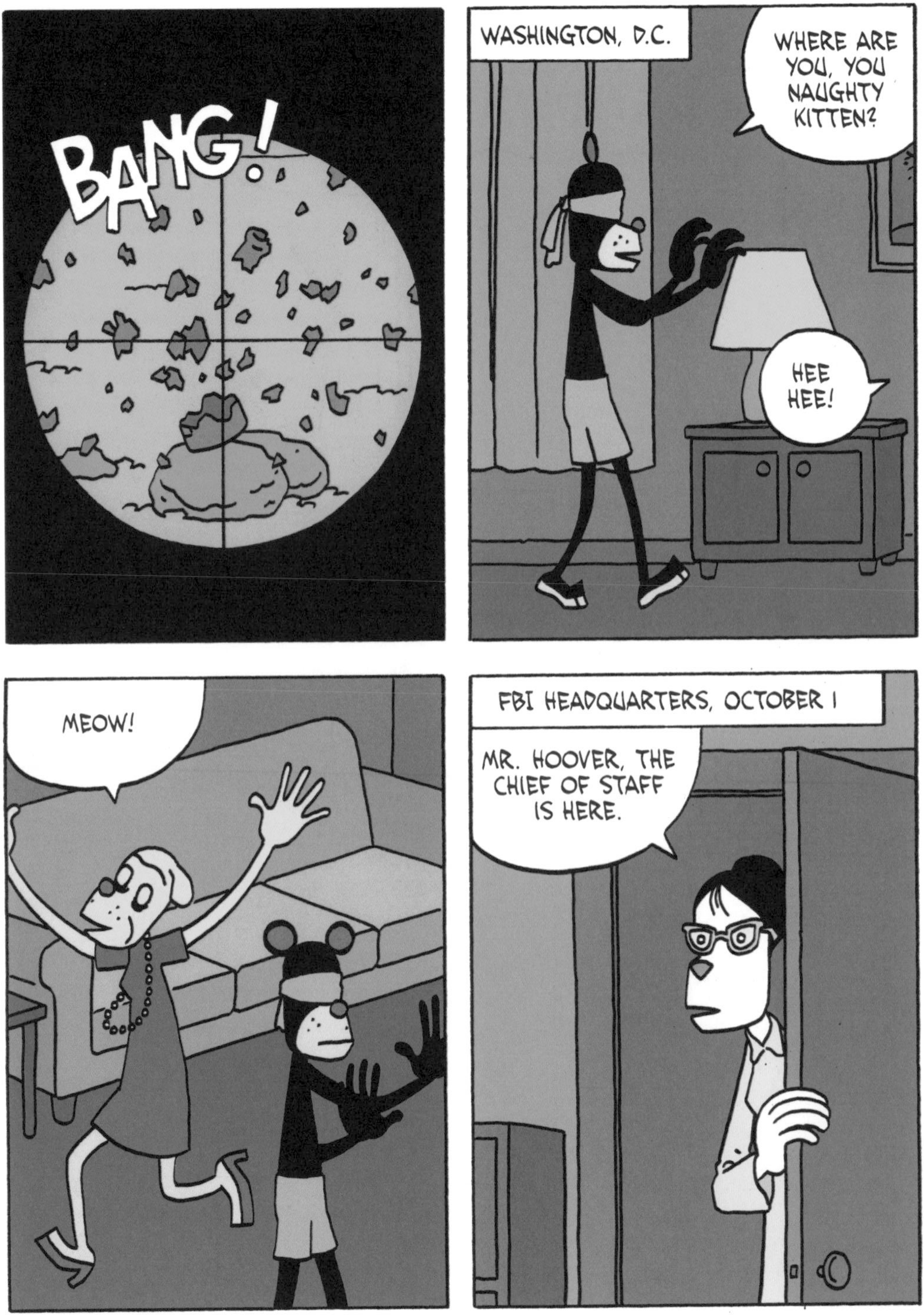
BANG!
WASHINGTON, D.C.
WHERE ARE YOU, YOU NAUGHTY KITTEN?
HEE HEE!
MEOW!
FBI HEADQUARTERS, OCTOBER 1
MR. HOOVER, THE CHIEF OF STAFF IS HERE.

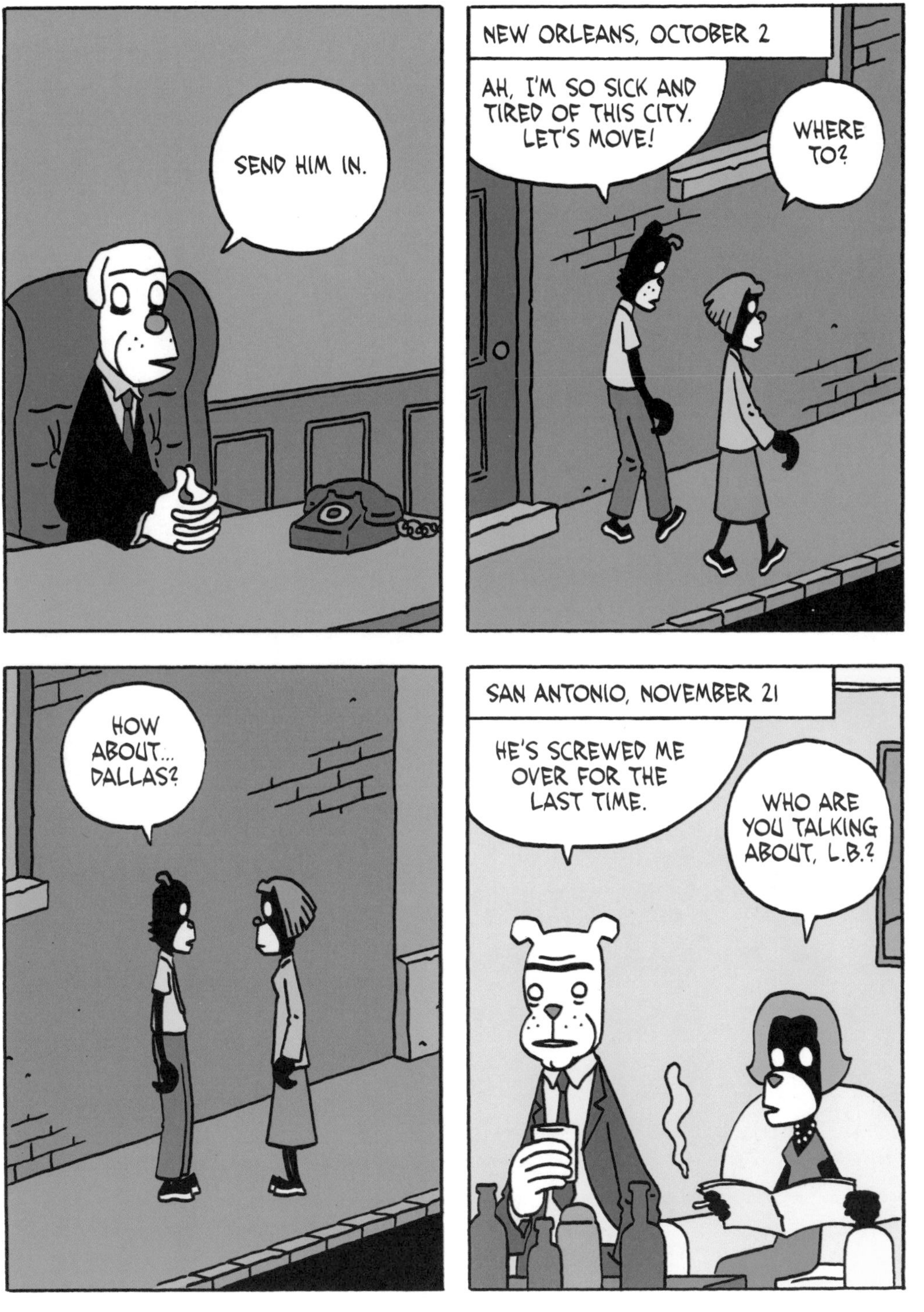
SEND HIM IN.
NEW ORLEANS, OCTOBER 2
AH, I'M SO SICK AND TIRED OF THIS CITY. LET'S MOVE!
WHERE TO?
HOW ABOUT... DALLAS?
SAN ANTONIO, NOVEMBER 21
HE'S SCREWED ME OVER FOR THE LAST TIME.
WHO ARE YOU TALKING ABOUT, L.B.?

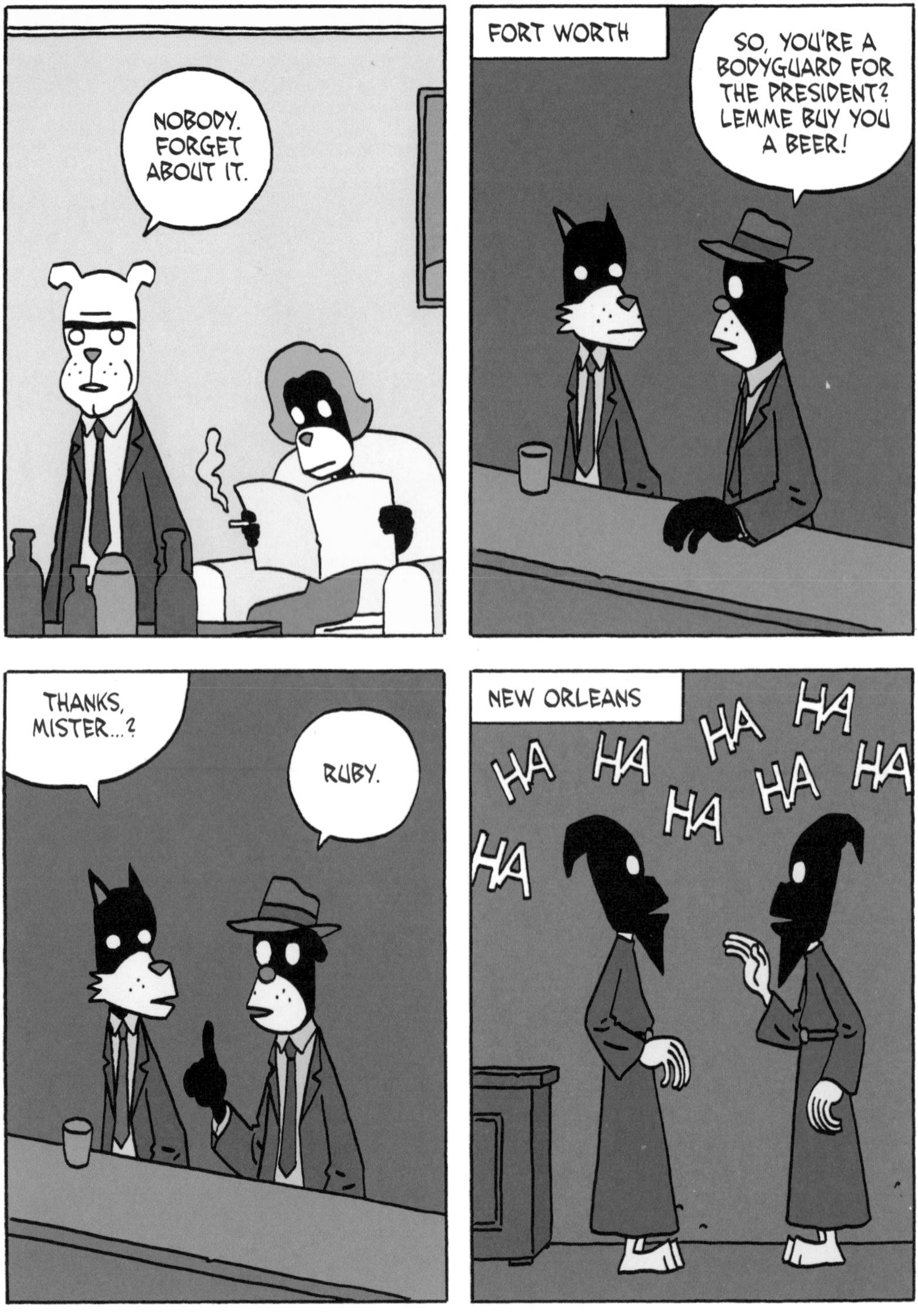
NOBODY. FORGET ABOUT IT.
FORT WORTH
SO, YOU'RE A BODYGUARD FOR THE PRESIDENT? LEMME BUY YOU A BEER!
THANKS, MISTER...?
RUBY.
NEW ORLEANS
HA HA HA HA HA HA HA HA HA

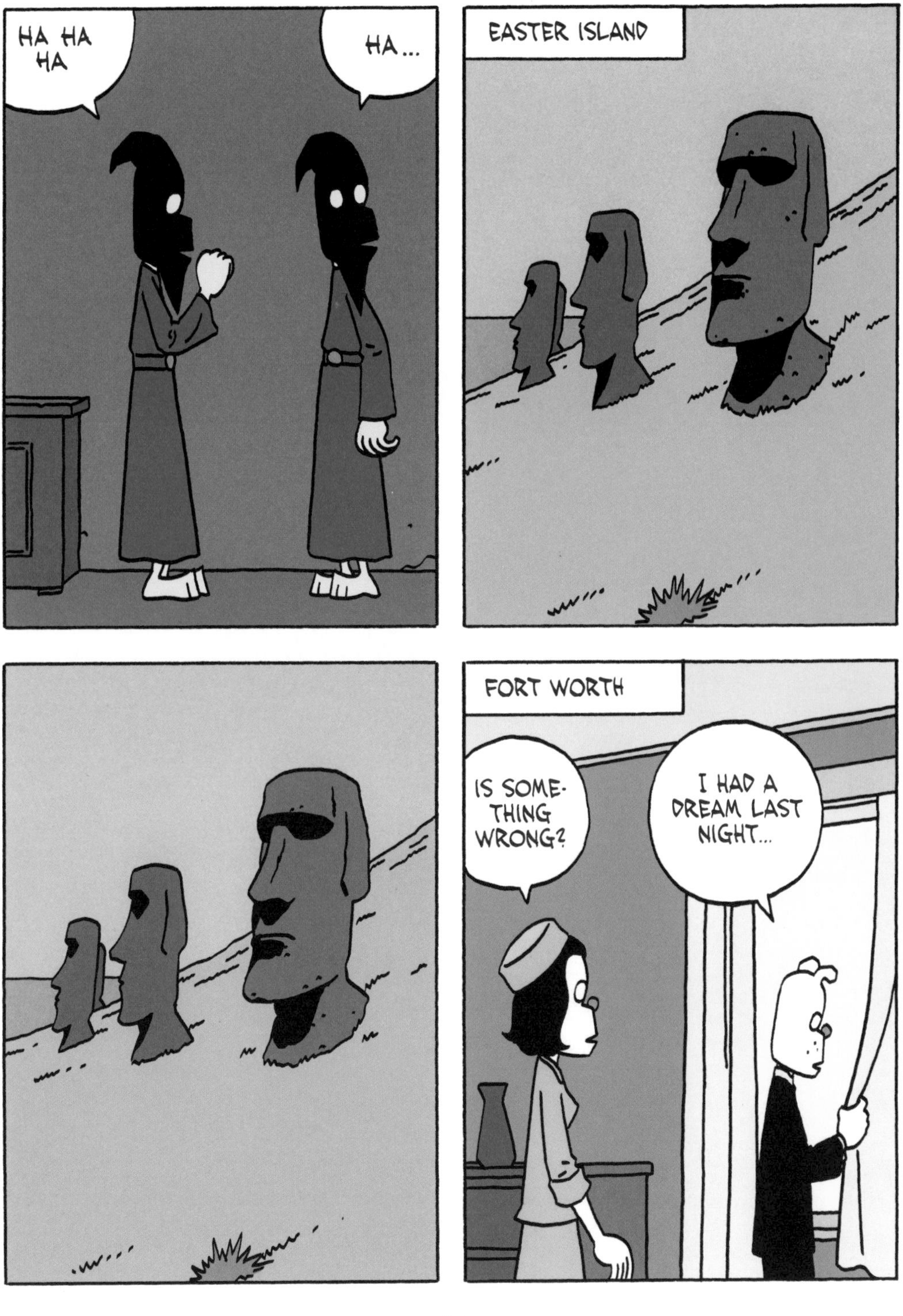
HA HA HA
HA...
EASTER ISLAND
FORT WORTH
IS SOME-THING WRONG?
I HAD A DREAM LAST NIGHT...

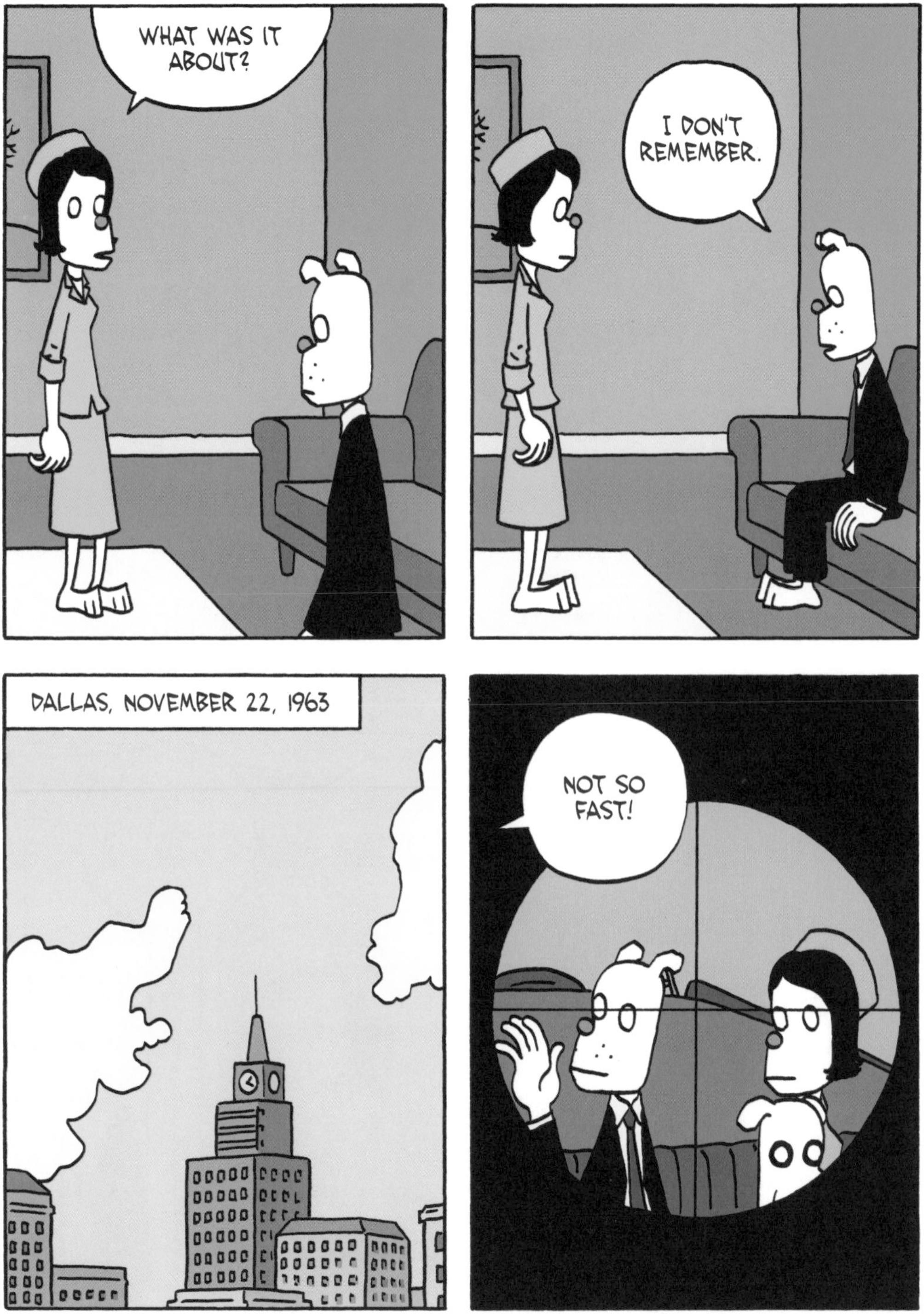
WHAT WAS IT ABOUT?
I DON'T REMEMBER.
DALLAS, NOVEMBER 22, 1963
NOT SO FAST!

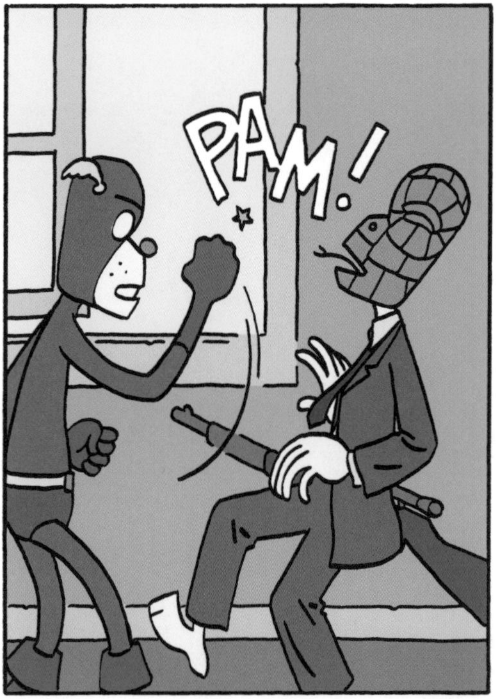
PAM!

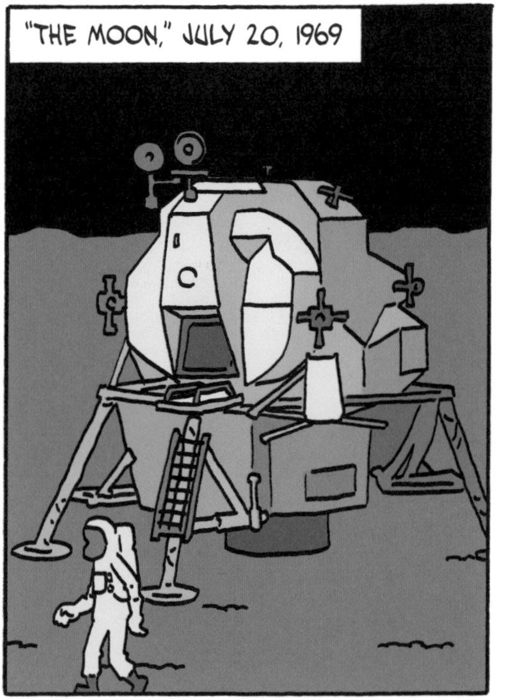
"THE MOON," JULY 20, 1969

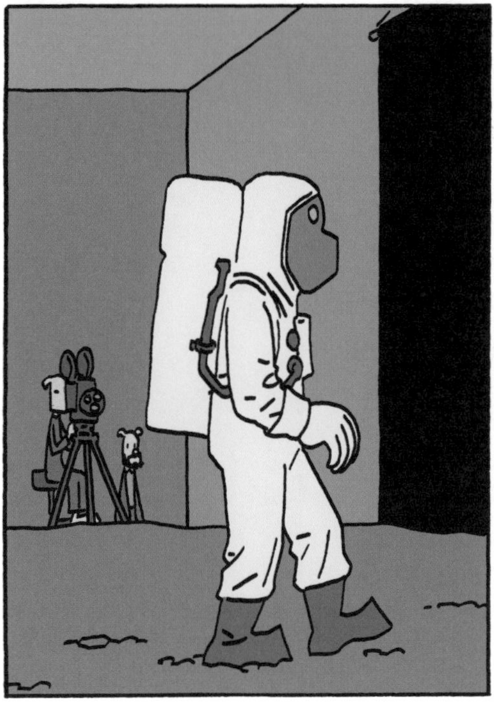

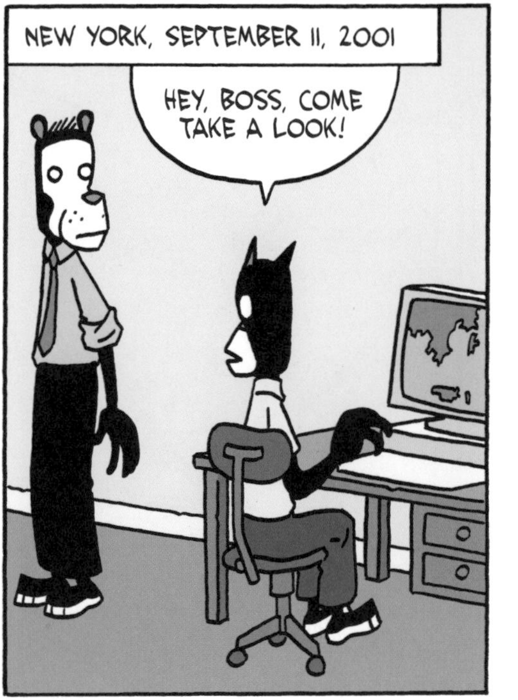
NEW YORK, SEPTEMBER 11, 2001
HEY, BOSS, COME TAKE A LOOK!

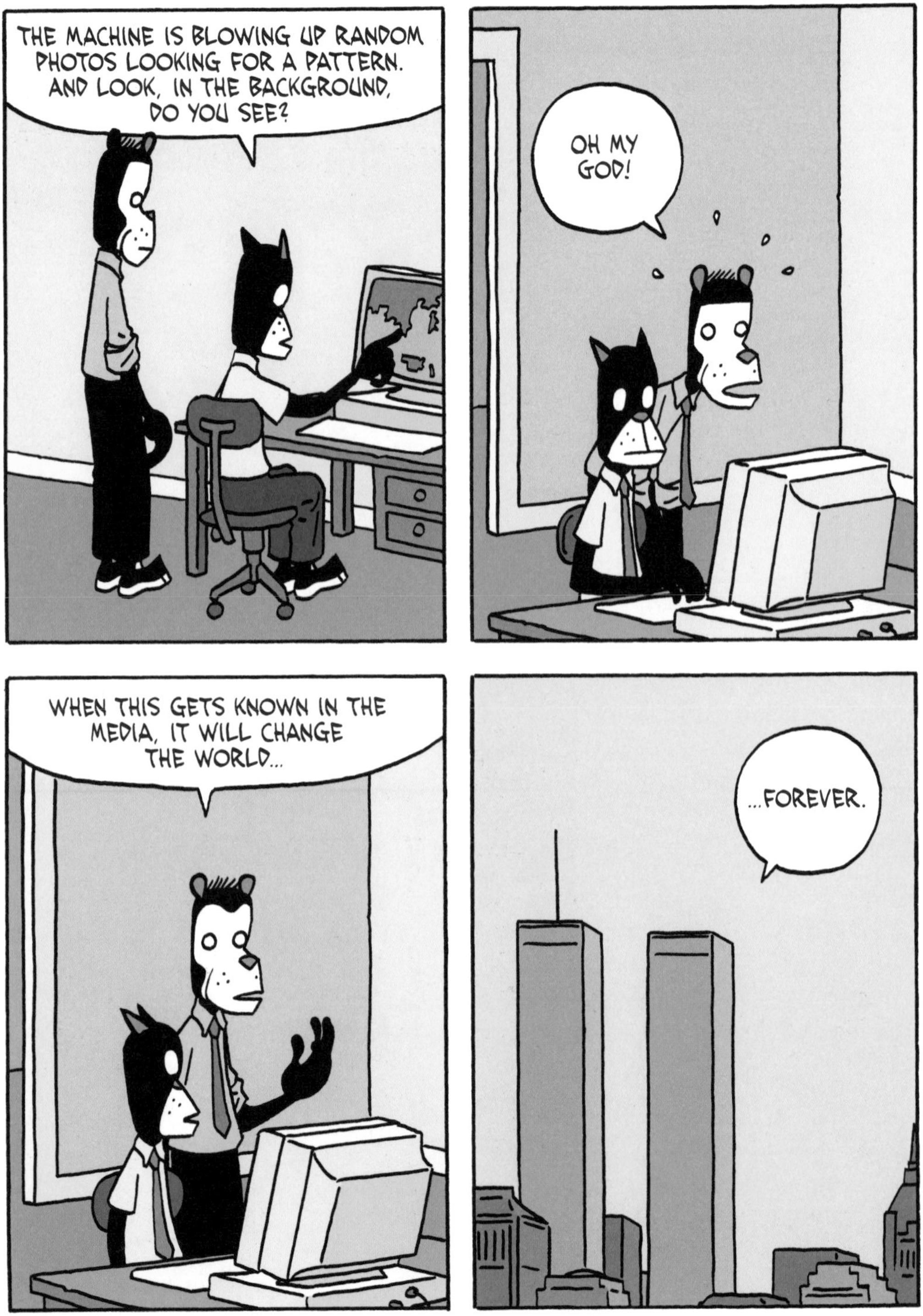
THE MACHINE IS BLOWING UP RANDOM PHOTOS LOOKING FOR A PATTERN. AND LOOK, IN THE BACKGROUND, DO YOU SEE?
OH MY GOD!
WHEN THIS GETS KNOWN IN THE MEDIA, IT WILL CHANGE THE WORLD...
...FOREVER.

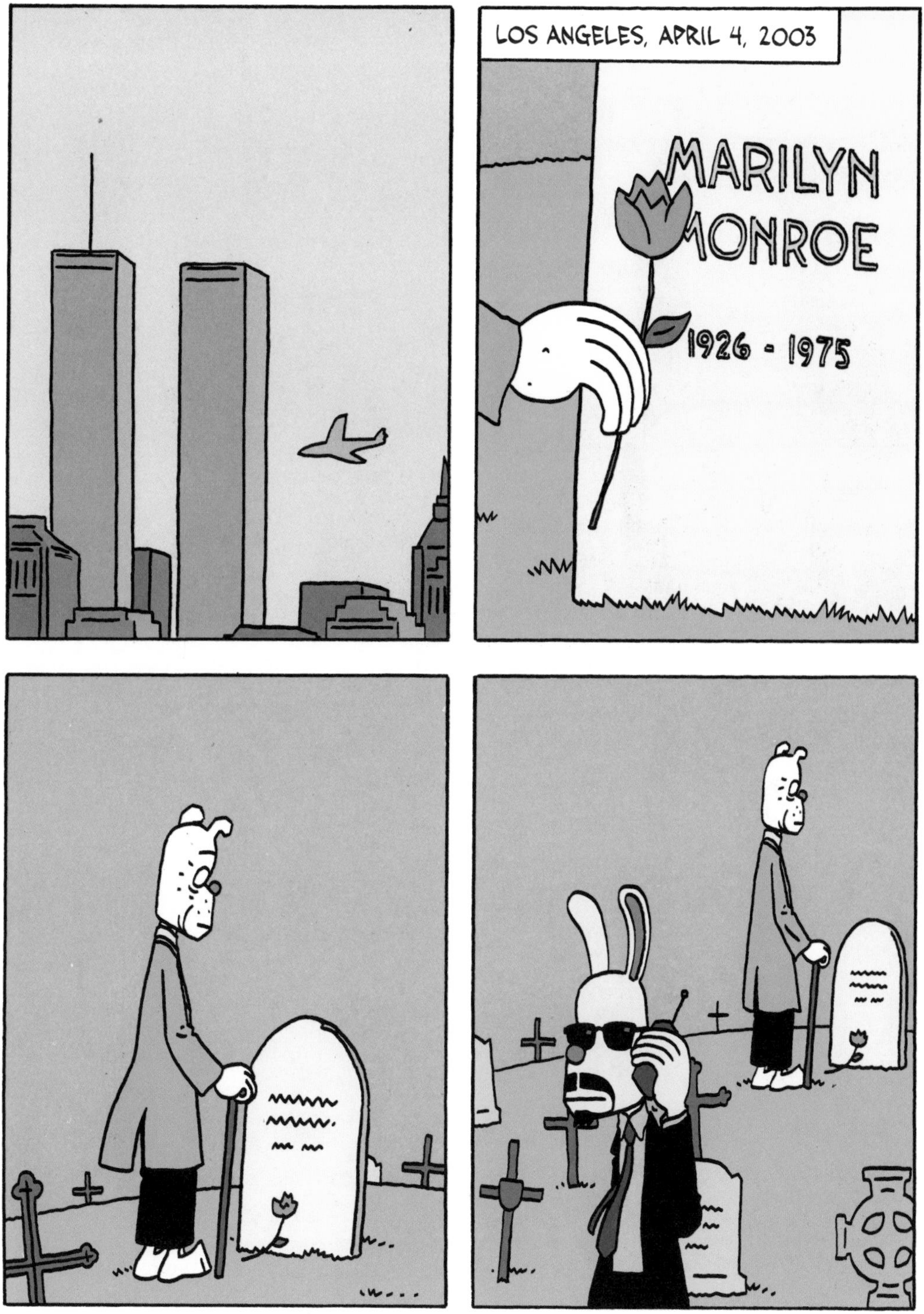
LOS ANGELES, APRIL 4, 2003
MARILYN MONROE
1926 - 1975

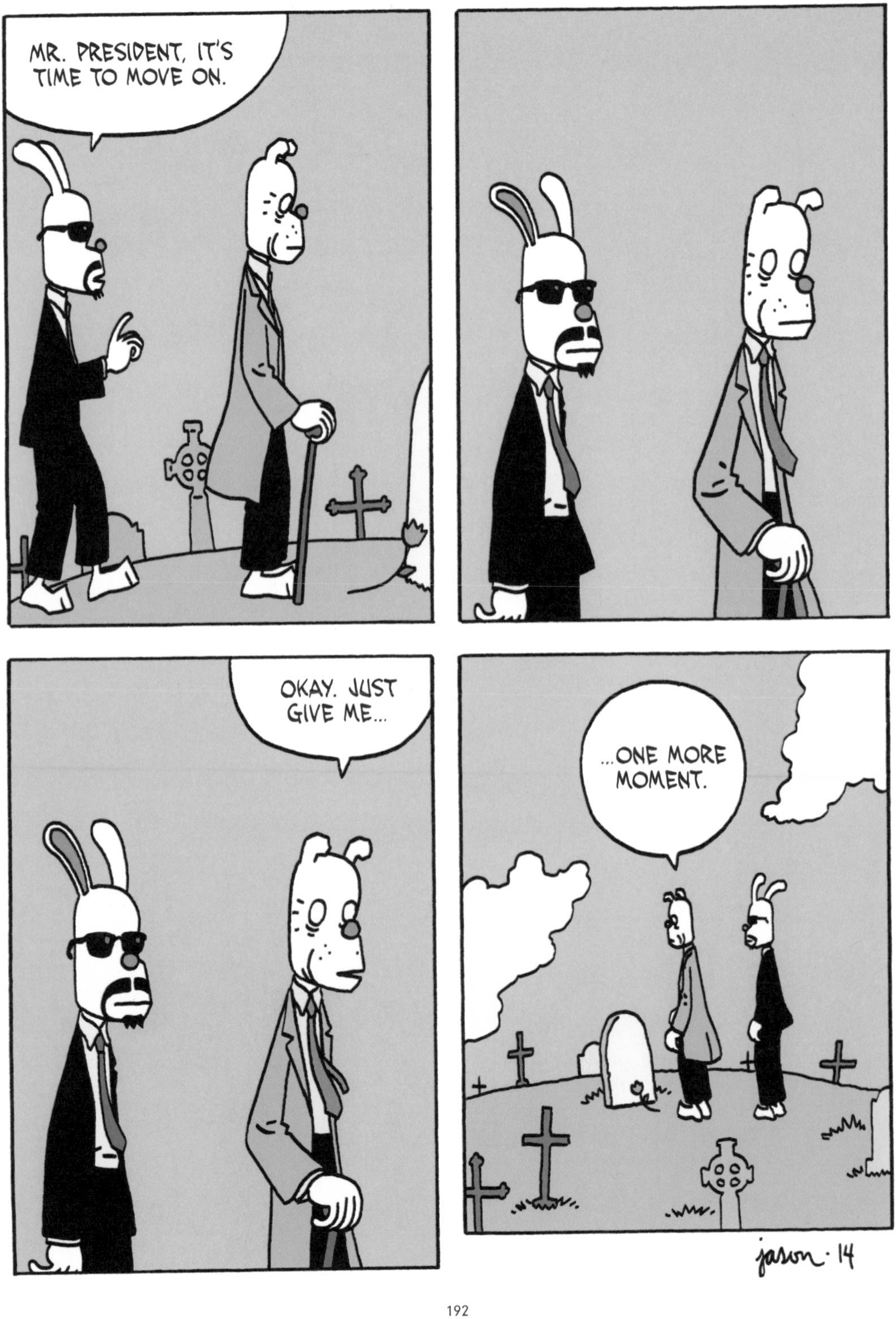
MR. PRESIDENT, IT'S TIME TO MOVE ON.
OKAY. JUST GIVE ME...
...ONE MORE MOMENT.
jason · 14

PRESENTING:

—

NOTHING

—

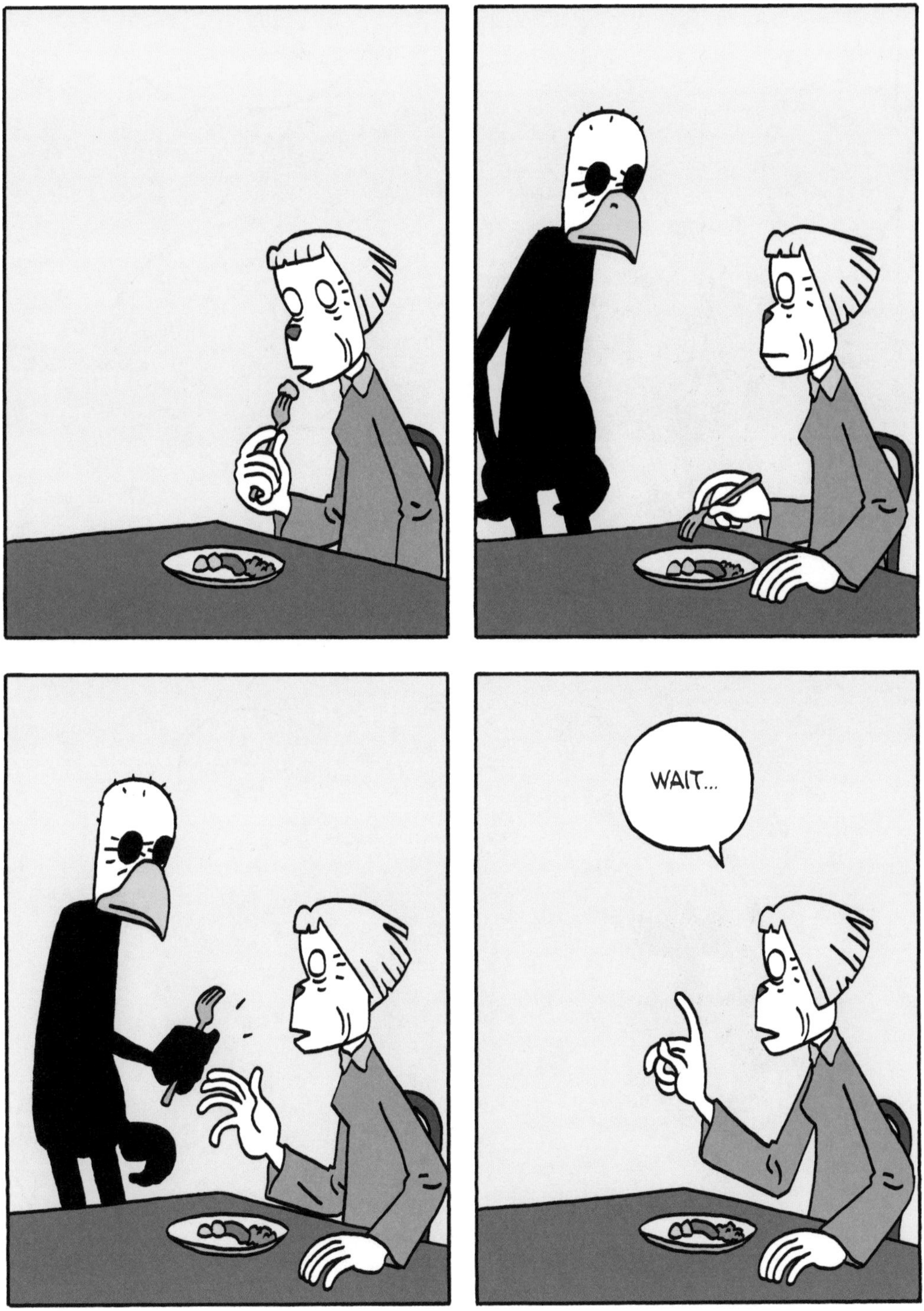
WAIT...

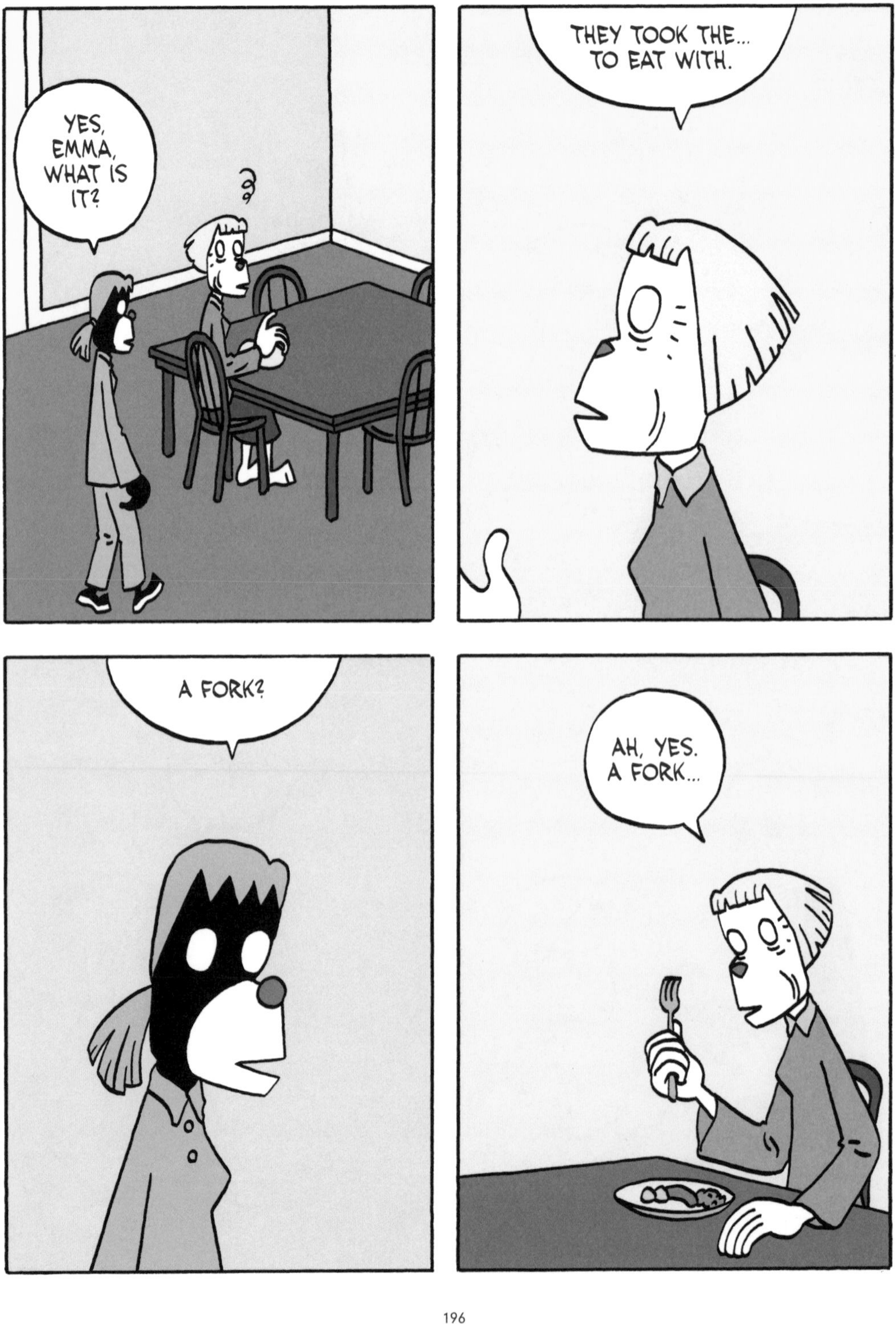
YES, EMMA, WHAT IS IT?
THEY TOOK THE... TO EAT WITH.
A FORK?
AH, YES. A FORK...

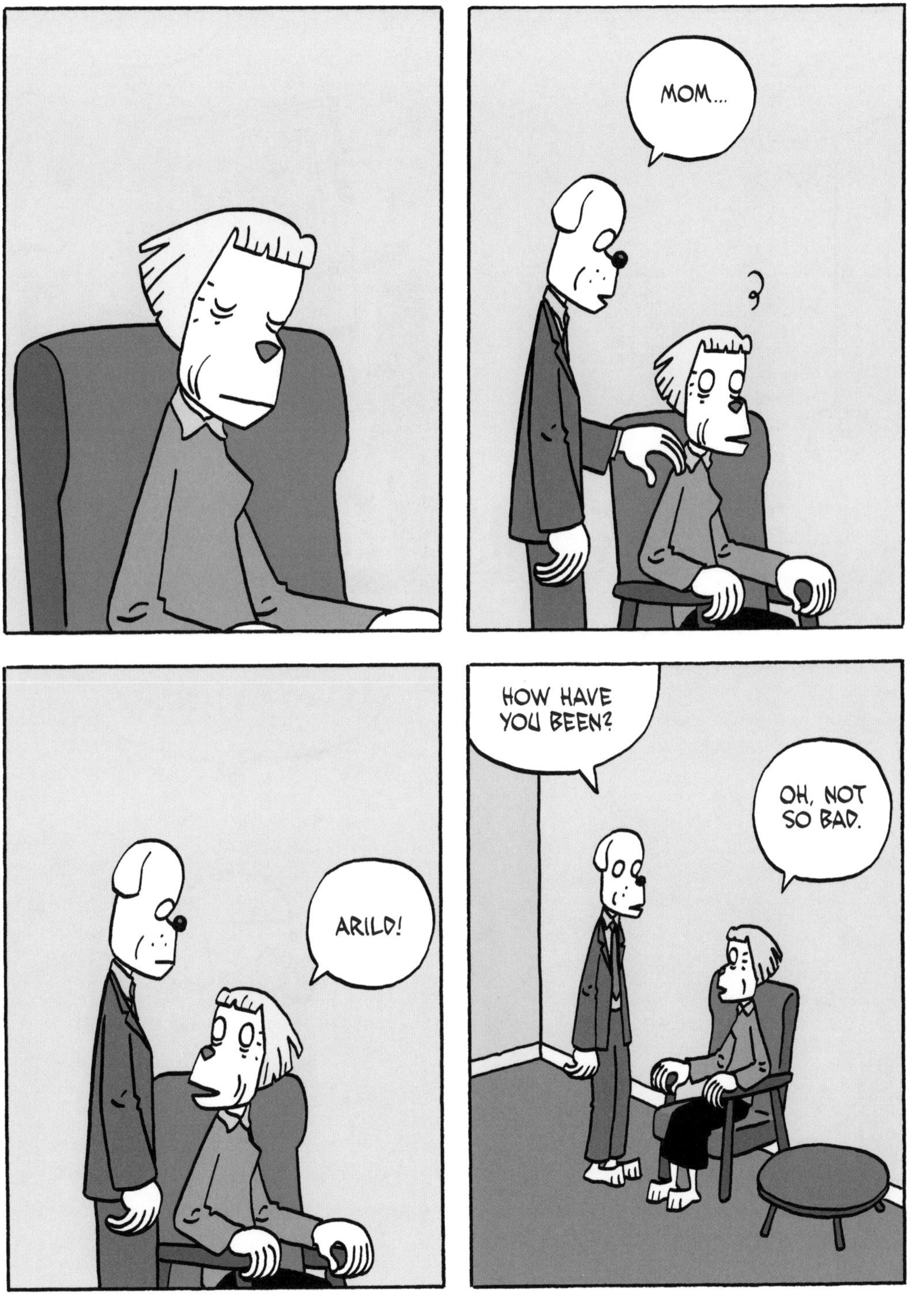
MOM...
ARILD!
HOW HAVE YOU BEEN?
OH, NOT SO BAD.

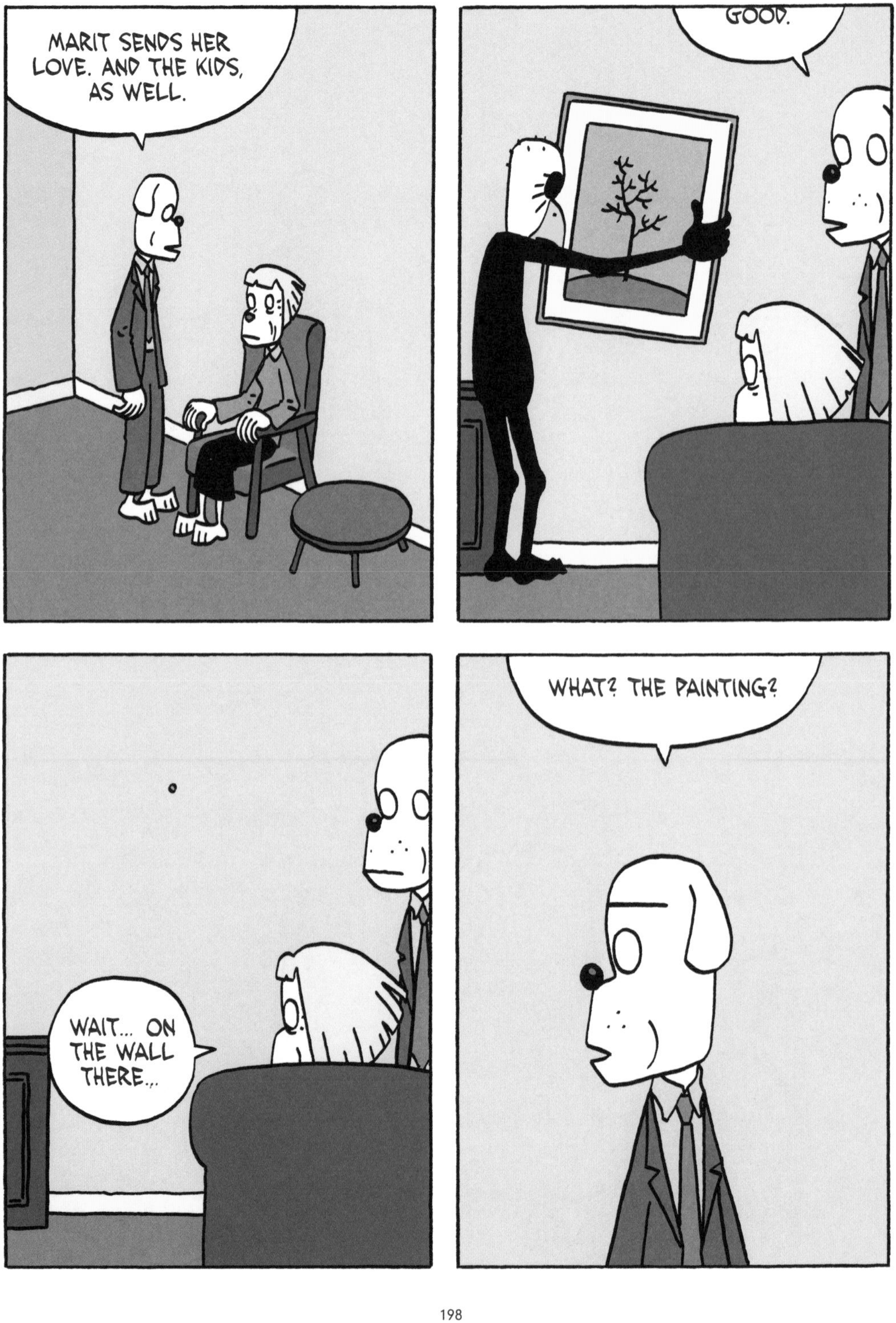
MARIT SENDS HER LOVE. AND THE KIDS, AS WELL.
GOOD.
WAIT... ON THE WALL THERE...
WHAT? THE PAINTING?

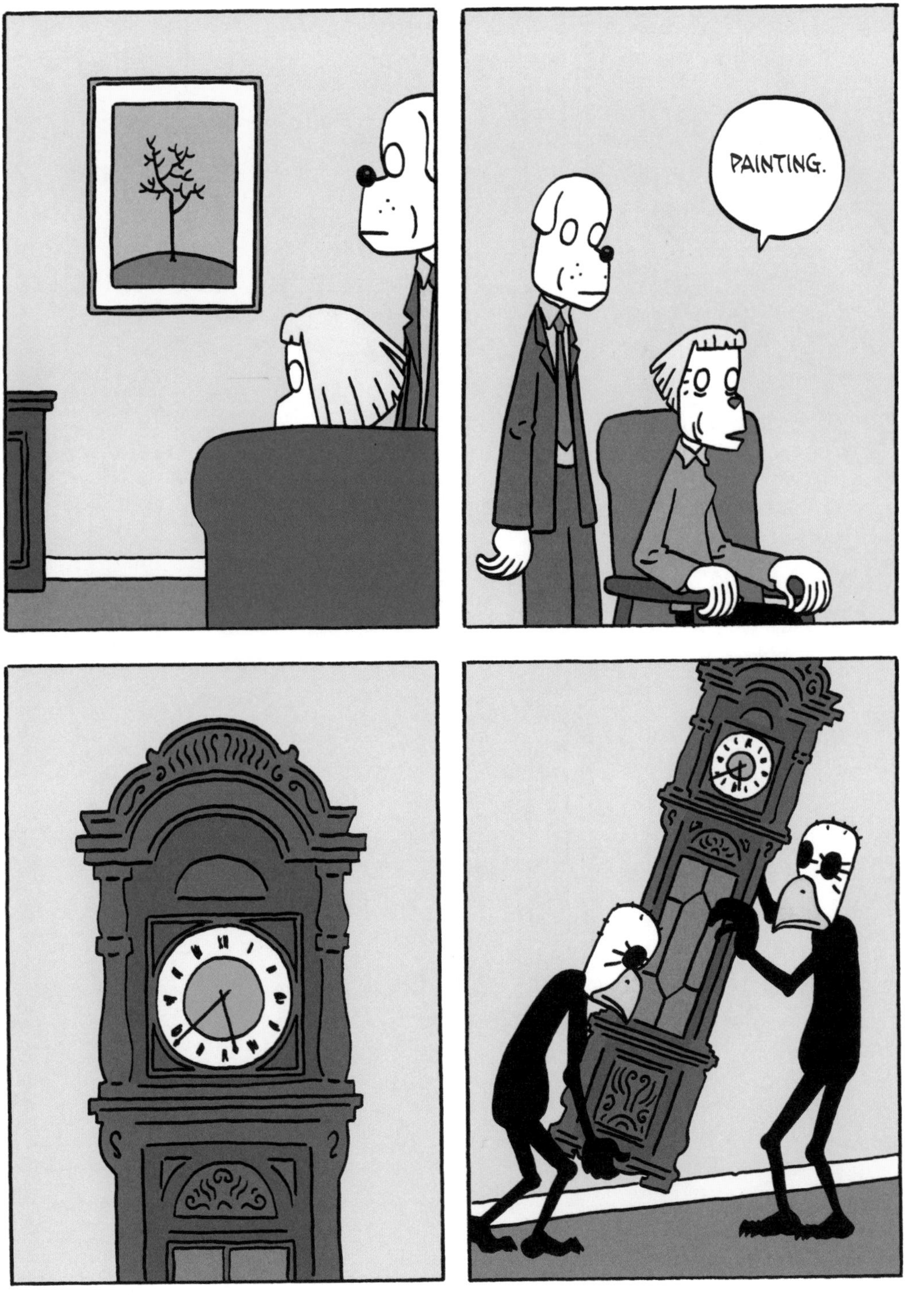
PAINTING.

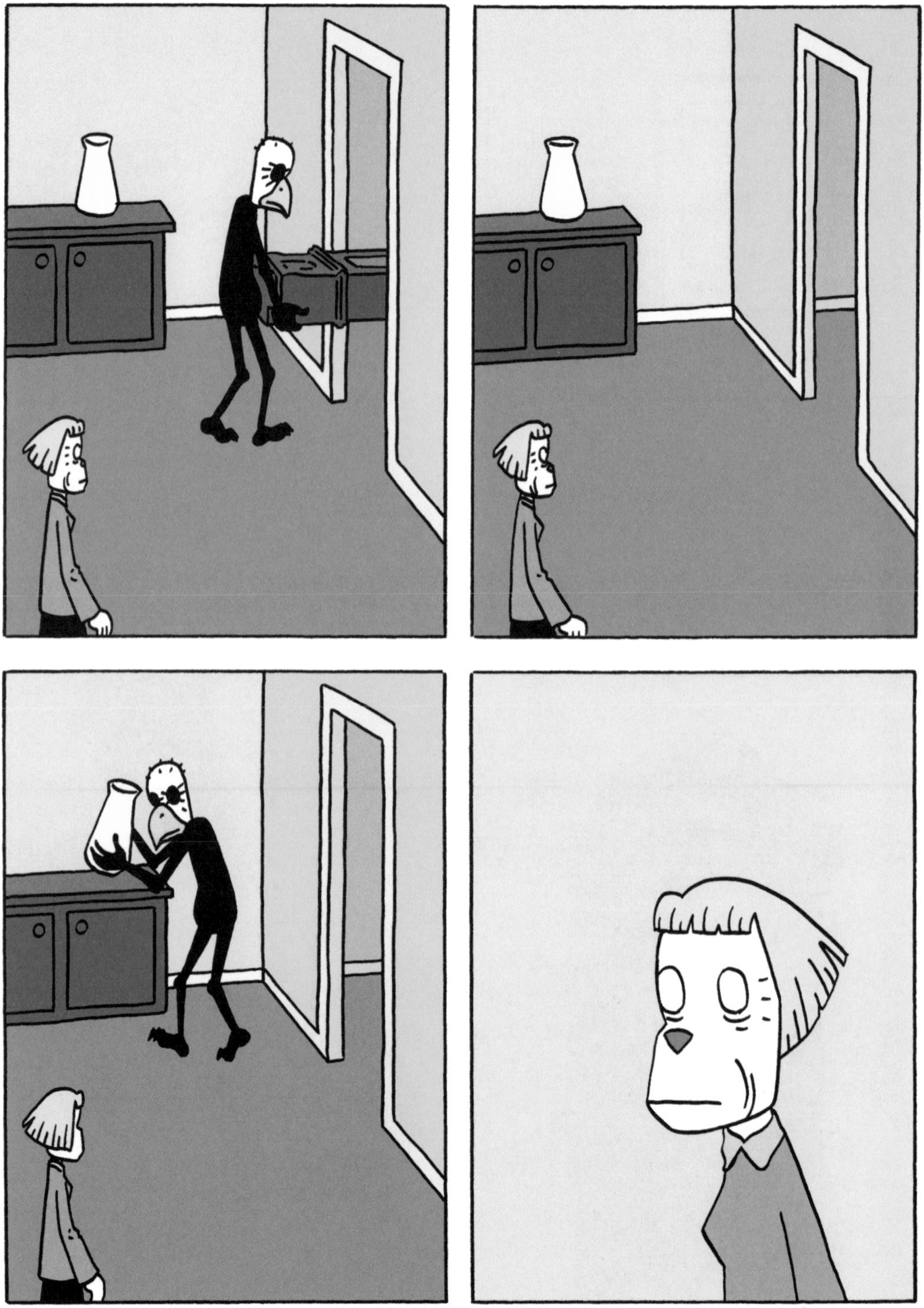

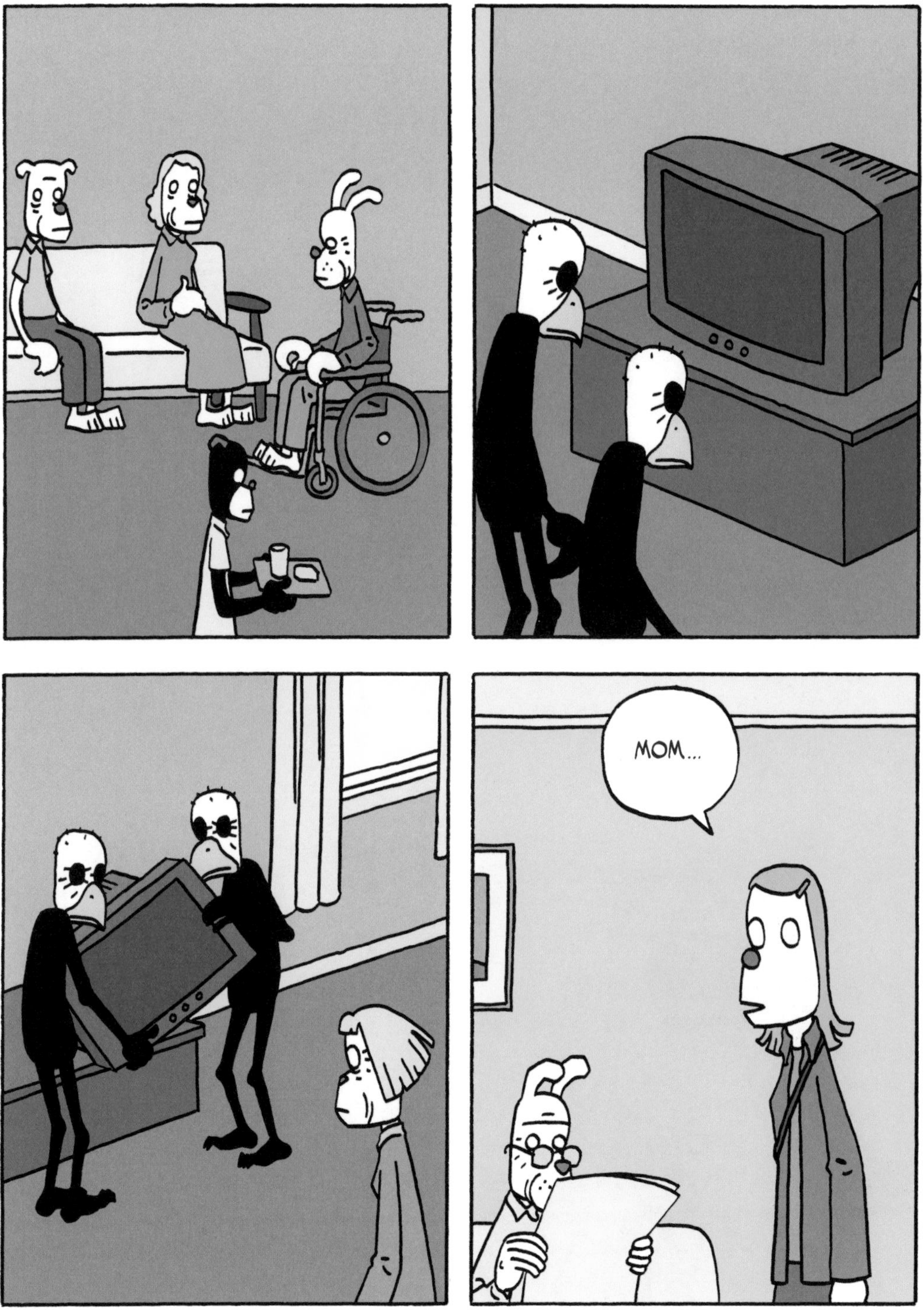
MOM...

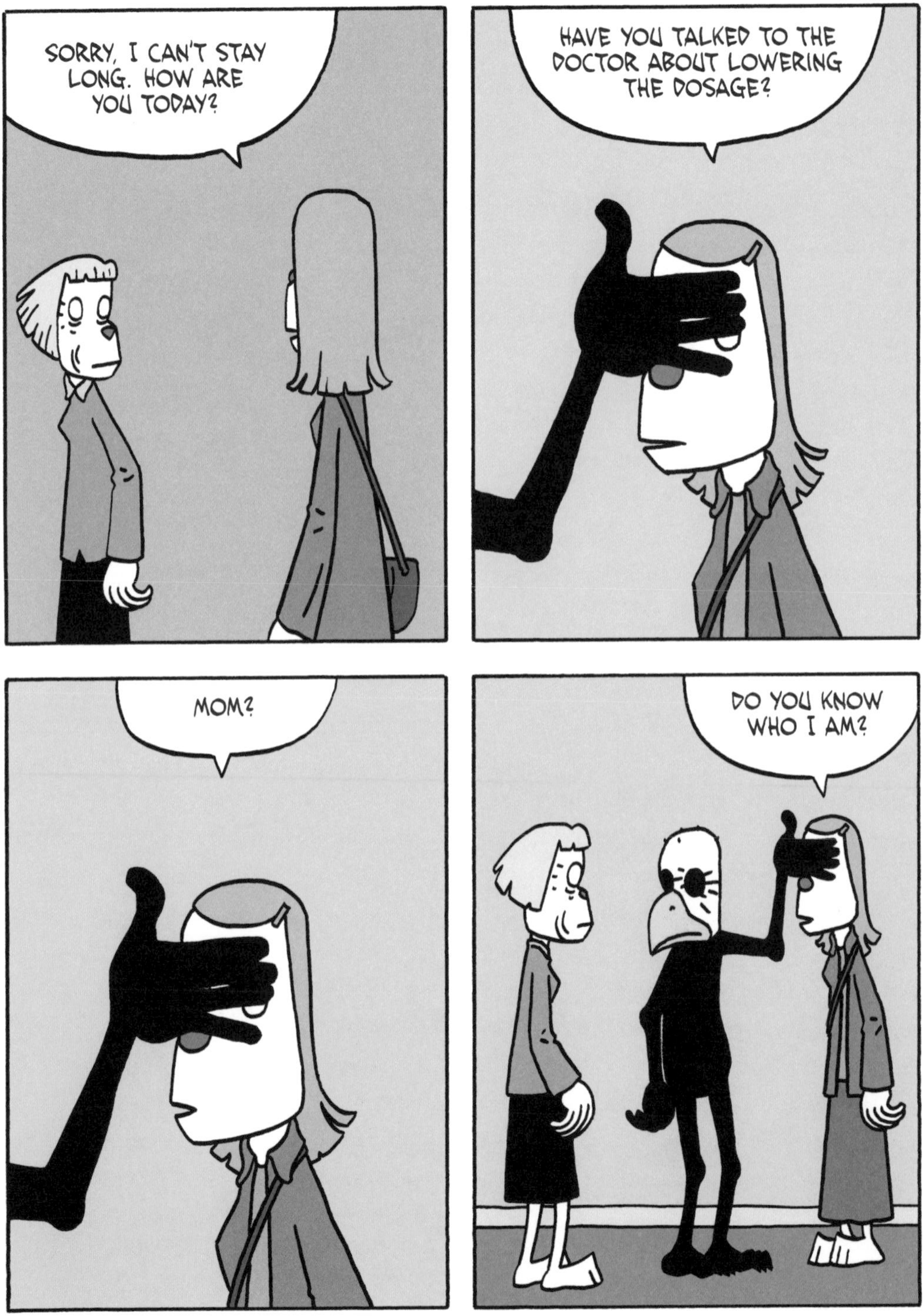
SORRY, I CAN'T STAY LONG. HOW ARE YOU TODAY?
HAVE YOU TALKED TO THE DOCTOR ABOUT LOWERING THE DOSAGE?
MOM?
DO YOU KNOW WHO I AM?

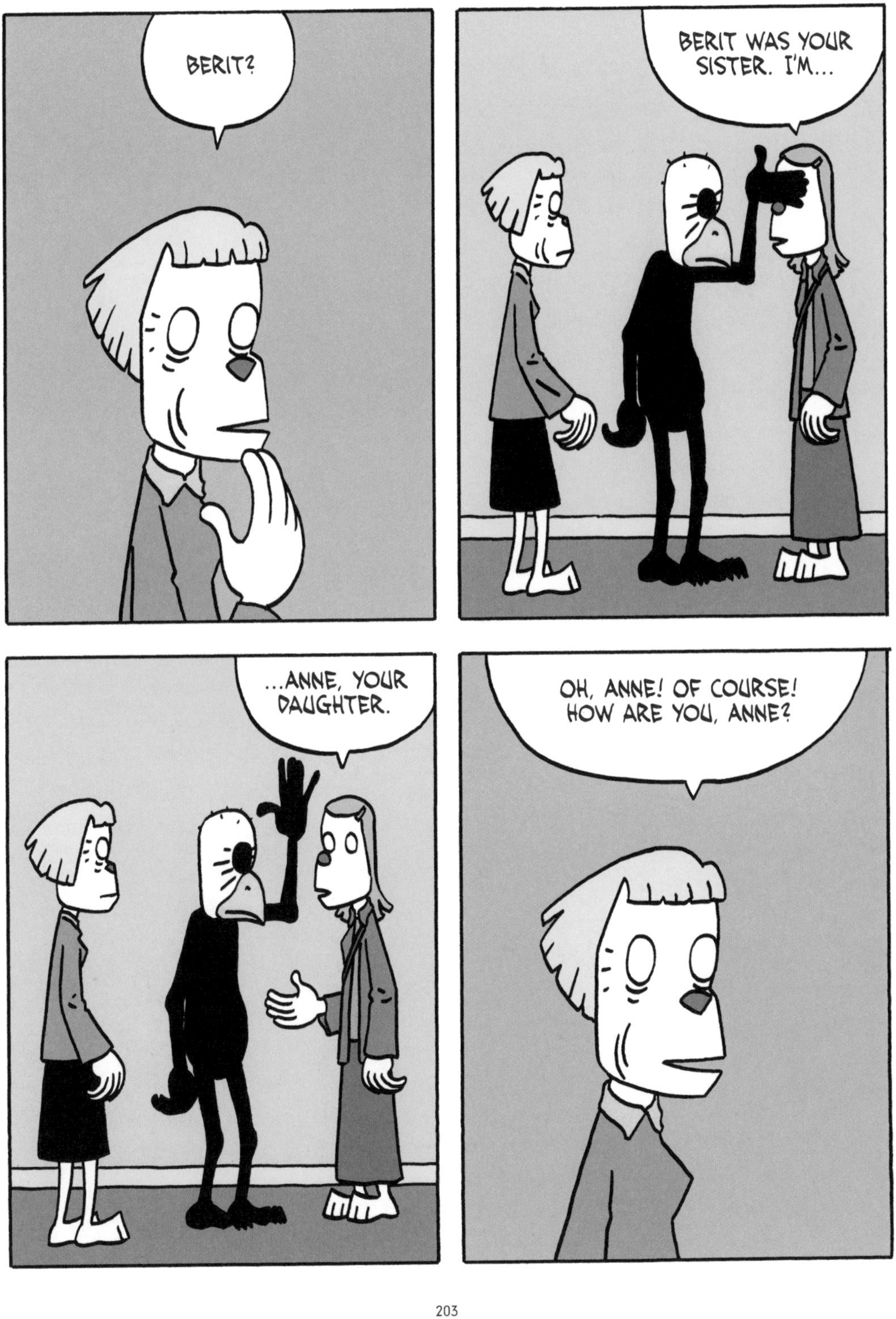
BERIT?
BERIT WAS YOUR SISTER. I'M...
...ANNE, YOUR DAUGHTER.
OH, ANNE! OF COURSE! HOW ARE YOU, ANNE?

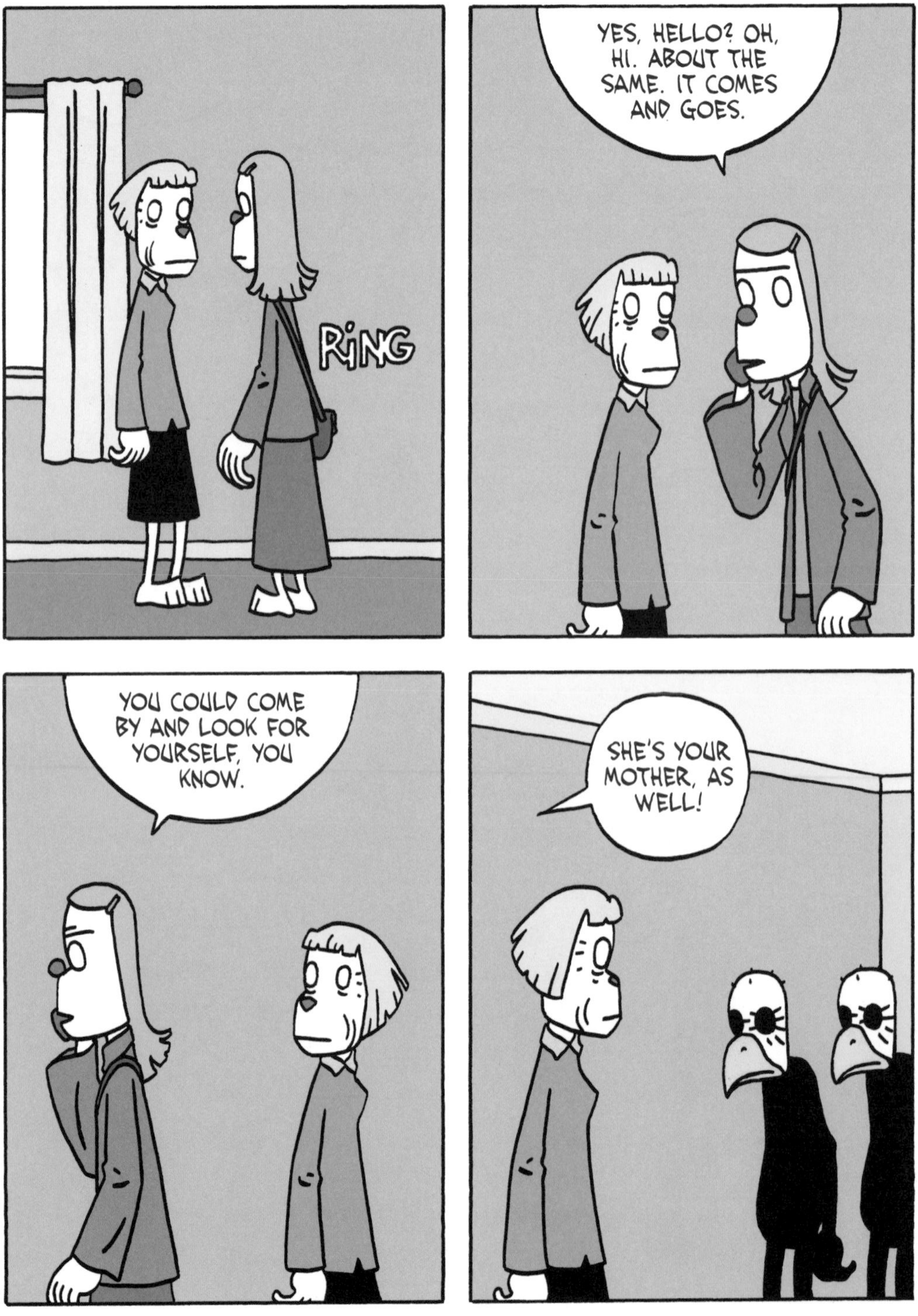
RING
YES, HELLO? OH, HI. ABOUT THE SAME. IT COMES AND GOES.
YOU COULD COME BY AND LOOK FOR YOURSELF, YOU KNOW.
SHE'S YOUR MOTHER, AS WELL!

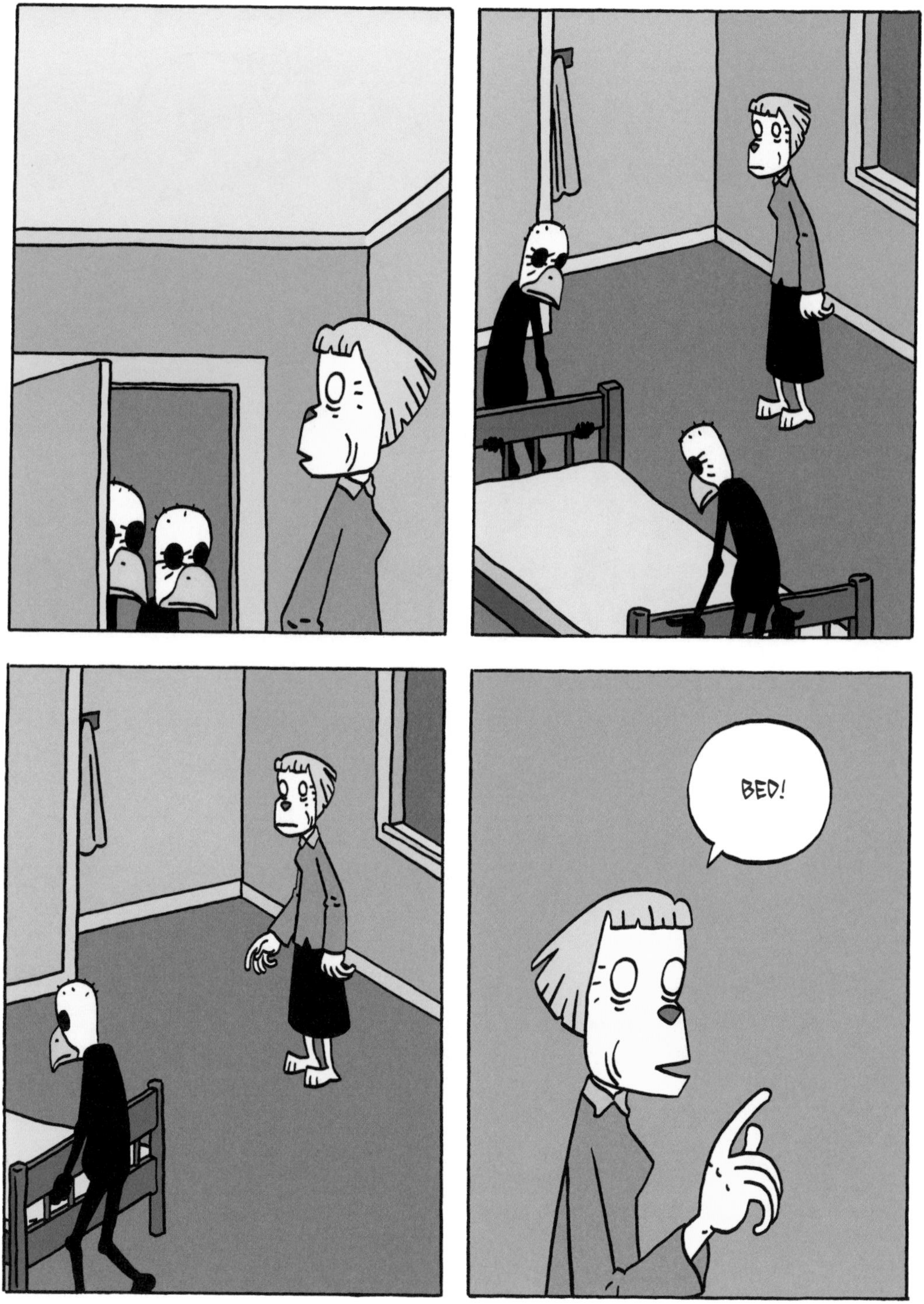
BED!

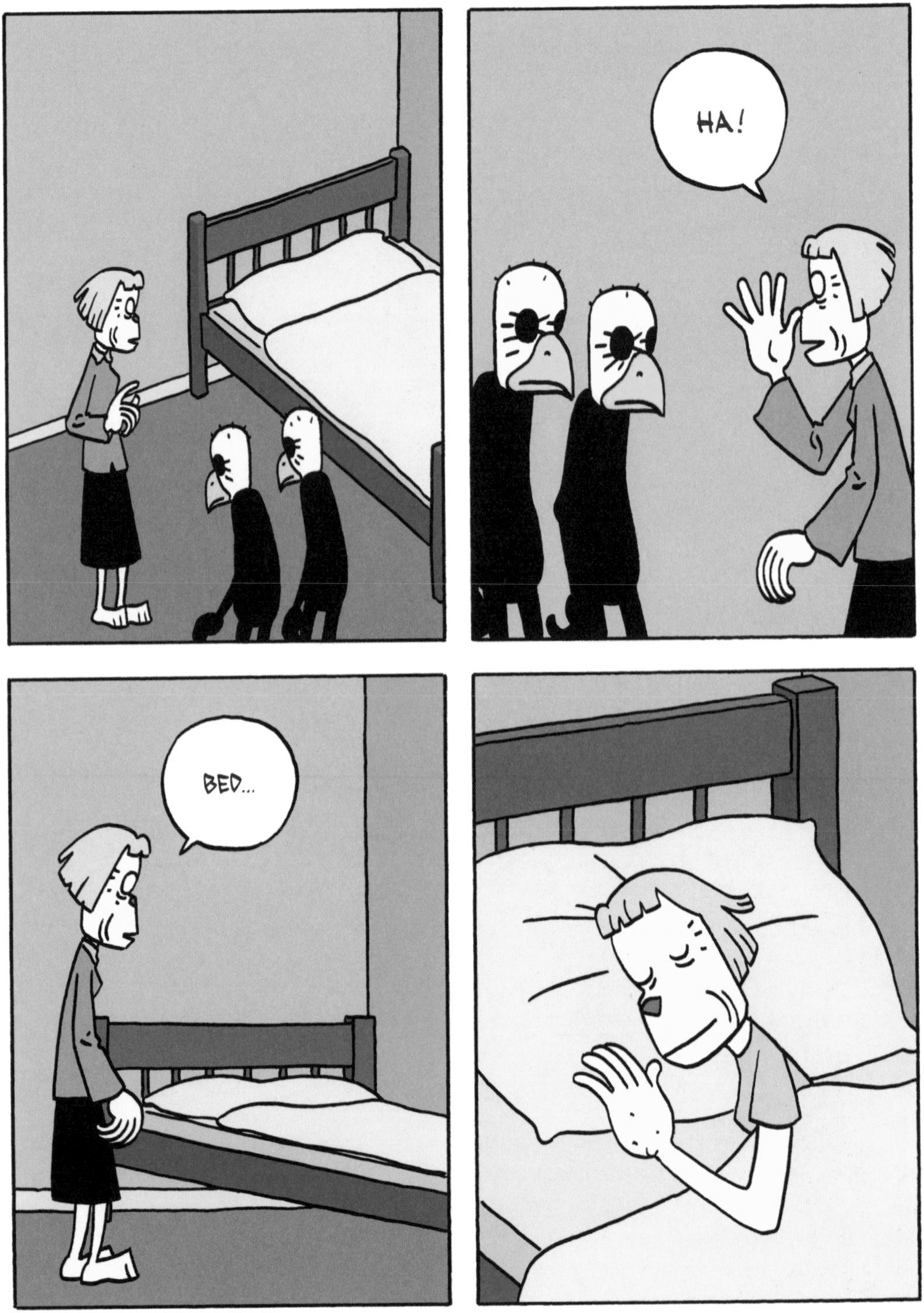
HA!
BED...

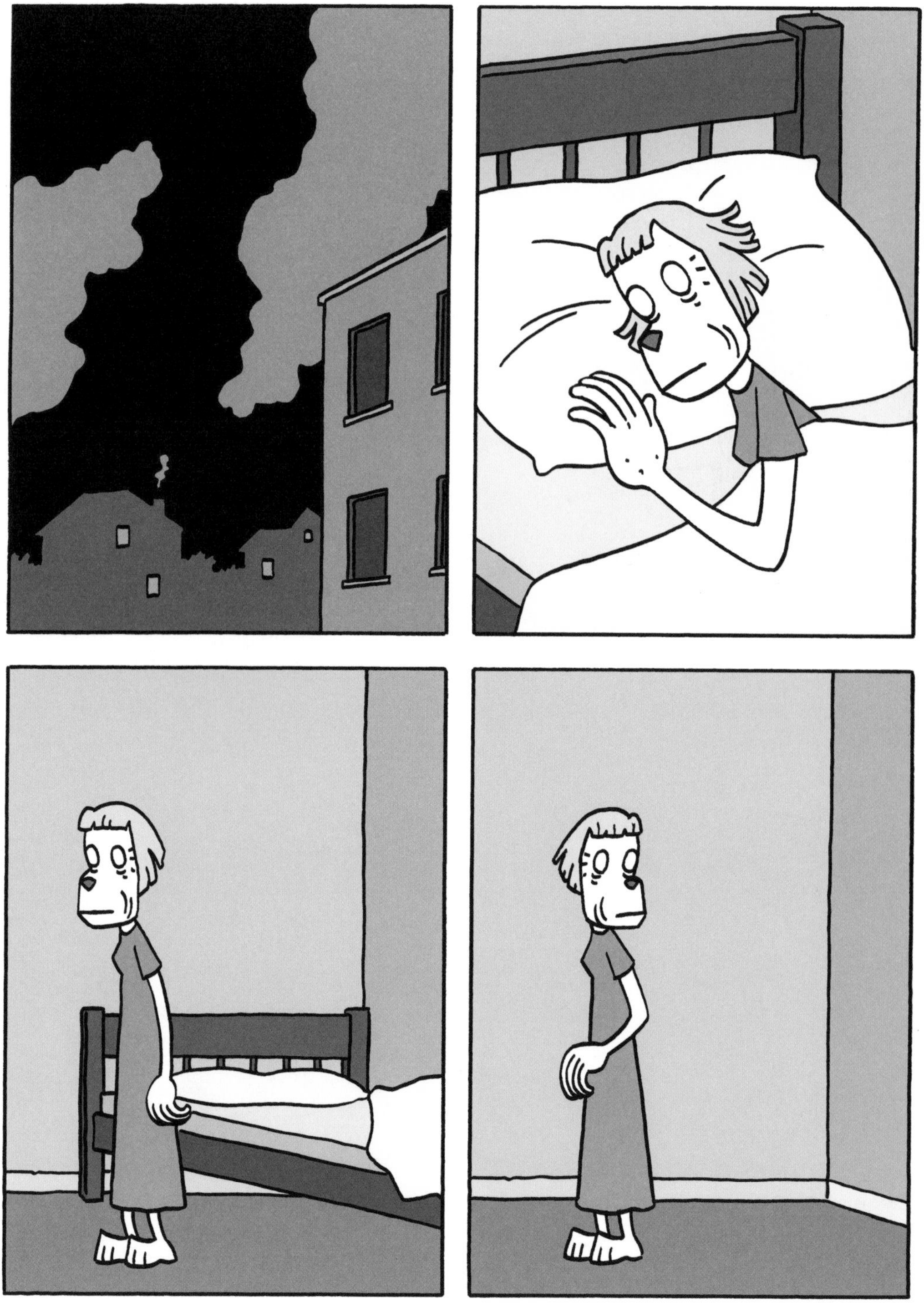

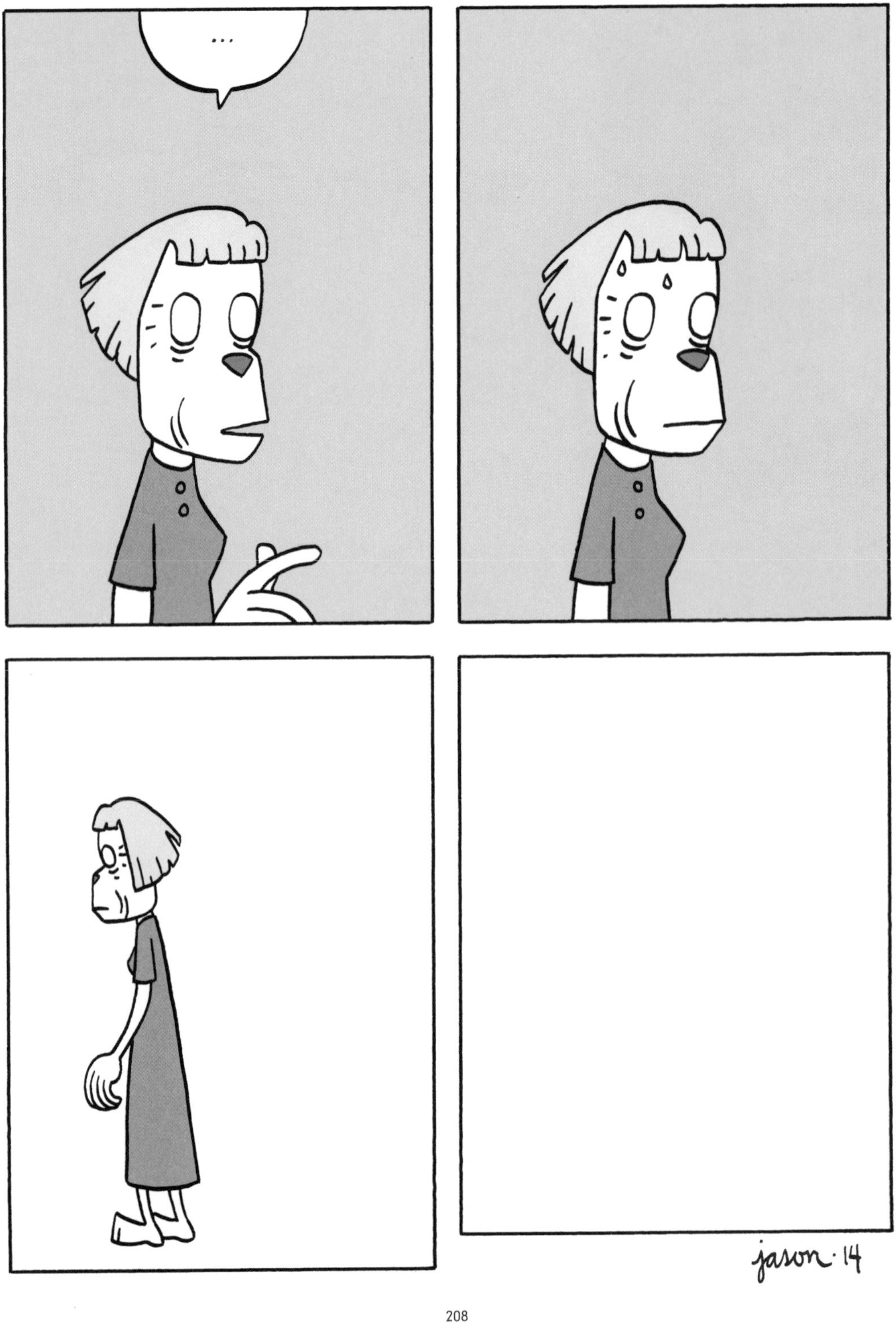
...
jason · 14